LIBRARY OF HEBREW BIBLE/
OLD TESTAMENT STUDIES

670

Formerly Journal for the Study of the Old Testament Supplement Series

Editors
Claudia V. Camp, Texas Christian University, USA
Andrew Mein, University of Durham, UK

Founding Editors
David J. A. Clines, Philip R. Davies and David M. Gunn

Editorial Board
Alan Cooper, Susan Gillingham, John Goldingay,
Norman K. Gottwald, James E. Harding, John Jarick, Carol Meyers,
Daniel L. Smith-Christopher, Francesca Stavrakopoulou,
James W. Watts

CHARACTERS AND CHARACTERIZATION IN THE BOOK OF KINGS

Edited by

Keith Bodner and Benjamin J. M. Johnson

LONDON • NEW YORK • OXFORD • NEW DELHI • SYDNEY

T&T CLARK
Bloomsbury Publishing Plc
50 Bedford Square, London, WC1B 3DP, UK
1385 Broadway, New York, NY 10018, USA
29 Earlsfort Terrace, Dublin 2, Ireland

BLOOMSBURY, T&T CLARK and the T&T Clark logo
are trademarks of Bloomsbury Publishing Plc

First published in Great Britain 2020
Paperback edition first published 2021

Volume Editors' Part of the Work © Keith Bodner and Benjamin J. M. Johnson, 2020
Each chapter © of Contributor

Keith Bodner, Benjamin J.M. Johnson, and contributors have asserted their right under the Copyright,
Designs and Patents Act, 1988, to be identified as Authors of this work.

All rights reserved. No part of this publication may be reproduced or
transmitted in any form or by any means, electronic or mechanical,
including photocopying, recording, or any information storage or retrieval
system, without prior permission in writing from the publishers.

Bloomsbury Publishing Plc does not have any control over, or responsibility for,
any third-party websites referred to or in this book. All internet addresses given
in this book were correct at the time of going to press. The author and publisher
regret any inconvenience caused if addresses have changed or sites have
ceased to exist, but can accept no responsibility for any such changes.

A catalogue record for this book is available from the British Library.

A catalog record for this book is available from the Library of Congress.

ISBN: HB: 978-0-5676-8090-7
PB: 978-0-5677-0207-4
ePDF: 978-0-5676-8091-4

Series: Library of Hebrew Bible/Old Testament Studies, ISSN 2513-8758, volume 670

Typeset by: Forthcoming Publications Ltd

To find out more about our authors and books visit
www.bloomsbury.com and sign up for our newsletters.

Contents

List of Contributors — vii
Preface — ix
List of Abbreviations — xiii

Chapter 1
CHARACTERIZATION AND ETHICS
   John Barton — 1

Chapter 2
AHAZ AND JEROBOAM
   A. Graeme Auld — 17

Chapter 3
BATHSHEBA BETWEEN THE LINES AND BENEATH THE SURFACE
   Sara Koenig — 32

Chapter 4
THE PORTRAIT OF SOLOMON IN THE BOOK OF KINGS
   Amos Frisch — 50

Chapter 5
REHABILITATING REHOBOAM
   Rachelle Gilmour — 65

Chapter 6
DECEIVING THE MAN OF GOD FROM JUDAH:
A QUESTION OF MOTIVE
   Paul Hedley Jones — 83

Chapter 7
DANCING WITH DEATH; DANCING WITH LIFE:
AHAB BETWEEN JEZEBEL AND ELIJAH
   Lissa M. Wray Beal — 103

Chapter 8
JEZEBEL NOW:
GAZING THROUGH MULTIPLE WINDOWS
   Athalya Brenner-Idan — 121

Chapter 9
AN AMBIVALENT HERO:
ELIJAH IN NARRATIVE-CRITICAL PERSPECTIVE
   Iain Provan   135

Chapter 10
THE CHARACTER OF ELISHA AND HIS BONES
   Stuart Lasine   152

Chapter 11
HE'S DRIVING LIKE JEHU—LIKE A MADMAN:
HUMOR AND VIOLENCE IN 2 KINGS 9–10
   Mark Roncace   167

Chapter 12
ATHALIAH: THE QUEEN WHO WAS NOT
   Patricia Dutcher-Walls   182

Chapter 13
ARTIFACTS OF SCENERY OR AGENTS OF CHANGE?
A SUBALTERN CHARACTER IN 2 KINGS 4:1-7
   Gina Hens-Piazza   199

Chapter 14
THE TRUST OF HEZEKIAH:
IN YHWH … AND ASSYRIA, EGYPT, AND BABYLON (2 KINGS 18–20)
   David T. Lamb   214

Chapter 15
MANASSEH THE BORING:
LACK OF CHARACTER IN 2 KINGS 21
   Alison L. Joseph   234

Chapter 16
TO REFORM OR NOT TO REFORM:
CHARACTERIZATION AND ETHICAL READING OF JOSIAH IN KINGS
   S. Min Chun   250

AFTERWORD   269

Bibliography   271
Index of References   289
Index of Authors   300

CONTRIBUTORS

A. Graeme Auld, Professor of Hebrew Bible, University of Edinburgh

John Barton, Emeritus Professor, Oxford University

Athalya Brenner-Idan, Professor Emerita of the Hebrew Bible / Old Testament Chair at the Universiteit van Amsterdam

S. Min Chun, Associate Professor of Worldview and Old Testament, Vancouver Institute for Evangelical Worldview

Patricia Dutcher-Walls, Professor of Hebrew Bible, Vancouver School of Theology

Amos Frisch, Professor of Bible, Bar-Ilan University

Rachelle Gilmour, Research Fellow, Charles Sturt University

Gina Hens-Piazza, Professor of Biblical Studies, Joseph C. Alemany Endowed Chair, Jesuit School of Theology of Santa Clara University, Graduate Theological Union

Paul Hedley Jones, Lecturer in Old Testament and Homiletics, Trinity College, Queensland

Alison L. Joseph, Adjunct Assistant Professor of Bible and its Interpretation, The Jewish Theological Seminary

Sara M. Koenig, Associate Professor of Biblical Studies, Seattle Pacific University

David T. Lamb, MacRae Professor of Old Testament, Missio Seminary

Stuart Lasine, Professor of Religion, Wichita State University

Iain W. Provan, Marshall Sheppard Professor of Biblical Studies, Regent College

Mark Roncace, Associate Professor of Religion, Wingate University

Lissa M. Wray-Beal, Professor of Old Testament, Providence Theological Seminary

Preface

In a pantomime play, it is important for the audience to know right away who are the heroes and who are the villains. Villains are to be booed, heroes are to be cheered. Knowing is part of the experience. It might be tempting to think that in a book such as Kings, where many of the characters get pass/fail scorecards, we are in a story world like that of a pantomime play. The heroes and villains must be obviously determinable, since knowing who is a bad king and who is a good king is part of the narrative's intent. We know Josiah is a good guy; Manasseh is a bad guy. Elijah is a hero; Ahab is a villain. However, although the pass/fail judgment of kings is a key thread running through the book, closer attention to the actual characterization of the various characters and various kings will show that the situation is not so simple or one-dimensional as it may appear. The book of Kings is not known as containing complex characters in the same way as its canonical counterpart, the book of Samuel. However, as this volume intends to show, giving due attention to the characters in the book of Kings shows that characters and their characterization are more complex, nuanced, and important than may be appreciated.

The importance of characters and characterization in Hebrew narrative has been recognized for a long time. Since Erich Auerbach argued that biblical narrative was "fraught with background" and that biblical characters were marked by "multilayeredness,"[1] most scholars offering literary analyses of biblical text have seen the importance and complexity of biblical characters. Robert Alter, for example, highlighted the way that biblical narrative was artfully reticent in its characterization and suggested a "scale of means" with which the biblical authors offered their characterizations, from direct to indirect.[2] Adele Berlin highlighted the different character types that can be found in biblical narrative, from type

---

1. Erich Auerbach, "Odysseus' Scar," in *Mimesis: The Representation of Reality in Western Thought* (Princeton: Princeton University Press, 2003), 12–13.
2. Robert Alter, *The Art of Biblical Narrative* (New York: Basic Books, 1981), 114–30. Pagination for the revised and updated version: *The Art of Biblical Narrative*, rev. ed. (New York: Basic Books, 2011), 143–62.

to agent to full-fledged character.³ Meir Sternberg offered an even more complex picture as he highlighted the surface-level characterization of a character that may be given in something like a characterizing epithet, and the in-depth characterization that is only possible by appreciating the whole narrative.⁴

While some characters in Kings have, over the years, received some treatment, most notably Solomon⁵ and the occasional treatment in two series,⁶ sustained attention to character and characterization in the Hebrew narrative in general and the book of Kings in particular have been relatively lacking. Recent studies have reinvigorated the treatment of character and characterization in New Testament narrative,⁷ and the time seems ripe to give sustained space to the analysis of characters in Hebrew narrative. The present volume and its companion volume on the book of Samuel⁸ attempt to do just that.

What we will find in this collection of studies is that the book of Kings contains a cast of characters that transcends the simple binary of whether or not this or that character did what was right in the eyes of Yhwh. We will see, for example, in John Barton's essay the complex way that characters in Samuel and Kings are useful as a resource for ethics. We will see in A. Graeme Auld's essay how the diachronic textual complexity

---

3. Adele Berlin, *Poetics and Interpretation of Biblical Narrative* (Sheffield: Almond, 1983), Chapter 2.

4. Meir Sternberg, *The Poetics of Biblical Narrative: Ideological Literature and the Drama of Reading* (Bloomington: Indiana University Press, 1985), esp. Chapters 9–10.

5. See Walter Brueggemann, *Solomon: Israel's Ironic Icon of Human Achievement*, Studies on Personalities of the Old Testament (Columbia: University of South Carolina Press, 2005); Steven Weitzman, *Solomon: The Lure of Wisdom* (New Haven: Yale University Press, 2011).

6. Patricia Dutcher-Walls, *Jezebel: Portraits of a Queen*, Interfaces (Collegeville: Liturgical Press, 2004); Jerome T. Walsh, *Ahab: The Construction of a King*, Interfaces (Collegeville: Liturgical Press, 2006); Sara Koenig, *Bathsheba Survives*, Studies on Personalities of the Old Testament (Columbia: University of South Carolina Press, 2018).

7. See Christopher W. Skinner, ed., *Characters and Characterization in the Gospel of John*, LNTS 461 (New York: Bloomsbury T&T Clark, 2013); Christopher W. Skinner and Matthew Ryan Hauge, eds, *Character Studies and the Gospel of Mark*, LNTS 290 (London: Bloomsbury T&T Clark, 2016); and Frank Dicken and Julia Snyder, *Characters and Characterization in Luke-Acts*, LNTS 548 (New York: Bloomsbury T&T Clark, 2016).

8. Keith Bodner and Benjamin J. M. Johnson, eds, *Characters and Characterization in the Book of Samuel*, LHBOTS 669 (London: Bloomsbury T&T Clark, 2020).

paints potentially complex characters. We will see in Rachelle Gilmour's essay that even Rehoboam, who is in many respects responsible for splitting the kingdom, may not be as straightforwardly villainous as first imagined. Lissa M. Wray Beal will show us that even Ahab is not a cookie-cutter character but is capable of his own complexity. We will see in Athalya Brenner-Idan's essay that one's opinion of the great villainess, Jezebel, depends entirely upon which set of eyes we use to look at her. Even the great prophet Elijah will be given an ambivalent presentation in Iain Provan's contribution.

In short, in this volume we will see that careful analysis of characters and characterization in the book of Kings rewards us with nuanced understanding of this literature which is not quite as simple as it may at first appear.

Keith Bodner
Benjamin J. M. Johnson
May 2018

ABBREVIATIONS

AB	The Anchor Bible
ABD	David Noel Freedman, ed., *The Anchor Bible Dictionary*, 6 vols. Garden City: Doubleday, 1992
ABRL	Anchor Bible Reference Library
AOTC	Abingdon Old Testament Commentary
ApOTC	Apollos Old Testament Commentary
ATD	Das Alte Testament Deutsch
AThANT	Abhandlungen zur Theologie des Alten und Neuen Testaments
BETL	Bibliotheca Ephemeridum Theologicarum Lovaniensium
Bib	*Biblica*
BibInt	*Biblical Interpretation*
BibInt	Biblical Interpretation
BKAT	Biblischer Kommentar, Altes Testament
BST	The Bible Speaks Today
BTB	*Biblical Theology Bulletin*
BTS	Biblical Tools and Studies
BZ	*Biblische Zeitschrift*
CBQ	*Catholic Biblical Quarterly*
CBQMS	Catholic Biblical Quarterly Monograph Series
CBR	*Currents in Biblical Research*
COS	*The Context of Scripture*, ed. William W. Hallo. 3 vols. Leiden: Brill, 1997–2002
CTQ	*Concordia Theological Quarterly*
DDD	Karel van der Toorn, Bob Becking, and Pieter W. van der Horst, eds. *Dictionary of Deities and Demons in the Bible*. Leiden: Brill, 1995; 2nd rev. ed. Grand Rapids: Eerdmans, 1999
ETL	*Ephemerides theologicae Lovanienses*
EUS	European University Studies
ExpTim	*The Expository Times*
FOTL	The Forms of the Old Testament Literature
HAR	*Hebrew Annual Review*
HSM	Harvard Semitic Monographs
HUCA	*Hebrew Union College Annual*
ITC	International Theological Commentary
JBL	*Journal of Biblical Literature*
JBQ	*Jewish Bible Quarterly*
JETS	*Journal of the Evangelical Theological Society*

JHS	*Journal of Hebrew Scriptures*
JJS	*Journal of Jewish Studies*
JSJ	*Journal for the Study of Judaism*
JSJSup	Journal for the Study of Judaism Supplement Series
JSNTSup	Journal for the Study of the New Testament Supplement Series
JSOT	*Journal for the Study of the Old Testament*
JSOTSup	Journal for the Study of the Old Testament Supplement Series
LHBOTS	Library of Hebrew Bible/Old Testament Studies
MJTM	*McMaster Journal of Theology and Ministry*
NCB	New Century Bible
NIBC	New International Bible Commentary
NICOT	New International Commentary on the Old Testament
OTE	*Old Testament Essays*
OTL	Old Testament Library
RBL	*Review of Biblical Literature*
SBT	Studies in Biblical Theology
SHBC	Smyth&Helwys Bible Commentary
SJOT	*Scandinavian Journal of the Old Testament*
ThZ	*Theologische Zeitschrift*
TynBul	*Tyndale Bulletin*
UF	*Ugarit-Forschungen*
VT	*Vetus Testamentum*
VTSup	Vetus Testamentum Supplement Series
WBC	Word Biblical Commentary
WBCom	Westminster Bible Companion
ZAH	*Zeitschrift für Althebräistik*
ZAW	*Zeitschrift für die alttestamentliche Wissenschaft*

Chapter 1

CHARACTERIZATION AND ETHICS

John Barton

Those who go to the Hebrew Bible/Old Testament as a resource for ethics most naturally gravitate towards the laws in the Pentateuch and the wisdom literature. The major twentieth-century authority on Old Testament ethics, Eckart Otto, argues that it is only in these two collections that ethics proper can be found, and accordingly his *Theologische Ethik des Alten Testaments*[1] cites very few biblical passages that do not come from either law or wisdom. Ethics is here seen as instructions on how to live, whether these come with divine authority (the law) or with the authority of a wise teacher (wisdom literature). Otto will not countenance the idea that ethics can be derived from narrative, poetry, or even prophecy. The prophets do not teach us ethics, as both Jews and Christians have traditionally believed, even though they do comment (adversely) on the behavior of their contemporaries: there is very little direct instruction to be had from the prophetic books. Psalmody and narrative texts, similarly, sometimes refer to ethical concerns, but their content does not amount to ethical teaching.

Many readers of the Hebrew Bible will find this rather counterintuitive, and I am certainly among them. Even if the prophets' role was not to teach, but more to denounce and to predict disaster,[2] we can easily deduce

---

1. Eckart Otto, *Theologische Ethik des Alten Testaments* (Stuttgart: Kohlhammer, 1994).
2. See my own discussion of this in John Barton, "Prophecy and Theodicy," in *Thus Says the Lord: Essays on the Former and Latter Prophets in Honor of Robert R. Wilson*, ed. J. J. Ahn and S. L. Cook (New York/London: T&T Clark, 2011), 73–86.

from the denunciations what they thought people ought to do, or ought to have done. Equally the Psalms often enshrine ethical principles: we have only to think of Psalms 15 and 24, sometimes described as "entrance liturgies," which contain brief ethical catechisms listing virtuous and vicious behavior and encouraging the reader (or hearer) to live an upright life. And narrative literature in the Hebrew Bible is full of stories that illustrate both vice and virtue, and can be used to encourage the reader to avoid one and follow the other. This is the burden of Gordon Wenham's *Story as Torah*,[3] in which he shows how there are many tales in the Bible (whether historical or fictitious) that have the function of illustrating moral behavior, just as much as have the overt laws and wisdom teachings. (This is close to Jewish tradition, in which *torah* does not refer only to the instructions in the Pentateuch but also to the generation of moral teaching from biblical texts of all kinds, and perhaps especially from narrative texts.) Narrative, he argues, goes beyond law strictly understood in that it often proposes ideals of conduct that exceed legal norms.[4] From narratives we learn not merely how to avoid sin, but how to practice virtue:

> Old Testament narrative books do have a didactic purpose, that is, they are trying to instil both theological truths and ethical ideals into their readers… the Bible storytellers are not advocating a minimalist conformity to the demands of the law in their storytelling, rather that they have an ideal of godly behaviour that they hoped their horoes and heroines would typify.[5]

3. See Gordon Wenham, *Story as Torah: Reading Old Testament Narrative Ethically* (Edinburgh: T. & T. Clark, 2000). On narrative ethics see also John Barton, *Ethics in Ancient Israel* (Oxford: Oxford University Press, 2014); "Reading for Life: The Use of the Bible in Ethics," in *The Bible in Ethics: The Second Sheffield Colloquium*, ed. J. W. Rogerson, M. Davies and M. D. Carroll R., JSOTSup 207 (Sheffield: Sheffield Academic, 1996), 66–76; reprinted in John Barton, *Understanding Old Testament Ethics: Approaches and Explorations* (Louisville: Westminster John Knox, 2003), 55–64; Bruce C. Birch, "Old Testament Narrative and Moral Address," in *Canon, Theology, and Old Testament Interpretation: Essays in Honor of Brevard S. Childs*, ed. G. M. Tucker (Philadelphia: Fortress, 1988), 75–91; M. Daniel Carroll R. and Jacqueline E. Lapsley, eds, *Character Ethics and the Old Testament: Moral Dimensions of Scripture* (Louisville: Westminster John Knox, 2007); Douglas A. Knight, "Moral Values and Literary Traditions: The Case of the Succession Narrative (2 Kings 9–20; 1 Kings 1–2)," *Semeia* 34 (1985): 7–23; Carol A. Newsom, "Narrative Ethics, Character, and the Prose Tale of Job," in *Character and Scripture: Moral Formation, Community, and Biblical Interpretation*, ed. W. P. Brown (Grand Rapids: Eerdmans, 2002), 121–34.

4. See also Gordon Wenham, "The Gap between Law and Ethics in the Bible," *JJS* 48 (1997): 17–29.

5. Wenham, *Story as Torah*, 3.

The characters in biblical narrative thus illustrate moral truths. They may serve as terrible warnings of what can go wrong in human behavior, but they may also show us what a really well-lived life would be like. Philo already had this conception of the people we meet in narrative texts. He uses characters in the Bible as examples. Hannah, for example, a particular favorite of his, is presented as a model to be imitated by those willing to embark on the way of virtue that leads to mystical ecstasy.[6] The historical reality of the characters he mentions often matters little to him; what is significant is their function as *exempla*. Thus he writes of the patriarchs:

> These are such men as lived good and blameless lives, whose virtues stand permanently recorded in the most holy scriptures, not merely to sound their praises but for the instruction of the reader and as an inducement to him to aspire to the same; for in these men we have laws endowed with life and reason, and Moses extolled them for two reasons. First he wished to show that the enacted ordinances are not inconsistent with nature; and secondly that those who wish to live in accordance with the laws as they stand have no difficult task, seeing that the first generations before any at all of the particular statutes was set in writing followed the unwritten law with perfect ease, so that one might properly say that the enacted laws are nothing else than memorials of the lives of the ancients, preserving to a later generation their actual words and deeds.[7]

The story of the reception of the Hebrew Bible is full of readers and preachers who have used the characters in it as *exempla*, either positive or negative: "enfleshed law" or wickedness personified. But treating them in this way amounts to seeing them, in E. M. Forster's classic distinction, essentially as "flat" characters rather than as "round" ones.[8] To take an example almost at random: the non-biblical *Testament of Joseph* presents the Joseph of Genesis as more or less an embodiment of chastity, and shows little interest in any other features of his character. Popular appeals to biblical personages are similar in concentrating on just one trait. The well-known worship song "Dare to Be a Daniel" summons up the biblical character as an example of courage in the face of persecution, and tries to get the person singing it to act with similar courage even when faced with the smaller temptations of everyday life. It is not concerned with Daniel as a visionary or dream-interpreter, which are equally important aspects

---

6. Philo, *de ebrietate* 144-53.
7. Philo, *de migratione Abrahami* 4-5.
8. See E. M. Forster, *Aspects of the Novel* (London: Penguin, 2005; original publication 1927), Chapter 3.

of the biblical Daniel. The characters in the Bible are thus often seen as instantiations of one particular virtue or vice, not as complex and varied personalities.

Now in this the Bible itself criticizes its own interpreters. For many biblical characters are not flat at all, but develop over time as real people do, and are not reducible to a single moral value. Some, certainly, are flat, introduced merely to move the plot along: Leah, for example, or Ben-hadad, or Zedekiah the son of Chenaanah. But many are round. And deducing ethical teaching from round characters is difficult, seldom attempted in the history of biblical reception. The usual course has been to flatten them out, as we have seen. But in presenting such characters as round, the biblical authors themselves challenge us to read them in a more complex way. The fact that it is only in modern times that there has been an explicit recognition in literary criticism of the fact of roundness in characterization does not make this challenge an anachronistic one. The evidence of the texts themselves contradicts any flattening out. The biblical authors were clearly aware that the people they described were not simple exemplars of this or that moral quality. If their work is to be a resource for ethical reading now, then the moral complexity of the round characters needs to be taken into account. As Forster himself noted, one of the salient features of round characters is that they can surprise us: they are not simply predictable even when they are consistent, and sometimes they are not consistent at all.[9]

I propose to look at a number of round characters in the books of Samuel and Kings and to ask how they might be useful to us in asking ethical questions—avoiding the temptation to flatten them into *exempla*.

Saul

Saul is perhaps the nearest the Hebrew Bible has to a tragic hero as defined by Aristotle, a great man who succumbs to a single fault. The fault is one that we would nowadays define as an illness rather than as a moral failing: Saul is presented as manifesting symptoms that would now be identified as justifying a diagnosis of bipolar disorder. He has spells of extreme elation and ecstasy in which he turns into a kind of prophet,[10] but also black times when his understandable jealousy of

---

9. Ibid., 81. For a thorough discussion of characterization in literary studies and its implications for the student of the Bible, a good source is Brian C. Small, *The Characterization of Jesus in the Book of Hebrews* (Leiden: Brill, 2014), which has a full bibliography.

10. 1 Samuel 10:9-12.

David turns to paranoia and leads him to threaten the life not only of David but even of his own son, Jonathan.[11] Whether Saul was in reality bipolar is a question that cannot be answered, but the narrator was quite clearly aware of the condition, though he could not of course have called it by its modern name, and he has no hesitation in attributing it to Saul. He gives it a theological explanation, attributing it to an "evil spirit from Yahweh," where we might speak in psychological or neurological terms. But however the condition is accounted for, it absolutely controls Saul's actions, driving him first to the reckless pursuit of war with the Ammonites and on to become king, but then plunging him into fear of the even greater ambitions of his own lieutenant, David—fears that are not ill-grounded, but which take him over and cloud his vision. In both mania and depression Saul is a larger-than-life figure, and he is one of the few characters in the Hebrew Bible whose physical size is mentioned; he is "head and shoulders" taller than anyone else.[12] His downfall comes about when he paradoxically refrains from killing the Amalekite king, Agag, for reasons he himself regards as fully justified—though as soon as Samuel points out that his act of mercy contradicts the direct command of God, he immediately sees the error of his ways.[13] Perhaps consistent with his earlier contact with the spirit-world when he prophesies after his anointing by Samuel, his last act before he is killed in battle at Aphek is to consult a medium, who brings up the shadowy spirit of Samuel himself to predict the disaster that the Philistines will wreak: "Tomorrow you and your sons will be with me."[14]

The complexity of Saul's character is obvious. In an ancient context a simple moralism endorsed Samuel's strictures on him and subscribed to the idea that his "madness" was a visitation by God for his sins. But a modern reader is likely to be more attuned to the ambiguities and difficulties, and to suspect that these were consciously in the mind of the original writer, even though later generations of readers missed them. We resist the idea that an "evil spirit from Yahweh" was responsible for Saul's illness, but we also see that the original writer was not necessarily condemning Saul by attributing it to this cause; for the writers of Samuel and Kings tended to trace evil as well as good back to God, rather than necessarily blaming it on the human actors. In other words, to say that Saul behaved as he did because of an evil spirit is probably not to condemn Saul, but to think rather of God as inscrutably causing suffering

11. 1 Samuel 19:8-10; 20:30-45.
12. 1 Samuel 10:23.
13. 1 Samuel 15.
14. 1 Samuel 28:19.

and misfortune. It is a spirit *from God*, not Saul's own fault, which causes him to lose his reason. Only David can calm the evil spirit by playing music to Saul,[15] yet it is David above all who provokes the paranoia that is so destructive to Saul's personality. Later readers would condemn Saul, but the writer was probably more merciful in tracing his problems back to what insurers call an "act of God."

On the other hand, the sin Saul does commit—the failure to kill Agag—is presented in the text as unequivocally wicked, since that is how it is seen by Samuel, who (I would argue) voices the ideas of the omniscient narrator. That sparing a conquered enemy, rather than subjecting him to the *herem*, is a fatal sin contradicts all our moral instincts, as it must have done those of many in ancient Israel.[16] There is also an underlying idea that there is a duty to do what God commands, irrespective of whether it coincides with human notions of morality, raising the same sorts of issues as Genesis 22, where Abraham is told to sacrifice Isaac and obeys without question (even though in the event God himself steps in to prevent the horror). It is hard to see how a modern reader can learn anything ethically wholesome from this story, taken as a paradigm for conduct. But it does fit with the overall presentation of Saul, whose fickleness of conduct may be caused here, as in the earlier story, by the "evil spirit" which makes him do things he would not otherwise think of doing. That his attitude towards God's orders has results—the sparing of an enemy—which we would regard as admirable rather than blameworthy, does not detract from the sense that he is essentially unreliable. A modern reader might perhaps wish to be as unreliable as Saul in a matter such as this, where ancient readers on the whole acquiesced in Samuel's judgement on his disobedience. But the character trait that underlies it all is a determination to be guided by his own counsel, which in many other cases certainly does lead him astray. For example, it makes him pursue pointlessly after David, and unable to see that David is bound to succeed him on the throne. He fails, in the writer's eyes, to accommodate himself to the divine plan for Israel. At the same time he is presented as admirable in many ways, as David recalls in his lament after Saul's death.[17] Many of his more obvious flaws are not of his own making.

---

15. 1 Samuel 16:14-23.

16. Thus when Elisha has trapped some Arameans in Samaria, his servant wants to kill them, but Elisha refuses: "Did you capture with your sword and your bow those whom you want to kill? Set food and water before them" (2 Kgs 6:22).

17. 2 Samuel 1:19-27.

It is even possible to read the story of Saul, though surely against the grain of the finished Hebrew Bible, as originally a defense of Israel's first king against David, the subordinate who supplanted Saul's line—possibly by supporting the Philistines in Saul's last battle, and then weeping crocodile tears at his death.[18] It is conceivable that underlying the accounts in 1 Samuel there is a pro-Saul narrative source that saw Saul as a flawed yet great king who was unjustly defeated, and so rendered unable to found the dynasty that would have been his deserved reward for saving the nation. In source-critical terms we might think of this as a northern Israelite document, supplanted and reworked by the southern, pro-David material that now overlays it. From a more literary perspective, we might regard the interweaving of pro- and anti-Saul material as an ingenious way of suspending judgement on the question of who should sit, or should have sat, on the throne of Israel. Saul was flawed yet had the just claim; David was talented and skillful, but was in the end a usurper. Neither was an ideal king, yet without them both the history of Israel and Judah could not have unfurled as it did. Morally both are somewhat murky characters; neither is to be imitated.

David

David is probably the most complex character in the Old Testament.[19] If we treat him as a flat character (simply an *exemplum*) we can certainly learn a few ethical truths, or truisms, from both positive and negative aspects of his life: be courageous, look after your parents, do not commit adultery, do not murder, keep your word, and so on. But if we consider him as the round character he certainly is, the account of his life becomes an extended reflection on ethical themes of a more complicated kind. The turning point in David's life, as 2 Samuel presents it, is his adultery with Bathsheba and the murder of Uriah the Hittite.[20] It is from then on that his family affairs start to go awry, and that, in the context of ancient politics, means that national affairs do so, too. After the Bathsheba episode his family breaks up, with Amnon's rape of Tamar followed by Absalom's revenge, and then Absalom's own rebellion and assumption of the kingship. David eventually emerges from this major crisis through the

---

18. See Simcha Shalom Brooks, *Saul and the Monarchy: A New Look* (Aldershot: Ashgate, 2005).
19. There is an excellent treatment of the portrayal of David in Shimon Bar-Efrat, *Narrative Art in the Bible* (Sheffield: Sheffield Academic, 1989).
20. 2 Samuel 11.

skills of Hushai the Archite in persuading Absalom to delay in following through on his success in leading a large majority of the population to follow him; but he does so only through the loss of Absalom himself, his beloved son.[21] A simple sin followed by simple repentance and divine forgiveness turns out to have all kinds of ramifications, into which many other people—indeed the whole nation—are ineluctably drawn.

But it is more complicated still, because the death of Bathsheba's first (unnamed) child by David as punishment for his murder of Uriah clears the way for her later son, Solomon, eventually to succeed David on the throne. As many commentators have noted, the divine "plan" here, if that is the right word, is immensely convoluted.[22] But from the ethical point of view, too, matters are far from simple. Especially if sections of 2 Samuel are correctly read as a Succession Narrative, that is, an account of how Solomon came, through divine providence, to become king and to have the kingdom firmly established in his hand, then the route to that outcome lies across a heap of corpses. Perhaps, as Joseph says to his brothers of their attempt to dispose of him, "You intended to do harm to me, but God intended it for good."[23] But that does not excuse the plots and assassinations and war that lead up to the desired climax of Solomon sitting on the throne. 2 Samuel is not a story with a moral, and David is surely not an example of any straightforward ethical precepts. His story shows how good and bad intentions, good and bad actions, and good and bad advice interact to create complex historical situations in which praise and blame cannot readily be assigned. The main useful ethical advice to be drawn from David's story is perhaps this: be aware that single, apparently random acts can lead to whole complexes of interactive consequences that no-one can foresee.

David's moral character is highly complicated. He does keep his word, for example when he honors his promise to Shimei not to kill him in revenge for siding with Absalom and cursing David;[24] but he makes sure that Solomon will kill him after all, when David himself is dead.[25] Thus he has a vindictive side, which comes out also in his dealings with Nabal, who has refused to cooperate in what looks very like a protection racket.[26]

---

21. 2 Samuel 13–19.
22. See the discussion in David M. Gunn, *The Story of King David* (Sheffield: JSOT Press, 1978) for a classic discussion.
23. Genesis 50:20.
24. 2 Samuel 19:18-23.
25. 1 Kings 2:8-9.
26. 1 Samuel 25.

He is also ruthless in his dealings with rivals, forcing Ishbaal, Saul's son, to take Michal from Paltiel, her husband, and give her back to him:

> Ishbaal sent and took her from her husband Paltiel the son of Laish. But her husband went with her, weeping as he walked behind her all the way to Bahurim. Then Abner said to him, "Go back home!" So he went back.[27]

How we are meant to react to these character traits depends on whether we are intended to read the storyline in the books of Samuel and Kings as pro-David or anti-David. The later historian who compiled Kings regarded David as the norm of an admirable king; but the actual narratives are much more ambiguous. Just as we know that David's affair with Bathsheba and his taking of her as his wife after he has disposed of Uriah is disapproved of by the writer—since he tells us that God himself, through Nathan, expressed his abhorrence of it—so we may be meant to see a similar judgement in the way David takes not only Michal but also Abigail from her husband, though Abigail herself takes much more of an initiative than Bathsheba. The moral world of David and Abigail is not one of strict loyalty to one's spouse, but of deals and counter-deals, and of maximizing one's life chances and opportunities.

On the other hand there is considerable magnanimity in David's character, as we see in the two incidents when he could have killed Saul but did not do so.[28] Whether this really proceeded from respect for "Yahweh's anointed," as he says, or from a residual affection for Saul, the narrator does not tell us, though his address to Saul as "my father" might lead us to think that he really cared for Saul. David, we know, has strong personal attachments to other people: certainly to Saul, whose illness he treats with "music therapy," but also to Michal (till it turns to bitterness over the incident of his dancing before the ark[29]) and of course to Absalom, despite all the injuries Absalom has inflicted on him. Then there is his friendship with Jonathan, the nature of which is disputed by commentators: was it a homosexual relationship or not? Either way it is certainly portrayed as extremely strong, and is described in the lament in 2 Sam. 1:26 as "passing the love of women." David is presented as a man of strong passions, both for good and ill—impetuous and not always consistent, but inspiring loyalty and admiration in many around him.

---

27. 2 Samuel 3:15-16.
28. 1 Samuel 23 and 24.
29. 2 Samuel 6:20-23.

How might one today use the story of David in moral discernment? Perhaps a point made by E. M. Forster could help here. He points out that we sometimes know more about fictional characters than we do about our real contemporaries, because omniscient authors can choose to reveal more about them than we can deduce about the people we meet in real life.[30] A caveat must at once be entered where the biblical narratives are concerned, to the effect that biblical authors often conceal much (just as some novelists do), and do not let us know what is going on in their characters' hearts. Nevertheless the point is an important one. We know, for example, that David loved Jonathan because the narrator tells us he did; we do not have to deduce it from observing them, as we so often do in real life. This means that fictional characters can sometimes inform us less ambiguously than do real people about dealing with ethical situations. That is why Greek tragedy is so often felt to shine a light on to the human condition: it shows us people in extreme situations and reveals how they react. And the biblical account of someone as complex as David can have the same kind of value. It can open us up to understand humanity, in temptation, evil-doing, and sometimes even in virtuous living, in a way that observing human life in the real world sometimes fails to do. This is miles away from treating biblical characters as *exempla*.

Solomon

Solomon is a less round character than Saul and David, and arrives on the throne entirely through the machinations of others, so that we might think of him as an entirely virtuous, or perhaps a merely vacuous, person. But soon he starts to show interesting features, though it is unclear how we are meant to assess him. To begin with he shows the great wisdom for which he has prayed in the story of the two women and the baby.[31] But when it comes to his building works and the splendor of his court, the narrative becomes ambiguous. As a matter of source analysis, I would assume that the narrative began as a document praising a great and glorious

---

30. Forster, *Aspects of the Novel*, Chapter 4; see also Wayne C. Booth, *The Rhetoric of Fiction* (Chicago: University of Chicago Press, 1961; 2nd ed., 1983), 3: "In life we never know anyone but ourselves by thoroughly reliable internal signs, and most of us achieve an all too partial view even of ourselves. It is in a way strange, then, that in literature from the very beginning we have been told motives directly and authoritatively without being forced to rely on those shaky inferences about other men which we cannot avoid in our own lives."

31. 1 Kings 3:16-28.

king, perhaps taken from the "book of the acts of Solomon." But in its present setting in the Deuteronomistic History it serves to illustrate how Solomon fell into sin, disobeying the law of the king in Deuteronomy 17 by amassing silver and gold, "returning to Egypt" to obtain horses, and marrying too many wives, many of them foreign.[32] Historically speaking this law is perhaps based on the account in Kings, but as it now stands it serves as a criterion by which to assess the king, and find him wanting. The building of the temple is in many ways the high point of Solomon's reign; from then on, he goes steadily downhill. But surely even his settling of accounts with David's enemies and with Adonijah[33] as soon he is on the throne bespeaks a less-than-admirable character. At least if the author is correctly seen as critical of David for taking vengeance on enemies, then Solomon must be tarred with the same brush. His wisdom turns to folly in the end and leads him to leave the kingdom in a far worse state than he found it. He remains, however, a less clearly drawn character than either Saul or David, and he does not exactly develop over time; rather, he switches from wisdom to folly in a more simplistic way than his father, a much more complex character.

Bathsheba and Michal

Bathsheba appears in the stories of both David and Solomon. When we first meet her, she is a pawn in David's plans, and tends to be referred to as "the wife of Uriah" or "the woman" rather than by her name, which is mentioned in 2 Samuel only when David's servants identify her after he has seen her bathing. But in 1 Kings she emerges as a character in her own right. Her intervention (at Nathan's urging) is crucial in ensuring that Solomon is anointed king. But then she makes a fatal mistake—unless it is a piece of cunning—in trying to get Abishag as a wife for Adonijah, which leads to his execution. She is not drawn any more fully than this, but she is more than merely a device in the plot—she is a person we should like to know more about.[34] Similar things might be said of another important woman in David's life, Michal, passed from hand to hand by Saul but clearly loving David and prepared to risk death for him, as we see in the incident where she hides a teraphim in the bed to give Saul's servants the

---

32. 1 Kings 9:10-28.
33. 1 Kings 2:19-25.
34. See Sara Koenig, *Isn't This Bathsheba?* (Princeton: Princeton University Press, 2011), and her contribution on Bathsheba in the present volume.

impression that he is at home when in fact he has fled.[35] Yet later she is alienated by David's exposure of himself when dancing before the ark, and this leads to a permanent rift: the note that she "had no child to the day of her death" is perhaps meant to imply that the affronted David had no further intercourse with her.[36]

Neither of these women is anything like as round a character as the three men in whose lives they are entwined, but they are both far more than ciphers. Like women in ancient Israel in historical reality, they have no independent sphere of action, but are determined by the men who take them as wives or concubines. Yet both demonstrate that this kind of subordinate status can still be manipulated for good or ill, and perhaps that such people need not allow themselves to be simply sidelined.

Elijah

In the century after Solomon we encounter Elijah, Ahab, and Jezebel, and their stories also reveal ethical aspects of characterization. Elijah emerges suddenly, already fully fledged as a prophet, announcing (or commanding) that there shall be no rain because of the sins of Ahab,[37] and he is a powerful, indeed irresistible, figure. He can cause rain as well as prevent it, it seems,[38] and he has the authority to kill the prophets of Baal,[39] with the king apparently powerless to prevent him. Yet he pre-eminently demonstrates the capacity to surprise us that Forster identifies as typical of round characters, since he experiences despair and depression alongside his supernatural abilities—less unlike Saul than one might think on a first impression. He is no cardboard prophet, but a nuanced individual whose almost magical powers co-exist with personal doubts and fears, fears which lead him to exaggerate his own isolation, saying "I alone am left" when God says, on the contrary, "I will leave seven thousand in Israel, all the knees that have not bowed to Baal, and every mouth that has not kissed him."[40] Paradoxically, this extraordinary wonder-worker turns out also to be a real human being with very human failings. If there is a "moral" in the stories of Elijah, it is that a sense of divine vocation can exist alongside depression and a sense of isolation. Of course there are miraculous elements in the Elijah cycle, as there are not so much in the

---

35. 1 Samuel 29:11-17.
36. 2 Samuel 6:23.
37. 1 Kings 17:1.
38. 1 Kings 18:41-46.
39. 1 Kings 18:40.
40. 1 Kings 19:10, 14, and 18.

tales of Saul, David, and Solomon; but it is nevertheless an account of a human figure drawn from life, not of a plaster saint. Elijah has an inner life, which we are allowed glimpses into from time to time.

Elijah combines power and authority and ruthlessness with diffidence and despair, inspired not by wind and fire but by the "still, small voice" (or "sound of sheer silence," NRSV) in which God is present.[41] Ahab fears him, Jezebel hates him; both try to kill him. He is presented as God's representative in a time of national apostasy, who escapes plots and violent assaults yet fears them at the same time, since it is never clear how far his quasi-magical powers will reach to keep him safe. From him we learn what it is like to be called to stand up for the cause of God in a hostile environment, with no certainty that God will provide protection. Even at the last, when he is to be assumed into heaven by horses and a chariot of fire, he does not know for sure what will be his legacy: will Elisha inherit a double portion of his spirit or not?[42]

As with Samuel, Saul, David, and many others, the tales about Elijah are complex, and they may reflect different perspectives on the prophet from partly mutually inconsistent traditions. Elijah is both a figure like the "classical" prophets, denouncing sin, yet also a rain-maker and magician. Where the latter aspect of Elijah is concerned, the narrator reveals few personal features, whereas with the former we learn of his inner turmoil. But as the texts now stand, the result is a rich blend of prophecy and magic, which appears in at least one of the classical prophets too: Isaiah, who denounced national injustice yet also miraculously healed Hezekiah, and caused the sun to move back in the sky.[43] Like Isaiah, Elijah not only reveals the power of the true God but also engages in criticism of the king and his policies, against a background of personal vulnerability. His vocation is to ignore his inner doubts and go in the strength of the sustenance that God provides, and this seems to make him a model to be imitated. Yet it is never quite clear how far the Hebrew Bible actually sets up people like Elijah as ideal types for imitation, or regards them as wholly unusual, and so not models at all. At all events the reader is surely meant to learn from them what serving God can entail, even if few people are going to share Elijah's special mission. That mission, of course, includes elements we would have grave doubts about, such as killing hundreds of prophets of Baal. Hearing the "still small voice of calm," as the well-known hymn "Dear Lord and Father of Mankind" puts it, results in Elijah's enabling the assassination of the king of Aram and Jehu's

41. 1 Kings 19:12.
42. 2 Kings 2:10.
43. Isaiah 38:1-8, cf. 2 Kgs 20:1-11.

bloody coup.[44] This is not the kind of action of which most strands in the Old Testament recommend imitation, but that it is one strand cannot be denied. God's general commands in the Hebrew Bible are mostly benign, but some of his particular ones can be brutal and murderous. We can hardly learn from Elijah, an exceptional figure, how to live an ordinary day-to-day life in society.

Ahab and Jezebel

Ahab and Jezebel, Elijah's contemporaries, are also interesting from an ethical point of view. Both are presented as unequivocally wicked, not only because they are Baal-worshippers, but also because they are socially oppressive, as we see in the story of Naboth's vineyard.[45] Like the rich people later condemned by Isaiah for enclosing the land of the poor,[46] Ahab seeks to acquire a plot of land that belongs by ancestral right to Naboth and which ought not to be alienated even for adequate monetary compensation: the king of Israel has no right of compulsory purchase. But Ahab is presented as inept even in his wickedness, and it takes the advice he receives from Jezebel—a sort of Lady Macbeth before her time—to hatch a plot that will ensure he gets what he wants. Jezebel writes letters, sealed with Ahab's seal, that cause Naboth to be indicted and tried on a trumped-up charge of having cursed God and the king, in contravention of Exod. 22:28. The result is that he is executed by stoning, and consequently his land reverts to the king. Ahab, however, repents, and (as with David after the murder of Uriah) the punishment he deserves is immediately postponed by God—as revealed to Elijah, Ahab's greatest adversary.

Ahab is pictured as a sullen and disagreeable figure, a feeble man dependent on his wife even for a plan to carry out his own evil designs; while Jezebel is the brains behind the king's actions, and seen as unequivocally evil. Yet Jezebel has her moment of bravado when Jehu comes to kill her, doing her make-up and refusing to hide, instead watching from her window till Jehu gets her eunuchs to throw her down and kill her.[47] It seems that the narrator could not resist a certain admiration for Jezebel's refusal to be cowed even in her last moments: she is a strong character, and her strength may be being presented as something to be imitated, even though she uses it in such bad causes.

44. 1 Kings 19:17.
45. 1 Kings 21.
46. Isaiah 5:5-10.
47. 2 Kings 9:30-37.

Hezekiah

After Ahab there are few round characters in Kings, which becomes increasingly a catalogue of monarchs who imitate the sins of Jeroboam I or Solomon in encouraging "pagan" worship. One exception, however, is Hezekiah, a "good" king who attempted to centralize worship at Jerusalem, anticipating the reforms of Josiah.[48] Hezekiah is commended also for showing faith in Yahweh during the Assyrian invasion and siege of Jerusalem, trusting in the advice of Isaiah, and finally escaping when the Assyrian army withdraws because of the miraculous "rumor" that causes it to flee.[49] Yet he is also not uncomplicated, since afterwards he behaves foolishly in letting a Babylonian delegation see the treasures in Jerusalem—a boastful action that naturally alerts the Babylonians to the rich pickings they might have there in time to come.[50] But, like Ahab, Hezekiah is told that the Babylonian invasion will not happen in his own days. There is thus a pattern in Samuel-Kings according to which even serious sins, such as those of David, Ahab, and Hezekiah, can be at least temporarily passed over, and their consequences mitigated or postponed—at least on the surface. At a deeper level, God is revealed as one who, though forgiving, also punishes: "you were a forgiving God to them, but an avenger of their wrongdoings," as Ps. 99:8 puts it. David is forgiven, yet his family is riven apart by the effects of his sin; Ahab is forgiven, but he is killed in battle and Jezebel is assassinated; Hezekiah's stupidity is overlooked, but in the next generation Babylon invades and puts an end to the kingdom of Judah. The idea—pervasive in the Deuteronomistic History, though rejected in Chronicles—that guilt builds up down the generations and is eventually avenged, is seen in all three of these kings' lives and heritages. They may at least in some measure escape themselves, but there is a taint on them and their families that cannot really be expunged. Whether a modern reading of the Bible permits us to affirm this as just, readers will differ about, but there can be little doubt that, as an empirical observation about how life actually unfolds, it has a certain truth. William Blake's dictum "Some are born to sweet delight, some are born to endless night" is unfortunately all too true to life as we see it around us, even if we insist that this is not the product of divine justice.

---

48. 2 Kings 18:1-8.
49. 2 Kings 18:9–19:37.
50. 2 Kings 20:12-19.

The characterization in the narrative books of the Hebrew Bible is often subtle and complex, and we have seen that it sometimes shows deep reflection on ethical matters. It undermines any idea that ethics in the Bible is simple or even crude: the interplay of complicated characters creates all sorts of interesting ethical situations, and God's place in the overall scheme is often hard to discern. The more highly developed biblical characters are far from being simple or obvious, and in thinking about their lives and deeds we can reflect on morality in a three-dimensional way, not resting content with a simple moralism but going on to think about the ways in which ethics is concerned with grey areas.

Chapter 2

AHAZ AND JEROBOAM

A. Graeme Auld

Two Bad Kings

Ahaz and Jeroboam "enjoy" two of the worst reputations in the book of Kings. About one half of David's successors in Jerusalem are introduced as having done "what was right in the eyes of Yahweh." Among them, Hezekiah (2 Kgs 18–20) and Josiah (22–23) are explicitly ranked alongside David. The other half are said to have done "what was evil in the eyes of Yahweh." Ahaz (2 Kgs 16) must be ranked alongside this latter group but is doubly unique. First of all, the preliminary assessment of him is in two parts: "He did not do what is right in the eyes of Yahweh his God, as his father David had done, but he walked in the way of the kings of Israel." Next, the first of these is not said of any other king. Unlike these kings of Judah with their different ratings, each successor of David and Solomon in (northern) Israel after the first is introduced the same way: "He did what was evil in the eyes of Yahweh; he did not turn from the sins of Jeroboam son of Nebat, which he caused Israel to sin." What complicates this plot is the fact that Jeroboam himself is presented as something of a second David (1 Kgs 11–14).

We have wicked Ahaz who is *not like* David and sinful Jeroboam who is *like* David. David of course figures much more largely in biblical tradition and is a much more complex character than either Ahaz or Jeroboam. Yet at least part of this conundrum is likely down to different stages in the writing of Samuel and Kings. Ahaz is unlike one (more favourable) presentation of David; and Jeroboam is part of another (less positive) David story. David was always a nuanced character as far back as we can probe the tradition. However, as part of the general discrediting of kingship in the Former Prophets, more and more doubts and negatives accumulated in his record. Ahaz was contrasted with "good old David," while the Jeroboam of the familiar book of Kings has his place in a fresh development of the story of Israel's kings. The older story of Jeroboam had not mentioned David, though the discerning reader might have noted parallels between them—David had been in Saul's service and Jeroboam in Solomon's. However, the newer expanded story is explicit about the links.

There are many differences between the ancient texts available to us: between Kings and Chronicles; between the standard Hebrew text and fragments in the Dead Sea Scrolls; between each of these and the ancient translations of these books into Greek). Most of them are small; yet they help us to glimpse, and occasionally see more clearly, how the books of Kings and Chronicles were edited and rewritten. The following essay will take account of the rewriting of both Ahaz and Jeroboam within biblical tradition.

Ahaz

Sometimes explicitly and sometimes implicitly, Ahaz is compared and contrasted with several other kings.[1] The introduction starts in standard fashion: Ahaz was 20 years old when he succeeded as king on the death of his father Jotham; and he reigned for 16 years (2 Kgs 16:2a). But it goes its own way when it comes to assessing Ahaz. Ahaz is doubly unique: he is accorded a negative assessment in two parts, and the first part is not repeated elsewhere: (a) he did *not* do what was right in Yahweh's eyes like David his father; (b) he walked in the way of the kings of Israel. It may be that the narrator is less interested in a contrast between Ahaz and the David of the distant past, but more in a contrast with Hezekiah his own son and Josiah in the immediate future, both of whom *did* what was right just like David his father. The second part, walking in the ways of the kings of Israel, aligned Ahaz instead with Jehoram and his son Ahaziah (namesake of Ahaz), who had been reported as walking in the ways of the house of Ahab (2 Kgs 8:18, 27). Ahaz is *not* like David, or Hezekiah,

---

1. For further discussion of Ahaz see A. Graeme Auld, *Life in Kings: Reshaping the Royal Story in the Hebrew Bible*, Ancient Israel and its Literature 30 (Atlanta: SBL Press, 2017), 69–76 and 150–1.

or Josiah; but he *is* like Jehoram and Ahaziah of Israel. As he moves to specifics, the narrator continues to suggest comparisons and contrasts. Ahaz (16:3) anticipated wicked Manasseh (21:6): "he even made his son pass in/through fire." And such behavior was "according to the abominations of the nations who Yahweh drove out in face of the sons of Israel," another formula found only in the introduction to Manasseh (21:2). There can be no doubt about the two comparisons with Manasseh: they are stated in exactly the same terms.

The contrast with Solomon that follows is, however, less than fully explicit (though rather more suggestive in Hebrew than in English). "He sacrificed...on the 'high places' on the hills" (16:4) alludes to two elements of the Solomon story: Solomon had offered sacrifice at the great "high place" at Gibeon before receiving a first vision from Yahweh (1 Kgs 3:4)—and, in its very name, Gibeon (*gb'wn*), the peak that towers over Jerusalem from the NW, was a "hill" (*gb'h*) *par excellence*. Then, though Solomon had sacrificed (*zbḥ*) at Gibeon, a more intensive form of the same verb is used to describe his "enthusiastic sacrificing" as the divine ark was brought into the new temple in Jerusalem (1 Kgs 8:5)— and exactly this (piel) form of the verb "sacrifice" is now used to describe Ahaz's cultic behavior "on the 'high places' on the hills." Solomon had *pro*gressed from Gibeon to the new national sanctuary in Jerusalem; but Ahaz's cultic practices were *re*gressive and were carried out at several sites. The synoptic tradition certainly observes that "high places" were not removed in the time of Kings Asa and Jehoshaphat; but none of the kings between Solomon and Ahaz is said to have sacrificed at one of these—the book of Kings states (and the book of Chronicles may well imply) that it was just the people that frequented such local sanctuaries. Ahaz was unlike David and Hezekiah and Josiah, but like the kings of Israel; like Manasseh (whose long reign would follow between Hezekiah and Josiah), but unlike Solomon. With these broad stroke introductory comparisons 2 Kings 16 and 2 Chronicles 28 are in full agreement: this is the common or assured biblical tradition. This so-called "synoptic" tradition offers a further unique royal pairing: it mentions Assyria and its king(s) only in connection with Ahaz and his son Hezekiah, so inviting readers to compare or contrast these kings as they relate to the great imperial power.

Between this introduction and the largely formulaic conclusion (2 Kgs 16:17-18//2 Chron. 28:26-27), Kings and Chronicles tell a story with several shared elements, but very differently.

	2 Kings 16		*2 Chronicles 28*
5	War with Aram and Israel	5-15	War with Aram and Israel
7	Appeal to Assyria	16	Appeal to Assyria
6	Trouble with Edom	17	Trouble with Edom
		18	Philistine raids
		19	Judah brought low by Ahaz
8	Treasures sent from Jerusalem	21	Treasures sent from Jerusalem
9	Assyria does respond	20	Assyria does NOT respond
10-16	Copy made of Damascus altar		
		22	Ahaz still more faithless
		23	Ahaz sacrificed to gods of Aram
17	Cut up temple furniture (detail)	24	Cut up temple furniture (summary)
18	Other Jerusalem changes		
		25	'High places' in every city of Judah

Figure 1. 2 Kings 16/2 Chronicles 28

It is a useful principle that the shorter version of a shared tradition is the older. On that basis, we would see the summary statement of the war with Aram and Israel (2 Kgs 16:5) as prior, with 2 Chron. 28:5-15 as secondary expansion. On the other hand, Chronicles states the appeal to Assyria more briefly (28:16), while Kings includes the terms of Ahaz's message to the Assyrian king (16:7). His words are quite extraordinary: "I am your servant and your son. Come up and rescue me…" Out of all the kings in Jerusalem, only David and Solomon have ever called themselves "your servant"—and only when speaking to Yahweh—or been called "my servant" by Yahweh. Then, except for its regular, literal genealogical sense, "son" only appears in that synoptic tradition where Yahweh makes a promise to David: he will be "father" to one of David's offspring who in turn will be "son" to Yahweh (2 Sam. 7:14). In this longer version of the appeal for help (2 Kgs 16:7), Ahaz is making a commitment to the king of Assyria in terms that he would have used only before Yahweh, had he been like David or Solomon. Furthermore, in synoptic narratives, "rescue" and "save" are only found in narratives about David and Hezekiah. Now the Chronicler has not a single good word to say about Ahaz. We have already noted that Ahaz and Manasseh share key elements of negative assessment. Yet, according to 2 Chron. 33:12-19, even wicked Manasseh will come to see the error of his ways. This king does not. On his death, 2 Kgs 16:20 reports the burial of Ahaz in "the city of David"—the royal necropolis; but 2 Chron. 28:27 insists he was *not* brought into "the tombs of the kings." There was therefore no reason for the Chronicler to delete this compromising passage from 2 Kgs 16:7, if it was part of his source. It is more sensible to conclude that the author of 2 Kgs 16:7b has added "I am your servant and your son; come up and rescue me," to blacken Ahaz still further. For the same reason, he added the pejorative word "bribe" (or "present") to the report in 16:8 of sending state treasures to Assyria in return for help.

Quite the largest "plus" in 2 Kings 16 vis-à-vis 2 Chronicles 28 serves the same function. According to this extended report (vv. 10-16), Ahaz visits Tiglath-Pileser of Assyria in Damascus, sees an impressive altar there, and sends a model of it to Uriah his priest in Jerusalem with instructions to make a precise copy. On his return to Jerusalem, he inspects it and offers various sacrifices on it. Having inaugurated the new altar, he moves the old bronze altar to its side, and gives extended instructions to Uriah: the new "great altar" should be used for the morning and evening sacrifices of king and people—and the bronze altar will be for the king's own use (for exactly what purpose is not clear). When the synoptic introduction to the Ahaz story invoked memories of Solomon, it was only in order to suggest a clear distinction between how each of these kings resorted to "high places." Ahaz himself, and not just his people, had been involved in cultic practices at a plurality of "high places"—presumably outside Jerusalem. This added narrative in Kings now does concern Jerusalem and makes further allusions to the king who had built its temple: (1) No other king since Solomon has been reported as presiding at sacrifice there. (2) The altar Ahaz describes as "great" is a striking reminder of the "great high place" visited by Solomon at Gibeon. (3) In synoptic tradition, only David and Solomon offered the sacrifices called *shelamim* ("offerings of wellbeing" in 2 Kgs 16:13, NRSV). And in Samuel-Kings as a whole, apart from David and Solomon, no other king but Saul has offered these sacrifices. Ahaz is presented as a large-scale innovator. Indeed, the detailed ritual instructions from this king to his priestly deputy remind us not so much of Solomon as of Moses passing divine instructions to Aaron.

The detailed report on the new altar is followed by a couple of verses (17-18) that are clearly related to 2 Chron. 28:24a but say something very different. Most obviously, both state that Ahaz "cut up" or "cut off" something that had to do with "the house of Yahweh." Kings talks of removing a king's outer entrance to the temple, Chronicles simply of closing the doors (of Yahweh's house). Most puzzling, the verb "close" (*sgr*) in 2 Chron. 28:24 is cognate with the plural noun *msgrwt* in 2 Kgs 16:17. These were some attribute or accompaniment of the "stands" or "supports" by which the great "sea" was held clear of the ground and are often translated "frames." Whatever earlier form of words had linked these shared elements, Kings reports radical alterations within the Jerusalem temple while Chronicles states clearly that Ahaz closed it: in its place "he made himself altars in every corner of Jerusalem"—the multiple "high places" he supported outside the city were now matched by multiple altars within it.

The opening overview (shared by Kings and Chronicles) sketches an Ahaz who is not like Hezekiah and Josiah but is aligned instead with Jehoram and Ahaziah and Manasseh. It also hints at a contrast between Ahaz and Solomon. However, in the narrative in Kings about Ahaz's new "great" altar in Jerusalem, this king has taken on Solomonic—and even Mosaic—pretensions. On the two occasions when the added material introduces Ahaz's own words, we must deduce that they are being cited against him: his readiness to replace loyalty to Yahweh with loyalty to the king of Assyria (16:7) and to impose new cultic arrangements on his priest (16:15).[2]

Jeroboam

There are two (obviously related) versions of Ahaz, one in Kings and the other in Chronicles. For Jeroboam, the textual evidence is more complicated. We shall concentrate here on the two different versions within Kings—at least in the ancient Greek translation of that book. The standard Hebrew text preserves just one; and that means that in 1 Kings 11–14 our English Bibles also make only that one available to us. Greek Kings includes a translation of most of this longer Jeroboam account, but not the final part about the sickness and death of his first son in 1 Kgs 14:1-18. However, at the heart of the remainder (between 12:24 and 12:25), Kings in Greek also contains an alternative, shorter, and quite differently arranged, Jeroboam story. This story, though available to us only in Greek, clearly did have a Hebrew original; and this was presumably part of the edition of the Hebrew book of Kings available to the Greek translator.[3] Partly because it is shorter, partly because its range is more restricted,

---

2. For a more sympathetic account of a historical Ahaz, see Marvin A. Sweeney, *I & II Kings*, OTL (Louisville: Westminster John Knox, 2007), 378–86.

3. Zipora Talshir has been widely commended for her study, *The Alternative Story: 3 Kingdoms 12:24 A–Z*, Jerusalem Biblical Studies 6 (Jerusalem: Simor, 1993). The divisions of this story, mostly longer than traditional biblical verses, are normally numbered a to z. An English translation is also available in Sweeney, *I & II Kings*,

but partly also because of the nature of the main "pluses" in the longer version, I suspect that the alternative text preserved in Greek gives us access to an older account of Jeroboam than we find in our Hebrew or English Bibles.[4] Be that as it may, reading the two versions of Jeroboam together helps our appreciation of each.

The shorter, less familiar, account is presented in three stages. (1) We learn first (b-f) that Jeroboam had responsibility for Solomon's building works both in Ephraim and in Jerusalem, and that he aspired to kingship. Solomon sought to kill this potential rival, and Jeroboam took refuge in Egypt till Solomon's death. When he asked permission to return, the pharaoh offered him a relative of his own wife in marriage. They married and had a child in Egypt. On his return to Ephraim, his whole tribe gathered to him and he built a castle in his home town. (2) The second act (g-n1) tells of the serious illness of his son by the princess. Jeroboam asked his wife to ask God about the child: she should take a gift of several foodstuffs to Ahijah, the man of God in Shiloh. As she approached, Ahijah asked his lad to meet her and tell her that Yahweh had a bad message for her. When she came before the man of God, Ahijah said to her: "Why have you brought me the foodstuffs, for I have bad news for you? When you come to your town, your maidens will meet you and tell you your child has died." A divine threat against Jeroboam's wider progeny followed. As Jeroboam's wife reached her town, she was met by lamentation. (3) Jeroboam's next move was to assemble all Israel's tribes to Shechem, in Ephraim's hill-country (n2-u). They were joined there by "Rehoboam son of Solomon." The word of Yahweh came to Shemaiah, "Take to yourself a new garment that has not entered water and tear it into twelve tatters before you put it on. Give Jeroboam ten tatters and say to him, 'This is what Yahweh says: "Take to yourself ten tatters to put on."'" And Jeroboam took

---

165–7—but without comment. However, in the same year, Sweeney sought to defend the priority of the MT in "A Reassessment of the Masoretic and Septuagint Versions of the Jeroboam Narratives in 1 Kings/3 Kingdoms 11–14," *JSJ* 38 (2007): 165–95.

4. Adrian Schenker has argued strongly for the priority of the shorter variant account, notably in "Jeroboam and the Division of the Kingdom in the Ancient Septuagint," in *Israel constructs its History*, ed. Albert de Pury, Thomas Römer, and Jean-Daniel Macchi, JSOTSup 34 (Sheffield: Sheffield Academic, 2000), 193–236. And he could be said to have refuted Sweeney's 2007 article (see note above) in "Jeroboam's Rise and Fall in the Hebrew and Greek Bible: Methodological Reflections on a Recent Article…," *JSJ* 38 (2008): 367–73. A. Graeme Auld develops Schenker's argument in light of his *Life in Kings* (n. 1 above) in "Some Thoughts on the First Jeroboam," *Biblische Notizen* (forthcoming).

them, and Shemaiah said to him, 'This is what Yahweh says, "Over the ten tribes of Israel shall you be king."'" The people then probed Rehoboam about his style of government in terms familiar from 1 Kgs 12:4-14. On his harsh response, they rejected the family of David, and Jeroboam returned to Jerusalem to rule over Judah and Benjamin only.

This account of Jeroboam has the Rehoboam story as its outer frame. At its start, we have the formal report of Solomon's death and burial and the succession of his son, who "did what was evil in the eyes of Yahweh and did not walk in the way of David his father" (a). And it ends in the year following the debacle in Shechem (x-z), when Rehoboam assembles Judah and Benjamin and goes up to Shechem to make war on Jeroboam but is prevented by Yahweh's word to Shemaiah (almost exactly as in 1 Kgs 12:21-24//2 Chron. 11:1-4). This version of the Jeroboam story is framed by the Rehoboam story. Its contribution within the larger house of David/Jerusalem narrative is to offer a part-explanation of how Rehoboam's kingdom lost the north, the majority of its territory—the rest was down to Rehoboam's own folly.

The clues to Jeroboam's characterization are ambiguous from the start of the shorter account. To start with his mother: she is introduced as a prostitute, and there is no mention of his father. We are inevitably reminded of Jephthah (Judg. 11:1-11), another bastard son who was also forced into exile. On the other hand, we are told his mother's name (b), and the actual form of words used ("and the name of his mother was X") is only used within the Bible's royal story (from Rehoboam onwards, in both Kings and Chronicles) where a new king is being introduced. In fact, we find this formula only once more in all the Hebrew Bible: in Lev. 24:10-12, a piece of legislation that appears to include some coded references to the story of Jeroboam. It may be significant that when Rehoboam "comes up" (n) to join the assembly at Shechem he is called "son of Solomon," so stressing his legitimate birth. Then, when Jeroboam is described as "exalting himself as far as the kingship" (b), the wording is very similar to 1 Kgs 1:5, where we read of the failed attempt by Adonijah (David's eldest surviving son) to become king when his father's strength is failing; and his many chariots (also b) recall Absalom at the start of his revolt (2 Sam. 15:1). Marrying a close relative of Pharaoh (e) compares Jeroboam with Solomon himself, just as favor shown to him in Egypt evokes memories of Joseph. [Re-]Building his own town, on his return to Ephraim from Egypt, is typical business of a king (f). And Shishak's spoiling of the Jerusalem temple in Rehoboam's fifth year (1 Kgs 14:25-26) can be read as the Pharaoh's reaction to the events at Shechem not long before.

The response Jeroboam's wife receives from the man of God in Shiloh is much worse than they could have expected. Not only will the sick child die as soon as she returns home (l), but all Jeroboam's male offspring will be "cut off" and their corpses scavenged by dogs in the towns and birds in the country (m). The first part of the divine threat is validated by the lamentation that greets her return home. However, undaunted, Jeroboam assembles all the tribes (or scepters) of Israel in Shechem; and Rehoboam too "went up" (n). This common verb often implies attack, but there is nothing to suggest hostility here: when David "went up" to Hebron (2 Sam. 2:2), he was simply making a journey with his two wives.

Before any more is reported, Jeroboam receives a second divine oracle (o). This comes in the form of an acted parable; and, as in other biblical stories, it involves a torn garment (see below on 1 Sam. 15). The type of cloak is part of the message; for the same four Hebrew letters (*slmh*) can be read one way as *salmah* (cloak) and another way as *Shelomoh* (Solomon). Shemaiah's tearing of the pristine cloak is deliberate, and twin conclusions are implied: Jeroboam will receive only (the larger) part of the whole kingdom; and even that part will be severely damaged—in ten tatters. Jeroboam had convoked the tribes and may have been involved in their discussion with Rehoboam (p-t). But he is not actually mentioned again till the very end, where he is the target of Rehoboam's planned invasion of the north (x). In the shorter story, David is mentioned only twice: Rehoboam does not follow David's example (a); and, when the people reject Rehoboam, what they say is "we have no portion in David" (t).

In the longer and more familiar account within 1 Kings 11–14 (MT), Jeroboam is also introduced as responsible for Solomon's labor-gangs (11:28). But in this version the start of the Jeroboam story is told within the parameters of the whole Solomon narrative.[5] On one occasion, as he was on the way from Jerusalem, Ahijah the prophet found him, grasped the garment he was wearing, and tore it in twelve tatters, and said: "Take to yourself ten tatters; for this is what Yahweh has said, 'I am tearing the kingdom from the hand of Solomon and shall give you the ten tribes…'" (11:29-39). Solomon sought to kill him, and he escaped to Egypt (11:40). However, in this version, Jeroboam is only the third of three such troublemakers for Solomon; and it is the first of them, an Edomite prince and also a refugee in Egypt, that marries the Egyptian princess (11:14-22).

---

5. Keith Bodner offers a very fine reading of this longer version in *Jeroboam's Royal Drama*, Biblical Refigurations (Oxford: Oxford University Press, 2012), but does not enter the discussion of alternative texts (n. 7 on p. 7).

Then comes the formulaic report of Solomon's death and burial and the succession of Rehoboam (11:41-43); and that is followed by Rehoboam going to Shechem, where "all Israel" had come to "king" him (12:1). As in the shorter version, but without mention of an Egyptian royal marriage, Jeroboam comes home on learning of Solomon's death (12:2). Jeroboam is mentioned among the representatives of Israel who put critical questions to Rehoboam (12:3). The new king's rejection of their concerns is attributed to Yahweh turning events to establish his own word spoken through Ahijah to Jeroboam (12:15). Before the shared account of Rehoboam's return to Jerusalem and subsequent attempt to recoup his losses by force, we read of his sending Adoram, who was [taskmaster] over the forced labor, whom "all Israel" stoned to death (12:18).

The story of Jeroboam's sick son is not told in 1 Kings till 14:1-18, after the account of his cultic activities at Bethel and Dan (12:25-33), and after the narrative about the visit to Bethel of the man of God from Judah and its lengthy aftermath (13). It is followed by a summary of Jeroboam's reign and the succession of Nadab his son (14:19-20). Neither longer nor shorter element of 14:1-20 (in Hebrew, or English) is represented in the Greek rendering of the (mostly) longer Jeroboam narrative. LXX mentions Nadab for the first time in 15:25, at the start of its short report on his reign. That means that the only report preserved in Greek on the son who died despite appeal to the man of God is the second "act" of the shorter alternative history.

In each of the episodes that are (broadly) shared between the shorter and longer narratives, there are small differences and also several ambiguities; and these bear on our assessment of characterization. The larger contrasts are of two sorts and both are "theological"—though quite differently—in that they concern the prophetic interpretations of the action. Shemaiah explains his acted parable of the torn garment only in terms of Jeroboam becoming king over part(s) of Israel (o); and the people then turn to bargain with Rehoboam. All of this takes place within the assembly at Shechem; and readers of the shorter version may fairly assume that both people and Rehoboam witnessed or were made quickly aware of what Shemaiah had done and said. In the longer version of the acted parable (this time ascribed to Ahijah), Solomon is still alive and Jeroboam (somewhere not far from Jerusalem) is still his servant. Ahijah starts his explanation with an extended indictment of Solomon (11:31-33) and moves on to offer Jeroboam (11:37) terms like Abner had offered David over northern Israel (2 Sam. 3:21). The immediate result is that Jeroboam must flee to Egypt till his king dies.

The shorter (alternative) history has nothing to say about the implications of the (Rehoboam and) Jeroboam narratives for the larger storyline in Kings about the divine promises to David and the divine demands on his house. However, in the longer (familiar) history, these implications are spelled out in great detail, most densely in 1 Kgs 11:31b-39 but also within the prophecy about the sick child (14:7-9). Such theological/ dynastic explanations are not only completely absent from the shorter alternative version but are also integrally related to the order in which the whole longer narrative is presented. It is not just that the longer (Ahijah) form of the parable (the earlier of the divine words in the familiar version) blames Solomon, offers Jeroboam a role as a part-replacement David, and hence leads to his immediate exile. The shorter (Shemaiah) form of the ten tatters comes on the heels of Ahijah's oracle delivered to Jeroboam's wife, warning that the death of their first son will be only the start of the divine threat to his house. Heard against that threatening background, the offer of ten tatters to wear from a larger garment is less a promise than a threat. It is not that the longer narrative has a religious component while the shorter does not, but rather that the shared prophetic actions are quite differently arranged and developed in each. Only in the longer version do the extended prophetic oracles explain how the story of Jeroboam relates to the divine promises to David and the iniquitous behavior of Solomon.

The Jeroboam who will receive a promise analogous to David is differently introduced in the longer version: his father is named (Nebat) and his mother is not a prostitute but a widow (11:26). "All Israel" had come to Shechem to "king" Rehoboam; Jeroboam had returned from Egypt; Israel summoned him, and they jointly put questions to Rehoboam (12:2-3, 12). After the threat of invasion from the south was averted on prophetic advice, we learn of building operations by Jeroboam: not at his own town of Zeredah, as in the alternative version (f), but at Shechem which he made his residence, and at Penuel (12:25). Penuel (Gen. 32), Shechem (Gen. 33), and of course Bethel (Gen. 28), all have positive resonance in the story of Jacob/Israel. Like the comparison with David, these echoes tie this Jeroboam son of Nebat positively into the larger biblical narrative. However, fearing that continuing worship in Jerusalem will lure his people back to Rehoboam, he furnishes cult-centers at Bethel and Dan with golden calves (12:26-30). And this time the echo from the books of Moses is quite negative: the golden calf fashioned by Aaron in the absence of Moses, that nearly led to the destruction of the people (Exod. 32; Deut. 9). Jeroboam's people did worship before his calves; and this "became a sin." And this "sin" was the only element of the Jeroboam story to be recalled throughout the account of northern Israel in the books of Kings: each of his successors, without exception, is blamed for continuing "in the sin which Jeroboam caused Israel to sin." David had also sinned (2 Sam. 24:10); but he had sought to clear his own sin by building an altar in Jerusalem and sacrificing at it (24:25). Adding iniquity to iniquity, Jeroboam appointed priests who were not Levites and instituted a fresh sacral timetable (12:30-33).

When Jeroboam himself was presiding at the altar over offerings by fire, a man of God from Judah arrived and proclaimed a divine oracle against the Bethel altar itself. The king stretched out his hand, commanding that the intruder be seized, and his hand withered—echoing the fate of the worthless shepherd in Zechariah's vision, who deserted the flock (11:17). Jeroboam making such offerings is in dubious company in the book of Kings: with Solomon at the "high places" (1 Kgs 3:3), with Solomon's wives to their several gods (11:8), with "the priests of the high places" (13:2), and with Ahaz at his new altar (2 Kgs 16:13, 15). At the same time as he lost power in his hand, the altar was "torn" (1 Kgs 13:3, 5). This verb is most often used of tearing clothing, as in the acted parable, where it symbolized tearing the kingdom. Jeroboam was the beneficiary then but is the loser now.

Jeroboam now asks the man of God to "soften Yahweh's face" (13:6), to entreat him to change his mind. It is a phrase with significant echoes. Yahweh tells Moses when still on the mountain that his people are worshipping a golden calf, that he will destroy them, and start a new people from Moses. But Moses successfully softens his face (Exod. 32:11). Saul tells Samuel that, in expectation of a Philistine advance, he knew he had not softened Yahweh's face; and he forced himself to offer up a holocaust. Another golden calf, and another rejected king. In this instance, the man of God did successfully intercede—as had Moses. The king now offers the man of God a meal and a gift, but these are roundly rejected: even for half the king's house he would neither eat nor drink in this place. It is another uncanny echo: again, in the temple in Bethel but now in the time of the much later king Jeroboam, Amos (also from Judah) is warned by the priest to return south and eat his bread there—not practice his prophetic craft in the national shrine of the Northern Kingdom (Amos 7:10-17).

We meet Jeroboam for the last time, anxious about his sick son. As in the alternative shorter version, he does not go himself but sends his wife to the man of God in Shiloh. Again, she should take gifts of food; but, in this version, she should also not be recognized: she should "alter herself" (14:2). The words are different, but we are inevitably reminded of Saul who "disguised himself and put on other clothes" before going to En-Dor to consult the medium (1 Sam. 28:6). Jeroboam also remarks to his wife that it was Ahijah who had said of him that he would be "king over this people." This note may well have a double function. On the surface, consulting the prophet who had promised him kingship again compares the relationship between Jeroboam and Ahijah with that between Saul and Samuel. However, the narrator may also be using Jeroboam to tell readers aware of the other version, which told that Shemaiah made the prediction to him, that it had really been one and the same Ahijah. There is a similar tell-tale note in 1 Kgs 12:6. The shorter version simply reports that Rehoboam consulted the elders (q); but the longer continues "who had attended his father Solomon while he was still alive." The longer version makes more of Solomon in the story; and, as a general rule, the words "live," "life," and "alive" play a much larger role in later than earlier elements of Samuel and Kings.[6]

Yahweh briefs Ahijah in advance, telling him that his visitor is "playing a stranger"—the verb is used just once more in the Bible: at the first meeting of Joseph with his brothers in Egypt, he recognizes them but to them he seems a stranger (Gen. 42:7). Ahijah's response to Jeroboam's wife is much more extensive than in the other version. As with Samuel and Saul at Endor, the divine response goes far beyond the immediate enquiry, be it Philistine pressure there or a child's illness here. Whether Saul or Jeroboam, in both cases the royal house is lost. The sick child dies and is buried and mourned by the people. But we are told nothing about any involvement of his father; and, in fact, we do not meet Jeroboam himself again.

In the shorter version, Jeroboam is a social nobody who is given status by Solomon and then Pharaoh. Despite a prophetic threat to his house and a "torn" warning about his prospects, he gains what is forfeited through Rehoboam's stubborn folly. In the familiar and much longer version, his father Nebat is acknowledged and again he becomes Solomon's servant, responsible for construction labor. He has to flee to Egypt, not because of his own royal pretensions, but because of a detailed divine oracle predicting that he will reign over most of Solomon's kingdom: ten tribes will be lost to the house of David because of *Solomon's* behavior. Rehoboam's folly at Shechem simply eases the process of realizing of the divine promise to Jeroboam and its counterpart, the threat to the house of David. In what follows, Jeroboam is presented as cultic innovator, along with Solomon's wives and King Ahaz; and he also uncannily echoes Saul who lost divine favor—and his kingdom to David.

---

6. Auld, *Life in Kings*, 29–38.

A Balance Struck?

Neither Kings nor Chronicles has a good word to say about Ahaz. The tradition they share contrasts him with both David and Solomon. Kings attributes to him two statements. In one he makes a pledge to the king of Assyria in terms David and Solomon only used in relation to their God. In the other, he institutes new ritual instructions. Bad has become worse.

Jeroboam is more complex. In the shorter and less familiar account, told wholly within the Rehoboam story, he is not a cultic innovator, but he does have royal pretensions. Rehoboam may have himself to blame for losing much of his kingdom; but Jeroboam, despite prophetic warnings, is very ready to gain what Solomon's son is losing. This narrative helps to explain how, in human terms, much of Israel was lost to Jerusalem and the line of David. But the longer and familiar story locates Jeroboam within a much larger narrative, stretching back to David and even Jacob. Solomon's faults are now in play, and not just those of his son. Jeroboam's own father is now named. The ten tatters are clearly presented as promise and not threat—Jeroboam will be something of a new Davidic king of Israel while at the same time the genealogically Davidic line will not lose everything. However, because of his cultic innovations, Jeroboam becomes a failure. In the one account, he is a self-server; in the other, he is a servant of God gone bad.

We noted as we began that the fame of David is differently used in the presentations of Ahaz and Jeroboam. As we proceeded, we found that the reputation of Solomon is also important in both. He is never mentioned in so many words in connection with Ahaz; but the attentive reader of the synoptic introduction understands that the king who sacrifices with enthusiasm at "high places" on hills is as unlike synoptic Solomon as he is unlike David. He has lapsed and returned to behavior from which Solomon had moved on. On the other hand, the Ahaz who built the new great altar was aping Solomon. Yet Solomon too was re-evaluated—for the worse—as the whole progression of kings became increasingly blamed for the collapse of Jerusalem. Whereas Ahaz in all versions was distanced from synoptic Solomon, now Solomon actually takes on traits of wicked Ahaz. The older Solomon story had told of his visit to the great "high place" at Gibeon (1 Kgs 3:4//2 Chron. 1:3); but now we are told that this was just one of many such visits, for "he sacrificed and offered incense at the high places" (3:3, not shared by 2 Chron. 1). This new preliminary verse is an interesting mix: it starts by saying that Solomon *loved* Yahweh and walked by David's statutes (3:3a)—just the opposite of Ahaz who was not like David but walked in the ways of the kings of Israel; but it goes on (3:3b) to compare Solomon with Ahaz who *sacrificed at "high places."* And it foreshadows 1 Kgs 11:1-8 (also not in Chronicles), which starts by saying that Solomon *loved* many foreign women and finishes by noting that these women burned incense and *sacrificed to their gods at the "high places"* he built for them around Jerusalem. Solomon's behavior in 1 Kgs (3:3) 11:1-8 is precisely what Ahijah complains about in his oracle to Jeroboam (11:33). The Solomon who now resembles wicked Ahaz is part of the background to the divine promise to Jeroboam in the longer of the two accounts.

Jeroboam is promised an "enduring" or "sure" house (11:38) just like David (2 Sam. 7:16), provided he is loyal to Yahweh as David had been. The parable of the twelve tatters had been something of a poisoned chalice when uttered by Shemaiah at Shechem in the shorter account. But in the longer version re-ascribed to Ahijah near Solomon's Jerusalem (11:29-31) there is no hint of curse; instead the parable introduces an explicit promise. And the acted promise has complex resonances. Like what had once passed between Saul and Samuel (1 Sam. 15:30-31), it concerns a torn garment. There, as Samuel turned to leave Saul, the king grabbed his cloak and it tore; and Samuel responded that Yahweh similarly was to tear his kingdom from Saul and give it to another—in this case, all his kingdom. At this early stage in the story, Jeroboam corresponds to the David who inherited another's kingdom. Rather like David and Jonathan with Saul, Jeroboam is Solomon's agent while Rehoboam is his son. But, by the time his wife hears Ahijah's words about their son(s), Jeroboam is more like Saul than David—a promise wasted and a dynasty without a future. The prophetic voice is already significant, when expressed first by Shemaiah and then by Ahijah at the heart of the shorter version. But its importance is even greater when both expanded oracles are voiced by Ahijah, promise at the start and threat at the end of the whole story.

The alternative and shorter story of Jeroboam preserved in the Greek Bible is simply a component, though an important one, of the story of Rehoboam; it is only a footnote within the larger story of the Jerusalem royal house from David to the fall of Jerusalem. This Jeroboam, like several subsequent kings of northern Israel, has a "walk-on" part in the southern story. But the expansively rewritten Jeroboam story constitutes a principal scene within an extensive re-presentation of the Bible's royal story in which a connected account of northern Israel's kings has been created and interleaved with the Jerusalem story. The new rebuilt Jeroboam heads that fresh account. Unable to establish a dynasty, he did inaugurate a lasting fateful trend.

Chapter 3

BATHSHEBA BETWEEN THE LINES AND BENEATH THE SURFACE

Sara Koenig

> How to make a bagel? First you take a hole… And how to make a narrative text? In exactly the same way.
>
> —Shlomith Rimmon-Kenan, *Narrative Fiction*[1]

Bathsheba only appears in seventy-six verses in the Hebrew Bible, is the subject of a mere thirty-three verbs, and speaks just 103 words.[2] The lines written about her are brief: though Hebrew narrative is typically laconic, Meir Sternberg describes 2 Samuel 11, the chapter in which Bathsheba first appears, as "frugal to excess even relative to the biblical norm."[3] Surface readings of Bathsheba's character are, unsurprisingly, flat and superficial. But within and between the lines are gaps about Bathsheba's motives, thoughts, and feelings, and those gaps get filled by readers in various and varying ways. Under the surface of the text are possibilities and potentialities for more complexity about Bathsheba's character. This

---

1. Shlomith Rimmon-Kenan's *Narrative Fiction*, 2nd ed. (London: Routledge, 2002), 128.
2. In addition to the narrative in 2 Sam. 11–12 and 1 Kgs 1–2, Bathsheba also is referenced in the superscription to Ps. 51. I express some of these ideas and claims about Bathsheba's characterization more fully in my works, *Isn't This Bathsheba? A Study in Characterization* (Eugene: Pickwick, 2011), and *Bathsheba Survives* (Columbia: University of South Carolina Press, 2018).
3. Meir Sternberg, *The Poetics of Biblical Narrative* (Bloomington: Indiana University Press, 1987), 191.

seemingly simplistic character Bathsheba is in fact multifaceted and interesting, presented in the text in such a way that she can be—and has been—characterized in multiple, disparate ways.

My own methodology is primarily narratological, drawing both on classical narratology's focus on the features and properties of a text, as well as "post-classical" narratology's attention to the dynamics of the reading process, interpretive possibilities, and dialogical negotiation of meaning.[4] As the epigraph above suggests, gaps are present in every narrative text, but the gapped nature of the narrative about Bathsheba may be its most distinguishing feature. Some readers have filled in the gaps in such a way that Bathsheba is interpreted as a seductress, bathing in the open to entice David's lust. Others interpret the terse description in 2 Sam. 11:4, "and he lay with her," as signaling her victimization, even rape. Such varying and even contradictory interpretations of Bathsheba's character are possible because this gapped text not only lacks details about her, but even lacks interest in her perspective: she is a minor character in a narrative focused on David and Solomon.

Interpretive decisions made about gaps early in the plot tend to have a domino effect. For example, George Nicol characterized Bathsheba in 2 Samuel as a "clever and resourceful woman who in marrying David evidently achieves her goal,"[5] and interpreted her actions in 1 Kings to get Solomon on the throne as similarly clever and resourceful. In contrast, Roger Norman Whybray read Bathsheba as victimized by David in 2 Samuel 11, and also understand her to be a victim of Nathan's plot to get Solomon on the throne in 1 Kings 1, describing Bathsheba as "a good natured, rather stupid woman who was a natural prey both to more passionate and to cleverer men."[6] Yet it need not be the case that a particular choice to fill a gap leads automatically to a similar choice: women in literary texts and the real world can be seductive and still be raped, for example. As Frank Kermode explained regarding the filling of gaps, "we may have to content ourselves with coexistent possibilities."[7]

---

4. These descriptions of "classical" and "postclassical" narratologies come from Ansgar Nünning, but are reproduced in Shlomith Rimmon-Kenan's *Narrative Fiction*, 142.

5. George Nicol, "The Alleged Rape of Bathsheba: Some Observations on Ambiguity in Biblical Narrative," *JSOT* 22 (1997): 53.

6. R. N. Whybray, *The Succession Narrative: A Study of II Samuel 9–20, [and] I Kings 1 and 2* (Naperville: A. R. Allenson, 1968), 40.

7. Frank Kermode, "New Ways with Biblical Stories," in *Parable and Story in Judaism and Christianity*, ed. Clemens Thoma and Michael Wyschogrod (Mahwah: Paulist Press, 1989), 125.

This article will present possibilities for Bathsheba's characterization yielded by the text of 2 Samuel 11–12 and 1 Kings 1–2. Using classical and postclassical narratology, I will exegete the text—the relevant words and phrases as well as the gaps—and also show examples of how interpreters have negotiated Bathsheba's character through filling the gaps.

Bathsheba Bathing and Beautiful

The reader encounters the first gap in the story when Bathsheba first appears in the narrative and David sees her bathing. Where does this bath take place? Is she aware that David sees her? What type of bath is it? How the reader fills this gap becomes central to Bathsheba's characterization. Understood one way, Bathsheba is an exhibitionist, publically displaying her nakedness where she could be seen.[8] Art and music have her "bathing on the roof,"[9] or, as in the Book of Hours produced for Louis XVI, explicitly and graphically naked, coyly watching David watching her.[10] Understood another way, David is a "peeping Tom," spying on a woman who is unaware that she is being watched. Because the setting is when kings go to war (2 Sam. 11:1), Bathsheba might suppose that David would not be present in Jerusalem, let alone on his roof, when she goes to her bath. Hans Memling's 1485 painting *Bathsheba at Her Bath* depicts Bathsheba topless stepping out of the bath into a towel; another strategically placed towel covers her pubic area. Memling's Bathsheba could not see David, and even his David could see virtually nothing of her, as he is too far away in the upper right corner of the image, and the towel is between them.[11] If the artistic interpretations demonstrate

---

8. The censure of nakedness in Ezek. 16:7 might mitigate against such an idea, however. In fact, nakedness throughout the Hebrew Bible is something to avoid.

9. This line comes from Leonard Cohen's song, "Hallelujah."

10. Thomas Kren describes this image as follows, "…while Bathsheba is immersed in her bath at the hips, her body below that point is still visible through the cool, blue water. Indeed her genitalia are precisely rendered, showing the labia, and originally they must have seemed even more strongly a focus of the miniature than today, because Bourdichon used silver paint, now tarnished, to convey the shimmer of light across the surface of the water… In relation to the biblical narrative, this depiction takes liberties…" Kren, "Looking at Louis XII's Bathsheba," in *A Masterpiece Constructed: The Hours of Louis XII*, ed. Thomas Kren and Mark Evans (Los Angeles: The J. Paul Getty Museum, 2005), 44.

11. J. Cheryl Exum makes the point that even if David in art cannot see Bathsheba, we viewers are made into voyeurs of her nudity. *Plotted, Shot and Painted: Cultural Representations of Biblical Women* (Sheffield: Sheffield Academic, 1996), 25. Cf.

various possibilities for understanding Bathsheba's bath, so also does the intertextual comparisons with Susannah. In the deuterocanonical text of Daniel, Susannah takes a bath in a place she thinks is private when the evil elders spy on her, but Susannah could be similar to Bathsheba, or different.[12]

The Hebrew verb that describes Bathsheba's bathing, רחץ, can connote purification (Lev. 14:5), but also refers to general "washing." The clause in 2 Sam. 11:4, "and she was purifying herself of her uncleanness," has been read as a reference back to Bathsheba's bath in 2 Sam. 11:2 as a ritual bath for purification after menstrual discharge, mentioned to clarify that there can be no question about the paternity of the child.[13] In Lev. 15:28, however, there is no bath or other cleansing ritual; a woman is automatically clean after she waits for seven days. Later rabbinic law prescribes bathing for purification after menstruation, so Tikvah Frymer-Kensky suggests that it is anachronistic to interpret Bathsheba's bath in 2 Sam. 11:2 as such purification. She writes that the bath discussed in 2 Sam. 11:4 is a second bath in which Bathsheba is "washing off the impurity that comes from all sexual relations, even licit ones...the phrase does not refer back to the bath that she was taking when she was first introduced, but to postcoital purification."[14] Because the version of 2 Samuel 11 found

also David Gunn, "Bathsheba Goes Bathing in Hollywood: Words, Images and Social Locations," *Semeia* 74 (1996): 75–9.

12. John Calvin seems to do both: he first explains that Bathsheba ought not to be condemned for the act of bathing, invoking Susannah as a positive example. But then Calvin criticizes the way in which Bathsheba—apparently unlike Susannah—bathed, saying, "But she should have exercised discretion, so as not to be seen. For a chaste and upright woman will not show herself in such a way as to allure men, nor be like a net of the devil to 'start a fire.' Bathsheba, therefore, was immodest in that regard." *Sermons on 2 Samuel: Chapters 1–13* (Edinburgh: The Banner of Truth Trust, 1992), 481.

13. Cf. Stephen L. McKenzie, *King David: A Biography* (Oxford: Oxford University Press, 2000), 157; Elna Solvang, *A Woman's Place is in the House: Royal Women of Judah and their Involvement in the House of David* (Sheffield: Sheffield Academic, 2003), 178. Lest I cast stones, I must admit I also explained Bathsheba's bath in that way in my *Isn't This Bathsheba?*, 37.

14. Tikvah Frymer-Kensky, *Reading the Women of the Bible* (New York: Schocken, 2002), 147. In contrast, S. R. Driver explains that because the verb "and she was purifying herself" in 2 Sam. 11:4 is a participle amidst a sequence of *waw*-consecutive 3rd person verbs, the action is not subsequent to the clause, "and he lay with her." Driver argues that a finite verb would be used instead if the narrator intended to convey that Bathsheba washed herself after their sexual encounter. *Notes on the Hebrew Text of the Books of Samuel* (Oxford: Clarendon, 1890), 223.

at Qumran lacks the phrase in v. 4, "from her impurity," Helen Leneman suggests that a later editor added the phrase to reflect changing attitudes towards menstruation and impurity.[15] If Bathsheba's bath in 2 Sam. 11:2 is a sponge bath or a footbath, that would have less sexual innuendoes than if she is bathing naked or cleaning her genitals for ritual purification.[16] During the patristic era, Bathsheba's bath was allegorized as a baptism. David was a figure of Christ, and Bathsheba as David's bride was a figure of the church, therefore her bath represented being washed for sins in the waters of baptism.[17] While the patristic tendency to allegorize most things can seem strange to those steeped in a more historical critical approach to the text, this reading illustrates that there are multiple possibilities for understanding Bathsheba's bath.

When David sees Bathsheba in 2 Sam. 11:2, she is directly described by the narrator as טובת מראה מאד, "very beautiful."[18] This, however, is hardly an unequivocal characterization. Shimon Bar-Efrat writes that Bathsheba's beauty "is mentioned solely because it plays the central role in the course of events, providing the motivation for David's...licentious behavior."[19] The only other woman described by the same phrase as Bathsheba is Rebekah (Gen. 24:16), who like Bathsheba has been characterized in varying ways.

In 2 Sam. 11:3, when David inquires about Bathsheba, an anonymous source responds, "Isn't this Bathsheba, the daughter of Eliam, the wife of Uriah the Hittite?"[20] Marti Steussy suggests that David is the one to identify Bathsheba, noting that the three consecutive verbs in Hebrew do not indicate any change of subject, and she translates the verse as, "David sent...and he inquired...and he said, 'Isn't this Bathsheba...?'"[21] If David

---

15. Helen Leneman, *Love, Lust and Lunacy: The Stories of David and Saul in Music* (Sheffield: Sheffield Phoenix, 2010), 275.

16. Bathsheba is depicted taking a footbath in several medieval Books of Hours, as well as in Pablo Picasso's 1949 lithograph "David and Bathsheba."

17. *Cassiodorus: Explanation of the Psalms*. Vol. 1. *Psalms 1–50*, trans. P. G. Walsh (New York: Paulist Press, 1990), 492–3.

18. David is described in similar terms in 1 Sam. 16:12, such that there is a linguistic connection between the physical appearance of David and Bathsheba.

19. Shimon Bar-Efrat, *Narrative Art in the Bible* (London: T&T Clark International, 2004), 49.

20. It is possible to translate the Hebrew interrogative הלוא as a definitive statement, as does JPS and NRSV. I prefer to translate it as a question, consistent with other places this interrogative is used in the narrative (2 Sam. 11:21; 1 Kgs 1:13), as well as to reflect some of the uncertainty about Bathsheba.

21. Marti Steussy, *David: Biblical Portraits of Power* (Columbia: University of South Carolina Press, 1999), 62.

is not the one to speak about Bathsheba, the source remains unknown. Perhaps it matters less who tells David about Bathsheba's identity than it matters that before he takes her, he knows who she is: married to one of his elite fighting men and the daughter of another (2 Sam. 23). Bathsheba's Hittite husband causes some to suppose that she herself is a foreigner,[22] but nowhere are her father Eliam and grandfather Ahithophel identified as non-Israelites.[23]

Bathsheba Sent for, Coming, Lain with, Returning

Even within a heavily gapped text, 2 Sam. 11:4 is notable for its lack of details. Four events are narrated in quick succession (he sent messengers to get her, she came to him, he lay with her, and she returned to her house) without any indication of feelings or motives. Much interpretive weight is placed on the phrase in 2 Sam. 11:4, "and she came to him." The phrase's relatively small narrative size—only two Hebrew words—does not match the enormity of the implication that Bathsheba is either complicit or compliant in the act of adultery. A number of late nineteenth- and early twentieth-century commentaries highlight that implication because there are no words to suggest any hesitation on Bathsheba's part in coming to David. John Peter Lange wrote, "The narrative leads us to infer that Bathsheba came and submitted herself to David without opposition. This undoubtedly proves her participation in the guilt..."[24] Keil and Delitzsch explain that in 2 Sam. 11:4,

---

22. For example, Luther refers to Bathsheba along with the other three women in Jesus' Matthean genealogy in his discussion of Gentile inclusion into the chosen of Israel. *Luther's Works: Lectures on Genesis, Chapters 38–44*, ed. Jaroslav Pelikan and Walter Hansen (St. Louis: Concordia, 1965), 14.

23. Uriah Kim argues that because Bathsheba is an Israelite, she is the "right" wife to David, able to help legitimatize David's dynasty. "Uriah the Hittite: A (Con)Text of Struggle for Identity," *Semeia* 90/91 (2002): 78–9. Bathsheba's relation to Ahithophel is not made explicitly in 2 Sam. 15:12 when Ahithophel is introduced, but Ahithophel is named as Eliam's father in 2 Sam. 23:34. Ahithophel is Absalom's advisor during his attempted coup against David, and a number of scholars ascribe motivation to Ahithophel based on what had happened to Bathsheba. For example, David Daube asserts that Ahithophel tells Absalom to sleep with his father's concubines (2 Sam. 16:20-22) because David treated Bathsheba "with the same ruthlessness." "Absalom and the Ideal King," *VT* 48 (1998): 320.

24. John Peter Lange, *Commentary on the Holy Scriptures: Critical, Doctrinal and Homiletical: Samuel*, trans. Philip Schaff (Grand Rapids: Zondervan, 1877), 466.

there is no intimation whatever that David brought Bathsheba into his palace through craft or violence, but rather that she came at his request without any hesitation, and offered no resistance to his desires. Consequently Bathsheba is not to be regarded as free of blame.[25]

Of course, many current readers will note that these writers do not acknowledge power dynamics of ruler and subject. Bathsheba's action of coming to David is likely connected with the previous clause in 2 Sam. 11:4; he sent for her, and it is unlikely that one could refuse the summons of the king. Strikingly, Greek manuscripts of 2 Sam. 11:4, notably Codex Vaticanus, reads, και εισηλθεν προς αυτην ("and *he* went in to her") instead of "and she came to him."[26] In this version, David is the subject of the verbs: he sent for her, he came to her, he lay with her. Bathsheba does not come to David; she is the object of his actions. It is harder to argue for any compliance on Bathsheba's part if she is not the subject of the verbs.

The nature of the sexual encounter in the words "he lay with her" is another gap: was this adultery, or rape?[27] Was Bathsheba a willing participant with David, or a victim of his violence? In the three narratives about rape (of Dinah in Gen. 34, the Levite's concubine in Judg. 19, and Tamar in 2 Sam. 13), the piel of ענה is used, so the lack of that verb in 2 Sam. 11:4 has been understood to mean that David did not rape Bathsheba.[28] The legal texts in the Hebrew Bible have been utilized to argue for and against rape and adultery. The rape laws in Deut. 22:23-27 connect rape with the location where the violation occurred: if in the city, the woman is

---

25. Carl Friedrich Keil and F. Delitzsch, *Biblical Commentary on the Books of Samuel*, trans. James Martin (Edinburgh: T. & T. Clark, 1868), 383.

26. The Greek και εισηλθεν προς αυτον does occur in mss c, s. The phrase is entirely omitted in mss h, a2 and Ethiopic.

27. Even that question may be overly polarized. Rachel Adelman explains, "A grey area lies between the binary of 'active' and 'passive' subject, which disrupts the categorical reading of their intercourse as either seduction or rape." *The Female Ruse: Women's Deception and Divine Sanction in the Hebrew Bible* (Sheffield: Sheffield Phoenix, 2015), 180.

28. Of course, it could also be that the biblical author deliberately chose to use the verb שכב, instead of ענה, to preserve the ambiguity in the narrative, as Benjamin J. M. Johnson pointed out to me in a private correspondence. Sandie Gravett asserts that no single Hebrew verb, not even ענה, corresponds exactly to contemporary understandings of rape. "Reading 'Rape' in the Hebrew Bible: A Consideration of Language," *JSOT* 28 (2004): 279. Based on the verbs in 2 Sam. 11:4—David "lay with" (שכב) Bathsheba after he sent (שלח) messengers and "took" (לקח) her—Brent Emery argues that Bathsheba was not raped. http://www.thenewstribune.com/news/local/community/gateway/g-living/article44756976.html.

presumed to have consented, for she did not cry for help. If it took place in the country, she presumably resisted. Therefore, because David "lay with" Bathsheba in Jerusalem, according to the ancient legal standpoint it would not be rape. However, both Deut. 22:22 and Lev. 20:10 clarify that both parties who commit adultery—the adulterer and adulteress—are to be put to death. Steussy writes, "The fact that no one mentions a death penalty for Bathsheba…suggests that she was not considered at fault."[29] Not only have the legal texts been used as evidence both for and against rape, but the narrative about Amnon and Tamar has been used in a similar way. Some scholars see connections between David's sexual behavior in 2 Samuel 11 and that of his son Amnon in 2 Samuel 13.[30] Others read the juxtaposition of the two narratives as more of a contrast.[31]

Even those who have noted a similarity in the actions of David and Amnon have been reticent to refer to it as rape,[32] but in her 2010 book, Suzanne Scholz emphasized the power differential between David and Bathsheba, arguing, "Since her consent does not matter, his action equals rape…"[33] In 2015, in a paper presented at the annual SBL conference, Anne Létourneau similarly pointed out how problematic—and even dangerous—it is to equate the absence of protest with consent, asserting

---

29. Steussy, *David*, 78. Steussy argues that David's action might be called "sexual harassment," in the modern sense of that term, especially because his action involves his abuse of power, though she acknowledges that the text's approach to such issues does not mirror the kind of responses we might have today. Ibid.

30. Cf. David Noel Freedman, "Dinah and Shechem: Tamar and Amnon," *Austin Seminary Bulletin Faculty Edition* 105 (1990): 60, and Frank Yamada, *Configurations of Rape in the Hebrew Bible: A Literary Analysis of Three Rape Narratives* (New York: Lang, 2008), 136.

31. Mark Gray concludes that, based on the verbs, the sexual encounters in the two narratives are different, but he does note how Amnon intensifies the actions against women previously done by his father. "Amnon: A Chip Off the Old Block? Rhetorical Strategy in 2 Samuel 13.7-15: The Rape of Tamar and the Humiliation of the Poor," *JSOT* 77 (1993): 48.

32. Though Freedman and Yamada do see connections between David and Amnon, neither use the language of rape to describe what happened to Bathsheba. The title of George Nicol's article is indicative of his position, "The Alleged Rape of Bathsheba: Some Observations on Ambiguity in Biblical Narrative." J. Cheryl Exum's *Fragmented Women: Feminist (Sub)versions of Biblical Narratives* (Sheffield: JSOT Press, 1993), includes a chapter about Bathsheba titled, "'Raped by the Pen'!", but Exum uses that language metaphorically to describe Bathsheba's treatment by "the androcentric biblical narrator", 171.

33. Suzanne Scholz, *Sacred Witness: Rape in the Hebrew Bible* (Minneapolis: Fortress, 2010), 100.

that David raped Bathsheba.[34] In that same year, David T. Lamb acknowledged the text's lack of explicit statement that David forced Bathsheba to have sex, but writes,

> the fact that the text places all of the blame for what happened on him and none of it on her, and that the crime warranted a death sentence for him, makes a highly compelling argument that he raped her. I'd call it a power rape.[35]

Also in 2015, Geraldine Brooks's novel *The Secret Chord* has Bathsheba in angry dialogue with Nathan about what happened: "Do you have any idea what he was like, that night? He used me like some—receptacle. The bruises on my breasts took a month to fade." Brooks's Nathan then thinks, "[David] had been raping her. And I had let myself call it a seduction. As I looked at her now, I was shamed by my own thoughts. In a way, I, too, had violated her."[36] These recent arguments that Bathsheba was a victim of rape are noteworthy because throughout most of reception history about Bathsheba, rape was not mentioned.[37] Scholz categorized the narrative of 2 Samuel 11 as a "biblical rape fantasy" in which a wife has sex with a man not her husband. Scholz writes, "she appears mostly as his object whose consent does not matter… This classic characteristic of rape, whether fantasized or practiced, needs to be recognized so that its pervasive influence can be brought to an end."[38] In the world after #metoo, Bathsheba may be increasingly characterized as a nonconsenting individual in an act of rape.

The final event in the plot-rich verse of 2 Sam. 11:4 is Bathsheba's return to her house; she is the subject of this action. Though Bathsheba is the object of David's actions in the verse—he took her, he lay with

---

34. Anne Létourneau, "Bathing Beauty: Concealment of Bathsheba's Rape and Counter-Power in 2 Sam 11:1-5," paper presented at Society of Biblical Literature meeting, Atlanta, 21 November 2015.

35. David T. Lamb, *Prostitutes and Polygamists: A Look at Love, Old Testament Style* (Grand Rapids: Zondervan, 2015), 134.

36. Geraldine Brooks, *The Secret Chord* (New York: Viking, 2015), 232.

37. No interpreter of Bathsheba from the patristic era up through the enlightenment suggested that Bathsheba was raped by David. The Talmud asserts that Bathsheba was not married to Uriah at the time of 2 Sam. 11. For example, in *b. Šabb.* 56a, R. Samuel b. Naḥmani said in R. Jonathan's name, "Everyone who went out in the wars of the house of David wrote a bill of divorcement for his wife." The idea was that Uriah had divorced Bathsheba before going to war, so therefore David could not have committed adultery with her.

38. Scholz, *Sacred Witness*, 103.

her—she also is a subject. In fact, from a structuralist perspective, in the MT David and Bathsheba alternate as the subject with three verbs each: he sent and took, she came, he lay with, she was purifying herself and returned. As noted above, there has been some debate about the timing of Bathsheba's washing described in 2 Sam. 11:4, including the possibility that it describes her bath in 2 Sam. 11:2. The narrative, however, never specifies timing for any event in 2 Samuel 11–12 or 1 Kings 1–2. Even if the washing described in 2 Sam. 11:4 happened after David lay with her and before she returned home, there is no indication how long this took. Did Bathsheba remain in the house of the king, or quickly leave? Moreover, while the plain sense of the verse suggests that this was a one-time encounter, certain movies and novels that paint the sexual act as a seduction and not a victimization recount a number of dalliances between Bathsheba and David.[39]

Bathsheba Conceiving, Sending, Telling

After Bathsheba conceives, she sends a message and tells David of her pregnancy (2 Sam. 11:5). What is not clear, again, is her motivation. Josephus describes the events as follows, "she became pregnant and sent to the king, asking him to contrive some way of concealing her sin, for according to the laws of the fathers she was deserving of death as an adulteress" (*Ant.* 7.131). In the nineteenth century, Methodist minister Joseph Benson explains, "She was afraid of infamy, and perhaps of the severity of her husband, who might cause her to be stoned."[40] The biblical text does not indicate whether or not Bathsheba wanted to cover up the paternity of her child, nor does it describe any feelings between David and Bathsheba. As Leneman observes,

> The question of whether David ever loves Bathsheba (or vice versa) is left unanswered. The minute she announces her pregnancy, his interest is in the paternity of the child, conceding her to Uriah from the start, which does not suggest great love.[41]

---

39. Cf. the 1951 movie "David and Bathsheba" with Gregory Peck and Susan Hayward; Joseph Heller's *God Knows* (New York: Alfred A. Knopf, 1984); and Jill Eileen Smith's *Bathsheba* (Grand Rapids MI: Revell, 2011).
40. Joseph Benson, *Critical and Explanatory Notes, Vol. 1: Genesis to the Second Book of Samuel* (New York: T. Mason & G. Lane, 1841), 893.
41. Helen Leneman, "Portrayals of Power in the Stories of Delilah and Bathsheba: Seduction in Song," in *Culture, Entertainment and the Bible*, ed. George Aichele (Sheffield: Sheffield Academic, 2000), 147.

Because Bathsheba sends a message to David and does not speak directly to him, Chloe Sun wonders if Bathsheba was afraid to confront David.[42] Another possibility, however, is that by sending the message, Bathsheba is expressing some power.[43] Though her words are few, Bathsheba is not silent.

Bathsheba Mourning, Marrying, Bearing

Gaps about Bathsheba's emotions are particularly open in 2 Sam. 11:26-27. In 2 Sam. 11:26 Bathsheba is the subject of the verb ספד, which can be translated as "mourn," "wail," or "lament." In a text so devoid of any description of emotions, it is interesting that some read this as only an action and not a feeling. For example, John Calvin described Bathsheba's tears as merely for show,[44] and eighteenth-century commentator Matthew Henry wrote, "What vile mockery! Only God knows how often the outward 'mourning' over the departed is but a hypocritical veil to cover satisfaction of heart for being rid of their presence."[45] In contrast, Bathsheba could be honestly grieved at Uriah's death.[46] Again, the filling in of previous gaps has a domino effect: if a reader understands Bathsheba's marriage with Uriah to be a good one, that same reader will likely interpret Bathsheba's grief as genuine. In 2 Sam. 11:26 the marriage relationship between Uriah and Bathsheba is repeatedly highlighted, saying, "And the *wife* of Uriah heard that her *husband* was dead, she mourned for her *husband*" (emphasis mine).[47]

---

42. Chloe Sun, "Bathsheba Transformed: From Silence to Voice," in *Mirrored Reflections: Reframing Biblical Characters*, ed. Young Lee Hertig and Chloe Sun (Eugene: Wipf & Stock, 2010), 30. Sun describes Bathsheba's sending someone to speak as "the first step toward the journey of voice," 35.

43. In 2 Sam. 11:5 Bathsheba "sent (שׁלח) and she told to David, and she said, 'I am pregnant.'" Mieke Bal draws on the work of A. J. Greimas who uses the French terms *destinateur* and *destinataire* ("sender" and receiver") to distinguish between actors in a narrative. Bal's own terminology is "power" and "receiver," indicating that the one who "sends" in a narrative is in a position of power. Bal, *Narratology: Introduction to the Theory of Narrative* (Toronto: University of Toronto Press, 1997), 198.

44. Calvin, *Sermons on 2 Samuel*, 516.

45. Matthew Henry, *An Exposition of the Old and New Testaments* (Philadelphia: Alexander Towar, and Hogan & Thompson, 1833), 402.

46. Such is the assumption made by Jill Eileen Smith, who in her novel *Bathsheba* spends two entire pages describing Bathsheba's grief at Uriah's death.

47. Two words in the verse get used for husband, אישׁ and בעל. Several English translations only use the word "husband" once, which avoids repetition but also

Another domino effect has to do with the Bathsheba's feelings about being taken by David as his wife (2 Sam. 11:27), nowhere mentioned in the text. Those who understood Bathsheba as wanting to be seen bathing by David, and read consent into their sexual interaction, assume that she is happy to become David's wife.[48] Suffragist Elizabeth Cady Stanton resists describing Bathsheba's feelings about David, instead writing, "to be transferred from the cottage of a poor soldier to the palace of a king was a sufficient compensation for the loss of the love of a true and faithful man."[49] Bathsheba's feelings about the birth of their son are similarly absent in the text, perhaps intentionally overshadowed by the narrator's description of God's response to the thing that David had done.

Bathsheba Comforted, Bearing, Naming

Bathsheba is not directly present in 2 Sam. 12:1-23, but she is directly referenced three times as "the wife of Uriah" (2 Sam. 12:9, 10, 15). Although Bathsheba becomes David's wife in 2 Sam. 11:17, the text refers to her in most of 2 Samuel 12 as Uriah's wife. Only after the death of their first son is Bathsheba again referred to as David's wife. Cheryl Kirk-Duggan observes, "the narrator silences [Bathsheba's] grief by describing only David's pain at the loss of their first child."[50] Certainly, David is the focus; Bathsheba is not present as a character in the bulk of 2 Samuel 12. But even though Bathsheba's grief is not directly narrated, it gets acknowledged in the description in 2 Sam. 12:24 that David comforted Bathsheba. In 2 Sam. 12:24, she is the object of David's actions: he comforts her, comes to her, lays with her.[51] Bathsheba is the subject of two verbs in 2 Sam. 12:24: she bears a second son, and names

---

misses the threefold emphasis on their relationship. One could translate בעל as "master" instead of "husband," which might be where some get the idea of a domineering Uriah.

48. Cf. Yochi Brandes, *The Secret Book of Kings: A Novel*, trans. Yardenne Greenspan (New York: St. Martins, 2016), 243.

49. Cady Stanton, *The Woman's Bible* (Seattle: Coalition Task Force on Women and Religion, 1974), 57. Cady Stanton's tone is itself a gap: could she be writing from a purely pragmatic perspective, or even be sarcastic?

50. Cheryl Kirk-Duggan, "Slingshots, Ships, and Personal Psychosis: Murder, Sexual Intrigue, and Power in the Lives of David and Othello," in *Pregnant Passion: Gender, Sex and Violence in the Bible*, ed. Cheryl Kirk-Duggan (Leiden: Brill, 2004), 56.

51. Two out of the three verbs, "come" (בוא) and "lay with" (שכב), are repeated from 2 Sam. 11:4, but in the MT of 2 Sam. 11 she came to him.

him Solomon. Bathsheba's "naming" is a *Ketib/Qere* in the MT: what is written is ויקרא, "and he called," but what is to be read is ותקרא, "and she called."[52] At the end of 2 Samuel 12, Bathsheba is in the role of mother, an aspect of her characterization that becomes increasingly important in 1 Kings.

Bathsheba Bowing, Speaking, Sworn to

Bathsheba is absent in the first ten verses of 1 Kings, when the "young and beautiful" Abishag is brought to warm David in bed. David, however, "did not know" Abishag (1 Kgs 1:4), which is another gap. Maybe David is impotent, unable to "know" the woman put under his covers. Or, perhaps the still virile David chooses to refrain from sexual relationships with her, as the Talmud affirms. In *b. Sanh.* 22a, Rab Judah describes David declaring to Abishag that she is forbidden to him, then having sex with Bathsheba thirteen times in a row. Rab Judah read between the lines of David's not knowing Abishag, and inserted Bathsheba in his explanation of the narrative.

Bathsheba's character development between Samuel and Kings is evident in her increased speech and action: in Samuel, she is the subject of thirteen verbs and speaks only two words, but in Kings she is the subject of twenty verbs, and speaks 101 words. She had been identified in Samuel as "wife" of Uriah and David, and "daughter" of Eliam, but in Kings she is known as "mother" of Solomon. Bathsheba's role as mother gets emphasized when Nathan comes to her in 1 Kgs 1:11-14 to solicit her help in placing Solomon, not Adonijah, on the throne: the text refers to her as Solomon's mother (1 Kgs 1:11) and Nathan refers to "your son, Solomon" (1 Kgs 1:12). Keith Bodner notes how, when speaking to Bathsheba, Nathan refers to Adonijah as "son of Haggith," and suggests that Nathan does so not because there are multiple Adonijahs, but because Nathan intends to exploit a maternal rivalry between Bathsheba and Haggith.[53]

---

52. The *Qere* is supported by Syriac, Targum and Vulgate, while the *Ketib* was possibly influenced by the following verse in which Nathan "called" the name of the child Jedediah. P. Kyle McCarter asserts, "In the time to which our story refers it seems to have been the mother's prerogative to name a newborn child (1 Sam. 1:20; 4:21, etc.)." *II Samuel* (New York: Doubleday, 1984), 303.

53. Keith Bodner, "Nathan: Prophet, Politician, and Novelist?" *JSOT* 26 (2001): 50. The text itself introduces Adonijah in relation to his mother in 1 Kgs 1:5.

Nathan tells Bathsheba to say to David, "Did you not, my lord the king, swear to your maidservant saying, 'Solomon your son will be king after me, and *he* will sit on my throne'?" (1 Kgs 1:13). This question, and how it gets answered, is the central gap in this chapter, with differing implications for Bathsheba's character. Was such a promise made, or did Nathan—or Bathsheba—invent one? The lack of such a promise in the text of Samuel-Kings causes many to say that it never occurred.[54] Nathan, who declared God's favor for Solomon in 2 Sam. 11:25, certainly could have vested interest in Solomon's kingship. David Marcus suggests that David had promised Bathsheba that her son would be king, but "deceived" Bathsheba by not following up on the promise. Marcus therefore understands Bathsheba to be motivated by revenge to "act in consort with Nathan to deceive David…"[55] Bathsheba could also have been motivated by her own desire to have power in the role of Queen Mother, or by a concern for her son.

Walter Brueggemann believes that Nathan is in charge of the entire scene, going so far as to script for Bathsheba what she is to say to David.[56] Yet the text in 1 Kings 1 would mitigate an overly literal reading of Brueggemann's description, for Bathsheba does not merely repeat the lines Nathan gave to her. She bows to David in homage before making a speech of her own, changing Nathan's words in seven ways.[57]

---

54. Walter Brueggemann believes David never made the promise. Brueggemann, *1 & 2 Kings* (Macon: Smyth & Helwys, 2000), 14. Choon-Leong Seow is also skeptical because of "the importance of such a tradition to the Davidic monarchy." "The First and Second Books of Kings," in *The New Interpreter's Bible, Vol. 3* (Nashville: Abingdon, 1999), 19. However, in 1 Chron. 22:7-16, David gives Solomon building plans for the temple, and tells him that he will be king, a promise made known to the assembly of Israel in 1 Chron. 28. The legacy of biblical criticism from the enlightenment means that many scholars will not utilize Chronicles to explain Samuel-Kings, but the rabbis, who read discrete biblical texts as interconnected, assert that David made the promise referenced by Nathan and Bathsheba in 1 Kings.

55. David Marcus, "David the Deceiver and David the Dupe," *Prooftexts* 6 (1986): 167.

56. Brueggemann, *1 & 2 Kings*, 20.

57. First, Bathsheba makes Nathan's question into a statement, "my lord, you swore to your servant"; second, she adds that David swore to her "by YHWH your God" (1 Kgs 1:17); third, Bathsheba tells David he did not know about Adonijah's actions; fourth, she gives David details about what Adonijah has done; fifth, Bathsheba refers to Solomon—the person whom Adonijah did not invite to his feast—as David's "servant"; sixth, Bathsheba tells David "the eyes of all Israel" are on him to tell them who will succeed him on the throne; and seventh, she tells David that when he dies, she and her son Solomon will be counted as offenders (1 Kgs 1:21).

Choon-Leong Seow asks, "Is Bathsheba merely a nice old woman who is easily manipulated? Or is she coldly calculating and shrewder than she seems at first blush?"[58] Nehama Ashkenasy argues, however, that Bathsheba is in control. She writes,

> Although Natan and the uninitiated reader may think that the prophet is manipulating her, perhaps the opposite is right. By playing the helpless mother, Batsheba empowers Natan to take a bolder, more decisive action in her favor and force the issue on David.[59]

It is interesting that while Nathan could have colluded with a number of other people, such as Zadok, Benaiah, Shimei, Rei, or "the fighting men" mentioned in 1 Kgs 1:8, he chose to appeal to Bathsheba, whose own name can be explained etymologically as "daughter of oath."[60]

Notably, it is Bathsheba whom David calls before he calls Zadok, Nathan, and Benaiah, and she is the one to whom David swears that Solomon will become king (1 Kgs 1:28-30). Bathsheba responds to David's oath by bowing to him a second time, and saying, "May my lord the king David live forever" (1 Kgs 1:31). Brueggemann believes that her wish "is less than earnest,"[61] but Seow reads her statement as genuine and connected to God's promise to David of an eternal dynasty in 2 Samuel 7.[62] Such different readings about Bathsheba's tone or intent in her speech in 1 Kgs 1:31 continue to illustrate the varying possibilities for this character.

Bathsheba Speaking, Saying, Asking

Bathsheba is absent in 1 Kgs 1:32–2:12, but reappears in 1 Kgs 2:13 when "Adonijah son of Haggith" comes to her; she is identified in the same verse as "Bathsheba, mother of Solomon." The central gap in

---

58. Seow, "Kings," 33.

59. Nehama Ashkenasy, *Woman at the Window: Biblical Tales of Oppression and Escape* (Detroit: Wayne State University Press, 1998), 115.

60. As Bodner discusses the seven scenes in 1 Kgs 1–2 in which oaths are sworn, he writes, "The reader will notice a triangular word-play on Bathsheba's name (בת־שבע), the number 'seven' (שבע), and the verbal root 'swear an oath' (שבע)." Bodner, *David Observed: A King in the Eyes of His Court* (Sheffield: Sheffield Phoenix, 2005), 154. Iain Provan and Moshe Garsiel also suggests that Bathsheba's name is a literary device used to emphasize the significance of the oaths in 1 Kgs 1–2. Cf. Provan, *1 and Kings* (Peabody: Hendrickson, 1995), 30; Garsiel, "Puns upon Names as a Literary Device in 1 Kings 1–2," *Bib* 72 (1991): 381.

61. Brueggemann, *1 & 2 Kings*, 16.

62. Seow, "Kings," 19.

1 Kings 2 has to do with why Adonijah comes to her to request Abishag's hand in marriage. Adonijah gives a partial answer in 1 Kgs 2:17 when he expresses his confidence that Solomon will not refuse the request from Bathsheba.[63] Indeed, Bathsheba's status and power is evident in the way Solomon arises to meet his mother, bows to her, and sets a throne for her at a position of honor on his right.[64] But perhaps Adonijah also thinks that Bathsheba is more easily persuaded than her son, or assumes she will not hear his request as Solomon does, as a bid for the kingdom. Nineteenth-century commentator J. Rawson Lumby wrote that Adonijah may have chosen to speak to Bathsheba for "this simplicity of hers…and thought that his petition, coming to Solomon through her, might appear less dangerous."[65] In contrast, Nicol and Aschkenasy view Adonijah as naïve in his approach to clever and cunning Bathsheba, arguing that she knew Adonijah's request for Abishag would give her son Solomon the warrant for deposing his half-brother and consolidating his reign.[66]

When Adonijah first approaches Bathsheba, she asks him if he comes peaceably (1 Kgs 2:13). That Bathsheba even asks such a question indicates a level of political awareness on her part, which might not therefore support her characterization as naïve. Adonijah's reply is affirmative, and he asks if he might have a word with her. She then commands him to "speak" (1 Kgs 2:14). Adonijah first describes his failed succession to the throne and then asks Bathsheba not to refuse. She responds by commanding him a second time, "speak" (1 Kgs 2:17). This wonderfully brief response does not commit her to anything, nor is there any indication of her tone; she could be amused, frightened, curious, or suspicious. Adonijah then presents his request: he asks Bathsheba to ask Solomon to give him Abishag. Bathsheba's response to this request is less brief but no less gapped; she says, "Good, *I* will speak to the king about

---

63. Solomon says as much in 1 Kgs 2:20.

64. Some compare Bathsheba with a *gebîrâ*, or "mighty lady," though the text does not use that term for her. Nancy Bowen concludes that while Bathsheba is an extraordinary woman who plays a pivotal role in the outcome of the succession, she is not a gebîrâ. "The Quest for the Historical Gĕbîrǎ," *CBQ* 63 (2001): 606. Beverly Cushman argues that Bathsheba functions as a gebîrâ in both chapters of 1 Kings, as one of the particular roles of a gebîrâ was to administrate the palace household, with special authority over the harem. "The Politics of the Royal Harem and the Case of Bat-Sheba," *JSOT* 30 (2006): 330.

65. J. Rawsom Lumby, *The First Book of the Kings* (Cambridge: Cambridge University Press, 1898), 21.

66. George Nicol, "Bathsheba: A Clever Woman?" *ExpTim* 99 (1988): 362–3; Ashkenasy, *Woman at the Window*, 112–17.

you" (1 Kgs 2:18). The word "good" (טוב) could mean that Adonijah's request is a good one, appropriate, or fair. It could also mean that what will happen to Adonijah—his death—is good for her son. Or, it could mean simply that she will relay Adonijah's position.

A similar gap is present in Bathsheba's description of the request to Solomon in 1 Kgs 2:20; she explains that she has "one small request." She may be trying to minimize something that she knows is major; she may honestly believe the request is not a large one;[67] she may also be speaking sarcastically. Marcus writes, "We are disposed to regard [Bathsheba] as devious, seeing an opportunity to get rid of an always potentially dangerous rival to Solomon."[68] Nancy Bowen, however, seems to be willing to hold the gap open as she writes, "What cannot be determined is if Bathsheba is acting in good faith or with cunning deviousness."[69] Solomon's response to Bathsheba's request that Abishag be given to Adonijah, however, is unequivocally negative, concluding with his own vow to kill Adonijah (1 Kgs 2:22-24). At this point, Bathsheba disappears. There is no mention of her exiting the throne room; there is no record even of her death. Bathsheba gets named in the superscription to Psalm 51, but is never again mentioned by name.[70]

Bathsheba Read and Reread

That Bathsheba fades away in the narrative without any explanation is consistent with this ambiguous and gapped text. But this is a strength, not a liability. As Gale Yee asserts, literary ambiguity involves a reader in the process of meaning making, even forcing "readers to become more actively involved with the characters."[71] Readers filling in gaps about Bathsheba's character have not only read below the surface, but have brought Bathsheba's character to the surface in different ways. The various potentials and possibilities for characterizing Bathsheba do not mean that her character is inexhaustible, or unknowable. Rather, the choices made

---

67. In Francine Rivers's novel, Bathsheba is confused by Solomon's wrath, and after Solomon orders Adonijah's execution, she tearfully says, "I didn't know. I never thought this would happen." *Unspoken: Bathsheba* (Carol Stream: Tyndale House, 2001), 402.

68. Marcus, "David the Deceiver," 167.

69. Bowen, "Historical Gebîra," 605.

70. In the book of Chronicles she gets named "Bathshua," and in the Matthean genealogy of Jesus, she gets mentioned, but as "wife of Uriah the Hittite" (Mt. 1:6).

71. Gale Yee, "Fraught with Background: Literary Ambiguity in II Samuel 11," *Interpretation* 42 (1988): 251.

to fill in gaps have varying implications and consequences for the rest of the narrative, as noted above. Moreover, while a reader has the freedom to fill in gaps in various ways,[72] not all gap-filling is equal: some require reading against the grain of the text, as in the example of those interpreters who read Bathsheba's grief for Uriah as mere pretense. Sternberg goes so far as to critique what he refers to as "illegitimate gap filling," which he defines as "launched and sustained by the reader's subjective concerns (or dictated by more general preconceptions) rather than by the text's own norms and directives."[73] Again, using narratological methods requires taking into account the features of a text, but against Sternberg, I would highlight how the dynamics of the reading process ultimately yield characterizations of Bathsheba more complex than initially thought.

---

72. Wolfgang Iser refers to all readers filling in the gaps in their own ways, in "The Reading Process: A Phenomenological Approach," *New Literary History* 3 (1972): 285.

73. Sternberg, *The Poetics of Biblical Narrative*, 188; cf. also 249–63.

Chapter 4

THE PORTRAIT OF SOLOMON IN
THE BOOK OF KINGS

Amos Frisch

One of the most important monarchs in the book of Kings is Solomon, the son and heir of the founder of the Davidic dynasty and the builder of the Temple in Jerusalem. The chronicle of his reign occupies the first section of the book. Solomon's importance for the book's author-redactor[1] is clear, both from the extensive coverage of his reign[2] and the many references to him in the book.[3] In the present article I will consider

---

1. I accept the notion of a single Deuteronomist redactor, as proposed by Martin Noth (but not every detail of his thesis, and certainly not the supposed pessimism of the composition). For a survey of the literature, see T. Römer, *The So-called Deuteronomistic History: A Sociological, Historical and Literary Introduction* (London: T&T Clark International, 2005). See also G. N. Knoppers, "Theories of the Redaction(s) of Kings," in *The Books of Kings: Sources, Composition, Historiography and Reception*, ed. A. Lemaire and B. Halpern (Leiden: Brill, 2010), 69–88.

2. The account of Solomon's reign (1 Kgs 1–11) stretches over 434 verses. In my reading, which sees the story as continuing through 12:24, there are 458 verses. This means 28.25% (or 29.81%) of the entire book (1536 verses). For ch. 1 as part of the Solomon pericope, see: J. T. Walsh, *1 Kings*, Berit Olam (Collegeville: Liturgical Press, 1996), v, 3; Z. Zevit, "First Kings," in *The Jewish Study Bible*, ed. A. Berlin and M. Z. Brettler, 2nd ed. (New York: Oxford University Press, 2014), 653; R. L. Cohn, "The Literary Structure of Kings," in Lemaire and Halpern, eds, *The Books of Kings*, 110. For a different approach, see M. A. Sweeney, *1 & II Kings*, OTL (Louisville: Westminster John Knox, 2007), 47.

3. His name appears 152 times in chs. 1–11, four more times in 12:1-24, and another six times in the rest of the book: a total of 162 times. For comparison's sake,

his depiction in the book of Kings, with special attention to his religious and moral evaluation, both explicit and between the lines.[4] This is a literary reading, not a historical study, with the goal of extracting the character from the text and not of reconstructing his career. Due to space limitations I cannot address every point in depth and will consider some only briefly.

The book of Kings employs standard formulas to introduce and sum up its account of each monarch's reign. The introductory formula comprises not only technical details, such as the year of the king's accession to the throne and the duration of his reign, but also a religious appraisal of his conduct—whether his actions were pleasing or displeasing to the Lord, along with an evaluation of his fealty to the Lord, especially in cultic matters. But there is no such introduction to the account of Solomon's reign (and so too for Jeroboam I).

Instead, Solomon's reign is evaluated twice, and in very clear terms: (1) there is a very favorable assessment in 1 Kgs 3:3a:[5] "Solomon loved the Lord, walking in the statutes of David his father." Here the standard "he did what was right in the eyes of the Lord" is "upgraded" by the use of by the verb "loved." (2) But there is also harsh and critical assessment in 1 Kgs 11:6a: "Solomon did what was evil in the sight of the Lord." As I have shown elsewhere, this bald statement comes at the midpoint of a concentric passage that runs from 11:4b to 11:8[6]—a location that makes it stand out in its context. It is preceded by a name midrash in v. 4 that amplifies the explicit judgment: "For when Solomon (שלמה) was old... his heart was not wholly true (שלם) to the Lord his God"; that is, he did not realize the implicit promise of his name. If we accept Zakovitch's

---

the name David is found only 96 times (including in collocations such as "City of David" and "House of David"); Jeroboam I, 71 times; and Ahab, 76 times. I would like to thank my friend Gilad Har-Shoshanim for most of the data in this and the previous note.

4. On means of evaluation in the Bible, see M. Sternberg, *The Poetics of Biblical Narrative* (Bloomington: Indiana University Press, 1985), 475–81; R. Schiff, "The Stylistic Means for the Ethical Evaluation of the Characters in the Narratives of the Book of II Samuel," MA thesis (Bar-Ilan University, Ramat-Gan, 1977), esp. 4–33 (Hebrew); A. Frisch, "The Narrative of Solomon's Reign in the Book of Kings" (PhD diss., Bar-Ilan University, Ramat-Gan, 1986), 65–126 (Hebrew).

5. Unless otherwise specified, the translation employed is the RSV. The chapter/verse references, however, are those of the MT, with those of RSV (where they differ) in square brackets.

6. A. Frisch, "A Literary and Theological Analysis of the Account of Solomon's Sins (1 Kings 11:1-8)," *Shnaton* 11 (1997): 167–79, on 176 (Hebrew).

idea,[7] a name midrash is present in the first evaluation, too: "Solomon loved (ויאהב) the Lord," where the root אה"ב can be seen as alluding to its synonym יד"ד and thus to Solomon's other name, Jedidiah (Hebrew *yedidiah*; 2 Sam. 12:25): Solomon did realize the meaning of this name, for he loved the Lord.[8] The link between 1 Kgs 3:3 and 2 Samuel 12 goes further, because the previous verse in the latter is, "he (Q: she) called his name Solomon. And the Lord loved him (אהבו)." Thus the name reflects not only Solomon's love for the Lord, but also the Lord's love for him.

Let us set aside for now the evaluation of Solomon and focus on the portrayal of his character and presentation of his reign, by reviewing the most important statements about him. We will try to separate the characterization from the evaluation, even though they are closely linked.

In the concluding formula, alongside the standard reference to the prebiblical source of the information, there is one word that is not part of the standard phrase: "Now the rest of the acts of Solomon, and all that he did, and his *wisdom*, are they not written in the book of the acts of Solomon?" (1 Kgs 11:41). The king's wisdom is the thread running throughout the narrative of Solomon's reign (hereinafter "NSR"):[9] all 21 occurrences of the root חכ"ם in Kings are in NSR.[10] Except for the reference to the artisan who created the vessels for the Temple (7:14), all of them relate to Solomon himself (or appear in a comparison with him—the second and third references in 5:10 [4:30]).[11]

Solomon's wisdom is represented as a divine endowment granted in his dream-vision at Gibeon at the start of his reign, as a reward for his reply to the Lord's invitation, "Ask what I shall give you" (3:5), because he does

---

7. Y. Zakovitch, "The Synonymous Word and Synonymous Name in Name Midrashim," *Shnaton* 2 (1977): 100–115, on 107 (Hebrew).

8. On the midrashim on the name Solomon, see A. Frisch, "Midrashic Derivations of Solomon's Name in the Book of Kings," *Beit Mikra* 45 (1999): 84–96.

9. We can mention Liver's interesting idea that the work cited in 11:41, the "Acts of Solomon," was the principal source for the biblical account of Solomon and his reign, and that it focused on the king's wisdom. See J. Liver, "The Book of the Acts of Solomon," *Bib* 48 (1967): 75–101; cf. A. Lemaire, "Wisdom in Solomonic Historiography," in J. Day et al., eds, *Wisdom in Ancient Israel: Essays in Honour of J. A. Emerton* (Cambridge: Cambridge University Press, 1995), 106–18, esp. 116–18.

10. See 1 Kgs 2:1, 9; 3:12, 28; 5:9 [4:29], 10 [30] (×3), 11 [31], 14 [34] (×2), 21 [5:7], 26 [12]; 7:14; 10:4, 6, 7, 8, 23, 24; 11:18.

11. On the centrality of the several categories of wisdom in NSR, see Lemaire, "Wisdom in Solomonic Historiography," 108–10. He also compares various matters with what is mentioned in the historical literature of the ancient Near East (ibid., 110–13).

not request some personal boon but a gift that will help him fulfill his obligations to his people (vv. 9-12). Solomon requests discernment and judicial wisdom (v. 11),[12] and receives far more—every sort of wisdom ("a wise and discerning mind"; v. 12), and to an extraordinary degree, as conveyed by the extravagant language that refers both to history and the future: "none like you has been before you and none like you shall arise after you" (v. 12).[13]

The author-redactor follows the story of the promise at Gibeon (3:4-15) with that of the famous Judgment, in which the king's wisdom allows him to identify which of the two women is telling the truth. This scene is the only explicit example of Solomon as a judge, although the Queen of Sheba does refer to his judicial role: "the Lord...has made you king, that you may execute justice and righteousness" (10:9). Important testimony that he does fulfill this mission comes incidentally, in the technical description of the construction of his palace: "And he made the Hall of the Throne where he was to pronounce judgment, even the Hall of Judgment" (7:7).

But we must not infer from the famous Judgment that Solomon's wisdom was limited to his role as judge. In fact, the story demonstrates that he was granted his wish; but he received much more, as we discover as NSR proceeds. In addition to judicial sagacity, NSR highlights his "encyclopedic" wisdom, to which an entire passage is devoted (5:9-14 [4:29-34]). The root חכ"ם occurs seven times in these six verses, both at the start (the third word in the Hebrew) and at the end (the very last word). Solomon is represented as the wisest man of all times and all places, exceeding the sages of every other civilization and the four famous sages, culminating in "he was wiser than all other men" (5:11 [4:31]). Not only that, but his literary output was vast: "He also uttered three thousand proverbs; and his songs were a thousand and five" (5:12 [4:32]). The account of the visit by the Queen of Sheba, too, highlights his theoretical wisdom. Here the accent is placed on his wisdom, which overshadows the economic and political aspects. The reference to his wisdom in the account of Solomon's cooperation with King Hiram of Tyre (5:21[7],

---

12. Cf.: J. A. Montgomery and H. S. Gehman, *A Critical and Exegetical Commentary on the Book of Kings*, ICC (Edinburgh: T. & T. Clark, 1951), 107; M. Noth, *Könige*, BKAT (Neukirchen-Vluyn: Neukirchener Verlag, 1968), 51; S. Zalewski, *Solomon's Ascension to Throne: Studies in the Books of Kings and Chronicles* (Jerusalem: Y. Markus, 1981), 171–2 (Hebrew)

13. See G. N. Knoppers, "'There Was None Like Him': Incomparability in the Books of Kings," *CBQ* 54 (1992): 411–31.

26[12]) evidently has political savvy in mind.[14] Here too we find the name midrash: "There was peace (שלם) between Hiram and Solomon (שלמה)" (v. 26[12]).

As we have seen, Solomon's wisdom can be traced to the divine promise made at Gibeon. However, even before then he is described as wise—twice in David's deathbed charge to him (2:6, 9), which refers to political acumen. Evidently this is an example of the talmudic dictum that "the Holy One Blessed Be He grants wisdom only to the wise":[15] that is, Solomon started out with a certain measure of wisdom, but this was reinforced by the promise at Gibeon.

NSR links Solomon's wisdom to his rule over Israel and his international prestige. The scene of the Judgment, which epitomizes his judicial wisdom, concludes with the narrator's observation: "And all Israel heard of the judgment which the king had rendered; and they stood in awe of the king, because they perceived that the wisdom of God was in him, to render justice" (3:28). This is followed immediately by "King Solomon was king over all Israel" (4:1) and the list of his senior officials (vv. 2-6) and twelve district prefects (vv. 7-19). This sequence suggests that his judicial wisdom helped him establish his rule over the people. Doing justice, including the display of brilliance in difficult cases, consolidates the king's standing (contrast Absalom's criticism of David as a judge as the start of his rebellion [2 Sam. 15:2-6]).[16] Solomon is "king over all Israel," but the two main segments of the people, "Judah and Israel" (4:20; cf. 1:35 and 5:5 [4:25]), are mentioned explicitly.

Solomon's theoretical wisdom raises his prestige throughout the world and stimulates other rulers to visit him to have first-hand experience of his wisdom—as we are informed at the end of the passage that extols his wisdom (5:14 [4:34]). Their "pilgrimage" reflects his international standing, which foreshadows Isaiah's description of the ideal king: "him shall the nations seek, and his dwellings shall be glorious" (Isa. 11:10)

Solomon's reign was an era of peace and prosperity for Israel. When he requests Hiram's assistance for his building project, he himself notes the difference between his father's reign, a time of war, and his own, which is

---

14. Another passage hints at (but does not state explicitly) his political sagacity. In his reply to Bathsheba (2:22), he alludes to the political preamble in Adonijah's petition to her (v. 15), even though she did not repeat it to Solomon (v. 20). His ability to reconstruct his rival's thought process, without hearing him, reflects his political skills. See Frisch, "The Narrative of Solomon's Reign," 199.

15. R. Johanan in *b. Ber.* 55a.

16. See Zalewski, *Solomon's Ascension to Throne*, 172.

one of peace (5:17-18 [3-4]).¹⁷ Not only does Solomon harvest the fruits of David's policy; he also makes his own contribution to the material abundance and prosperity, in part by forging alliances with neighboring kingdoms (notably Egypt and Sheba), extensive international trade, both overland and maritime, an improved administrative system, and more. The practical outcome of all this for the man in the street is: "And Judah and Israel dwelt in safety, from Dan even to Beer-sheba, every man under his vine and under his fig tree, all the days of Solomon" (5:5 [4:25]). The people, too, benefit: "Judah and Israel were as many as the sand by the sea; they ate and drank and were happy" (4:20). The people's comfort and contentment are noted both at the time of his coronation (1:40, 45) and at the conclusion of the dedication of the Temple (8:66).¹⁸

Another motif is Solomon's righteousness and his fealty to the covenant with the Lord. This is a classic component of the moral and religious evaluation in the book of Kings. The story of the dream-vision at Gibeon highlights his wisdom, but it also emphasizes his righteousness. Solomon's request of the Lord is appraised favorably: "It pleased the Lord that Solomon had asked this" (3:10). This divine approval leads to the granting of the larger gift. But in addition to this overt aspect of his righteousness, the content of Solomon's request (3:6-9) also reflects, I believe, his righteousness. It indicates his idea of the ideal monarch, in three domains: his relationships with the Lord above him, with the people beneath him, and with himself and his position.¹⁹ Solomon's request expresses humility towards the Lord and recognition of Him as master. It expresses humility towards the people, whom he sees as the chosen people. And it reflects modesty about himself, as not yet ready for his job, in the shadow of his father. The motif of righteousness is manifested once again in the story of the construction of the Temple: the initiative itself, the vast enterprise described in great detail, and Solomon's speeches at its dedication. Several points in his address bear emphasis: (1) his invocation of the Lord's unique status (8:23); (2) his observation that the

---

17. A name midrash that links Solomon's name to peaceful climate that prevailed in his time appears in Chronicles: "his name shall be Solomon (שלמה), and I will give peace (שלום) and quiet to Israel in his days" (1 Chron. 22:9). Compare the above-mentioned name midrash on the relations between Solomon and Hiram (1 Kgs 5:26[12]).

18. The root שמ"ח "happy" with reference to the people occurs six times in NSR (twice in 1:40); this does not include Hiram's joy (5:21[7]). In the rest of Kings the root appears only twice, in the account of Joash's enthronement (2 Kgs 21:14, 20).

19. See Frisch, "The Narrative of Solomon's Reign," 242–6.

Lord keeps His promises (8:20, 23-24, 56); (3) his reference to the Lord's transcendence (8:27); (4) his reference to the Lord's control over history and payment of a just return to all human beings as a function of their deeds, whether punishment or forgiveness (8:31-32, 33-34, 35-36, 39, et passim); (5) his vision that all humankind, and not only the Israelites, will revere the Lord (8:43, 60).[20]

As part of this motif we find the other side of the coin as well—sinning and disloyalty to the covenant with the Lord. At first merely an option (9:6-9), it later becomes a reality. Solomon sins not only by marrying many foreign women (evidently political marriages) but also by erecting shrines to their gods in Jerusalem (11:7-8), for which the kingdom was condemned to punishment.

Unlike the motif of righteousness, which appears in NSR with its reverse as well, the wisdom motif is only favorable. This might entice us to accept Porten's idea that Solomon's sin reflects the absence of wisdom,[21] so that this antithesis, too, is in the text. But there is no solid evidence of a link in the text between sin and folly, so we had best not introduce it ourselves. Solomon's punishment for his sins is the loss of his kingdom (11:11); but the verdict is softened so that the secession by the northern tribes is postponed to his son's reign (11:12-13; cf. vv. 31-32 and 34-36). Thus Solomon, at the peak of his glory, unites the Israelites through the construction of the Temple and the festivities of its consecration (8:1-3).[22] It is his sin that causes the rupture between Judah, the king's own tribe, and the ten tribes, replacing the united empire with two smaller kingdoms that will sometimes be at war with each other.

---

20. The principle enunciated here is that Solomon is not voicing the author-redactor's view, but is expressing his own ideas as an independent character. See M. Greenberg, "תפלה," in *Encyclopaedia Biblica, Vol. 8* (Jerusalem: Bialik Institute, 1982), cols. 896–922, in 918–20 (Hebrew). Solomon's perspective during his righteous phase is close to but not identical with the "authorized" view. The most conspicuous difference relates to the eternity of the Temple (contrast Solomon's declaration in 8:13 [and the implication of 8:46-48, where he envisions that the people in exile will pray in the direction of the Temple, whose destruction is not mentioned] and the Lord's reply in 9:7). For the view I reject, see, e.g., R. D. Nelson, *First and Second Kings* (Louisville: John Knox, 1987), 5–6.

21. See: B. Porten, "The Structure and Theme of the Solomon Narrative (1 Kings 3–11)," *HUCA* 38 (1967): 93–128, on 98.

22. Garsiel believes that Solomon's excursion to Gibeon (3:4), in the territory of Benjamin, was a political act intended to bind the northern tribes to his kingdom. See M. Garsiel, "King Solomon's Trip to Gibeon and His Dream," in *Ben-Yehudah Jubilee Volume*, ed. B. Lurie (Tel Aviv: Israel Society for Biblical Research, 1981), 191–271, esp. 191–8 (Hebrew).

And what was Solomon's transgression? It is stated explicitly and falls into the domain of the cult, which is so important to the author-redactor of Kings. I would argue, however, that in addition to the religious transgression, which is indeed paramount, there is also subsidiary criticism of Solomon's social policies. The heavy burden he imposed on the people is mentioned no fewer than five times in the story of the northern tribes' secession (12:4, 9, 10, 11, 14); they demand that Rehoboam reduce their taxes as a condition for their continued fealty to the House of David. Several loci in NSR and the story of the split compare the burden of the corvée under Solomon with the bondage in Egypt: (1) The words of the people's request of Rehoboam, "lighten the harsh labor and the heavy yoke which your father laid on us" (עבדת אביך הקשה...אשר נתן עלינו; 1 Kgs 12:4 [NJPS]) inevitably bring to mind the description of the Egyptian bondage in Deuteronomy: "The Egyptians...laid harsh labor on us" (ויתנו עלינו עבדה קשה; Deut. 26:6 [NJPS]).[23] (2) Jeroboam's position in Solomon's bureaucracy as the overseer of the "forced labor (סבל) of the House of Joseph" (11:28) echoes the "burdens" (סבלות) of the Israelites in Egypt.[24] (3) The description of Solomon's vast building project: "Solomon built (ויבן)... and all the store-cities (ערי המסכנות) that Solomon had," with the long list of cities linked by "and (ואת)" (1 Kgs 9:17-19) echoes Exod. 1:11: "they built (ויבן) for Pharaoh store-cities (ערי מסכנות), Pithom and Raamses (את...ואת)." (4) There is a set of inverted analogies between Solomon and Jeroboam, on one side, and Moses and Pharaoh, on the other side: Solomon, after having been compared to Moses, is in his twilight years compared to Pharaoh, while Jeroboam plays the role of Moses.[25] All of these paint us a negative portrait of Solomon against the backdrop of his socioeconomic policy.

This perception that part of Solomon's sin derived from his socioeconomic policy can help us understand the link between the transgression and the punishment. The division of the united kingdom is not merely a technical result of a complex divine decree, beginning with the deposition

---

23. Outside the story of the division of the kingdom (and its parallel in Chronicles), the expression "harsh labor" (עבודה קשה) occurs four times in the Bible; three of them relate to the bondage in Egypt. The fourth occurrence is Isa. 14:3. The root כב"ד "heavy" found in our verse may also bring to mind the Egyptian bondage (Exod. 5:9; 7:14; 8:11, etc.) and then the measure for measure punishment of the Egyptians (14:4, 17, 18, 25).

24. See Exod. 1:11; 2:11; 5:5; 6:6, 7.

25. See the extensive discussion in A. Frisch, "The Narrative of Solomon's Reign," 96–102; and, more briefly, Frisch, "The Exodus Motif in 1 Kings 1–14," *JSOT* 87 (2000): 3–21, on 13–15.

of the king, followed by two expressions of clemency (explained by the merits of David and of Jerusalem); it can also be seen as a natural outcome of the conduct of a Judahite king who infringes the liberty and prosperity of the other tribes and incites against himself especially a prominent leader of the tribe of Ephraim, which has borne a tradition of leadership since ancient times.[26]

The last motif to be addressed here is that of building. Solomon is the great builder, notably of the Temple, his monumental project for the ages. He also builds his palace, fortifies several cities, and erects store-cities and chariot and cavalry towns all over the country (9:15-25). Late in life, however, he sins precisely by building: "Then Solomon *built* (אז יבנה) a high place for Chemosh the abomination of Moab, and for Molech the abomination of the Ammonites, on the mountain east of Jerusalem. And so he did for all his foreign wives, who burned incense and sacrificed to their gods" (11:7-8). His mission was to build: "he shall *build* the house (הוא יבנה) for My name" (5:19[5]; 8:19). He indeed fulfilled this destiny, but also built idolatrous shrines. The building motif is also part of his punishment, as Ahijah tells Jeroboam: "I will be with you, and will *build* you (ובניתי לך) a sure house" (11:38).[27]

After this discussion of the recurrent motifs in NSR, we return to the issue of the assessment of the king and the two antithetical judgments incorporated into the initial account and summation of his reign. We can add the verse from the Gibeon scene, already mentioned, "It pleased the Lord that Solomon had asked this" (3:10), as well as several critical assessments in ch. 11. These are the only explicit religious evaluations of Solomon in the text; everything else seems to be neutral descriptions. We must realize, however, that the biblical narrator does not just report what happened; in addition, and no less important, he takes a stand on events and offers a religious and moral appraisal thereof. Hence we should address two questions: (1) Where else in NSR is there religious assessment (positive or negative) of him? (2) Is there any regularity or system in the location of such assessments, or are they scattered randomly in the text?

With regard to the first question, various scholars have indeed pointed out many evaluations of Solomon and his deeds, most of them critical,

---

26. For social issues as a factor leading to the breakup of the kingdom, see A. Frisch, *Torn Asunder: The Division of the Kingdom Narrative in the Book of Kings* (Beer Sheva: Ben-Gurion University of the Negev Press, 2013), 26–31 (Hebrew).

27. Another motif picked up by Walsh should be mentioned: the frequent references to David. See Walsh, *1 Kings*, 155–6.

scattered throughout the story.²⁸ But precisely this abundance of negative comments arouses suspicion. Is every passage in which modern readers detect a note of criticism indeed critical of Solomon? Perhaps they are reading their own ideas into the text.²⁹ This leads to my second question, about the systematic placement of the assessments. My thesis, which is

---

28. For a list of scholars who find criticism of Solomon throughout the story, see Y. H. Jeon, "The Retroactive Re-evaluation Technique with Pharaoh's Daughter and the Nature of Solomon's Corruption in 1 Kings 1–12," *TynBul* 62 (2011): 15–40, on 20 n. 16.

29. I will briefly present one representative example: Commentators and modern scholars have found criticism of Solomon in various elements of the short passage 3:1-3: (1) his marriage to Pharaoh's daughter; (2) the use in vv. 2-3 of רק "however, only," seen as setting a limit to the praise; (3) the mention of the high places (condemned throughout Kings after the building of the Temple); (4) oblique criticism within the positive assessment: the statement that "Solomon loved the Lord," rather than the standard formula, "he did what was right in the eyes of the Lord," alludes to the negative connotations of the verb in connection with his foreign wives in ch. 11; and (5) the comparison of the structure of these verses with the opening of the censure of Solomon in ch. 11—foreign wives and worship on the high places.

I find none of this persuasive. (1) The reference to his marriage with Pharaoh's daughter is written from a political perspective. By contrast to ch. 11, where the verb "love" applies to the foreign women, here it refers to the Lord. In ch. 3 we find only that he made a marriage alliance. (2) As for רק, Kaufmann long ago noted its use as an emphatic particle, like its synonym אך, applying to what follows and not as a limiting modifier (Yehezkel Kaufmann, *From the Secrets of the Biblical Art: A Collection of Essays* [Tel Aviv: Dvir, 1966], 199 [Hebrew]). Cf. Gen. 20:11; Deut. 4:6; Judg. 3:2, 19:20; 1 Kgs 21:25. (3) With regard to the high places, the text explicitly justifies their existence, because the Temple has not yet been built. (4) The unusual phrasing of the positive assessment here reflects a more favorable view than the standard formula. The appearance of the verb "love" in ch. 11 has no implications for its use here; on the contrary, it emphasized the contrast, in keeping with the respective contexts (as we will see immediately). (5) Hence there is no room for the comparison with ch. 11, where the high places are meant for idolatry and not for the worship of the Lord. In ch. 11 they are a result of the marriage with foreign women; in ch. 3 there is no link between the foreign wife and the high places. What is more, it is obvious that the context of 3:1-3 is very positive. Not only, as already mentioned, is it extravagant in its praise of Solomon (v. 3), it also serves to prepare for the dream-vision at Gibeon; he has gone to the high place there, and the Lord's appearance to him is a reward for his conduct. There is also the consideration noted by Brosh: "It is difficult to posit that the narrator wanted to disparage Solomon in advance, given the fear that a stain on the builder of the Temple, Solomon, might carry over to his deed, the construction of the Temple" (B.-Sh. Brosh, "Complex Royal Characters in the Book of Kings" [PhD diss., Tel Aviv University, 2005], 118 [Hebrew]).

not original to me, is that there is a good reason for where the two contradictory evaluations with which I began (3:3 and 11:6) are located in NSR; namely, that the story is fashioned as a diptych of contrasting "panels," in which the first section is all light and brilliance and the second part increasingly dark.[30]

In addition to the favorable judgments already noted here, I believe that there are additional positive appraisals of Solomon in the first half of NSR. Here are several in chs. 1 and 2.

1. In the story of Solomon's enthronement (ch. 1), a positive assessment of the young prince emerges from the contrast between Solomon and his brother and rival Adonijah. Their confrontation plays out on three levels. The first is the pursuit of power: Adonijah aspires to the scepter and attracts a loyal following. The narrator paints this in negative terms: "Now Adonijah son of Haggith went about boasting, 'I will be king!'" (1:5 [NJPS]). Solomon, by contrast, is passive.[31] The second contrast is in their attitude towards their royal father: whereas Adonijah exploits David's old age and frailty and schemes without his knowledge, Solomon's loyalists take their case to the king and emphasize their allegiance to him. The third has to do with the rival brother—each of them fears that, should he lose the contest, the victor will have him killed. But after Solomon succeeds to the throne and his brother flees, he does not order Adonijah's execution, but promises him his life if he refrains from opposing him. These are the first words Solomon speaks in NSR, and they express clemency and mercy towards his rival, but with royal sternness.

2. In the story of the consolidation of Solomon's power (2:13-46), the penultimate verse, which immediately follows Shim'ei's condemnation, is Solomon's blessing to himself: "But King Solomon (המלך שלמה) shall be blessed, and the throne of David shall be established (נכון) before the Lord for ever" (v. 45). Given this wording, and especially the third-person reference, I would see the verse as an example of the rare instance of a judgment that can be

---

30. As will be clarified below, I read NSR as having a concentric structure, with three main sections. To simplify the discussion, however, of two contrasting appraisals, it is easier to speak of a diptych, one panel favorable and the other critical.

31. The books of the Former Prophets view the fact that a man does not make an effort to obtain the crown as a virtue. In this he resembles the authentic prophets, whose vocation was forced on them rather than sought for.

heard as expressed both by the character and by the authoritative narrator,[32] which of course lends greater force to the evaluation. What is more, the next verse, the last in this episode, concludes with a phrase that indicates the fulfillment of the self-blessing: "So the kingdom was established (והממלכה נכונה) in the hand of Solomon" (v. 46). This certainly reflects the heavenly approval of the new king.

There are also positive evaluations in the second half of NSR (such as in the account of the Queen of Sheba's visit and the descriptions of Solomon's wealth and wisdom), which we have postulated is critical of him. The question, of course, is where to draw the line between the two parts of the story. It is clear that ch. 11 is wholly unfavorable in its assessment of Solomon. We might, then, limit the negative section of NSR to that chapter. The two sections do not have to be of equal length; indeed, the fact that the first and positive section is much longer gives added weight to the favorable judgment. I believe, however, that there is criticism of Solomon, albeit implicit, already at the end of the pinnacle of his achievements.[33] The construction of the Temple and its consecration are the zenith of his career, and conveyed with abundant details (chs. 6–8). I propose that these chapters, with the prophecy linked to them that responds to the construction of the Temple (9:1-9), is the hinge point of the concentric structure.[34] The line between the positive and negative attitudes towards Solomon runs through the third and last part of the prophecy (vv. 6-9). Here the negative element is unmistakable, with the long reference to sin and the punishment that will follow it—the destruction of the Temple. This stands out not only in comparison to the shorter attention to the favorable option (vv. 4-5) but no less so against the background of what I see as the parallel prophecy at the start of the construction project (6:11-13), where we encounter only the positive option: loyalty to the Lord and its reward. From this point on (9:6) the text is strewn with critical allusions, even if the explicit criticism is deferred until ch. 11.

In addition to the prophecy that opens the second section, I would like to note, by way of example, three other implicit criticisms in that section.

---

32. On this device, see Sternberg, *The Poetics of Biblical Narrative*, 476, §4.
33. This has been designated the "middle stage corruption view" (Jeon, "The Retroactive Re-evaluation Technique," 21–3).
34. See A. Frisch, "Structure and its Significance: The Narrative of Solomon's Reign (1 Kings 1–12.24)," *JSOT* 51 (1991): 3–14.

1. Solomon's negotiations with Hiram after the construction of the Temple (9:10-14) are presented with implicit censure of the deal by which Solomon trades "twenty towns in the Galilee" for building materials—land for goods. Ironically, Hiram is not happy with the deal, and the last word in the story is his. Comparison with the parallel passage before the construction of the Temple reveals the deterioration in the standing of Solomon's kingdom. There Solomon paid with agricultural produce (5:24-25[10-11]), and not with territory.
2. In the account of the Queen of Sheba's visit (10:1-13), her praise of Solomon's justice contains hidden criticism. Of David, whose path Solomon is supposed to be continuing, we were told: "David *administered justice and righteousness* for all his people" (2 Sam. 8:15). But the Queen says of Solomon, "He made you king to *administer justice and righteousness*" (1 Kgs 10:9 [NJPS]). The administration of justice is Solomon's mission, but she does not say that he fulfills it. What is more, she says that Solomon was elected "because of the Lord's everlasting love for Israel" (ibid.). But readers remember that Solomon-Jedidiah is the *individual* whom the Lord loved (2 Sam. 11:24).
3. When we are told of his acquisition of many horses and chariots and of the abundance of silver and gold (10:10-29), the tone is indeed laudatory. But the immediate sequel, the report of his many foreign wives, puts readers in mind of the Law of the King in Deuteronomy 17; it is hard to escape the feeling that the appearance here of all five motifs mentioned there—many horses, Egypt, many wives, his heart turning astray, and the accumulation of silver and gold—is deliberate.[35]

Why did the author-redactor choose the method of direct praise and covert criticism? I do not believe the technical solution, which attributes this to the nature of the sources on which he drew, is enough. Rather, the reason is literary and theological: to wit, his ambivalent attitude towards Solomon's material achievements. The author-redactor acknowledges that they are important, and all the more so because wealth and glory were included in the Lord's promise to Solomon at Gibeon. On the other hand, he is aware of their problematic nature, including their contravention of the

---

35. Cf. M. Weinfeld, *Deuteronomy and the Deuteronomic School* (Oxford: Clarendon, 1972), 168 n. 4; M. Brettler, "The Structure of 1 Kings 1–11," *JSOT* 49 (1991): 87–97; M. Cogan, *1 Kings*, AB 10 (New York: Doubleday, 2001), 323.

provisions of the Deuteronomic Law of the King. He focuses his explicit criticism on his many foreign wives, because this led to the most severe transgression of all—turning away from the Lord—and because Solomon was active in contracting these alliances (whereas the accumulation of wealth derived in part from gifts he received from other monarchs).[36]

This method of casting a story as a diptych, in which one panel highlights the positive and the other the negative, is not unique to NSR, and is applied to other kings as well: Saul and David in the book of Samuel, and several kings in Chronicles, notably Rehoboam (2 Chron. 10–12), Asa (chs. 14–16), and Joash (24). It can also be found in Kings itself, though less conspicuously and with less contrast between the praise and the criticism: Jeroboam I (1 Kgs 11:26–14:20), Uzziah (2 Kgs 15:1-7),[37] and perhaps also Hezekiah (2 Kgs 17–20).

The problem with the idea that there is criticism of Solomon from the very start of NSR is that such a reading frequently requires isolating verses or even words from their immediate and clearly positive context; modern readers or scholars are in fact reading their own values and worldview into the text. We are not looking for our own position, however, but for that expressed by the text.[38]

To avoid any misunderstanding, let me make it plain that I do not overlook implicit hints; I myself find them in the second part of our story. What distinguished those I acknowledge and those I reject is their context: the burden of proof lies on those who allege to have found a negative implication in the middle of a clearly favorable passage (such as alongside "Solomon loved the Lord"). The insinuations I highlight are fully integrated into their context and appear throughout the second part of NSR, beginning with the prophecy that closes the account of the construction of the Temple and continuing through the explicit censure in ch. 11. After beginning with the theoretical possibility of exile and destruction of the Temple, the second part of NSR concludes with overt

---

36. Seibert (Eric Seibert, *Subversive Scribes and the Solomonic Narrative: A Rereading of 1 Kings 1–11* [New York: T&T Clark, 2006]) understands the situation differently. He believes that the author does hold an unambiguous position, but, afraid to say so explicitly, merely hints at it. I think that the author's position is complex and reflects the tension in his theological thought.

37. The short account of his reign ends with the notice that he was stricken with leprosy. The phrase "the Lord smote the king" would seem to indicate punishment.

38. For a thorough discussion of the "intention" we are seeking, that is, "what is written in the text?," see M. Weiss, *The Bible from Within: The Method of Total Interpretation* (Jerusalem: Magnes, 1984), 12–17.

criticism and announcement of the punishment to follow—the division of the kingdom. This creates a negative frame around all the positive references in this section and is what distinguishes allusions that are significant and others that I believe exist mainly in the reader's mind.

Solomon, the king of wisdom, is also the king of love: initially the love of the Lord and of Israel, but later of pagan women. The moral assessment of Solomon in the book of Kings falls into two parts: a first section that is all light, and a second in which there are still rays of light but which darkens at the end. My proposal, though, is that the darkness does not fall suddenly; the change is gradual, and positive statements in the second part conceal elements of criticism. This is the method that the author-redactor of Kings employed to present the extremely complex figure of one of the greatest rulers of Israel, who built the Temple in Jerusalem and oversaw a period of peace and prosperity for his people, but who was also responsible for the erection of pagan shrines in Jerusalem[39] and for an intolerable tax burden on his people, which ultimately shattered the national unity. The criticism is not political, but rather religious and didactic. It is meant to teach readers the lesson that there is no assurance that a person will continue down the path of righteous behavior; instead, throughout our lives we must cope with religious and moral challenges while relating appropriately not only to the Lord but also to our fellow human beings.

---

39. This complexity also appears in Nehemiah: "Did not Solomon king of Israel sin on account of such women? Among the many nations there was no king like him, and he was beloved by his God, and God made him king over all Israel; nevertheless foreign women made even him to sin" (Neh. 13:26).

Chapter 5

Rehabilitating Rehoboam

Rachelle Gilmour

A man is known by the company he keeps, or so the proverb goes. Rehoboam is remarkable in biblical narrative for the extent to which his characterization is conveyed through the direct speech of his friends, as much as his own speech and actions. The story of Rehoboam is interwoven with the drama of Jeroboam in 1 Kings 12–14, but the narrative focus rests on Rehoboam in 1 Kgs 12:1-24 and 14:21-31. During his reign, the kingdom of Israel splits into North and South after being united during the time of his father Solomon. His characterization is at the narrative center, and yet ultimately irrelevant in the political changes that take place at the beginning of his reign, because God intervenes in his attempts to retain and regain the Northern Kingdom.

In this essay, we will begin by diagnosing a tension in the interpretation of Rehoboam's characterization. Most interpreters evaluate Rehoboam's character negatively, based on his role in the schism of the kingdom, and our reading will confirm that Rehoboam is a cruel and oppressive king. However, in contrast to this characterization, the narrator includes a remarkable example of Rehoboam's obedience to God in 1 Kgs 12:21-24 and omits either a positive or negative evaluation of Rehoboam in 1 Kgs 14:22. In response to the diagnosis, firstly this essay will challenge the interpretation that Rehoboam is foolish for rejecting the advice of the elders; secondly, Rehoboam's characterization is examined in its wider context of divine determination and comparisons to the character of Solomon.

Diagnosing Rehoboam

Although Rehoboam has little more than a cameo in 1 Kings in comparison to his father Solomon and rival Jeroboam, his character is colorful and gains notice in ancient interpretations. The teacher of Ben Sira[1] evaluates Rehoboam as "broad in folly and lacking in sense, Rehoboam whose policy drove the people to revolt," the epithet "broad in folly" a play on Rehoboam's name. In contrast, Josephus (*Ant.* 8.212-224, 246-265) finds redeeming features in his portrait of Rehoboam. Josephus considers the advice from the elders to be good but also suggests Rehoboam's motivations for refusing it: it was unbefitting to the grandeur of the king. Josephus portrays the crowd as a rabble, which is fickle and unreliable, and lays ultimate causation with divine will in accordance with 1 Kgs 12:15. He emphasizes Rehoboam's obedience to the prophecy of Shemaiah, underlining the contrast to Jeroboam who is portrayed as impious and lawless.[2]

Reading 1 Kgs 12:1-20, many modern commentators agree with Ben Sira's assessment of Rehoboam's character. R. Nelson describes Rehoboam as "a thoroughly unlikeable character. He is arrogant, impulsive and tactless";[3] S. J. DeVries finds "senseless obstinacy of Rehoboam and its calamitous effects";[4] and J. Walsh evaluates the characterization of Rehoboam:

> …the narrator has little respect for Rehoboam. He presents him as foolish, arrogant, insensitive, self-serving, and politically obtuse. There are also indications that his diplomatic gaffe is not due to simple bad judgement but to a much more fundamental weakness of character.[5]

---

1. See Markus Witte, "'What Share Do We Have in David…?' Ben Sira's Perspectives on 1 Kings 12," in *One God–One Cult–One Nation: Archaeological and Biblical Perspectives*, ed. Reinhard G. Kratz and Hermann Spieckermann (Berlin: de Gruyter, 2010), 91–117 (108). Witte suggests that Ben Sira largely reflects the Hebrew MT text, although he makes no mention of 12:15. Cf. Witte also notes (p. 103) that the overall attitude towards kingship in Ben Sira is negative.

2. See Louis H. Feldman, *Studies in Josephus' Rewritten Bible*, JSJSup 58 (Leiden: Brill, 1998), 244–62.

3. Richard D. Nelson, *First and Second Kings,* Interpretation (Louisville: John Knox, 1987), 78.

4. Simon J. DeVries, *1 Kings*, 2nd ed., WBC 12 (Nashville: Thomas Nelson, 2003), 156.

5. Jerome T. Walsh, *1 Kings*, Berit Olam (Collegeville: Liturgical Press, 1996), 168.

Similarly, B. O. Long describes the characterization of Rehoboam as "arrogant, brash, politically naive, and insensitive."[6]

There is plentiful textual evidence in 1 Kgs 12:1-20 to support negative evaluations of Rehoboam's character. The scene is dominated by dialogue and, through this means, the characterization of Rehoboam is vividly developed.[7] For example, Walsh attends to small variations when one character's speech is reported by another character. When Rehoboam paraphrases the request of the northern people in v. 9 ("lighten the yoke that your father put on us"), he omits their repeated claim from v. 4 that the service imposed on them is "heavy" ("your father made our yoke heavy [הקשה]; now therefore lighten the hard [הקשה] service of your father and his heavy [הכבד] yoke that he placed on us"), the root קשה repeated twice and כבד used once in their request in emphasis.[8] This reflects Rehoboam's blindness to, or even deliberate obfuscation of, their oppression.

The centerpiece of this dialogue is the crudity and harshness of Rehoboam's young friends. They are introduced as "the children" (הילדים) in v. 10 in contrast to the "elders" (הזקנים) in v. 6. The term "children" establishes the immaturity of their wisdom.[9] The language of the young advisors is colorful, giving insight into their collective character in only a few words. The response in v. 10, translated in the NRSV "my little finger is thicker than my father's loins" (קטני עבה ממתני אבי), is difficult to interpret on account of its euphemisms. "My little finger" (קטני) is a reference to Rehoboam's penis rather than finger, as recognized by most modern interpreters.[10] The phrase, "my father's loins" (ממתני אבי), is

---

6. B. O. Long, *1 Kings with an Introduction to the Historical Literature*, FOTL 9 (Grand Rapids: Eerdmans, 1984), 136.

7. On the importance of dialogue for characterization, see Shimon Bar-Efrat, *Narrative Art in the Bible*, JSOTSup 70 (Sheffield: Almond, 1989), 64–77.

8. Walsh, *1 Kings*, 163.

9. As Sweeney notes, Rehoboam is 41 years old according to the chronology in Kings and so this label for his contemporaries is "striking" (Marvin A. Sweeney, *I & II Kings*, OTL [Louisville: Westminster John Knox, 2007], 170). Cf. Alexander Rofé, "Elders or Youngsters? Critical Remarks on 1 Kings 12," in Kratz and Spieckermann, eds, *One God–One Cult–One Nation*, 79–89 (82–3). Rofé compares the usage of "children" (ילדים) to Dan. 1:4, 10, 13, 15, and 17, where the term means "youngsters," and on this basis he proposes a late Persian period date of composition.

10. For interpreters who understand this to be his penis, see Ze'ev Weisman, *Political Satire in the Bible*, Semeia Studies (Atlanta: Scholars Press, 1998), 108; Keith Bodner, *Jeroboam's Royal Drama* (Oxford: Oxford University Press, 2012), 67; Sweeney, *Kings*, 170; Also, Mordechai Cogan, *1 Kings: A New Translation with Introduction and Commentary*, AB 10 (New York: Doubleday, 2001), 349. Cogan

less discussed in scholarship, but could either be "waist" if literally the loins,[11] or a euphemism for his father's testicles.[12] Nevertheless, as R. Boer observes, if a euphemism for genitalia is used, even for its more technical sense, the usage inevitably evokes its full cluster of meanings.[13] In other words, the comparison might be primarily between Rehoboam's penis and his father's waist, but an allusion is inevitably also made to his father's testicles. Both comparisons, to Solomon's waist and testicles, have a comic effect because of their absurdity in size and comparison to Solomon's large number of progeny. Walsh describes this as "gutter language"[14] and the coarseness and crude absurdity contributes to the depiction of the young advisors' immaturity.

The crude image in the advice of the young men is also an assertion of power, particularly Rehoboam's power to subject the people. As evidenced from Ezek. 16:26 and 23:20, where the Egyptians are described as having large penises, genital size was a sign of potency in ancient Israel.[15] Yet, at the same time as asserting Rehoboam's power, their response humorously deconstructs the basis for his power: rather than claiming divine right, popular selection, or wisdom of rule, the response asserts the most basic foundation for male power: brute force. Another backhanded compliment could be suggested by their choice of euphemism for Rehoboam's penis, "my little" (קטני), which presumably is not erect and so not as suggestive

---

notes that Qimchi, alone among medieval interpreters, understands the word this way. Cf. DeVries, *1 Kings*, 153, who translates the word as "my little finger." One difficulty in interpreting the word as "my penis" is that the adjective "thicker" (עבה) in v. 10 is feminine, suggesting it may refer to a body part that comes in pairs. However, as many of the euphemisms in Hebrew for penis are feminine, this may also explain the form, e.g., "legs" (רגלים), "knees" (ברכים), "thigh" (ירך), "fluid duct" (שפכה). See the list of terms in John H. Elliot, "Deuteronomy—Shameful Encroachment on Shameful Parts," in *Ancient Israel: The Old Testament in its Social Context*, ed. Philip F. Esler (London: SCM, 2005), 161–90 (168–9).

11. E.g. DeVries, *1 Kings*, 153.
12. Roland Boer, *The Earthy Nature of the Bible: Fleshly Readings of Sex, Masculinity, and Carnality* (Houndsmill: Palgrave Macmillan, 2012), 52.
13. Ibid., 50.
14. Walsh, *1 Kings*, 164.
15. See Hilary Lipka, "Shaved Beards and Bared Buttocks: Shame and the Undermining of Masculine Performance in Biblical Texts," in *Being a Man: Negotiating Ancient Constructs of Masculinity*, ed. Ilona Zsolnay (London: Routledge, 2017), 176–97 (178–9); Also, Elliot, "Deuteronomy," 170. Bodner, *Jeroboam*, 68, points to a different aspect of the assertion of power: he compares this vulgarity to other "ruptures" in the story of David that are marked by rape and adultery, namely David taking Bathsheba and Amnon raping Tamar.

of virility as it might be.[16] By complimenting Rehoboam's physique and power, they simultaneously insult his capacity for any more laudable elements of kingly rule. Significantly, Rehoboam does not repeat this part of the advice to the people.[17] Nevertheless, it contributes to his characterization, both because of the insight into his friends' collective character, and into their perception of his power.

The second part of the young men's advice is given in v. 11, "Now, whereas my father laid on you a heavy yoke, I will add to your yoke." There is cruelty in taking the people's request in v. 4 to "lighten the heavy service of your father and his heavy yoke (ועלו הכבד)" and reusing the same language, now "I will add to your yoke (ואני אוסיף על עלכם)." The reversal suggests that the people are being punished for making the request and that silent submission would have been better for them. Furthermore, in v. 11, the additional labor will be enforced with greater severity than the whips used by Solomon, "My father disciplined you with whips, but I will discipline you with scorpions." "Scorpions" (עקרבים) are thought to be a type of vicious whip,[18] but, as with the multiple meanings alluded to by the euphemism for genitalia, the literal meaning of an aggressive and painful animal is simultaneously evoked. Alongside a threat of power, this image is another reference to Rehoboam's masculinity and personal potency: use of weapons was a key attribute of masculinity in ancient Israel and so the claim is virtually synonymous with the claim about his penis size.[19] The people will not serve Rehoboam willingly but their submission will be enforced by his masculine power.

When Rehoboam follows the advice of the young advisors, he is associated with their crudity and he takes on their cruelty. According to Ben Sira and many modern interpreters, following crude and cruel advice is foolish. However, as the narrative continues in 1 Kgs 12:21-24, a different, albeit less colorful, characterization of Rehoboam emerges and Josephus's more generous interpretation of Rehoboam's character finds support in

---

16. See Boer, *Earthy Nature*, 52.

17. Walsh, *1 Kings*, 164, finds that Rehoboam's foolishness has its limits; Bodner, *Jeroboam*, 69, suggests that Rehoboam did not quite have the courage to make this bold claim. I wonder if the reason is twofold: firstly because of the back-handed compliment; and secondly, because the claim about his penis size is synonymous with the threat of whips, symbols of masculinity and power (see below), and therefore redundant in repetition.

18. Cogan, *1 Kings*, 349, describes "scorpions" as "an apt term for a barbed whip, consider the thorny nature of the 'scorpion-plant.'"

19. Lipka, "Shaved Beards," 179. Thank you to Dr. Anthony Rees for pointing this out to me.

the text. We will now change our course in Rehoboam's diagnosis, and suggest another, more positive, characterization of Rehoboam in 1 Kgs 12:21-24 and 1 Kgs 14:21-34.

DeVries cautiously describes 1 Kgs 12:21-24 as "an apologia" for Rehoboam not moving against the Northern Kingdom,[20] and describes Rehoboam heeding God's command as, "cowardly and indecisive when the time came to fight" rather than as obedience to God.[21] Walsh supposes, "the narrator's generalization of the obedience to a plural 'they' enables him to avoid attributing expressly to Rehoboam anything that might elicit our admiration."[22] For DeVries and Walsh, Rehoboam's later actions, including his obedience in 12:21-24, must be interpreted negatively because of Rehoboam's characterization in the dialogue with his advisors. However, Nelson acknowledges a shift in Rehoboam's characterization when Rehoboam and the people obediently respond to Shemaiah's prophecy. He grants that the effect of 1 Kgs 12:21-24 is, "to rehabilitate the obedient Rehoboam in the reader's opinion especially in light of Jeroboam's coming acts of disobedience."[23]

In addition to 1 Kgs 12:21-24, the return to Rehoboam in 1 Kgs 14:21-31 further expands the depiction of Rehoboam. At first sight, the evaluation of Rehoboam is negative when the evaluation of his subjects is given in v. 22: "Judah did what was evil in the sight of the Lord; they provoked him to jealousy with their sins that they committed, more than all that their ancestors had done," followed by a litany of cultic sins. A case can be made that Rehoboam was responsible for preventing his people's cultic misdemeanors even though direct blame is avoided. However, comparison to other versions of the story suggests that the absence of Rehoboam's name is significant for his characterization.

2 Chronicles 10–12 largely aligns with 1 Kings 12–14, until the withdrawal of Rehoboam's army in 1 Kgs 12:24//2 Chron. 11:4.[24] However, the latter part of Rehoboam's reign in 2 Chronicles 11 diverges from the Kings account and Rehoboam is portrayed as very successful: he builds cities of defense, and the priests and Levites support him. Significantly,

---

20. DeVries, *1 Kings*, 156.
21. Ibid., 159.
22. Walsh, *1 Kings*, 170.
23. Nelson, *Kings*, 80.
24. Cf. Japheth points out that the northern claim of a heavy yoke of service upon them is not confirmed by the narrator of Chronicles earlier in the narrative and so their behavior is not justified as it is in Kings (Sara Japheth, *I & II Chronicles*, OTL (Louisville: Westminster John Knox, 1993], 653).

Rehoboam repents after Shishak attacks, and God turns his wrath from Rehoboam in 2 Chron. 12:12. Overall, in S. Japheth's judgement, "[Rehoboam's] rule is sketched in moderate contrast to the severely negative view of I Kings 14.22-24."[25] However, the closing evaluation of Rehoboam's reign in 2 Chron. 12:14 reads, "[Rehoboam] did evil for he did not set his heart to seek the Lord."

Similarly, Rehoboam is attributed direct blame in LXX (Old Greek) 1 Kings 12–14. There are a number of variations from the MT, in particular a lengthy supplement in LXX 1 Kgs 12:24. The LXX additions in v. 24 characterize Rehoboam more negatively than the MT,[26] and, accordingly, it too has a reading in LXX 1 Kgs 14:22, "Rehoboam did evil in the sight of the Lord." Therefore, the absence of Rehoboam's name in MT 1 Kgs 14:22 is conspicuous and it is significant that direct blame has been avoided.[27]

Another conspicuous absence of blame for Rehoboam is found in 1 Kgs 15:3, "[Abijam] committed all the sins of his father (אביו) which he did before him; his heart was not true (שלם) to the Lord his God, like the heart of David, his father (אביו)." The sins of "his father" (אביו) could equally refer to the sins of Solomon as to the sins of Rehoboam, particularly as Abijam's great grandfather David is also referred to as "his father" (אביו). Moreover, the description of David's heart as "true" (שלם) creates a play with the name Solomon (שלמה), suggesting Solomon is alluded to in the first half of the verse.

One possible explanation for this less negative view of Rehoboam's characterization may be that his characterization develops throughout 1 Kings 12–14. The latter part of his reign is placed in juxtaposition with the evil deeds of Jeroboam, and this explains why Rehoboam is evaluated

---

25. Ibid., 682.
26. Charles S. Shaw, "The Sins of Rehoboam: The Purpose of 3 Kingdoms 12.24a-z," *JSOT* 73 (1997): 55–64. The addition is thought to be an expansion of the MT, using the MT as a base text rather than reflecting an earlier tradition (see Z. Talshir, *The Alternative Story of the Division of the Kingdom: 3 Kingdoms 12.24 A–Z*, Jerusalem Bible Studies 6 [Jerusalem: Simor, 1993]; Cogan, *1 Kings*, 355–6; Marvin A. Sweeney, "A Reassessment of the Masoretic and Septuagint Versions of the Jeroboam Narratives in 1 Kings/3 Kingdoms 11–14," *JSJ* 38 [2007]: 165–95).
27. Cf. in the book of Kings, where there are a number of examples of a king who is evaluated as doing evil in the eyes of the Lord and causing the people to sin (e.g. Jeroboam in 1 Kgs 14:6; 15:26, 30, 34). However, apart from the somewhat different formulation in 2 Kgs 17 (see especially 2 Kgs 17:17), it is otherwise unattested that the people, but not the king, do evil in the eyes of the Lord.

generously in comparison to Jeroboam later in the narrative.[28] However, I propose a reading that rehabilitates Rehoboam's image in 1 Kgs 12:1-20 and suggests that it coheres with 1 Kgs 12:21-24 and 1 Kgs 14:22. The colorful portrait of Rehoboam and his young advisors is retained, and further evidence will demonstrate faults in Rehoboam's rule. But one fundamental point of interpretation in Rehoboam's characterization is reassessed: that Rehoboam was foolish to reject the advice of the elders and accept the advice of the young men.

Rehabilitating Rehoboam

Rehoboam's character might be instantly rehabilitated by pointing to the role of divine intervention in the drama. In 12:15, the narrator reveals, "But the king did not listen to the people, because it was a turn of affairs by the Lord so that he might fulfill his word, which the Lord had spoken by Ahijah the Shilonite to Jeroboam son of Nebat." Rehoboam's reign and characterization lie within the wider context of the division of the kingdom. Rehoboam's political role is subservient to God's purposes in bringing about the division of the kingdom; and so God explicitly intervenes in Rehoboam's drama because of his condemnation of Solomon and his election of Jeroboam to start a new dynasty in the Northern Kingdom. However, dual causality, where divine determination and human actions are simultaneously represented in the narrative as bringing about an outcome, is a common feature of biblical narrative.[29] Rehoboam's decision-making is not simply theatre; he is responsible for his actions and

---

28. The contrast in style (and possibly characterization) may also have a diachronic explanation. Weismann analyzes 12:1-19 separately from its context. He identifies a satirical wisdom story which gives an anthropocentric view of the schism in 12:1-19, and which blames the division on the character failings of Rehoboam. The story has later historiographic remarks in vv. 2-3, 17 and the "teleological remark" in v. 15 to harmonize the wisdom story with the surrounding story in Kings, which places blame on Solomon for the schism (Weisman, *Satire*, 101–11). Weisman follows the form-critical analysis in Long, *1 Kings*, 134–40 and the redaction proposed by Ina Plein, "Erwägungen zur Überlieferung von 1Reg.11,26-14,20," *ZAW* 78 (1966): 8–24. See also Cogan, *1 Kings*, 350–2, 354, who considers the wisdom tale in 1 Kgs 12:1-20 (now containing a number of glosses) as separate from vv. 21-24, a late didactic addition to exculpate Rehoboam; and Volkmar Fritz, *1 & 2 Kings*, trans. Anselm Hagedorn, Continental Commentary (Minneapolis: Fortress, 2003), 140–1.

29. See Yairah Amit, "The Dual Causality Principle and Its Effects on Biblical Literature," *VT* 37 (1987): 385–400. Note also the cautions of Jaco Gericke, "Rethinking the 'Dual Causality Principle' in Old Testament Research—a Philosophical Perspective,"

these actions are important for his characterization,[30] even if, somewhat ironically, they are also in line with the will of God that the kingdom be divided. We will first examine Rehoboam's characterization from the point of view of human causality, before returning to the additional implications of divine intervention.

Consistent amongst almost every modern reading of 1 Kings 12 is the conclusion that Rehoboam should have listened to the advice of the elders.[31] However, this is not the evaluation of the narrator in 1 Kings, who identifies the failure in v. 15 as "the king did not listen to the people." The king ought to have listened to the people of Israel in v. 4, not the elders in v. 7. The advice of the elders and the request of the people are not identical, especially not in rhetoric, and there is good cause for Rehoboam's rejection of the elders' advice. Although the wise decision would have been to lighten the yoke of the people, Rehoboam is not characterized as inept for following the advice of the young men.

The elders are described in v. 6 as those "who stood before Solomon his father when he was alive." It is unclear whether this is an endorsement by the narrator: it may be a reference to the elders' long experience and wisdom from old age;[32] or it may be reminiscent of Solomon's disastrous marital decisions and the oppression of the northern tribes in Solomon's reign. Some commentators see the rejection of the advice of elders as

---

OTE 28 (2015): 86–112. Gericke warns against understanding dual causality as a principle and highlights that causation is much more complex than formulations of the "dual causality principle" often presuppose.

30. A reading of dual causality is applied in the Rehoboam story by Bodner, *Jeroboam*, 70; and Walter Brueggemann, *1 & 2 Kings*, Smyth & Helwys Bible Commentary (Macon: Smyth & Helwys, 2000), 158. Roland Boer, *Jameson and Jeroboam*, Semeia (Atlanta: Scholars Press, 1996), 155–8 (156), suggests 1 Kgs 12:1-15 "comes close to achieving a believable dual causality." Kojo Okyere, "An Empowered People: A Literary Reading of 1 Kings 12:1-20," *MJTM* 14 (2012–2013): 124–47, points out that the causality is not only attributed to God and to Rehoboam, but also Jeroboam and the northern tribes. This reading goes some way towards acknowledging the many different types of causes involved in a story, as highlighted by Gericke, "Rethinking the 'Dual Causality Principle.'"

31. For example: Weisman, *Satire*, 103; Barbara E. Organ, "'The Man Who Would Be King': Irony in the Story of Rehoboam," in *From Babel to Babylon: Essays on Biblical History and Literature in Honour of Brian* Peckham, ed. Joyce Rilett Wood, John E. Harvey, and Mark Leuchter (New York: T&T Clark, 2006), 124–32 (126); Bodner, *Jeroboam*, 68; Nelson, *Kings*, 79; DeVries, *1 Kings*, 157, 158; Cogan, *1 Kings*, 351. Cf. Rofé, "Elders or Youngsters?" 79–89.

32. E.g. Bodner, *Jeroboam*, 64–5.

inherently foolish because wisdom comes with age,[33] but the reference to Solomon mitigates this assumption. Solomon himself was wise in his youth but condemned for his sins later in his reign.

The advice of the elders does not directly grant the request of the people, nor does it use the same rhetoric. Rather, the elders advise Rehoboam to adopt a position radically more humble than what the people have asked. "All Israel" in v. 4 ask: "Now therefore lighten the hard service of your father and his heavy yoke that he placed on us, and we will serve you" (עתה הקל מעבדת אביך הקשה ומעלו הכבד אשר נתן עלינו ונעבדך). The implication of "lightening" (הקל) the load of service, is that the service and yoke remain in place.[34] However, the elders' advice in v. 7 is to overthrow the yoke completely, not suggesting lightening their service (הקל מעבדת), but actually serving them (תהיה עבד לעם הזה ועבדתם). The removal of the service is emphasized in the elders' advice in v. 7 by the repetition of the root עבד, advocating becoming a "servant" (עבד) and serving them (ועבדתם).

Leaving aside a modern moral standpoint, servant kingship is never lauded in the narrative of Samuel-Kings nor is it equated elsewhere with listening or obeying the request of the people.[35] As J. Gray points out, it is a very unusual proposal that the king serve the people rather than serve God, such that Gray even emends the text, omitting in v. 7 "and will serve them" (ועבדתם).[36] Although kings are frequently called a servant, it is always a servant of God, never of the people. M. Weinfeld

---

33. E.g. Cogan, *1 Kings*, 351; Nelson, *Kings*, 78. Both Cogan and Nelson also style the scene as a stereotypical opposition between wise and foolish advice. However, significantly, two similar scenes in 1 Kgs 3 and 2 Sam. 16–17 (cited by Cogan), do not have this dichotomy. In 2 Sam. 16–17, Ahithophel could hardly be called "wise" but yet his advice proves to be more strategic. Moreover, Absalom does not see the advice as a decision between two different options: he partially accepts Ahithophel's advice to rape David's concubines but accepts Hushai's battle tactic to delay and lead the army himself. Interestingly, Rofé, "Elders or Youngsters?" 79–89 points to a number of late texts which suggest wisdom is not necessarily found in old age (Eccl. 4:13-14 and Job 32:7-9) and argues that the story of Rehoboam argues against them. However, these same texts can be used to suggest old age is *not* automatically associated with wisdom in this story either.

34. As Bodner explains, the northern delegates are "acquiescent enough, and not overtly hostile." The presence of Jeroboam may be a veiled threat but they appear ready to accept Rehoboam if he accepts their demand (Bodner, *Jeroboam*, 63).

35. E.g. Samuel (1 Sam. 8:22) and Saul (1 Sam. 15:24) both listen to the voice of the people, but neither is called the people's "servant."

36. John Gray, *I & II Kings*, OTL, 3rd ed. (London: SCM, 1977), 302, 305. Cf. Josephus's interpretation that this advice was not befitting a king (see above).

argues that although the idea of a king as servant occurs only here in the Hebrew Bible, the concept finds ancient Near Eastern parallel in the first millennium Babylonian "Advice to the Prince."[37] However, the "Advice to the Prince" suggests only that the king should listen to the people, not that he should be their servant. B. Organ also directly addresses this anomaly and interprets being a servant only as "prudent words for prudent action" or, in other words, obey the people in this matter and remain subject to the law as commanded in Deut. 17:14-20.[38] Even so there is a disparity in how radically the king needs to humble himself before the people: the rhetoric of the elders' advice suggests that Rehoboam remove the yoke of oppression to become their servant; the request of the people is only that he lighten the yoke.

A king responding with capitulation to his people, giving them more than they asked, is also a problematic strategy for holding power. As M. Sweeney points out:

> The advice that he present himself as a servant to them would hardly provide a lasting basis for his rule; he would become a very weak ruler, and power within the coalition would clearly shift to the north.[39]

Sweeney suggests the solution that this approach would delay the revolt and give Rehoboam time to build up support in the Northern Kingdom. Similarly, Walsh and DeVries suggest that once Rehoboam has been made king, he will be free to ignore his promises and so may hold power.[40] However, although these strategies make good sense, they are different to the strategy of actually granting the people's request, as endorsed by the narrator in v. 15.

In summary, v. 15 reveals that the wise course of action was to listen to the people. However, the advice given to Rehoboam by the elders was to be (or seem to be) weaker than the people request, and the advice by the young men was to be harsher. I will now argue that Rehoboam was not inept in accepting the latter counsel. I examined earlier the colorful language that the young men use to advise Rehoboam to exert his power,

---

37. Moshe Weinfeld, "The King as the Servant of the People: The Source of the Idea," *JJS* 33 (1982): 27–53. He also cites 1 Sam. 12:2, "the king walking before you" (התהלכתי לפניכם), which he understands as being a servant (p. 190). However, this phrase is better understood as "act on behalf of you" (see David Tsumura, *The First Book of Samuel*, NICOT [Grand Rapids: Eerdmans, 2007], 317).

38. Organ, "Irony," 129.

39. Sweeney, *Kings*, 170.

40. Walsh, *1 Kings*, 162; DeVries, *1 Kings*, 158, 159.

and I accepted that the young advisors, and by association Rehoboam, are characterized as crude and cruel. However, the advice followed by Rehoboam is not cause for Rehoboam's condemnation in Kings and the advice even had the potential to be successful.

The basis for the evaluation of kings in the book of Kings is the adherence to worshipping God alone and fulfilling cultic requirements, not kindness to the people. Wise rule of the people is a concern in a number of the narratives in Kings, and is an important part of characterization, but it is not the primary factor in the status of the king before God. This claim is best illustrated by the exceptions to the rule, two kings who are guilty of harshness to the people, but for whom this sin is considered lightly compared to their cultic sins. In the condemnation of Manasseh's rule in 2 Kgs 21:1-18, there is a litany of cultic sins in vv. 3-9. In contrast, all that is said about his rule over the people is that he led Judah to sin (v. 9). The condemnation of Manasseh and description of what will befall Jerusalem comes immediately after this list of cultic sins in vv. 10-15. Finally, as a postscript in v. 16, it is reported, "Manasseh shed very much innocent blood until he had filled Jerusalem from one end to another." No details are given of this killing, nor is it listed in the sins leading to Manasseh's condemnation. Another example is King Ahab in 1 Kings 21 who is accused by Elijah of killing Naboth in order to take his vineyard. Although Ahab is condemned for this killing with the evaluation in 1 Kgs 21:20, "you have sold yourself to do what is evil in the sight of the Lord," the condemnation is interspersed with reminders that Ahab has also committed cultic sins. In v. 22, he has "caused Israel to sin" even though ostensibly he is being punished for killing Naboth, and in vv. 25-26, there is another reminder that he has worshipped idols. Overall the book of Kings includes violations of the people in its characterization of kings, implicitly evaluating them negatively.[41] However, these characterizations are always in conjunction with cultic violations when they are overtly condemned.

Moreover, the advice of the young men, although delivered in distasteful terms, has political merit. R. Boer raises this possibility in a reading of Rehoboam in Kings and Chronicles in dialogue with Machiavelli's *The*

---

41. Another possible example can be found in 2 Sam. 24, where David holds a census and as a result God punishes the people with a plague. It is possible that this census was in order to organize corvée labor and that this was the basis of the sin. However, note that it is the people who are punished by David's sin (the whole of Jerusalem is untouched by the plague), inflicting more pain on them than corvée. Furthermore, David remains the paradigm for a good king despite the holding census.

Prince.⁴² Boer suggests that Rehoboam takes a Machiavellian approach to power: a leader should be miserly with his own property but generous with others', and should aim to be feared with some limited cruelty. By being cruel to some, the Machiavellian prince can be merciful to many. For Machiavelli, the elders' advice to be a servant to the people is foolish advice. Boer then argues that this approach to power is evaluated positively in the Chronicles account where Rehoboam's rule over Judah is ultimately successful, but that the Kings account is "anti-Machiavellian."

I propose that, according to the narrator, Rehoboam's tactic had the potential to be successful and that success was prevented by the divine intervention in 1 Kgs 12:22-24. This can be demonstrated by reading 1 Kgs 12:1-24 with the Sheba story in 2 Sam. 19:42[41]–2 Samuel 20.⁴³ We will see that there are a number of parallels between these two stories, and David's success at holding together Judah and Israel in 2 Sam. 19:42[41]–2 Samuel 20 gives an example of how Rehoboam's negotiations could have proceeded without the intervention of God.

The initiating problem in 2 Sam. 19:42[41] is Judah's proximity to the king, and the people of Israel come to King David saying, "Why have our kindred the people of Judah stolen you away, and brought the king and his household over the Jordan, and all David's men with him?" In v. 43[42], the people of Judah respond in a way that suggests the real complaint is inequality of gifts as well as power, "Have we eaten at all at the king's expense? Or has he given us any gift?" This forms a close parallel to the scenario in 1 Kgs 12:1-24, where Israel complains of heavy service, but Judah is aligned with the king. The narrative in 2 Sam. 19:44[43] further describes the response of the people of Judah, "the words of the people of Judah were more harsh than the words of the people of Israel" (ויקש דבר איש יהודה מדבר איש ישראל). Significantly, the root קשה used in the verb "to be more harsh" (ויקש) is also used in 1 Kgs 12:13 to describe Rehoboam's response to the people, "the king answered the people harshly" (ויען המלך את העם קשה), when he takes the advice of the young men. This root is also highlighted in 1 Kings 12 as it is used in v. 4, and its antonym "to lighten, easy" (קלל) is repeated in vv. 4, 9, and 10.⁴⁴

---

42. Roland Boer, "Rehoboam Meets Machiavelli," in *Rewriting Biblical History: Essays on Chronicles and Ben Sira in Honor of Pancratius C. Beentjes*, ed. Jeremy Corley and Harm van Grol (Berlin: de Gruyter, 2011), 159–72.

43. See Organ, "Irony," 127–8, who suggests 1 Kgs 12 is patterned on the story of Sheba.

44. Note that this root is also used in the Israelites' complaint in 2 Sam. 19:44[43], "why do you despise me" (הקלתני), but with opposite intent: in Samuel the complaint

The harsh words spoken to the northern tribes have the same effect in both 2 Samuel 20 and 1 Kings 12: a rebellion occurs and the people say in 2 Sam. 20:1,

> We have no portion in David,
> no share in the son of Jesse!
> Everyone to your tents, O Israel!
> (אין לנו חלק בדוד ולא נחלה לנו בבן ישי איש לאהליו ישראל)

and in 1 Kgs 12:16,

> What share do we have in David?
> We have no inheritance in the son of Jesse.
> To your tents, O Israel!
> Look now to your own house, O David.
> (אין לנו חלק בדוד ולא נחלה לנו בבן ישי איש לאהליו ישראל).

After this cry of rebellion, both narratives proceed in a similar way, but with the events in a different order. In 2 Samuel 20, David first returns to Jerusalem in vv. 2-3, then sends his army to regain the rebellious people by brute force in v. 4. Finally, after a dramatic battle, Joab quashes the rebellion on behalf of David in v. 22. In v. 24, there is a note that "Adoram was over the forced labor" (ואדרם על המס). In 1 Kings 12, first Rehoboam sends his task master to Israel, who is also called Adoram (אדרם אשר על המס) in v. 18.[45] This action is quickly proved foolish when Adoram is stoned by the Israelites but it does not lose Rehoboam the kingdom. Rehoboam returns to Jerusalem in v. 18 and here the narrator interjects in vv. 19-20 to give the end of the story, that Israel remained in rebellion "to this day." Although the end of the story is given, the parallels with 2 Samuel 20 resume. Just as David sent his army to quash the rebellion after he had returned to Jerusalem, so too Rehoboam gathers 180,000 troops, a large number very likely to have achieved its goal, "to restore the kingdom to Rehoboam son of Solomon."

---

is that they make the people "light" or unimportant, in 1 Kgs 12 the request is to make their labor light.

45. It is not clear whether Adoram is the same person in 2 Sam. 20:24 and 1 Kgs 12:18 because of how old this would have made him, but nevertheless it appears to be an intentional reference (Bodner, *Jeroboam*, 75). Adoram may be a variant of the name Adoniram in 1 Kgs 4:6 and so could also be the name of Solomon's taskmaster.

Although the boast of Rehoboam and his young advisors about Rehoboam's power is framed in crude and unappealing language, it is proven accurate, at least in the short term.[46] Rehoboam has 180,000 troops whom he is able to call up to enforce the service of the northern tribes. A further reference to Rehoboam in 1 Kgs 12:27 confirms that he holds power. Jeroboam makes the golden calves because he fears the people will return to Rehoboam, whom he describes as "their lord" (אדניהם). Interestingly, later in Rehoboam's reign, Rehoboam is depicted as impotent, both in preventing Judah's sins (14:22-24) and against King Shishak of Egypt (14:25-28), and we will return to this unevenness in the next section.

This reading reframes Rehoboam's options for responding to the people's request in a way that is significant for Rehoboam's characterization. Rehoboam is not inept when he rejects the advice of the elders. Cruelty may not be morally wise but it has the potential for being politically effective at retaining power, and the cruelty shown by Rehoboam is not a failure judged harshly elsewhere in the book of Kings.

Unlike David, Rehoboam is prevented from successfully regaining the northern tribes by a command from God through the prophet Shemaiah. The command to return home is addressed to Rehoboam, along with the house of Judah and Benjamin and all the people (v. 21), and they immediately cease trying to regain the northern tribes through military strength. By analogy to the story in 2 Samuel 20, it is only with this retreat that Rehoboam has really experienced defeat. Rehoboam has followed the same successful strategy as David: a harsh response backed up by military strength after he returns to Jerusalem. An unsuccessful outcome is brought about only by divine intervention. Rehoboam's characterization and divine will directly intersect, and Rehoboam loses the northern tribes because of his obedience, not because of ineptitude.

However, in v. 15 Rehoboam's decision-making runs side by side with the fulfillment of prophecy. The text gives few clues for interpreting Rehoboam's rejection of the people's request. One possibility is that this course of action is clouded by receiving two sets of bad advice, one strategically ill-advised and the other morally. However, the colorful and clever strategy of the young men's advice suggests that Rehoboam's

---

46. Contra Weisman, *Satire*, 109. According to the Chronicles account, in 2 Chron. 11:21, Rehoboam has 18 wives, 60 concubines, 28 sons, and 60 daughters. Although these numbers are less than Solomon's "achievements," if read with the Kings account they attest further that a boast about Rehoboam's virility is not entirely empty.

susceptibility to the lure of exerting power distracts him from simply granting the request.[47] The absence of an evaluation at the close of Rehoboam's reign is fitting for this characterization: Rehoboam is not lauded because he oppresses the people, and does not grant their request; but he is also not condemned as doing evil, because he is neither apostate nor disobedient.

Rehoboam and Solomon Compared Once Again

Although these two instances of divine intervention point to two different characterizations of Rehoboam, there is a commonality in their purpose: they demonstrate that Rehoboam's drama is part of a wider context of prophecy against the house of Solomon. In terms of plot, Rehoboam is a "foil" to Jeroboam, the necessary failure for Jeroboam's success.[48] However, in terms of character, the structure of Rehoboam's characterization is built around an inversion of Solomon's character. Moreover, the tension in Rehoboam's characterization, between the dialogues with his advisors and the surrounding narrative, finds relative coherence through the consistent inversion of Solomon, either for good or for bad.

Although Solomon is held responsible for the division of the kingdom in 1 Kgs 11:11-13, the division does not happen during his reign and he wards off three potential adversaries, the third of which is Jeroboam. Thus the story of Rehoboam has a fundamental contrast to the story of Solomon: Solomon forces Jeroboam to flee, but Rehoboam loses the northern tribes to him.

The comparison between Solomon and Rehoboam is established through parallels between Rehoboam's impasse with the northern tribes in 1 Kgs 12:1-15 and the story of Solomon's wisdom in 1 Kings 3.[49] In 1 Kgs 3:16, two women come to the king and "they stand before him" (ותעמדנה לפניו), each giving her own version of a dispute over a baby boy. According to 1 Kgs 12:1-15, Rehoboam is given two sets of advice, also by elders who "stood before Solomon" (עמדים את פני שלמה) in v. 6, and the young men who "stood before him" (העמדים לפניו) in v. 8. Although

---

47. Conversely, taking advice demonstrates an act of caution, a distinct possibility if this story is read alongside Saul's condemnation for listening to the voice of the people (1 Sam. 15:24).

48. Bodner, *Jeroboam*, 59. There are several parallels between these two characters which highlight this opposition. For example, just as Rehoboam calls advisors and is "counselled" or asks for "counsel" (ויועץ, v. 6; נועצים, v. 9), so also Jeroboam is "counselled" (ויועץ) in 12:28.

49. Cf. Weisman, *Satire*, 106–7.

Rehoboam has advisors and Solomon has complainants, the parallel is set up by the repetition of the phrase "standing before..." In each case those standing before the king are not named but identified by their status: prostitutes in 1 Kgs 3:16; and elders in 1 Kgs 12:6 and children in 1 Kgs 12:10.

These parallels culminate in an inversion in the plot lines, each directed by the Divine. Solomon finds a third course of action due to divinely gifted wisdom, whereas Rehoboam chooses only the best of two bad options alongside a divine "turning" of events. Solomon asks in 1 Kgs 3:9 for a "discerning [lit.: listening] mind to judge your people" (לב שמע לשפט את עמך), whereas Rehoboam does not "listen to the people" (ולא שמע המלך אל העם) in 1 Kgs 12:15. When Rehoboam does not see that he should reject both sets of advisors, his characterization is in pointed contrast to Solomon. The back-handed compliments of the young advisors to Rehoboam suggest Rehoboam's masculine power is his only asset; and the wider context of divine determination against him confirms this.

Another inversion between Solomon and Rehoboam relates to the furnishing of the temple. Solomon fills the temple with gold, including making shields of gold in 1 Kgs 10:16-17 and, significantly, this gold is given to him by foreign monarchies. After the visit of the Queen of Sheba, the enormous amount of gold that Solomon received is reported, including the note that it came from "all the kings of Arabia and the governors of the land" (1 Kgs 10:15). Whereas Solomon receives gold from foreign kings and a foreign queen for the temple, the gold shields are taken away by a foreign king in the time of Rehoboam. In 1 Kgs 14:25-26, King Shishak of Egypt takes all the treasures, including Solomon's gold shields, from the temple. As was noted earlier, Rehoboam's impotence in the face of foreign aggression is arguably inconsistent with the summoning of 180,000 in 12:21. However, it is consistent with the ongoing inversion of the story of Solomon in Rehoboam's characterization.

Rehoboam is evaluated more positively in the final inversion of Solomon's character. Solomon is accused of following other gods in 1 Kgs 11:5, but there is no evidence that the people follow his lead. In 11:7-8, Solomon builds high places for other gods but he does so explicitly for his "foreign wives" (v. 8) not for the people of Israel. In contrast, the people of Judah build high places in 1 Kgs 14:23-24 and commit the abominations of the people around them, but there is no statement that Rehoboam did so too. Furthermore, unlike Solomon's large quantity of foreign wives, including Rehobaom's own mother who was an Ammonite (14:21), the mother of Rehoboam's heir Abijam, Maacah daughter of Abishalom (15:2), is Israelite, possibly the daughter of Rehoboam's own uncle Absalom, David's son. This contrast points to the intriguing avoidance of a negative characterization for Rehoboam, and blame upon the people of Judah for following other Gods. Solomon is apostate but the people are not, and Rehoboam is not apostate but the people are.

Conclusion

Regardless of the purported immense size of Rehoboam's physical assets, nothing is able to overcome the divine predetermination that his kingdom would be divided. In his boast to be greater than his father, the audience is directed to the realization that Rehoboam forever remains under the shadow of his father: he cannot match his father's wisdom and he bears the divine opposition that brings about retribution for his father's sins.

There is much to dislike in Rehoboam's characterization: he is cruel and oppressive in association with his friends. This characterization perhaps leaves little sympathy in an audience when Rehoboam bears the punishment for his father's sins in the disintegration of his kingdom. However, one aspect of Rehoboam's portrayal in 1 Kings 12 can be rehabilitated: the political astuteness of Rehoboam's rejection of the advice of the elders and strategy of responding with force. Monarchical oppression, whilst theoretically looked down upon in biblical law, receives little censure in the book of Kings. Instead, the book of Samuel offers an example of a parallel strategy bringing success. In the end, the division of the kingdom takes place because of both divine will and Rehoboam's characterization: except that responsibility rests with Rehoboam's obedience to the prophetic word, not his cruelty or foolishness.

Chapter 6

DECEIVING THE MAN OF GOD FROM JUDAH: A QUESTION OF MOTIVE

Paul Hedley Jones

In numerous ways—morally, literarily, theologically—the strange turn of affairs in 1 Kings 13 hinges on the Bethelite prophet's decision to seek out the man of God from Judah and dupe his southern "brother" into breaking God's threefold commandment. But since the narrator does not reveal what the Bethel prophet hopes to achieve through this act of deception, it is left to the reader to consider the possibilities and, as is the business of biblical exegetes, to speculate. This essay grapples with the characterization of the two anonymous prophets in 1 Kings 13, focusing especially on the older prophet's motive for deceiving the man of God from Judah. In addition, we shall consider how the Bethel prophet's actions relate to the story's function in Kings.

Minding the Gap

Gap-filling is an essential element in the poetics of biblical narrative, and a vital means of grappling with textual ambiguities with full, imaginative seriousness. Various kinds of gaps are possible—of knowledge, location, identity—many of which stimulate readerly speculation about the rationale or psychology undergirding certain behaviors. Some gaps are only temporarily withheld, to be disclosed by the narrator at an opportune moment for the reader's delight, but other details remain unknown, and unknowable. Did Uriah refuse to return home because he knew of

Bathsheba's affair? Was Elisha justified in cursing the forty-two youths who jeered at his baldness?[1] And so on.[2]

The plot in 1 Kings 13 hinges on a perplexing exchange between the man of God from Judah and the old Bethel prophet, wherein one anonymous prophet is deceived by the other. The scene at the Bethelite's house (vv. 20-23) is clearly central to the chapter, both sequentially and substantively. But while the narrator is clear about the Bethel prophet's malintent—כחש לו (he deceived him; v. 18b)—nothing is said of his motive for lying.[3] The reader's inability to determine the Bethelite's motive may lead to the (reluctant) acknowledgment of a distinction between meaningful *gaps*, i.e. details omitted for the *sake* of interest, and irrelevant *blanks*, i.e. details omitted for *lack* of interest.[4] To anticipate the discussion below, we shall consider whether the Bethel prophet's motive is an important *gap* or an irrelevant *blank*. But to pave the way for a meaningful discussion of motive, it is necessary to first establish who is whom in this narrative. This is especially important with regards to the two anonymous prophetic figures. Which, if either, is the implied reader prompted to trust? Does the narrator make it clear whether one prophet represents Yahweh's interests over and against the other?

Of the two prophetic characters, one hails from the north and the other from the south. This detail ultimately proves to be of tremendous significance, though in my judgment, it is simplistic to label the southerner "good" and the northerner "bad" simply on account of their geographic origins, as some have done.[5] After all, a number of genuine prophets of Yahweh hail from the north in the book of Kings (e.g., Elijah, Elisha, Micaiah, Ahijah), and since one prophet lies and the other is disobedient,

---

1. Meir Sternberg, *The Poetics of Biblical Narrative: Ideological Literature and the Drama of Reading* (Bloomington: Indiana University Press, 1985), describes a literary work as "a system of gaps" since so few of the details that readers require—or think they require—are explicitly given. He discusses a number of examples; cf. 186–90, 235–40.

2. See Stuart Lasine, *Weighing Hearts: Character, Judgment, and the Ethics of Reading the Bible*, LHBOTS 568 (London: T&T Clark, 2012) for one approach to the psychological evaluation of literary characters, 3–19; on 1 Kgs 13 in particular, see 93–114 (Chapter 4).

3. 1 Kgs 13:18b

4. Sternberg, *Poetics*, 236. However, as Sternberg rightly observes, one reader's gap is another's blank.

5. Karl Barth, *Church Dogmatics II.2: The Doctrine of God*, trans. G. W. Bromiley et al.; Edinburgh: T. & T. Clark, 1957), 398–400; so Marvin Sweeney, *I and II Kings*, OTL (Louisville: Westminster John Knox, 2007), 182.

one could argue that the story avoids distinguishing between protagonist and antagonist altogether.[6] Moreover, their anonymity prevents any direct identification with named prophets in the surrounding chapters, such as Shemaiah (south) or Ahijah (north) whose allegiances are less ambiguous. In spite of difficulties, however, the narrative contains enough clues for the reader to determine how these two prophetic figures align with the interests of other major characters in the book of Kings.[7] We consider them here in the order that they appear: the man of God from Judah (vv. 1-10) followed by the old Bethel prophet (v. 11).

Anonymity and Identity: A Who's Who

1 Kings 13 recounts a puzzling exchange between two anonymous prophets (Jeroboam sets the tone in vv. 1-10, but remains in the background) who, for unknown reasons, are depicted as being in tension with one another. Despite efforts to understand the distinction between איש האלהים ("man of God") and נביא ("prophet"), no real advances have been made that impact upon the meaning of the story.[8] That neither term indicates prophetic authenticity is evident from the fact that both the man of God and the old prophet fail in some respect even as both also speak a genuine word of the LORD. The narrative does not differentiate in any clear way between a "true" and "false" prophet, nor is it concerned with the issue of prophetic discernment. The simplest explanation seems the best: that the consistent use of different appellations throughout the story serves the simple purpose of avoiding confusion. Only the Bethel prophet seeks to undermine this distinction—"I am a prophet as you are" (v. 18); "Alas, my brother!" (v. 30)—and his words appear to deliberately disrupt the narrator's pattern. In spite of the anonymity of the two prophets, their allegiances are significant for understanding the story, as we shall see.

---

6. Barth's reading identifies this as the central dynamic: that neither character (yet both!) represents God's elect and non-elect/rejected.

7. I disagree with Crenshaw, who contends that the narrative's primary concern is with the issue of discernment. For a full critique of his interpretation, see Paul Hedley Jones, *Anonymous Prophets and Archetypal Kings: Reading 1 Kings 13* (London: T&T Clark, forthcoming).

8. Both terms are applied to the northern prophets, Elijah (1 Kgs 17:18; 18:22) and Elisha (1 Kgs 4:7; 9:1). But see Jay A. Holstein, "The Case of *'îš hā'ĕlōhîm* Reconsidered: Philological Analysis versus Historical Reconstruction," *HUCA* 48 (1977): 69–81.

1 Kings 13 begins rather abruptly with והנה ("But look!"), a presentative exclamation that serves "as a bridge for a logical connection between [the] preceding clause and the clause it introduces."[9] Since הנה signifies a change in perspective but never the beginning of a new textual unit,[10] what follows must be read in connection with the preceding context, which stresses that the newly established festival, date, and sacrificial rites in northern Israel are all of Jeroboam's design. As numerous scholars suggest, treating 12:33–13:34 as a textual unit provides והנה with a preceding clause and places Jeroboam's actions within an interpretive frame of reference.[11] Within the purposes and limits of this essay, it is sufficient to acknowledge that the preceding context effectively characterizes Jeroboam as a villain due to his cultic innovations.[12] Conversely, the man of God's sudden appearance and condemnation of the altar infers from the outset whose side this enigmatic figure is on. In an established context of false worship, the man of God is identified explicitly with Judah, the place of the LORD's choosing (cf. Deut. 12), and with Josiah, who will ultimately rid the nation of Jeroboam's cultic innovations (v. 3; cf. 2 Kgs 23:15). A number of other details also confirm that the man of God is characterized from the outset as Yahweh's authentic representative. For the sake of brevity, I list them here in outline:

- the man of God comes to denounce Jeroboam's illegitimate cultus;
- he comes '*in* the word of the LORD' (בדבר יהוה, v. 1);[13]
- he uses the classic prophetic formulation, "Thus says the LORD" (v. 2);

---

9. Waltke and O'Connor, *Introduction to Biblical Hebrew Syntax* (Winona Lake: Eisenbrauns, 1990), §40.2.d (677); also §40.2 (674f.) on the functions of *hinne* as a 'presentative exclamation.'

10. So Walter Gross, "Lying Prophet and Disobedient Man of God in 1 Kings 13: Role Analysis as an Instrument of Theological Interpretation of an OT Narrative Text," [trans. Robert Robinson] *Semeia* 15 (1979): 97–129.

11. So John Gray, *I & II Kings*, OTL, 1st ed. (London: SCM, 1964), 318f.; Simon DeVries, *1 Kings*, WBC 12, 2nd ed. (Nashville: Nelson, 2003), 164f.; Mordechai Cogan, *1 Kings*, AB 10 (New York: Doubleday, 2001), 365f.; Burke O. Long, *1 Kings with an Introduction to Historical Literature*, FOTL 9 (Grand Rapids: Eerdmans, 1984), 143f., et al.

12. See Keith Bodner, *Jeroboam's Royal Drama* (Oxford: Oxford University Press, 2012), for an extensive treatment of Jeroboam's characterization; cf. Aberbach and Smolar, "Aaron, Jeroboam & the Golden Calves," *JBL* 86 (1967): 129–40.

13. The more common formulation in OT narrative is כדבר יהוה (*according* to the word of the LORD; e.g., 2 Kgs 12:24); if the ב is read as a *beth* of identity, or *beth essentiae*, the idiom may suggest that the man of God comes in the spirit of that

- his prophecy associates him with the righteous Josiah (v. 2) in contrast to the Bethel prophet, who picks up where the wayward Jeroboam left off (see below);
- his prophecy about Josiah is ultimately fulfilled (2 Kgs 23:15-20; cf. Deut. 18.21-22);
- two signs (one of healing and one of destruction) are immediately fulfilled in the presence of Jeroboam, thus demonstrating his authenticity (vv. 3-6);
- he comes to Bethel subject to (and obedient to) a divine, threefold command (v. 9).

Previous appearances and pronouncements from "men of God" in the DH are also certified within their contexts as authentic (cf. Judg. 13:6; 1 Sam. 2:27; 9:6; 1 Kgs 12:22)

Just as the man of God is introduced as being "from Judah" in v. 1, so the old Bethel prophet is found "dwelling in Bethel" (ישב בבית־אל, v. 11). And while it is presumptuous to characterize these figures by their geography alone, the narrator's brief comment at the end of v. 18 (כחש לו) suggests that the Bethelite has taken up the flag that Jeroboam let fall in the opening scene.[14] From the beginning of the second scene (v. 11), it is evident that the Bethelite's interests are at odds with those of the man of God from Judah.[15] Following his sons' general report of what happened in Bethel that day, the narrator adds—quite emphatically—that "the words also that [the man of God from Judah] had spoken to the king [אל־המלך], they told to their father" (v. 11):

את־הדברים אשר דבר אל־המלך ויספרום לאביהם

What words is the narrator referring to? Given that the initial pronouncement is made *against the altar* (על־המזבח, vv. 2, 4), and that the prayer for the king's withered hand is prayed *to the LORD* (ויחל ... את־פני יהוה, v. 6), the only remaining words, which are explicitly recounted as being *to the king* (אל־המלך, v. 8), are these:

---

efficacious word, or even serving *as* the word of the LORD. Waltke and O'Connor, *Hebrew Syntax*, 198, §11.2.5e. Cf. W. Gesenius, *Gesenius' Hebrew Grammar*, ed. E Kautzsch, trans. E. Kautzsch, 2nd ed. (Oxford: Clarendon, 1910), 119.

14. I have borrowed this turn of phrase from Barth, *CD II.2*, 405.

15. Barth goes so far as to designate the Bethelite "the real Satan of the story." Ibid., 402.

If you give me half your kingdom, I will not go in with you; nor will I eat food or drink water in this place. For thus I was commanded by the word of the LORD: You shall not eat food, or drink water, or return by the way that you came. (vv. 8-9)

In other words, the Bethelite knows from the outset that the man of God has been prohibited from eating, drinking, and returning by the way he came.[16] What's more, his knowledge of these details appears to fuel a sense of urgency in the events that follow. The Bethel prophet's question, אי־זה הדרך הלך ("Which way did he go?") in v. 12 is immediately followed by an imperative, חבשו־לי החמור ("Saddle a donkey for me!") in v. 13. Verse 14 then begins, "And he went after [וילך אחרי][17] the man of God, and found him..." The flurry of speech and action indicates that when the Bethel prophet pursues the man of God on his donkey, he is—like the reader—fully aware of the threefold commandment.

Therefore, the Bethel prophet's invitation to the man of God, "Come home with me and eat some food" in v. 15 is neither friendly nor innocent, but rather a deliberate attempt to lure the man of God into breaking the commands.[18] When the Bethel prophet's hospitality is refused (as expected) and the divine command reiterated (v. 17), the Bethel prophet bolsters his invitation in three ways, each designed to impress upon the man of God their shared prophetic authority: (a) the Bethelite introduces himself to the man of God, saying, גם־אני נביא כמוך ("I also am a prophet like yourself"); (b) he claims to have received a word from an angel; and (c) he borrows the man of God's unusual phrase, claiming that the angel was authorized to speak "*in* the word of the LORD" (בדבר יהוה) (see

---

16. There is insufficient space to explore the particular prohibitions here; but for an excellent summary of proposals and an argument concerning the prohibition against returning, see Uriel Simon, "I Kings 13: A Prophetic Sign—Denial and Persistence," *HUCA* 47 (1976): 81–117 (revised and republished as "A Prophetic Sign Overcomes Those Who Would Defy It: The King of Israel, the Prophet from Bethel, and the Man of God from Judah," in *Reading Prophetic Narratives*, trans. Lenn. J. Schramm [Bloomington: Indiana University Press, 1997], 130–54).

17. Where the phrase הלך + אחר occurs in Hebrew narrative, the connotation tends either to be one of *pursuit* (see, e.g., Gen. 37:17; Josh. 6:8, 9, 13; 1 Sam. 6:12; Jer. 2:8, 23; 7:9; 11:10; Ezek. 20:16; Hos. 5:11) or of *behavior* (to walk in the manner of; 2 Kgs 13:2; see Waltke and O'Connor, *Hebrew Syntax*, 192–3 §11.2.1). The former connotation clearly applies here.

18. Contra Walsh, who thinks that the question of whether the old prophet is *for* Bethel, or simply residing *in* Bethel, is left open. J. T. Walsh, *1 Kings*, BO (Collegeville: Liturgical Press, 1996), 183–4.

n. 13). The false word that follows explicitly contradicts each part of the commandment: "Bring him back with you [השבהו] into your house so that he may eat food and drink water" (v. 18).

A close reading of this section thereby reveals that the narrator's statement at the end of v. 18—"he lied to him"—is less an abrupt reversal than curt confirmation of the attentive reader's suspicions: the Bethelite's invitation to the man of God is not extended as a friendly gesture but with malicious intent.[19] Verse 19 concludes the scene by stating baldly that the man of God acquiesces, breaking the threefold commandment in its entirety. The Bethel prophet's ruse achieves its purpose and the man of God is duped.

Considering Motive: Within the Text

So far, two things are clear: the man of God is presented as Yahweh's authentic representative; and the Bethel prophet deliberately sets out to cause the man of God to break the commands. What is not clear is the Bethel prophet's motive for doing so. The reader is thus invited, or indeed compelled, to consider how this particular gap in the narrative might be filled. On this question, a number of possibilities have been suggested:

(a) The most common explanation of the Bethelite's motive is that the elder prophet wished to test his younger colleague's prophetic authenticity.[20] If the man of God could be duped into disobedience and no consequences ensued for breaking the threefold commandment, then the man of God's prophecy against Bethel could be readily dismissed. From this perspective, the Bethel prophet is taken to be deliberately testing the man of God (since he was not an eyewitness to the signs reported by his

---

19. C. F. Keil, *The Book of the Kings*, trans. J. Martin, Biblical Commentary on the Old Testament (Grand Rapids: Eerdmans, 1950), 206–7, argues that without the Bethel prophet's intentional act of deceit, it is possible to see him in a much more positive light. But whether or not one follows Šanda in omitting the phrase "he lied to him" does not necessarily make any real interpretive difference. The tenor of the entire passage, even without כחש לו, is one of pursuit and deceit. Thus, Klopfenstein understands the concluding phrase to refer to "all his goal-oriented behaviour" in vv. 11-20a, and not just his words. Klopfenstein also notes that the angel, in contrast to the Judean's "word of the LORD" is not even an "angel of Yahweh" (658). See Martin Klopfenstein, "1. Könige 13," in *ΠΑΡΡΗΣΙΑ: K. Barth zum achtzigsten Geburtstag*, ed. E. Busch, J. Fangmeier, and M. Geiger (Zurich: EVZ-Verlag Zurich, 1966), 658. So also D. W. Van Winkle, "1 Kings XIII: True and False Prophecy," *VT* 39 (1989): 35.

20. So Gray, *I & II Kings*, 322; DeVries, *1 Kings*, 173; Gene Rice, *1 Kings: Nations Under God*, ITC (Grand Rapids: Eerdmans, 1990), 113; et al.

sons) to determine just how serious is this prophetic word of condemnation against Jeroboam's cultus. Having established that the Judean's prophetic mandate was indeed authentic (proven by his death!), the Bethel prophet then fetches his body, mourns his death, and asks to be buried alongside him in due course. In doing so, he offers an explanation for the death of his fellow prophet (v. 26) whilst affirming the prophetic word that was spoken in Bethel (v. 32). This interpretation of the old prophet's motives and actions makes sense of the world within the text, so long as the reader assumes that the Bethel prophet did not trust what his sons had reportedly seen "that day" (v. 11), and that the destruction of the altar and the withering of the king's hand were insufficient evidence of the man of God's authenticity.

(b) One of the more creative accounts of the Bethelite's motive comes from Dutch scholar Jaap van Dorp,[21] whose work is explained and developed somewhat by Erik Eynikel.[22] The logic and gist of van Dorp's argument is that the Bethel prophet deliberately entraps the man of God because he learns from his sons that one day King Josiah will remove human bones from their graves in order to desecrate illegal altars. "From their report he realises that his grave will be desecrated too, unless he finds some way to prevent it."[23] The Bethelite therefore concocts a plan to prevent the desecration of his own grave, and the only imaginable way to do so is to ensure that his bones are buried with a Judean of sufficient piety to ward off Josiah's acts of purification. "The old prophet therefore can do only one thing: get the man of God killed."[24] The Bethel prophet's demand

---

21. Jaap van Dorp, "Wat is die steenhoop daar? Het graf van de man Gods in 2 Koningen 23" [What is that pile of stone there? The grave of the man of God in 2 Kings 23], in *Amsterdamse Cahiers voor Exegese en Bijbelse Theologie* [ACEBT] 8, ed. K. A. Deurloo et al. (Kampen: Kok, 1987), 64–97.

22. Erik Eynikel, "Prophecy and Fulfillment in the Deuteronomistic History: 1 Kgs 13; 2 Kgs 23, 16-18," in *Pentateuchal and Deuteronomistic Studies*, ed. C. Brekelmans and J. Lust, BETL 94 (Leuven: Leuven University Press, 1990), 227–37. Eynikel devotes half of his article to a discussion of Van Dorp's reading. I am not proficient in Dutch and so do not have direct access to Van Dorp's work, thus I am reliant upon Eynikel's citations and explanation. Van Dorp's broader purpose is to reinforce the close connection between 1 Kgs 13:11-32 and 2 Kgs 23:16-20 and to show that 1 Kgs 13 is an original unit.

23. Ibid., 234.

24. Cited in ibid. Similarly, Eynikel, supporting Van Dorp, writes: "The simplest solution is to assume that the old prophet acted only to save his bones from desecration, because he was informed from the beginning (v. 11) what would happen with all the graves of Bethel," 234 n. 29.

that his own bones be placed with those of the Judean is motivated by self-preservation, since the Judean's tomb will undoubtedly be respected when Josiah comes (300 years later) to fulfil the word of the LORD.

Van Dorp's reading is certainly interesting and represents a serious engagement with certain aspects of the narrative. However, for the Bethelite to hear the report from his sons and immediately draw the conclusion that someday his own corpse would be included in Josiah's defilement of the altar (which would surely require only a few bones) seems rather extreme, even paranoid. Moreover, the Bethelite is presumably willing to lead another man to his death in order to (hopefully) preserve his own bones from defilement. The logic of Van Dorp's argument thus leads to a characterization of the Bethelite as a fearful and murderous old man, an evaluation that is not easy to justify from the text. Moreover, the Bethelite could not have known from the beginning that the man of God would die in a manner that kept his body intact for burial, nor that the Judean's bones would be spared from defilement. Van Dorp's reading is serious and imaginative, to be sure, but it leans heavily on a very particular characterization of the Bethel prophet. All things considered, van Dorp's gap-filling seems overly generous.

(c) A third possibility, and in my judgment the most preferable, is that the Bethel prophet sought to *subvert* the prophecy against Bethel by upending the man of God's integrity.[25] As Barth observes, the old prophet from Bethel is well aware that the theological justification for the Northern Kingdom's cultus would be restored if only the man of God would eat and drink in Bethel.[26] Similarly, in spite of a very different interpretive approach, Klopfenstein speaks of a "double victory" [*doppelten Sieg*] in the deception. That is, while the Bethelite may perhaps be testing the man of God's authenticity—as per (a) above—his deliberate act of seduction also has another goal in mind. Since the Judean's visit to the Bethelite's home could not have been done in secret—Klopfenstein repeatedly, and in my judgment, rightly, stresses the public nature of all these events—their communion together would be perceived as confirmation that Jeroboam's syncretism was a legitimate form of worship, perhaps even as evidence of a "transfer of religious rights from Jerusalem to

---

25. This view was favored by some early interpreters. Keil, *Book of the Kings*, notes "that Josephus and the Chald., and most of the Rabbins and of the earlier commentators both Catholic and Protestant, have regarded him as a false prophet, who tried to lay a trap for the prophet from Judah, in order to counteract the effect of his prophecy upon the king and the people" (206).

26. Barth, *CD II.2*, 400–401.

Bethel."[27] For the man of God to visit the old prophet in his home would almost certainly give the impression that Bethel and Jerusalem, like their prophets, stand on common ground. In the public eye, the Judean's earlier actions in profaning the cult could be disregarded, or at the very least, relativized significantly.

Ultimately, there is little in the text to arbitrate between these readings with much certainty, so that a consideration of the possibilities still fails to advance the reader beyond the realm of speculation. Indeed, it appears that we have drawn a *blank*, rather than a *gap*. Goldingay, for one, responds to the question we have been considering here—"Why did the second prophet do as he did?"—by saying, "The story doesn't say; it's not relevant to the story."[28] His initial observation is, of course, correct ("the story doesn't say"), but I am less certain that a lack of clarity regarding the Bethelite's motive necessarily signifies irrelevance. As we noted in the introduction, gap-filling is a vital element in the poetics of Hebrew narrative, a means by which readers are invited to grapple with interpretive possibilities. In so doing, I am inclined to agree with Walter Gross, who approaches the text via role analysis, drawing on Vladimir Propp's *Morphology of the Folktale* (1968). Gross observes: "The roles are more important than the characters. For *whatever reason*, YHWH forbade the man of God to eat or drink in Bethel. Both the king and the nabi, again for *whatever reasons*, assume the role of opponent through their actions."[29] That is to say, while the text may not present a clear motive for the Bethelite's deceptive actions, readers may nonetheless ascribe significance, or relevance, to his behavior.

In my view, Gross's assertion that in 1 Kings 13 "the roles are more important than the characters" is a helpful one that redirects readerly inquiry from plot elements *within* this "self-contained chapter"[30] to the creative intentions of the author-redactor *behind* the textual world.[31]

---

27. Klopfenstein, "1. Könige 13," 657–8: "die Übertragung von Jerusalemer Kultrechten auf Bethel und damit die Gemeinschaft unter Gleichberechtigten."

28. John Goldingay, *An Introduction to the Old Testament: Exploring Text, Approaches and Issues* (London: SPCK, 2016), 189.

29. Gross, "Lying Prophet," 123 (emphasis added).

30. Barth, *CD II.2*, 393.

31. To the contrary, Van Seters, "On Reading the Story of the Man of God from Judah in 1 Kings 13," in *The Labour of Reading: Desire, Alienation, and Biblical Interpretation*, ed. Robert C. Culley et al. (Atlanta: Scholars Press, 1999), 225–34, argues that any difficulties one has in understanding 1 Kgs 13 "are the result of a lack of literary skill by the author" (233). But see Jones, *Anonymous Prophets*, for an appraisal of Van Seters.

Indeed, it seems that the motive (and hence the character) of the anonymous northern prophet in 1 Kings 13 can be understood in terms of broader literary developments within Dtr's over-arching schema.

As I have argued above, the story is set within a context of division and opposition between north and south (1 Kgs 12:19; 14:30) so that, in terms of the story's symbolic significance, it may be expected that the Bethelite, a representative figure for Jeroboam and northern Israel, demonstrates loyalty to the north—for *whatever* reason. In light of this context and the opening scene, the narrative leads us to expect an alignment between the actions of Josiah and the man of God on one hand (representing right worship in God's chosen city of Jerusalem), and between Jeroboam and the Bethel prophet on the other (representing false worship in the cities of Samaria). This central tension between north and south is sustained in the unfolding narrative when the old Bethelite takes up Jeroboam's cause—however one chooses to fill the motive gap. Our inquiry is thus redirected from the *narrator's logic* in 1 Kings 13 to the *redactor's purpose* in recounting a tale of this sort at this particular point in the history of Israel and Judah. From this wider frame of reference, questions concerning genre, redaction, and literary structure guide the reader. We will discuss these exegetical elements briefly in what follows.

Considering Motive: Behind the Text

Vital to any discussion of a text's meaning and function is its genre. Though much could be said regarding 1 Kings 13, we will limit discussion to a few pertinent comments. A particular form of Hebrew narrative that has received significant attention in recent years (albeit under various designations) is that of narrative analogy.[32] Narrative analogies are stories woven into larger units, where the shorter story supplies a hermeneutical key to its wider context. Robert Alter, for instance, speaks of "narrative analogy, through which one part of the text provides oblique commentary

---

32. E.g., Moshe Garsiel, *The First book of Samuel: A Literary Study of Comparative Structures, Analogies and Parallels* (Ramat-Gan: Revivim, 1985); Joshua Berman, *Narrative Analogy in the Hebrew Bible: Battle Stories and their Equivalent Non-battle Narratives*, VTSup 103 (Leiden: Brill, 2004); Aulikki Nahkola, *Double Narratives in the Old Testament: The Foundations of Method in Biblical Criticism* (Berlin: de Gruyter, 2001); Peter Miscall, "The Jacob and Joseph Stories as Analogies," *JSOT* 6 (1978): 28–40; idem, *The Workings of Old Testament Narrative*, Semeia Studies (Chico, CA: Scholars Press, 1983); James G. Williams, "The Beautiful and the Barren: Conventions in Biblical Type-scenes," *JSOT* 17 (1980): 107–19.

on another."³³ Some examples, to name but a few, are Genesis 2–3,³⁴ 38;³⁵ Judg. 2:11f.; 9:7-15;³⁶ 1 Samuel 25;³⁷ 2 Sam. 12:1-6; and our story in 1 Kings 13. The most extensive study of 1 Kings 13 in this vein is by David Bosworth, who has sought to assimilate Barth's overtly theological reading within contemporary, mainstream scholarship.³⁸ However, he is certainly not alone in identifying 1 Kings 13 as a form of narrative analogy.³⁹

Redaction-critical evidence surrounding 1 Kings 13 also suggests that our story may be an interpolation (an instance of *wiederaufnahme*⁴⁰) that provides theological commentary on the division of the kingdoms. The

---

33. Robert Alter, *The Art of Biblical Narrative* (New York: Basic Books, 1981), 21; cf. 180. David A. Bosworth, *The Story within a Story in Biblical Hebrew Narrative*, CBQMS 45 (Washington: Catholic Biblical Association of America, 2008), describes 1 Kgs 13 as "a specific kind of narrative analogy" (vii).

34. Seth D. Postell, *Adam as Israel: Genesis 1–3 as the Introduction to the Torah and Tanakh* (Eugene: Wipf & Stock, 2011).

35. Bosworth, *Story*, Chapter 2.

36. David Jobling, *The Sense of Biblical Narrative, Vol. 2: Structural Analyses in the Hebrew Bible*, JSOTSup 39 (Sheffield: JSOT Press, 1986), 44–87, esp. 70f.

37. Robert P. Gordon, "David's Rise and Saul's Demise: Narrative Analogy in 1 Samuel 24–26," *TynBul* 31 (1980): 37–64; Bosworth, *Story*, Chapter 3.

38. Bosworth, *Story*, Chapter 4. This work further develops his earlier essay: "Revisiting Karl Barth's Exegesis of 1 Kings 13," *BibInt* 10 (2002): 360–83.

39. Robert Cohn, "Literary Technique," perceives 1 Kgs 13 within the Jeroboam story (1 Kgs 11–14) as "a kind of parable, a story within a story, that sets into relief the theological dynamics of the larger narrative" (33); Bodner, *Jeroboam's Royal Drama*, refers to the second part of the narrative (13:11-32) "as a 'play-within-a-play,' a type of *political allegory* that functions as a subtle reflection on the fate of Jeroboam's kingship" (97–8; original emphasis); Bosworth places 1 Kgs 13 as a "story within a story" in the much broader context of 1 Kgs 13–2 Kgs 23. Others use such terms as "parable" (Alexander Rofé, *The Prophetical Stories: The Narratives about the Prophets in the Hebrew Bible, their Literary Types and History*, trans. D. Levy [Jerusalem: Magnes, 1988]) and "political allegory" (Roland Boer, "National Allegory in the Hebrew Bible," *JSOT* 74 [1997]: 95–116). In spite of variations in terminology, what is being evoked and accented is the nature of the story as one that utilizes an unusual system of referentiality to illuminate broader national and political themes. Bodner and Cohn argue that the fate of the man of God reflects that of King Jeroboam, who in turn represents the nation of Israel.

40. I.e. "resumptive repetition." The German word literally means "taking up again." Where an interpolation has been made, the redactor uses a repeated phrase (or phrases) to draw the reader's attention back to the main subject matter; a literary device that effectively says, "Now, where were we?" On the similarities between *Wiederaufnahme* and ordinary conversation, see R. F. Person, "A Reassessment

repetition of the phrase ויהי הדבר הזה לחטאת ("and this thing became a sin") in 1 Kgs 12:30 and 1 Kgs 33:34 forms an *inclusio* around the story of the two prophets, as numerous scholars have observed.[41] Moreover, the placement of the Jeroboam cycle (1 Kgs 11–14) at the beginning of the history of the divided kingdoms has structural significance, since the history hearkens back to "the sin of Jeroboam" again and again in its evaluation of northern kings and in its explanation for the fall of the north (2 Kgs 17:21-22). Similarly, there is a general consensus among scholars about the importance of the Josiah narrative (2 Kgs 22–23) as a—and probably *the*—high point of Israel's gloomy monarchial record. The two pivotal figures of Jeroboam and Josiah, and their associated narratives, thus provide "bookends" to the history of the divided kingdom, as archetypal figures in the story of the man of God from Judah, which begins in 1 Kings 13 and reaches its conclusion in 2 Kgs 23:15-20.[42]

Jerome Walsh has helpfully articulated how the reader's task of establishing contextual parameters is critical for considering a text's function and thus its meaning in relation to the range and substance of its referents.[43] Accordingly, when 1 Kings 13 is treated as a narrative analogy

of Wiederaufnahme from the Perspective of Conversation Analysis," *BZ* 43, no. 2 (1999): 239–48. Also see Curt Kuhl, "Die 'Wiederaufnahme'—ein literarkritisches Prinzip?" *ZAW* 64 (2009): 1–11.

41. So Stephen McKenzie, *The Trouble with Kings: The Composition of the Book of Kings in the Deuteronomistic History*, VTSup 42 (Leiden: Brill, 1991), 51; Cogan, *1 Kings*, 367; Van Seters, "The Deuteronomistic History: Can it Avoid Death by Redaction?" in *The Future of the Deuteronomistic History*, ed. Thomas Römer, BETL 147 (Leuven: Leuven University Press, 2000), 216; Werner E. Lemke, "The Way of Obedience: I Kings 13 and the Structure of the Deuteronomistic History," in *Magnalia Dei: The Mighty Acts of God: Festschrift for G. E. Wright*, ed. F. M. Cross, W. E. Lemke, and P. D. Miller, Jr. (Garden City: Doubleday, 1976), 320 n. 31; Garry Knoppers, *Two Nations Under God: The Deuteronomistic History of Solomon and the Dual Monarchies, Vol. 2* (Atlanta: Scholars Press, 1994), 50–1; Van Winkle, "1 Kings XII 25–XIII 34: Jeroboam's Cultic Innovations and the Man of God from Judah," *VT* 46 (1996): 102–3; Thomas Römer, *The So-Called Deuteronomistic History: A Sociological, Historical and Literary Introduction* (London: T&T Clark, 2007), 153.

42. Note that each archetypal king is mentioned in the narrative about the other (1 Kgs 13:2; 2 Kgs 23:16). For a recent study of Kings that utilizes the literary technique of archetypes, see Alison L. Joseph, *Portrait of the Kings: The Davidic Prototype in Deuteronomistic Poetics* (Minneapolis: Fortress, 2015), and my review in *VT* 67 (2017): 153–7. Also see my *Anonymous Prophets*.

43. J. Walsh, "The Contexts of 1 Kings xiii," *VT* 39 (1989): 355–70; cf. idem, "Methods and Meanings: Multiple Studies of 1 Kings 21," *JBL* 111, no. 2 (1992): 193–211.

that introduces the history of the divided kingdoms and anticipates Josiah's cultic reforms, it functions less as a self-contained story with a "moral" (whether for Jeroboam, an exilic audience, or a contemporary one) than as an interpretive lens for the subsequent history. While all stories must necessarily sustain an internal logic, the literary placement of this episode suggests that it likely serves a particular hermeneutical function for a broader range of texts and ought therefore to be interpreted accordingly.

Well-known in this regard is Wellhausen's list of programmatic speeches that simultaneously recollect the past while looking to the nation's future. The retrospective/prospective function of certain texts, as described by Wellhausen and Noth, bear numerous similarities to the function that some scholars have attributed to 1 Kings 13. Wellhausen first identified the use of speeches as a unifying structural device throughout the DH in his *Prolegomena zur Geschichte Israels*:

> The great period thus marked off and artificially divided into sub-periods, is surveyed and appraised at every important epoch in sermon-like discourses. These are much more frequent in Kings than in Judges and Samuel. It makes no difference whether the writer speaks in his own person, or by the mouth of another; in reviews of the past he speaks himself, 2 Kings xvii.; in anticipations of the future he makes another speak (1 Kings viii. ix.). A few examples must be cited to show what we mean.[44]

Wellhausen goes on to cite from Solomon's prayer in 1 Kings 8, the prophecy of Ahijah[45] in 1 Kgs 11:31-35, and 2 Kings 17, as examples of programmatic texts. In light of the strategic placement of such texts, scholars such as Otto Plöger were perplexed by the unusual hiatus around 1 Kings 11–14, which narrates one of the worst political debacles in Israelite history.[46] Werner Lemke, however, observes that 1 Kings 13

---

44. J. Wellhausen, *Prolegomena to the History of Ancient Israel* (Cambridge: Cambridge University Press, 2013 [orig. 1885 ET]), 274.

45. The text [ET] actually reads, "a prophecy of Abijah to the first Jeroboam" (275), though it is clear that "Ahijah" is intended. The same error occurs on p. 279, and in both cases, the original German also erroneously reads "Abijah."

46. See Otto Plöger, "Speech and Prayer in the Deuteronomistic and the Chronicler's Histories," in *Reconsidering Israel and Judah: Recent Studies on the Deuteronomistic History*, ed. Gary N. Knoppers and J. Gordon McConville (Winona Lake: Eisenbrauns, 2000), 34.

fills a vacuum which has been felt by many. It would be remarkable, to say the least, if as important an event in the history of Israel as the division of the kingdom, with its ensuing religious schism, and the establishment of those cultic practices which led to the eventual downfall of Israel should have received only passing attention from the Deuteronomistic Historian...
If we are correct, however, 1 Kings 13 fulfills precisely the kind of function Plöger was looking for. To be sure, it is not a speech like 1 Sam. 12, nor a prayer like 1 Kings 8, nor a free commentary like II Kings 17:7-20. Rather, it is a narrative with considerable action, suspense and movement, but heavily interlaced with dialogue and speeches by its main characters. The particular vehicle chosen by the Deuteronomist to make his point was dictated, here as elsewhere, by his available sources.[47]

If the author-redactor's motive in depicting these representative, anonymous prophets in opposition to one another was indeed to segue into the history of the kingdoms with a prophetic legend that introduces certain key dynamics developed therein, then the Bethel prophet's *particular* motive is less important than the simple fact that he is characterized as a loyal representative of the north vis-à-vis the south. His representative role demands only that the old Bethel prophet speak and act in opposition to the man of God from Judah—which, clearly, he does (v. 18b).

This reframing of 1 Kings 13 helpfully shifts the reader's attention from moral injunction to literary function.[48] In its wider context, 1 Kings 13 may be read as a narrative analogy that explicates the recent division of the kingdoms and foreshadows the untimely death of Josiah (another man of God from Judah). As a story depicting tension between north and south, 1 Kings 13 "constitutes a kind of heading"[49] over the history of the kingdoms by introducing a central, relational dynamic between Israel and Judah. While the story's plot is fascinating in its own right, 1 Kings 13

---

47. Lemke, "Way of Obedience," 325–6 n. 103. Steven McKenzie also acknowledges the potential gains of adding 1 Kgs 13 (and 2 Sam. 7) "to the series of speeches and narratives in Deuteronomistic style which provide structure for the DH." S. McKenzie, *The Chronicler's Use of the Deuteronomistic History*, HSM 33 (Atlanta: Scholars Press, 1985), 2. Cf. Dennis McCarthy, "II Samuel 7 and the Structure of the Deuteronomistic History," *JBL* 84 (1965): 131–8, argues that 2 Sam. 7 is such a text as well. Cf. Frank Moore Cross, *Canaanite Myth and Hebrew Epic: Essays in the History of the Religion of Israel* (Cambridge: Harvard University Press, 1973), 241–64.

48. I say "helpfully" because numerous interpreters who insist on finding a moral injunction in the narrative find themselves at a loss to explain why both prophets ultimately fail to act in ways that appear ethically sound.

49. Barth, *CD II.2*, 403.

may also be understood to serve a comparable function to Wellhausen's list of programmatic texts by holding an interpretive lens over the subsequent history. In this final section, we explore this reading strategy by highlighting certain parallels between the Bethel prophet in 1 Kings 13 and northern Israel in 1 Kings 14–2 Kings 17.

Conclusion: Israel Turns Judah from the Way

When the narrative in 1 Kings 13 is read as a narrative analogy, or proleptic parable, that precedes and foreshadows the history of the kingdoms, certain details from the broader history are particularly noteworthy in connection with the characterization of the Bethel prophet.[50]

(a) *Like Israel, the Bethel prophet intentionally violates the prohibition of fellowship with (the man of God from) Judah.* Following the division of the kingdom in the Jeroboam cycle (1 Kgs 11–14), some prophetic narratives contain warnings concerning north–south fellowship (e.g. 1 Kgs 22; 2 Kgs 3),[51] and the hostility between kingdoms is expressed in repeated military conflict (1 Kgs 12:21; 14:30; 15:6, 16-17; 2 Kgs 14:11-14).[52] The same prohibition is reflected in 1 Kings 13, where the man of God is instructed to abstain from food and drink in Bethel.[53] And just as the Israelite kings in the broader history initiate the prohibited collaboration with the kings of Judah (cf. 1 Kgs 22:4; 2 Kgs 3:7), it is the Bethel prophet in 1 Kings 13 who deliberately instigates table fellowship with the man of God.

(b) *The history of the kingdoms follows the basic pattern established in 1 Kings 13; viz. Judah/the man of God is led into sin by Israel/the Bethel prophet.* In the history of the divided kingdoms, as Bosworth observes, "the [prohibited] alliance leads to intermarriage between the house of David and the house of Ahab. Ahab's marriage to Jezebel of Sidon leads to the worship of Baal in Israel. Similarly, Jehoshaphat's son Jehoram's marriage to Ahab's daughter Athaliah causes the house of David to walk in the ways of the House of Ahab (2 Kgs 8:18, 27). As the larger, wealthier,

---

50. Other parallels may be noted, especially concerning the fate of the man of God from Judah. Jones, *Anonymous Prophets*, presents a literary-theological reading of 1 Kgs 13 that accounts for numerous points of parallelism between the man of God from Judah and King Josiah.

51. Barth, *CD II.2*, 394, 400; Bosworth, *Story*, 143–4.

52. Bosworth, *Story*, 137.

53. The majority of interpreters understand the significance of the threefold commandment to reflect a prohibition from fellowship with the north.

and more powerful kingdom, Israel takes the lead in the alliance with Judah. Instead of Judah influencing Israel toward more correct worship, Judah is seduced into Baal worship."[54] By the same token, in 2 Kings 17, the narrator pauses when providing a theological rationale for Israel's defeat under Assyria to state that Judah will ultimately reach the same fate because of Israel's influence: "Judah also did not keep the commandments of the LORD their God but walked in the customs that Israel had introduced [וילכו בחקות ישראל אשר עשו]" (2 Kgs 17:19; cf. Mic. 1:13).[55]

Analogously, in 1 Kings 13 the Bethel prophet is described by the narrator as "the prophet who caused him to turn from the way" (v. 26; cf. v. 20). Moreover, numerous commentators have observed that the language of vv. 21 and 26 intentionally toy with the metaphorical ambiguity of words like "turn" (*shuv* in the *hiphil*), "way"/"path" (*derek*) and "command/ment" (*mitzvah*) to accomplish something more than simple narration.[56] The Bethel prophet is depicted in a negative light for causing (the man of God from) Judah to turn from the way of obedience.[57]

(c) *The 'hero' in 1 Kings 13 is neither the man of God nor the old prophet, but rather the efficacious word of God; this is true also within the history of the kingdoms.* One of the most challenging plot elements in 1 Kings 13 is the reversal of v. 20. With the narrator's report from v. 18 still fresh in our minds—"he deceived him"—we read that "the word of the LORD came to the prophet who caused him to turn" (ויהי דבר־יהוה אל־הנביא אשר השיבו). No sooner is the Bethel prophet characterized as a liar than he receives a true word! Walsh says of this jarring reversal

---

54. Bosworth, "Revisiting," 380.

55. These verses are often referred to as "intrusive" by historical-critical commentators (e.g., Cogan, *II Kings*, 206). In Bosworth's schema, the confusing reversal of 1 Kgs 13:20 is juxtaposed with the dynamics of 2 Kgs 9–11, so that what happens at the table of the Bethel prophet reflects how "[t]he roles of the two kingdoms are reversed in Jehu's coup." He notes that due to the intermarriage between north and south, Ahab's granddaughter Athaliah remains on the throne for 6 years (2 Kgs 11:3; ~841–835 BCE) and Baal worship is sustained in Judah. Thus, the "spreading" from north to south occurs especially through Athaliah. Bosworth, *Story*, 145.

56. See Lemke on מצנה in v. 21, "Way of Obedience," 311; also Gross, "Lying Prophet," 104; Van Winkle, "1 Kings XIII," 41; Thomas B. Dozeman, "The Way of the Man of God from Judah: True and False Prophecy in the Pre-Deuteronomic Legend of 1 Kings 13," *CBQ* 44, no. 3 (1982): 386–7.

57. Verse 26 also uses the distinctly Deuteronomistic phrase מָרָה אֶת־פִּי יְהוָה, "he rebelled against the mouth of the LORD" (cf. Deut. 1:26, 43; 9:23; also, Josh. 1:18; 1 Sam. 12:14-15; 1 Kgs 13:21, 26; see Lemke, "Way of Obedience," 308–9); Van Winkle, "1 Kings XII 25–XIII 34," 111.

of fates that the man of God "moves from obedience through unwitting disobedience to death" while the Bethel prophet moves "from narrow patriotism through sacrilege to true prophetic mission."[58] For many interpreters, however, this unpredictable twisting of fates is critical to a proper understanding of the story, for the reversal suggests that God's word is the primary driving force within the strange world of the narrative; the prophets remain secondary characters, as it were.

The same motif is evident in the monarchial account that follows, where Dtr's well-known prophecy-fulfilment schema accentuates the efficacious word of God throughout history. As we noted above, 1 Kings 13 and its epilogue in 2 Kgs 23:15-20 highlight YHWH's sovereignty over history in one of the most striking instances of this schema. The structure of the whole indicates that the word of the LORD, spoken by the man of God at the inception of the history of the divided kingdom, has enduring efficacy. That both Israel and Judah are doomed from the outset is manifested in 1 Kings 13, where the anonymous kingdom representatives (i.e. the man of God and the old prophet), who prove to be disobedient and deceptive, die separate deaths but share a common grave. (Similarly, Jeroboam and Josiah, who also serve as kingdom representatives, die in ways that bespeak the fates of their kingdoms, Israel and Judah.) As von Rad has shown, the "Deuteronomistic theology of history, the theology of the word finding certain fulfilment in history,"[59] is a pattern that appears frequently throughout the DH, and especially in the book of Kings. The Bethel prophet's unexpected reversal in v. 20 from liar to truth-teller thus echoes a broader theme: God's word finds fulfilment by any means necessary, including even ways that make a true prophet false or a false prophet true.

(d) Finally, *Israel's idolatrous influence upon Judah leads to exile/ death, just as the falsehood of the Bethel prophet leads to the untimely death of the man of God.* Following the fulfilment of the prophetic word concerning the man of God's untimely end, the old prophet mourns the death of his "brother" and requests a shared tomb (vv. 30-31). These words and actions, too, are best explained by observing the relation between Israel and Judah in the subsequent history. As Walsh makes the point, "both are doomed to overcome their separation only in death. Judah will be buried in an alien land, and Israel will be saved only so far as it is

---

58. Walsh, "Contexts," 360.
59. Gerhard von Rad, "The Deuteronomistic Theology of History in the Books of Kings," *Studies in Deuteronomy*, SBT 1.9, trans. David Stalker (London: SCM, 1953), 83.

joined to Judah."⁶⁰ Barth, too, perceives the Bethel prophet and the man of God as portents of the shared exilic demise of Israel and Judah:

Both here and in the whole sphere of the Old Testament history of kings and prophets there can be no visible consummation of the restored fellowship other than this common grave. It is Israel's grave into which Judah itself is first laid, and then Israel. The historical conclusion brings a reversal in the actual sequence of events. But either way, it is in this grave that the reunion of the separated brothers is completed.⁶¹

Even as Dtr's account of the divided kingdoms nears the tragic end that was prophesied at its inception, a hopeful note is sounded—not just in the reign and reforms of Josiah, but also in the union of the two anonymous prophets who represent the nations whence they come (cf. Ezek. 37:22-23).

Regarding the question of the Bethelite prophet's motive in 1 Kings 13, I have suggested that from a literary perspective *the deceptive actions of the Bethel prophet reflect the dynamic of hostility between Israel and Judah depicted in the wider narrative framework*. But since the motive of the Bethel prophet remains ambiguous, a range of possibilities is left open to the reader, and this applies subsequently to the precise nature of Judah's relation to Israel in the history that follows as well. This kind of reading (and writing?) strategy generates interpretive possibilities, both literarily and theologically, in much the same way that one might notice when regarding Abraham as a proleptic embodiment of Israel in Genesis,⁶² or Nabal as a representative figure for Saul in 1 Samuel 25.⁶³ We have also seen that where the logic of the *narrator* is not forthcoming (regarding a motive, for instance), the logic of the *narrative*—especially its literary placement—can establish contextual parameters that ascribe to it an alternative function and meaning.

---

60. Walsh, "Contexts," 367–8. Walsh acknowledges his indebtedness to Barth on this point. Affirming that Barth's work "remains a classic," he writes: "The proleptic character of the narrative is fundamental to Barth's justly famous exposition of the chapter. My reading is similar to his" (368 n. 25). The paragraph quoted above is also repeated (not quite verbatim) in Walsh's commentary on 1 Kgs 13, where Barth's influence is readily discernible. Walsh, *1 Kings*, 205.

61. Barth, *CD II.2*, 406.

62. See, e.g., Moberly, *The Bible, Theology, and Faith: A Study of Abraham and Jesus* (Cambridge: Cambridge University Press, 2000), 83f.

63. See Bosworth, *Story*, Chapter 3; Robert P. Gordon, "David's Rise and Saul's Demise: Narrative Analogy in 1 Samuel 24–26," *TynBul* 31 (1980): 37–64.

Certainly, one lesson that arises from our engagement with 1 Kings 13 is the recognition that biblical genres do not always comply with modes of analysis seeking an either/or distinction. There is ultimately no need to *determine* the text's origins, historicity, or even its genre, in order to read with full, imaginative seriousness. Rather, as Moberly makes the point, critical questions and judgments ought to aid the reader in "recognizing which questions a text will and will not constructively sustain, and [in] determining the uses to which a text is and is not put."[64]

In the case of 1 Kings 13, a self-contained chapter that immediately follows the division of the kingdom, the Bethel prophet's deliberate deception of the man of God from Judah provides a potential gloss on the ensuing history where Judah is said to follow in Israel's footsteps (2 Kgs 17:19). From this perspective, the actions of the Bethel prophet are consistent with the narrator's apt characterization: he is indeed הנביא אשר השיבו מן־הדרך "the prophet who caused him to turn from the way" (v. 26).

---

64. R. W. L. Moberly, *The Bible in a Disenchanted Age: The Enduring Possibility of Christian Faith* (Grand Rapids: Baker Academic, 2018), 194.

Chapter 7

Dancing with Death; Dancing with Life: Ahab between Jezebel and Elijah

Lissa M. Wray Beal

Dance Prelude

> See, I set before you today life and prosperity, death and destruction. For I command you today to love YHWH your God, to walk in his ways and keep his commandments, statutes, and judgments... But if your heart turns away and you do not listen, and you are led away and worship other gods and serve them...you shall surely perish. (Deut. 30:15-18)[1]

This is the choice set before Israel: life, or death; the worship of YHWH or other gods. The choice is the same throughout Israel's life in the land, and a king is to immerse himself in the law, choose rightly, and thus lead the people in covenant faithfulness (Deut. 17:18-19). On this foundational covenant issue, the north's first king, Jeroboam, fails. According to the Deuteronomic warning, worship of Jeroboam's golden calves leads to "death and destruction," ultimately experienced in exile (2 Kgs 17:21-23). Ahab, the Omride scion, follows Jeroboam's sin. To it, he adds the worship of Baal through his marriage to the foreign Jezebel. These events begin Ahab's reign, characterizing him immediately as evil (16:29-34).[2]

If the worship of the golden calves leads to death and destruction, the addition of Baal worship only confirms the prognosis, and it is this god that is the focus of Ahab's reign. As the storm god, Baal ruled the rain

---

1   Translations are the author's own.
2. Unless specified, chapter/verse refers to 1 Kings.

(and thunder and lightning). Through this, crops—and thus life—were considered under his control.[3] The localized manifestations of Baal, their visible representation in cult objects, and the social attraction to Israel of worshipping in ways aligned with their Canaanite neighbors apparently presented enticing alternatives to a national deity whose cult was focused in distant Jerusalem, and who was not to be represented in visible form. But despite such seeming attractions, worship of Baal was in direct conflict with YHWH's sole sovereignty over Israel (Exod. 20:3; Deut. 5:7), and a threat to Israel's covenant life and blessings (Deut. 16:21-22; 28:15-68; Hos. 2:13).

Despite popular belief in Baal's power over rain, crops, and life, Ahab's cycle shows Baal had no such power as it was held solely by YHWH, the Life-Giver. Peter Leithart clearly identifies the conundrum:

> [d]uring the time of the Omrides, Israel is living in a culture of death, a result of the Omride devotion to dead idols, and death permeates the daily lives of [Israel]. Yahweh had given Israel a living, fruitful land, flowing with milk and honey and watered with the rain from heaven, but idols make the land deadly.[4]

As Baal's narrative representative, Jezebel is aligned with death. Yet Ahab is not left wholly to her influence, or that of Baal. Standing against Jezebel and challenging Baal, Elijah represents YHWH and thus life. Ahab interacts with both these representatives repeatedly through five chapters (1 Kgs 16–19; 21).[5] By examining these alternating interactions, this study pursues the complex characterization of Ahab. Although initially characterized in the introduction as evil, he shows himself responsive both to Jezebel/Baal *and* Elijah/YHWH. Like Israel, he "wavers between two opinions" (2 Kgs 18:21), and cannot be characterized as merely a stereotypical evil character.[6]

---

3. W. Herrmann, "Baal," *DDD*, 132–9.
4. Peter J. Leithart, *1 & 2 Kings* (Grand Rapids: Brazos, 2006), 186.
5. LXX highlights the continuity of characters, placing ch. 21 after ch. 19. Chapters 20, 22 name Ahab, but Jezebel and Elijah do not appear and therefore these chapters are excluded from this study. For this same reason, redaction-critical and historical arguments that remove chs. 20, 22 from Ahab's account are not engaged (for this position see John Gray, *1 & II Kings*, OTL [Philadelphia: Westminster, 1970], 414–18; Jerome T. Walsh, *Ahab: The Construction of a King* [Collegeville: Liturgical Press, 2006], 108–10; a brief answer is provided in Lissa M. Wray Beal, *1 & 2 Kings*, AOTC 9 (Downers Grove: InterVarsity, 2014), 261–3.
6. Stuart Lasine, *Weighing Hearts: Character, Judgment, and the Ethics of Reading the Bible*, LHBOTS 568 (London: T&T Clark, 2012), rejects a flat characterization

The characterization can be construed as a dance, with Ahab partnered at times with Jezebel/Baal, at others with Elijah/YHWH. Sadly, the narrative finale (ch. 21) ends as it began: Ahab partnered with Jezebel/Baal and therefore faced with judgment and death. That death occurs outside the parameters of his interactions with Jezebel and Elijah (in ch. 22). Yet, there *is* a final dance in which all three appear together again and which effects the death foretold in ch. 21. This study, having traced the complex characterization of Ahab through his interactions with Jezebel and Elijah, briefly visits that final *danse macabre*, noting the reappearance of Elijah, the final pairing of Ahab with Jezebel/Baal, and the finality of Ahab's choice of dance partner.

Dance Partners (1 Kings 16:29-34; 17:1)

The dance begins with Ahab, one of the most important northern monarchs. Not only is his twenty-two year rule the longest of any northern king (except Jehu), his rule and dynasty receives the greatest narrative space of any northern king (sixteen chapters; from 1 Kgs 16–2 Kgs 9). His importance is, however, for the wrong reasons, as the opening of his narrative makes clear. Additionally, his daughter marries into the Davidic line (2 Kgs 8:18) and apparently by this connection Baalism enters Judah (2 Kgs 11:18; 18:4; 23:4-5). Ahab's influence is so great that one of the last Judahite kings is explicitly compared (albeit negatively) to Ahab (2 Kgs 21:4).

---

of Ahab through comparative analysis of classical Greek characterizations in his chapter "Kings Wicked and Weak: The Characterization of Ahab in Comparative Perspective" (171–91). The present study similarly rejects a flat characterization of Ahab by utilizing the lens of the interrelations of Ahab with Jezebel and Elijah. Likewise, both Jezebel and Elijah are complex characters, narratively presented not merely as flat stereotypes of good and evil. For instance, Jezebel shows strength of character and devotion in her defense of her deity, and attentive conjugal concern in her pursuit of her husband's desire, and Elijah's flight and rejection of the prophetic calling (1 Kgs 19) shows weakness, fear, or burnout. In these and other respects, the complexity of Jezebel and Elijah is apparent (a narrative and sociological analysis that explores the complexity of these two characters is found in Patricia Dutcher-Walls, *Jezebel: Portraits of a Queen* [Collegeville: Liturgical Press, 2004]). The present study focuses only on the role they play vis-à-vis Ahab and Deuteronomic concerns regarding worship practices and obedience to YHWH's word. For these reasons, the exploration of the complexity of these characters is not pursued.

Ahab's importance is apparent from the outset of his account as, within the first two verses, he is identified thrice with a patronym ("son of Omri"). Yet it is a dubious association, for the preceding conclusion of Omri's reign marks him as doing evil in YHWH's eyes (more than all who were before him), walking in the ways of Jeroboam, and causing Israel to sin (16:25-26). In this regard, Ahab will follow in his father's footsteps as a true "son of Omri." There is a sly reference here to Ahab's own name, which means "father's brother" or more literally, "one like the father."

A typical regnal formula opens Ahab's reign, with elements including the monarch's name, length and place of reign, concurrent southern monarch, and regnal evaluation.[7] In the mouth of the reliable narrator, the wholly negative evaluation of Ahab polemically shapes readers' expectations of his reign.[8]

Ahab is first described as doing evil in the eyes of YHWH. As if that is not bad enough, he does "more [evil] than all who were before him" (16:30), rhetorically advancing him beyond his own father and even Jeroboam, the arch-villain of the north. Thus, if Jeroboam's fate is sealed for doing evil (14:7-14), Ahab's greater evil alerts the reader to the likelihood of a similar judgment.

Whatever else this greater evil includes (and ch. 21 provides some details), the evaluation identifies three. First, Ahab continues in the sins of Jeroboam. From the narrator's perspective, these sins are egregious (12:30; 14:9, 16). Yet they are ironically described "as if…light" alongside his second sin. This is his marriage to Jezebel, the first of Ahab's dance partners. Narrative dismay at the king's choice is apparent as covenant law forbids marriage to a foreigner (Deut. 7:1-6). Her father's name (Ethbaal; Phoenician *Ittobaal*; "Baal exists") suggests close association with the foreign god. Jezebel herself may have served as a priestess of the deity.[9] The narrator's contempt is signaled as her name (originally vocalized as *ʾizəbūl*, "Where is the prince?") is now *ʾîzebel*, with a scatological play upon the word *zebel* ("dung"). Foreigner and idolater, Jezebel is dangerous and despicable. Ahab's choice depicts him as gravely in error.

Ahab's second sin leads to his third sin: Baal worship. Ahab "served" (from *ʿbd*) and "worshipped" (from *ḥwh*) Baal. Elsewhere, the verbal combination marks idol worship that arouses God's anger and causes

---

7. Detailed discussion of these formulae appears in Burke O. Long, *1 Kings*, FOTL 9 (Grand Rapids: Eerdmans, 1984), 159–61.

8. Yairah Amit, *Hidden Polemics in Biblical Narrative*, BibInt 25 (Leiden: Brill, 2000), 50–1, explores the phenomenon of polemical shaping of expectations.

9. Pauline A. Viviano, "Ethbaal," *ABD* 2:645; Gale A. Yee, "Jezebel," *ABD* 3:848–9.

Israel to perish (Deut. 4:19; 8:19; 11:16-17; 29:26; 30:17-18; Josh. 23:7, 16). The Baal altar and temple Ahab builds is against YHWH's will (Deut. 7:5; 12:2-7, 11-14), characterizing Ahab as the infamous Jeroboam, who built unorthodox altars and places of worship (1 Kgs 12:28-33). In further defiance of YHWH, Ahab erects a sacred pole for the goddess Asherah (v. 33; see Deut. 7:5; 12:3; 16:21).[10] Like northern kings before him, Ahab's sins "provoke" (from k's) YHWH's anger (v. 33; see 14:9; 15:30; 16:2, 7, 13, 26). Yet Ahab's provocation is "more than all the kings of Israel before him"—once again, he exceeds even Jeroboam.

The concluding notice activates Joshua's ancient curse (Josh. 6:26). Like Ahab, Hiel flaunts YHWH's word and receives punishment "according to the word of YHWH." That this occurs "in Ahab's days" implicates the king's reign as a context amenable to such action and thus confirms Ahab's evaluation while foreshadowing similar disaster for his reign, "according to the word of YHWH."

The king's reign thus begins under YHWH's judgment, for Ahab stands with Jezebel and her god, Baal. His choice will affect him, his dynasty, and YHWH's covenant people. For these reasons, YHWH does not leave the king—or Israel—without a witness.

Immediately following, and in answer to Ahab's introduction, Elijah appears (17:1). He proclaims the cessation of "dew" (*ṭal*) and "rain" (*māṭār*) and their return only at his word—not through Baal's power or even the seasonal cycle. The citation of "dew" and "rain" invokes covenant curses upon apostate Israel (the same words are found in Deut. 11:11, 14, 17; 28:12, 24; 33:28). Elijah's act disciplines apostate Ahab and Israel in the hope of renewed covenant faithfulness. He is Ahab's second potential dance partner.

Elijah claims the prophetic role for himself by announcing YHWH's word. This role is confirmed, however, only through the events of ch. 17 whereby YHWH sustains Elijah, and Elijah works miracles through YHWH. The chapter's conclusion, "Now I know that you are a man of God and the word of YHWH in your mouth is truth" (v. 24), confirms Elijah's claim. Thus confirmed, YHWH's prophet will proceed to confront Ahab, Jezebel, and Israel with YHWH's word.

Ahab stands, then, between two powerful people and the deity each represents. Committed to Jezebel and Baal (16:29-34), Elijah's ministry will invite him to repentance and covenant renewal. The question is whether Ahab will change dance partners, or not.

---

10. Part of the initial characterization of Ahab, Asherah features only occasionally (1 Kgs 18:19). Narrative focus is on Baal.

Who Leads? (18:1-20)

This episode brings Ahab into interaction with three characters. He comes face-to-face with Elijah, and their encounter activates the Mount Carmel contest. Jezebel appears, acting offstage, yet Ahab also interacts with her. Finally, Ahab interacts with his servant Obadiah who also mediates interactions with Jezebel and Elijah. Each interaction characterizes Ahab, at times in ambiguous ways. Throughout, the question is raised: will Jezebel or Elijah claim control of Ahab?

Ahab and Jezebel

Jezebel's actions take place before Ahab's meeting with Elijah. We learn through the narrator that Jezebel has been "destroying the prophets of YHWH" (v. 4), action that Obadiah later confirms (v. 13). Ahab is not implicated explicitly, but the possibility that this signals lingering respect for YHWH[11] is unlikely given Ahab's resistance to YHWH throughout the episode. Yet there is ambiguity as to whether Jezebel acts "with his approval" or while he "weakly and passively looked the other way."[12]

Given the pattern of YHWH's prophets challenging the king (Elijah; prophets in chs. 20, 22), it is difficult to imagine the king was unaware of them and thus their plight. More, would Ahab be ignorant when there are so many to be hidden away and fed in a time of famine? Particularly if Obadiah uses the king's stores, Ahab must have some inkling of events. Whether tacitly approving, passive, or weak, Ahab does nothing to stop the queen and has some culpability regarding her actions toward the prophets.

The defense of the prophets falls to Obadiah, aptly named "servant of YHWH." He "sustained" the prophets (vv. 4, 13, from *kwl*), which aligns him with YHWH by whom Elijah was "sustained" (*kwl*; 17:4, 9). Obadiah and the narrator claim the actions prove Obadiah's fear of YHWH (vv. 3-4, 12-13). By implication, Ahab's failure to act shows he does not fear YHWH. Obadiah acts righteously, and Ahab stands condemned through inaction.

Alongside Jezebel's attempt to kill YHWH's prophets, she feeds four hundred and fifty prophets of Baal and four hundred prophets of Asherah (v. 19). The contrast to Ahab condemns him. In the face of severe famine, she cares for the people of her god while the Israelite Ahab cares neither for the prophets or people of YHWH. Instead, Ahab searches the land,

---

11. So Walter A. Maier, "Reflections on the Ministry of Elijah," *CTQ* 80 (2016): 70.

12. Hayyim Angel, "Hopping Between Two Opinions: Understanding the Biblical Portrait of Ahab," *JBQ* 35 (2007): 4.

including even the "wadis" (v. 5—the same type of place at which Elijah had been sustained by the ravens [17:2-6]) in order to sustain the animals. Compared to Jezebel's concern for people, his priorities are misplaced. The narrator's judgment against Ahab is apparent, for while Jezebel is "destroying" (from *krt*) the prophets of YHWH and sustaining her own prophets, the king's concern is that he will not have to "kill" (from *krt*) any of the animals (v. 5).[13]

Although some ambiguity exists, interaction with Jezebel predominantly characterizes Ahab negatively. Jezebel is characterized as wicked but she at least acts to save her "people," the prophets of Baal and Asherah. Ahab does not similarly act for YHWH's prophets or people. Rather, Obadiah proves the true servant of YHWH, working behind the scenes at personal cost and risk.

Ahab and Elijah

For three years, Baal has produced neither water nor food and Ahab is left to search the land for water and grass. In this context, Elijah is sent to Ahab with the promise of "rain" (*māṭār*). Through Elijah, YHWH will challenge Ahab to acknowledge that YHWH is the true provider of rain and sustenance.

In the encounter of Ahab and Elijah, Ahab is characterized through the attribution to characters of roles and/or titles, and the characters' relationship to the deity. On both counts, Ahab is denigrated. He is never called king—not by the narrator, prophet, or even Obadiah (who does however reference Ahab as "my lord" in v. 10). The lack of title confirms Ahab's lack of power. Nor is his relationship to YHWH cited positively. Instead, he has "forsaken YHWH's commandments" (v. 18). On the other hand, Obadiah's role as palace steward is stated (v. 3) and his relationship to YHWH is "one who fears YHWH" (vv. 3, 12). Elijah likewise is contrasted to Ahab. Although not labeled a prophet, he holds the prophetic role for "the word of YHWH came to" him (v. 1). His relationship to YHWH is also positive. Obadiah names YHWH as "your [Elijah's] God" (v. 10), with the power of God's spirit able to transport Elijah (v. 12), and Elijah proclaims that it is he (and by implication, not Ahab), who stands before YHWH (v. 15). Obadiah and Elijah are named positively in their roles and in their relationship to YHWH. Ahab is not and thus he is subtly lowered in the reader's estimation.

---

13. Deborah A. Appler, "From Queen to Cuisine: Food Imagery in the Jezebel Narrative," *Semeia* 86 (1999): 58, notes "Ahab is more concerned about the welfare of his horses and mules than his own people."

The naming of characters also works to shape Ahab. He is named frequently (by YHWH in v. 1, the narrator repeatedly, Obadiah in vv. 9, 12). Elijah is named by the narrator and Obadiah, and Obadiah is named by the narrator. Even Jezebel is named by the narrator, Obadiah, and Elijah. By omission, Elijah and Ahab never name one another. Elijah references Ahab as "your [Obadiah's] lord" (v. 8; cf. v. 14), effectively rejecting personal association between himself and Ahab. The contrast is particularly acute as Obadiah's immediately prior and deferential "my lord Elijah" evokes a sense of personal relationship (v. 7; cf. vv. 12, 13).

The meeting of prophet and king occurs through Ahab's deference: he is summoned (v. 8) and comes to the prophet (v. 16). At this point of meeting, the name-calling turns vicious. "Troubler of Israel" appears elsewhere only twice, accusing Elijah alongside those who have distressed Israel: Achan (Josh. 6:18; 7:25; 1 Chron. 2:7) and Saul (1 Sam. 14:29). By accusing Elijah, Ahab takes no responsibility for Israel's trouble, despite the narrative making the connection by immediately placing the drought after Ahab's covenant failures (17:1). Elijah rejects the appellation, naming Ahab as the cause of Israel's trouble and giving further detail: Ahab has "forsaken YHWH's commandments and followed the Baals." Ahab is left in no doubt as to where the blame lies, and neither is the reader.

Elijah next commands Ahab to act. It will be Ahab's third action in this episode, and an evaluation of it will be furthered by considering it in light of Ahab's first two actions. The first (discussed above) is his impotent search for water—an action which negatively characterizes Ahab as unconcerned for his own people. The second is Ahab's determined search to find the troubler, Elijah (vv. 9-10), which aligns him with Jezebel's similar vendetta against YHWH's prophets. His search extends to the nations, involving them in sworn declarations. As in the search for water, however, Ahab is impotent to secure his objective.

Given Ahab's determined search, Obadiah fears for his life should Elijah disappear. It is an eventuality over which Obadiah has no control, and for which the king should not blame him. But so engrossing is Obadiah's fear it begins and ends his response to Elijah (vv. 9, 14). The servant's consternation arises from his estimation of Ahab's caprice and injustice—even against one who is working alongside the king to find water! Having worked closely with Ahab, his assessment of his master has credibility; more, Obadiah's credible witness is evident for he has otherwise "repeat[ed] information we have already learned from the reliable narrator (compare 18:12b–13 with 18:3b–4)."[14]

---

14. Walsh, *Construction of a King*, 28, notes the repetition's few differences "are explicable in ways that cast no doubt on Obadiah's veracity."

In light of the negative depiction of Ahab's first two actions, does his third action in the episode continue the negative depiction? His response to Elijah's command to "send...and gather" (v. 19) is surprising: Ahab complies and "sends...and gathers" (v. 20). The command-response sequence is immediate and identical. Has the drought had its intended effect and the king is now responsive to YHWH? If so, has the assessment of Ahab's prior two actions been too negative? Not at all, for the devil is in the details: Elijah demands the gathering of

- all Israel,
- the four hundred and fifty prophets of Baal, and
- the four hundred prophets of Asherah.

Ahab's response is immediate, but striking in what it lacks. He gathers *only* "the prophets."[15] The broken command-response sequence is jarring, revealing that Ahab has fudged on following through.

Thus, as this episode ends, Elijah is positively characterized: he is YHWH's prophet; he can attribute blame where it is due; he commands the rain and...he commands Ahab. He is in control, leading the dance. Yet Ahab is only somewhat compliant. He continues to resist YHWH's prophet. His character, revealed through interactions with Jezebel and Elijah, is cast in a negative light. That has not been reversed as this episode concludes.

Rejoining the Dance (18:41-46)

During the Mount Carmel contest, Ahab is narratively absent. Considering his limited compliance in v. 20, it is possible he chose not to attend. In light of his presence in the contest's immediate aftermath, it seems more likely he is present as Israel affirms that "YHWH, he is God!" (v. 39). Since the contest concerns the state of the covenant made with all the people of Israel, Ahab's narrative absence is appropriate. It points to what the king should be: one among equals (Deut. 17:15), part of Israel, and bound in the same covenant. It is this aspect of kingship that will be circumvented in ch. 21.

---

15. Only the Baal prophets appear at Carmel, and no mention is made of all four hundred and fifty. The prophets of Asherah are not mentioned at all; they may reappear in 1 Kgs 22:6. Walsh, *Construction of a King*, 30, labels the king's compliance as "grudging and imperfect."

The contest over, Elijah commands Ahab to "go up" and "eat and drink"—assumedly some form of ritual meal, although details are not provided.[16] The details are not the point, but Ahab's obedience is. He immediately responds and "went up to eat and drink" (the verbs in the command and response are the same root). The king's obedience is startlingly different than his accusation when last encountering Elijah (v. 17), a difference that suggests Ahab has had (along with Israel) a change of heart on Carmel.

Ahab is left narratively unattended on the mountain top while narrative attention is focused on the prophet's petition for rain. It is the prophet—not the king—who is important. When the promise of rain comes, further commands are given the king through Elijah's assistant. Again, Ahab's subservience is highlighted. YHWH communicates with the prophet; the prophet sends the assistant. It is the prophet—not the king—who is important.

Ahab is to "hitch up" and "go down." So wholly has the king changed his attitude that his compliance is too rapid to be narrated. The narrative skips over Ahab's compliance to catch him up en route to Jezreel. The omission also heightens the need for rapid action in light of the impending "pelting rain" (vv. 41, 44) brought about by the prophet—again, the one to whom YHWH attends.

Throughout this episode, Ahab is compliant and subservient to the prophet to whom YHWH attends. As a final illustration of the king's submission, the YHWH-empowered prophet runs ahead of the king's chariot preceding him to Jezreel. Ahab travels as an apostate king brought to heel by the prophet he sought to kill and whom he labeled "troubler." Elijah runs as one on whom the hand of YHWH rests (v. 46), who stands in YHWH's presence (v. 15), receives YHWH's word (v. 1), and throughout the chapter has effected YHWH's power. One can only imagine the glance that passes between king and prophet as Elijah runs by.

Changing Partners (19:1)

This one-verse interaction with Jezebel speaks volumes. Ahab relates the Mount Carmel events: the humiliation of Jezebel's Baal; the death of her prophets. Is his account *merely* a response to a conjugal "What did you

---

16. Herbert Chanan Brichto, *Toward a Grammar of Biblical Poetics: Tales of the Prophets* (Oxford: Oxford University Press, 1992), 136, calls it a "sacrificial meal," as does Marvin A. Sweeney, *I & II Kings*, OTL (Louisville: Westminster John Knox, 2007), 229, while Walsh, *Construction of a King*, 31–2, traces Elijah-Moses connections and suggests a Sinai-style covenant meal.

do today?" Or is his response calculated; a manipulative ploy to move Jezebel to act against Elijah? Ahab must know of her earlier deathly vendetta against YHWH's prophets. Surely he can anticipate she will act similarly when she hears the news.

Ahab is thus either clueless of Jezebel's past actions and the signaled potentiality of similar action against Elijah. Or, he is subtle in his assessment of Jezebel's deadly potential against the one who bested him. If the latter, this verse also suggests that Ahab's earlier compliance at Carmel may not include wholehearted or lasting repentance, and certainly that there is no *volte-face* in his animosity towards Elijah. Given his next encounter with Elijah, in which Ahab greets him as "my enemy" (21:20), the latter option appears likely.

Grand Finale (21:1-29)

Finally in this chapter Ahab directly interacts with both Jezebel and Elijah. The events begin "after these things," that is, after the Aramean wars of ch. 20, and the judgment leveled against Ahab (20:42).[17] Following on that judgment, ch. 21's judgment contributes to a growing picture of the king's covenant failure. After ch. 20's judgment, Ahab returns to Samaria "resentful and vexed" (20:43). It is the same attitude he adopts in the Naboth incident (v. 4), providing a further link to the preceding chapter.[18]

Ahab and Jezebel interact after the exchange between "Naboth the Jezreelite" and "Ahab the king of Samaria" (v. 1). Naboth speaks only in this exchange, but his importance throughout the chapter is signaled as he is named seventeen times; six of these add that he is "from Jezreel." Naboth will defend his ancestral inheritance. By contrast, Ahab is named only twelve times[19] and is introduced as "king of Samaria." This is a reference to the capital established by his father (16:24) and where Ahab was apparently born.[20] He has a palace in Jezreel, but the land he covets

---

17. The LXX places ch. 21 immediately following ch. 19, thus clustering the Ahab-Jezebel-Elijah materials together.

18. T. S. Hadjiev, "The King and the Reader: Hermeneutical Reflections on 1 Kings 20–21," *TynBul* 66 (2015): 68, notes the repetition indicates intentional placement of chs. 21 after ch. 20. As ch. 20 excludes Jezebel and Elijah, this paper agrees with Hadjiev's observation, but does not focus further on links between the chapters.

19. Jezebel is named eight times, and Elijah three.

20. Naboth the Jezreelite (v. 1), Elijah the Tishbite (v. 17), and Ahab of Samaria (vv. 1, 18) are each referenced by their birthplace, and (for Naboth and Ahab) primary residence. See Wray Beal, *Kings*, 271, 273.

is not within his patrimony: he is the interloper. Introduced as "king," the account presents Ahab's misunderstanding of kingly prerogatives and ends with judgment on Ahab's rule (vv. 20-22). Ironically, Omri bought Samaria and it became the dynasty's royal city, while Ahab's attempt to buy a vineyard will spark prophetic judgment against that dynasty.

Naboth defends his ancestral "inheritance" (*naḥalâ*; vv. 3-4), a word describing covenanted land gifted by YHWH according to Israel's tribes (Josh. 13:6-7). Such land is given as a sacred possession by YHWH and Naboth is loath to cede it. By contrast, Ahab (and Jezebel) only ever call it a "vineyard" (vv. 2, 6-7, 15-16), never an inheritance or possession. More, Ahab's desire to make it a "vegetable garden" is ominous, for the phrase is found elsewhere only in Deut. 11:10 where it describes Egypt, the place of slavery. These variant characterizations of the land show Naboth's regard for it as YHWH's possession, but Ahab's desire for it as an object for personal benefit. Naboth is mindful of covenant gifts; Ahab is not.[21]

In the exchange, Ahab's desire to purchase the land may not be inherently unlawful, but it does transgress Naboth's sense of "familial obligation."[22] Ahab is later judged for the means of achieving the land, not his desire for the land *per se*. Naboth refuses the king's generous offer, placing his conviction above the king's desire. Rather than be instructed by such covenant attentiveness, Ahab pouts. He is "resentful and vexed" as when earlier judged (20:43), turns to the wall, and refuses food.

Enter Jezebel, who shows immediate concern for her husband's disposition (v. 5). Ahab's response is artful in what it fails to communicate of his exchange with Naboth. He makes his offer appear generous but omits Naboth's reasons for refusal. The abrupt "I will not give you my vineyard!" makes Naboth appear unreasonable, and even churlish.[23] Beyond mischar-

---

21. Hadjiev, "King and the Reader," 69, argues the emphasis lies "not on the rationale behind Naboth's refusal but on the subsequent actions of the royal family." My argument places greater significance on the words applied to the land, but concurs on the import of subsequent royal action.

22. Helen Paynter, "Ahab—Heedless Father, Sullen Son: Humour and Intertextuality in 1 Kings 21," *JSOT* 41 (2017): 456, discusses scholarly disagreement on whether the sale is forbidden by patrimonial law (eg., Lev. 25:8-34) and concludes "[t]here appears to be broad consensus…that Naboth's refusal, whether he *could* or *would* not part with his patrimonial [*naḥalâ*], is rooted in a sense of familial obligation." Walsh, *Construction of a King*, 49, and Wray Beal, *Kings*, 274, understand the law does prohibit sale. However read, the point is that Ahab is not convinced by Naboth's reasons; if the law underlies Naboth's reasons, Ahab's character is further denigrated.

23. Paynter, "Ahab," 463, characterizes Ahab as a sullen son, a "wary dependent" who "tells [Jezebel] what she wants to hear."

acterizing Naboth, there is a more sinister intent behind Ahab's words. He has reason to anticipate Jezebel's response, for he had earlier told tales to Jezebel (19:1) and she had sought Elijah's death. Having witnessed her murderous streak against prophets who oppose royalty (18:4; 19:2) he has gauged action and speech to activate her as his agent. Thus later, Naboth's death is laid at his door.

Jezebel vows to obtain the vineyard for Ahab. Expressing her understanding of the exclusive rights of monarchy she exclaims: "Now you yourself are king over Israel!"[24] She will act on that conviction to achieve Ahab's desire. Surely, some such response is what Ahab counted on, and his culpability is supported by three additional narrative elements.

First, Ahab is the chapter's focus. Yairah Amit notes Ahab's prominence in six of the chapter's seven units, being absent only in the trial's climax (vv. 11-14). By comparison, Jezebel appears only in two scenes (vv. 4-10, 15-16), where she acts on the king's behalf, or communicates the acquisition of the king's desire.[25] In her appearances, she serves only as an agent in procuring the king's desire. She is culpable, but agentially so; narrative focus places greater culpability on Ahab.

Second, the focus of YHWH's judgment falls on Ahab (vv. 17-22, 24-26). Jezebel is not free from judgment (v. 23), but the sin against Naboth is specifically charged to Ahab's account, not Jezebel's (v. 19). It is Ahab's word that prompted Jezebel's action. And, while Jezebel is known as the author of the letters (v. 14) they bear the king's name and seal (v. 8). It is difficult to consider that Ahab is unaware of her actions.

Finally, Ahab's culpability is made by narrative implication. Jezebel (v. 15), the narrator (v. 16), and YHWH (vv. 18-19) all indicate Ahab has taken "possession" of Naboth's inheritance.[26] Naboth earlier cited the vineyard as his "inheritance" (*naḥalâ*), that is, land gifted by YHWH to be possessed within families. That Ahab is depicted as "possessing" Naboth's land utilizes the key word in a subtle reminder the king has

---

24. The phrase has various potential translational nuances, including sarcastic, interrogative, and emphatic/hortatory (as here); all express astonishment that a king may not demand his desire (see Paynter, "Ahab," 463–4).

25. Yairah Amit, *Reading Biblical Narratives: Literary Criticism and the Hebrew Bible* (Minneapolis: Fortress, 2001), 54–6, 87–8.

26. Nominal "possession," and verbal "to possess" and "dispossess" all derive from the root *yrš* and describe Israel's possession of gifted land (Josh. 1:11; 13:1, 6; 23:5; 24:4). The root is especially prominent in Josh. 13–21, where land is divided by tribal units. Israel's possession of land per YHWH's instruction is part of its covenant obedience.

circumvented YHWH's covenant not only through the murder, but by the possession of another's inheritance.

Whatever Jezebel's role, the king is not innocent.[27] When Jezebel communicates the success of her plot, the king asks no questions for he has anticipated such an outcome. He makes no remonstrance but moves immediately to possess the vineyard he coveted.

To answer the abuse of royal power, "the word of YHWH" comes to Elijah (v. 17). He is dispatched with the authority of "Thus says YHWH" (v. 19) to challenge Ahab the "king of Israel" (v. 18)[28] who has abused the prerogatives of Israelite kingship. Elijah is to accuse Ahab of "murder," a contravention of the covenant expressed in the Ten Commandments.[29] The prophesied judgment shows ironic justice, visiting upon Ahab Naboth's gruesome end (v. 19).

Ahab's "Have you found me, O my enemy?" shows the same hostility against the prophet as his earlier greeting, the "troubler of Israel" (18:17). The earlier greeting had addressed Elijah's relationship to Israel. Now, Ahab references a more personal relationship ("*my* enemy"), knowing the prophet comes to uncover Ahab's personal culpability.

The prophet is commissioned to give accusation and judgment (vv. 17-19), but the narrative omits their delivery. Instead, when prophet and king are face-to-face, Elijah names different sins (21:20-24), using YHWH's first-person voice to heighten the accusation's authority. The omission and the new accusation narratively contextualize the crime against Naboth within deeper covenant failures. The enumerated sins recall those named in the introduction (16:29-34) and for which the dynasties of Jeroboam (14:8-11) and Baasha (16:2-4, 7) have already been judged.

In a final summation (vv. 25-26), the narrator confirms Ahab's sin as "doing evil in the eyes of YHWH," for Jezebel "incited" him. The word "incite" refers primarily "to matters of religious policy, not the abuse of citizen rights and judicial corruption which are exemplified by the murder of Naboth."[30] The incitement is a reference to Jezebel's god Baal, as

---

27. Jezebel's motivations while worthy of exploration are outside the boundaries of this study. See Appler, "Queen to Cuisine," 62, who proposes different possibilities including "wifely duty and love for her husband…or disgust with Ahab's childish behavior."

28. The phrase is read, "Ahab the king of Israel [*who lives*] in Samaria." Samaria is understood as referencing his birthplace and primary residence. See also n. 20 above.

29. The verb has the root $rṣḥ$ as in the Ten Commandments (Exod. 20:13; Deut. 5:17).

30. Lasine, *Weighing Hearts*, 185, cf. n. 37 on p. 184. The verbal root *swt* is similarly used for religious deviance in Deut. 13:6.

confirmed in the next sentence: Ahab "went after idols." Ahab's idolatry includes Jeroboam's calves (16:31), but the focus here returns to the Baal worship introduced as Ahab's reign began. The sin is so terrible that Ahab is likened to the Amorites whom YHWH "dispossessed" (an ironic final occurrence of the root earlier translated as "possess"). The judgment against Ahab exhibits a similar level of severity as exhibited against the Amorites. There can be no doubt that Ahab is measured and found wanting for his sin against Naboth and (even more) God.

Ahab's sins (enumerated by YHWH, Elijah, and the narrator) reveal one hardened to YHWH, making his repentance surprising.[31] There have been no Mount Carmel fireworks (as had earlier precipitated Ahab's change of heart), but only the Word of YHWH spoken by the prophet. Yet that word has generated repentance that is surely genuine, for YHWH accepts it. Of what, however, does Ahab repent? Given that Baal worship is not eradicated until much later (2 Kgs 9–10), Ahab's humility is not an abdication of Baal worship, or at least not permanently. He and his house continue in that crime.[32] Rather, in light of the whole chapter, his act of repentance is for the specific crime of Naboth's murder.[33]

With this connection, it is instructive to compare Ahab's crime with David's crime against Bathsheba and Uriah, a kingly act that shows surprising parallels. Both kings covet another man's property. Both utilize an agent to achieve their desire, although David's active complicity casts him more negatively. Both crimes show an "effort to let the crime appear to be the natural result of an existing machinery or system."[34] Yet David does not see Nathan as a personal enemy, feels a "generous indignation"[35] at the parable which describes his crime, and repents before punishment is announced. On these measures, Ahab compares unfavorably to David: he labels Elijah a personal enemy, no "generous indignation" is evidenced, and repentance ensues only after he has heard the word of punishment.

---

31. Torn clothing, sackcloth, and fasting elsewhere signify repentance, eg., Gen. 37:34; Est. 4:1; Pss. 35:13; 69:11; Amos 8:10.

32. Maier, "Reflections," 73–4, argues similarly that it was not "repentance unto life" for there is no word of forgiveness, and Ahab continues committed to false prophets.

33. Hadjiev, "King and the Reader," 71, points here to the importance of the larger context, making a connection "between Ahab's idolatry and his apparent lack of mercy and justice."

34. H. P. Liddon, *Sermons on Old Testament Subjects* (London: Longmans, Green & Co., 1891), 221. For David, the "existing system" was the exigencies of warfare; for Ahab, the legal system (however falsely applied).

35. Ibid., 222.

It is as if he is "terrified at the *consequence* of his wrong-doing,—at the prophet's picture of the dogs licking his blood where they licked the blood of Naboth,—at the predicted ruin of his house."[36] And never does Ahab affirm with David that he has "sinned against YHWH" (2 Sam. 12:13). Most damning of all, Ahab's crime against Naboth stands within, and is evidentiary of, a greater crime: idolatry.

YHWH does receive Ahab's repentance for his role in Naboth's murder. But Ahab's idolatry remains untouched. No word of forgiveness is therefore given, and judgment is not removed, only delayed.[37]

Final Danse Macabre *(2 Kings 9–10)*

Ahab dies in 1 Kings 22, but his dynasty continues until Jehu usurps the crown (2 Kgs 9–10). Jehu's coup is a bloody *danse macabre*, destroying everyone attached to Ahab's house in fulfillment of Elijah's prophetic word. In these two chapters appears the final narrative collocation of Ahab with Jezebel and Elijah. We turn now to reflect briefly on each character's graphic appearance, noting through each the ongoing characterization of Ahab.

Jezebel (who alone of the three remains alive) haughtily challenges the usurper only to die gruesomely by Jehu's command (2 Kgs 9:30-37). Splattered and trampled, eaten by dogs with little left to reclaim, the prophetic word is fulfilled (21:23) and Jehu's final scatological reference consigns her to ignominy.

Jezebel's presence also is exerted through her influence. Named the source of non-peace within Israel, her "harlotries and sorceries" evidence her evil (2 Kgs 9:22). Her influence extends to her "house"—the Baal temple and cult. Like its patron queen, it is destroyed (10:15-28) and a final scatological reference (10:27) mirrors the queen's ignominious disposition.

These depictions carry carnivalesque overtones that include the overturning of hierarchies, juxtaposition of the sacred and profane, scatology, and mock crowning/decrowning.[38] Through them, Jezebel and her house

---

36. Ibid.

37. A similar delay of judgment is accorded Solomon (1 Kgs 11:35). See also 2 Chron. 12:12; 32:26; 33:12-13.

38. Francisco O. García-Treto, "The Fall of the House: A Carnivalesque Reading of 2 Kings 9 and 10," in *Reading Between Texts: Intertextuality and the Hebrew Bible*, ed. Danna Nolan Fewell (Louisville: Westminster John Knox, 1992), 153–71; Helen Paynter, *Reduced Laughter: Seriocomic Features and their Functions in the Book of Kings*, BibInt 142 (Leiden: Brill, 2016), 64–115; for a narrative study attentive to these traits see Lissa M. Wray Beal, *The Deuteronomist's Prophet: Narrative Control*

are mocked and cast aside. As in Ahab's introduction (1 Kgs 16:29-34) it is a polemic that also discredits the king who married her.

Although dead, Ahab's "ghost" appears in the dynasty that bears his name. Reference to the "house of Ahab" is highly concentrated in these chapters, highlighting its importance.[39] Ahab also appears through his descendants, Kings Jehoram and Ahaziah,[40] and Ahab's seventy sons. First Jehoram and Ahaziah are destroyed (2 Kgs 9:24-27), then in a bloody dispatching of heads in baskets, Ahab's sons (10:1-8). Their destruction is an exorable fulfillment of YHWH's word against Ahab and his house (21:21-22). The king partnered with Jezebel and Baal, and thus reaps Deuteronomic destruction (Deut. 30:15-18).

Finally, prophetic fulfillment communicates Elijah's presence. Not only is he named as the "prophet of record" throughout (2 Kgs 9:25-26, 36-37; 10:10, 17),[41] but it is by his word Jehu is anointed. The commission was given originally to Elijah (19:16); now, Elisha commissions a young prophet for the task (2 Kgs 9:1-3). Yet, when the young prophet anoints Jehu it is Elijah's words—not Elisha's—that he intones (compare 2 Kgs 9:6-10 with 1 Kgs 21:20-24).[42]

By this device, Elijah is present, and his words anoint Jehu. The usurper fulfills Elijah's word and in Jehu's zeal against Ahab, Jezebel, and Baal (2 Kgs 10:16), Elijah's own zeal against the house of Ahab (19:10, 14) is reconfigured in Jehu's action.[43] Jehu acts like an "avatar of Elijah," working destruction like that "severest of prophets."[44]

Dance Postlude

The concluding *dance macabre* once again brings together Ahab, Jezebel, and Elijah. In their final interaction, the narrative closes as it opened, proving the Deuteronomic warning with which this exploration began.

---

of Approval and Disapproval in the Story of Jehu (2 Kings 9 and 10), LHBOTS 478 (New York: T&T Clark, 2007).

39. Six of eleven occurrences in 2 Kings appear in these two chapters (2 Kgs 8:18, 27 [three times]; 9:7, 8, 9; 10:10, 11, 30; 21:13).

40. The southern Ahaziah is related to Ahab by marriage (2 Kgs 8:18).

41. Wray Beal, *Kings*, 373.

42. Explored in Wray Beal, *Deuteronomist's Prophet*, 60–8.

43. An exploration of Jehu's zeal identifying him with Elijah is found in Wray Beal, *Deuteronomist's Prophet*, 127–8.

44. Burke O. Long, *2 Kings*, FOTL 10 (Grand Rapids; Eerdmans, 1991), 121 and 138; similarly Lasine, *Weighing Hearts*, 126.

Ahab is introduced as exceedingly wicked. In his choice of Jezebel and Baal idolatry he aligns himself not with the Living God who alone controls the rain, crops, and life, but with the impotent Baal, and thus with death. The succeeding narrative draws Ahab in complex ways. It is a reminder that biblical narrative attends to the complexities of living within covenant—a complexity that is no less pertinent today. Even the wicked are not always wholly villainous, nor the faithful wholly righteous. At times Ahab continues to be responsive to Jezebel and Baal. At times he is responsive to the lead of Elijah, the representative of YHWH and life. Ahab even shows repentance—however partial or transitory. Yet by his ongoing commitment to Jezebel's Baal, his fate is sealed and death and destruction overtake his later house. The queen who incited him is dispatched brutally, as is her house. All leave the dance floor in ignominy.

Only Elijah remains on the floor, representing YHWH and life. If only Ahab had chosen *this* partner, his dance would not have met with death and destruction, but the life and prosperity Deuteronomy promised.

Chapter 8

JEZEBEL NOW:
GAZING THROUGH MULTIPLE WINDOWS

Athalya Brenner-Idan

The reader can interpret—indeed, can pass judgment on the character. That is because, in one way or another, the character is readable, or shall we say "visible": the reader "sees" it. The reader sees it through the medium of an agent other than the character, an agent that sees and, seeing, causes to be seen… [T]he focalizer influences how the reader perceives the character seen. But our game does not stop there: we cannot determine "who sees" without taking into account the medium through which we perceive that sight: the narrating. So we must know "who speaks." "The one who speaks" is the narrating agent, set in motion by and representing the author (the answer to the question "Who writes?")…[1]

Focalization is, then, the relation between the vision and what is seen, perceived.[2]

To Begin: Guidelines

"In interpreting narratives, too often—it seems needless to say—critics pass directly from the author to the character."[3] This is especially applicable to biblical literature. The biblical authors and narrators, external to the text and internal to it, seem to pull us in the direction of their agenda,

---

1. Meike Bal, "Narration and Focalization," in *Narrative Theory: Critical Concepts in Literary and Cultural Studies, Vol. 1*, ed. M. Bal (London/New York: Routledge, 2004), 272–3.
2. Mieke Bal, *Narratology: Introduction to the Theory of Narrative*, 4th ed. (Toronto: University of Toronto Press, 2017), 133.
3. Bal, "Narration and Focalization," 273.

to entice us to their corner, and all too often we gladly comply. We take their value judgment for granted, and make do with analyzing technicalities and devices; and in focusing on the artistry of *how* this is done.

Going beyond this position into the recognition that readers' perception of characters depends on what the reader *sees*, as well as on what the author/narrator *shows*; and that a narrative, any narrative or text, may contain more than one "focalization," to substitute for the older point-of-view term, is well explained by Mieke Bal.[4] In the following reading, I use her wise counsel as a first guide for seeing, listening to, and assessing the humanoid apparitions that inhabit a biblical text.

If a narrative may contain more than one focalizer, in fact every time a character is seen/heard/acts she is the focus—albeit temporary—of the plot, then an interesting exercise is to imagine a different focalization for each character; while recognizing the pull of the author that cannot be ignored, it can be put aside for the duration, in the sense that the narrator's focalization will not be privileged over narratees' focalizations—at least for the duration. This is my second guideline, and here the film *Rashomon* and its relative open-end presentation are helpful as a third guide (as will be shown in a little while).

A transparent, if somewhat limiting, way of presenting a character as focalizing her or his angle is to pretend to tell that angle in the first-person mode. A pretense, certainly, substituting an omniscient reader/critic for the omniscient and judgmental author/narrator. However, this may flesh out the character and take it beyond the author's intent. I've done it before[5] and find it liberating as a clarifying reading technique. This is my fourth guide.

A fifth guide is to choose a text one has read before, many times, in order to ask: now that I look at it differently, what gain have I achieved?

And finally, a general guide: this is surely reading against the grain, so is it worth trying?

The Characters in the Text

Gazing at "Jezebel" as she is last seen alive inside the biblical text, all made up and gazing at Jehu through the lattice of the royal palace in

---

4. For instance, see the quotations at the head of this chapter, and Bal, *Narratology*, 104–24, 132–49.

5. Athalya Brenner, *I Am: Biblical Woman Tell Their Own Stories* (Minneapolis: Fortress, 2004); idem, "Michal and David: Love between Enemies?" in *The Fate of King David: The Past and Present of a Biblical Icon*, ed. T. Linafelt, C. Camp, and T. Beal (New York/London: Continuum, 2010), 260–70.

Jezreel, and then she's dead, can be done from various perspectives, or focal points. You, the reader of "her" story, please consider:

1. Which character do you mostly identify with? With King Ahab? With Jezebel? With Naboth? With the accusers and elders in Naboth's trial? With Jehu? With the prophet Elijah? Or with Athaliah[u], J[eh]oram, Ahaziah[u]?
2. Are you from Tyre, identifying with a foreigner who witnesses the events from another land?
3. Do you believe the biblical narrator in-the-text?
4. Or do you believe that the biblical author[s], that elusive entity, know[s] best?
5. Do you wonder about lacunae—where, for instance, is Naboth's wife in this story? Presumably his children had a mother or mothers?
6. And finally, is a multiple-focalization of the narrative characters in any way more convincing than one adhering to the adopted author/narrator focalization?

Looking at the Characters

Much has been written by feminist scholars on Jezebel[6]—present company included[7]—in recent decades. The general if not exclusive trend has

---

6. For instance, Susan Ackerman, "On Queen Mothers," in *Warrior, Dancer, Seductress, Queen: Women in Judges and Biblical Israel*, ABRL (New York: Doubleday, 1998), 128–80; Eleanor Ferris Beach, *The Jezebel Letters: Religion and Politics in Ninth-Century Israel* (Minneapolis: Fortress, 2005); Fernando Candido da Silva, "To Whom Do Jezebel's Remains Belong?" in *Texts@Contexts: Samuel, Kings and Chronicles, Vol. 1*, ed. Athalya Brenner-Idan and Archie C. C. Lee (London: Bloomsbury T&T Clark, 2017), 24–45; Patricia Dutcher-Walls, *Jezebel: Portraits of a Queen* (Collegeville: Liturgical Press, 2004); Janet Howe Gaines, *Music in the Old Bones: Jezebel through the Ages* (Carbondale: Southern Illinois University Press, 1999); Lesley Hazleton, *Jezebel: The Untold Story of the Bible's Harlot Queen* (New York: Doubleday, 2007); Jennifer L. Koosed, "Death of Jezebel," *Bible Odyssey*, http://www.bibleodyssey.org/people/related-articles/death-of-jezebel.aspx; Judith E. McKinlay, *Reframing Her: Biblical Women in Postcolonial Focus*, Bible in the Modern World 1 (Sheffield: Sheffield Phoenix, 2004); Tina Pippin, "Jezebel Re-Vamped," in *A Feminist Companion to Samuel and Kings*, ed. A. Brenner (Sheffield: Sheffield Academic, 1994), 196–206; Phyllis Trible, "Exegesis for Storytellers and Other Strangers," *JBL* 114 (1995): 3–19; Gale A. Yee, "Coveting the Vineyard: An Asian American Reading of 1 Kings 21," in Brenner-Idan and Lee, eds, *Texts@Contexts*, 46–64.

7. Athalya Brenner, "Jezebel," *Shnaton* 5/6 (1981–82): 27–39 (Hebrew); idem, *The Israelite Woman: Social Role and Literary Type in Biblical Narrative*, BibSem 2

been a departure from previous bible[8] commentary agreement. Jezebel has previously been considered by commentators as an evil woman,[9] in collaboration with the biblical fragments that tell her story: a foreigner although of royal blood (1 Kgs 16:21; 2 Kgs 9:34), one who led her husband astray after foreign gods (1 Kgs 16:21-23), persecuted Elijah (19:1-2), caused the unlawful murder of Naboth (ch. 21), and was finally killed for her sins as a prostitute and sorcerer by Jehu and eaten by dogs (2 Kgs 9). And yet, as in so many biblical passages, other readings are possible, and perhaps synchronously valid even if they seem contradictory. Let us remind ourselves that stories are informed by their readers and their readers' agendas as much as by their authors, narrators and editors. And so are the characters within those stories.

In this contribution I shall try to refer to these different and at times conflicted portraits of Jezebel the wife, parent and monarch, Rashomon-style,[10] relying on past and present Jezebel scholarship, but also striving to clarify through this case study readerly roles and contextual positions.

(Sheffield: JSOT Press, 1985); Athalya Brenner-Idan, "On Scholarship and Related Animals: A Personal View from and for the Here and Now," *JBL* 135 (2016): 6–17.

8. This reader/writer habitually refers to the Hebrew god as Yhwh, and spells "bible" in the lower case (unless citing secondary literature). These are ideological choices, even though they do not agree with the more common formats of "Bible/s" and Yhwh/YHWH privileging both with uppercase and/or small caps.

9. For instance, John Gray, *I & II Kings*, OTL, 3rd ed. (London: SCM, 1977); J. A. Montgomery and H. S. Gehman, *A Critical and Exegetical Commentary on the Book of Kings*, ICC (Edinburgh: T. & T. Clark, 1951); Joseph Robinson, *The First Book of Kings*, CBC (Cambridge: Cambridge University Press, 1972). For comprehensive bibliographies see Patrick T. Cronauer, *The Stories about Naboth the Jezreelite: A Source, Composition, and Redaction Investigation of 1 Kings 21 and Passages in 2 Kings 9*, LHBOTS 424 (New York: T&T Clark, 2005); Dagmar Pruin, *Geschichten und Geschichte: Isebel als literarische und historische Gestalt*, OBO 222 (Fribourg: Academic Press; Göttingen: Vandenhoeck & Ruprecht, 2006).

10. The following paragraphs are quoted from the pages of the IMDB website (https://www.imdb.com/title/tt0042876/ and further) dealing with the well-appreciated Japanese film directed by Akira Kurosawa (1950). The film is called *Rashomon*, after the place where the action or rather its different memories unfold. The point of the film is, indeed, how events seem to change when different characters/voices narrate them—even beyond the grave. More information can be found on the site. Below are two summaries of the plotline, which—once more—proves the point.

(1) "In twelfth-century Japan, a samurai and his wife are attacked by the notorious bandit Tajomaru, and the samurai ends up dead. Tajomaru is captured shortly afterward and is put on trial, but his story and the wife's are so completely different that a psychic is brought in to allow the murdered man to give his own testimony.

I shall not delve into intricacies of authorly intentions and literary techniques, but attempt to uncover, even if in a cursory manner, what "happens" to a biblical character when viewed through specific readerly lenses. The situation is: you, as a reader, are drawn to identify with some characters in the text and dissociate yourself from their opponents or enemies. The question is: whose side are you on, which side do you own, when you read stories linked to Jezebel? Obviously, more than one identification with one character is possible. However, a sliding scale from relatively positive to relatively negative assessment of a story's character is always present, consciously or otherwise, in the readerly [re] construction of a story. In order to make my intentions clear, I shall take the theoretical need for readerly identification with a story's characters one step further, by fictitiously endeavoring to "speak" the biblical characters in the first-person mode.

With Ahab, Who Says: Jezebel Is My beloved and Reliable Spouse

According to 1 Kgs 16:31-33 I took Jezebel the Tyrian as a wife and worshipped her god, the Baal. Please note: this was a diplomatic marriage, embodying a pact with her original Tyre city state. And yet, to say that I neglected Yhwh's worship is ridiculous: both sons I had

---

He tells yet another completely different story. Finally, a woodcutter who found the body reveals that he saw the whole thing, and his version is again completely different from the others."

(2) "Sheltering from a rainstorm in the derelict Rashomon gatehouse, a commoner wants to hear the strange story that has horrified a priest and confounded a woodcutter. They tell him about a murder inquiry at which they have just appeared as witnesses. Tajomaru (a bandit with a reputation for murder and lust) had managed to tie up a samurai and rape his wife. The woodcutter had discovered the dead body of the samurai in the forest, and the bandit was arrested the following day. But how the samurai was killed was unclear. Strangely, the three people involved all claim to be responsible. The bandit describes winning a dramatic sword fight. The distraught woman all but admits she was driven to stab her husband in desperation. Through a medium, the dead samurai claims his wife was treacherous, and that this drove him to suicide. Something has motivated at least two of them to lie, grotesquely subverting truth, justice, and decency. Even the woodcutter has not been forthright, and ironically, he feels that he too must lie. He changes his story, claims to have witnessed the crime, and gives yet another (the fourth) wild version of the samurai's death. The commoner is not fooled, and it only reinforces his cynical view of life. Then the men make a discovery, and their reactions reveal that, though there is terrible evil and mistrust in the world, there is also goodness."

with Jezebel, and who briefly reigned as monarchs after my death, had Yhwh-theophoric names (Ahazuah[u], 2 Kgs 1:52; Jehoram, 2 Kgs 3:1), not to mention Athaliah. It would be more accurate to state that we directed between us two official worships: mine, the dominant one, a Yhwh-worship; and Jezebel's, the secondary one, a Baal-Asherah worship. This way we had a dual religious establishment under our shared control. And note, unlike Jezebel, personally, I'm never accused of victimizing Yhwh's prophets.

According to 1 Kings 21, I get angry then descend into depression when Naboth declines to sell his vineyard to me. Jezebel is quick to notice my mood, then promises to give me my wish: why shouldn't I have the land closest to my palace, for security and other reasons? This she does, taking care to do it legally: Naboth is accused of treason and killed. I am then free to "inherit" Naboth's vineyard, which I do (v. 16). I am not involved in the process, which seems to be legal (treason is rewarded by death; the culprit's property then reverts to the king), although it is, from the narrator's viewpoint, fabricated. I get my wish. Jezebel gives it to me, as I implicitly trust her to do. It is only when I hear Elijah's sharp rebuke that I go into mourning (vv. 19-27). For what? For Yhwh's verdict? For the prophet's harsh forecast of mine and Jezebel's death? This is not stated. Do I regret the whole affair, do I admonish or punish Jezebel, do I limit her authority, do I take away her authority to act for me (vv. 8-9)? You readers are not told. She remains my honored spouse, and probably a $g^e b\hat{i}r\bar{a}h$—at least an influential King's mother, if not formally a Queen mother—after my death at war. Sure, it would seem that the narrator would not wish to whitewash my silent complicity with Jezebel's actions. However, this leaves you, the readers, with the impression that I, Ahab, has trusted Jezebel as a personal and professional partner. Also, I do not return the vineyard to the original family owners by way of rectification—at least, as far as you are [not] told.

With Jezebel, Who Says:
I Don't Understand What All the Fuss Is About

Ahab has told you: I was his trusted queen.[11] He had other wives, certainly, but not one of them had my influence, or fortune, or education, or savvy.

---

11. Unproblematically admitted by Montgomery and Gehman, *Book of Kings*, 312, but they are in the minority! See also Zafrira Ben Barak, "The Status and Right of the *Gebīrâ*," in Brenner, ed., *A Feminist Companion to Samuel and Kings*, 170–85.

He relied on me, totally. I deserved his devotion, as I proved during his lifetime and also when I acted as regent after his death.

It seems pointless to try and defend my position further, what with the hostile manner my story is told, and centuries of reception history cooperating with the bible's negative assessment.[12] And yet, as you can clearly understand, for instance, from Beach's imaginative yet insightful book about me,[13] what was at stake here was a different vision of Israelite monarchy. This should be emphasized. My own vision, and to a certain extent Ahab's, was copied on what I learnt as a royal child: the land belongs to its king and this is a civil matter; and religious worship is sponsored by royalty as well. The biblical writers' vision was: the land belongs to Yhwh and is a religious matter; religious life is or should be dictated by Yhwh's prophets and self-proclaimed emissaries. Such conflicting ideologies had to clash. I was first a winner, then historically a loser. And yet, as you can learn from Jehu's actions, his usurping of the Crown—even though he claimed divine sponsorship—was not complete until after murdering me. Such was my power.

With Naboth: A Man Wronged?

I'm sure most of you identify with me and my reasons for not giving up my vineyard. At least those of you who feel connected to the land you inherited, family land for generations, and against powerful neighboring landlords. And the way I was disposed of, and what happened to my property as a result.

Do you nevertheless entertain a faint notion that I simply didn't want to give in, or that my stand was the beginning of negotiations?[14] I can assure you this is wrong.[15] See, the story's narrator and the prophet Elijah

---

12. See Yairah Amit, "Design and Meaning in the Story of Naboth," *Beit Miqra'* (2015): 19–36 (Hebrew); Yael Shemesh, "A Gendered View," *Beit Miqra'* (2015): 117–40 (Hebrew).

13. Eleanor Ferris Beach, *The Jezebel Letters: Religion and Politics in Ninth-Century Israel* (Minneapolis: Fortress, 2005).

14. Brenner-Idan, "On Scholarship," 11, 13; Phillippe Guillaume, "Naboth's Vineyard," *Bible Odyssey*, http://www.bibleodyssey.org/en/passages/main-articles/naboths-vineyard-1-kgs-21.aspx; idem, "Naboth the Nabob: A View from Assyrian Jezreel," *UF* 46 (2015): 161–82.

15. So most older commentators. Also newer ones: for instance Y. Fleishman, "Ahab's Request and Naboth's Response," *Beit Miqra'* (2015): 92–116 (Hebrew); Gilbert Okuro Ojwang, "Juridical Impotence in the Naboth Story in the Context of Kenya's New Land Laws," in Brenner-Idan and Lee, eds, *Texts@Contexts*, 65–94;

and, most significant of all, Yhwh, are on my side.[16] I deserve pity and empathy and admiration for my ideological stance, and for my end. Yes, I wasn't poor but a landlord and a man of substance. But even the rich deserve justice.

Let me add one more note. I had a vineyard. Ahab wanted to make it into a garden, a food-producing field, or perhaps a recreational ground, or a secure ground next to his palace. It's my revenge that his palace is no more. But even now, at the Jezreel dig, a wine press has been found.[17] My legacy, even if it's not my own press.

With Participants in Naboth's Trial: We Had No Choice

We, the elders and dignitaries and commoners of Jezreel, had no choice. What Jezebel commanded, we had to do. True, we knew her demand was immoral and against our customs, but we couldn't resist. We were under pressure. Even the narrator understands that and doesn't condemn us directly.

As for our two "witnesses," the accusers against Naboth, well, they are defined as "scoundrels" (1 Kgs 21:10, 13-14); there is no way to even consider their viewpoint on the story.

With Jehu, Who Says: I Believe, at Least Proclaim to Believe, that Jezebel Is a Whore and Sorceress

I was just a military officer in Ramoth Gilead, the important defense line against the Arameans east of the Jordan river, when a man claiming Yhwh's authority through the prophet Elisha came to crown me privately as the Israelite king, with a mission to destroy Ahab and his dynasty and their Baal worship. At first I thought he was either crazy or joking; however, my colleagues' response soon made me accept (2 Kgs 9:1-14).

Anne Marie Kitz, "Naboth's Vineyard after Mari and Amarna," *JBL* 134 (2015): 529–45; Stephen C. Russell, "Ideologies of Attachment in the Story of Naboth's Vineyard," *BTB* 44 (2014): 29–39.

16. See Amit, "Design and Meaning"; Alexander Rofé, "Naboth's Vineyard: The Story's Origin and Its Purpose," *Mishpatim* 14 (1985): 521–6 (Hebrew); idem, "The Vineyard of Naboth: The Origin and Message of the Story," *VT* 38 (1988): 104–89.

17. N. Franklin, J. Ebeling, and P. Guillaume, "An Ancient Winery in Jezreel," *Beit Miqra'* (2015): 9–18 (Hebrew); Norma Franklin, "Jezreel before and after Jezebel," in *Israel in Transition: From Late Bronze II to Iron IIa (c. 1250–850 B.C.E.), Vol. 1: The Archaeology*, ed. Lester L. Grabbe, LHBOTS 491 (London: Bloomsbury T&T Clark, 2010), 45–53.

Why was I chosen for this mission? Truthfully, I don't know. Neither does anybody else. I was an army commander, not a politician or a religious leader. But why should I not seize the chance for power, thus legitimated? The audience with "one of the sons of the prophets" (9:1) was private; nobody could dispute my claims as to its contents. I had enough army support to carry it out. So I murdered my way through the related royal houses of Israel and Judah, and didn't stop until everybody was out of the way—necessary cruelty, all this bloodshed, accepted by my contemporaries as zealousness for Yhwh, no doubt.

Why did I not rest until I had Jezebel killed? I hate to admit it but this should be obvious. Although a mere woman, she was of royal blood, thus symbolic of a connection to Tyre, which I wanted stopped. But, more importantly, and I do hate to admit it, her power was so great that without killing her I couldn't achieve my mission and ambition.

So I branded her a whore and witch (9:22); had her killed by her own eunuchs (9:32-33). Note how, even when she knew her end was near, she put on makeup and taunted me verbally (9:30-32). She had guts. Only after that could I have a treaty meal as the new sovereign, pointedly burying Jezebel's remains only after the meal (9:34-37). Only after that could I continue in the killing trajectory of Ahab's dynasty (ch. 10).

I hate to admit it, truly. It annoys me. But Jezebel was important. I had to get her out of the way in order to realize my ambition of a complete takeover. She was more of an obstacle than her royal sons. Shame on the kingdom of Israel for allowing such a situation! Oh well. Now, was she more wicked, shall we say, than I was, in my cruelty to Ahab's relations? Well sure, do believe that, since, as the bible tells you, Yhwh was on my side, not hers.

With Elijah, Who Says: Jezebel Is a Rival to Fear

I didn't see Ahab as my chief adversary. I was never afraid of appearing before him and delivering shocking prophesies: not before I killed the Baal prophets on Mount Carmel and not after (1 Kgs 18), not after the Naboth affair when I prophesied doom for his dynasty (21:18-22). He never threatened me, even as he saw me as a threat; and hearing Yhwh's response to the Naboth affair, he regretted it and thus saved his dynasty till after his death (21:25). Also, please note: before he goes to his last battle, he consults with Yhwh's prophets, not any other "prophets" (if the nameless "king of Israel" in 22:5-28 indeed refers to Ahab, as it appears to do in this context).

But Jezebel was another story. She was the patroness of Baal/Asherah worship. She decimated Yhwh's prophets (18:4a). She incited Ahab to follow her ways (21:25, the narrator's remark). So when she sent messengers to me, swearing by Yhwh's name that she would kill me (19:1-2), I believed her. I was afraid for my life.[18] I left for Judah and then went to the desert in order to save my life (v. 3). There I had an important divine revelation that named Elisha as my successor and Jehu as the next king of Israel. If I returned to Israelite country, that was only to deliver god's response to the Naboth affair to Ahab. I never clashed with Jezebel again.

This is to say: the adversary I was fighting against wasn't Ahab. My adversary was Jezebel. A woman; a foreigner; a Baal and Asherah worshipper; wicked and immoral. Nevertheless, she yielded power, and not only in her husband's name. I had to flee, especially if I wanted to carry out my prophetic mission. I had to admit that she could get me. This is the real measure of her power. This is why my prophecy to Ahab about his end was also extended to her (21:23), and carried out by Jehu (2 Kgs 9:36-37).

Luckily, history and commentary are on my side too: until recently, nobody paid much attention to Jezebel. The stories in Kings were considered mine, and Ahab's. Fortunately.[19]

With Athaliah[u], J[eh]oram and Ahaziah[u]: Jezebel Is Family, our Mother or Grandmother, a Strong and Supportive Woman

We, Ahaziah[u] and J[eh]oram, are Ahab's and Jezebel's sons. It's not clear to us why the bible mentions Ahab as our father (1 Kgs 22:41 and 52 for Ahaziah[u]; 2 Kgs 3:1 for J[eh]oram) but declines to

---

18. "I was afraid": the MT here has the consonants *wyr'*, pointed to mean "and he [Elijah] *saw.*" However, as is clear from the context, it should have been pointed to read *wa-yirā'*, "he was afraid." So the LXX, other ancient translation and modern English translations (for instance the JPS 1985 and the NRSV).

19. It has been customary for commentators to look for the different strands of the Kings story and define them mainly as an Elijah cycle (Gray, *I & II Kings*, following Fohrer and others) and Ahab sources combined with some secondary sources. This may be correct from the perspective of source criticism. However, it misses the point in the sense that, as consumers, we share in the final product, the combined story, whether we do it critically or otherwise, and this is how we help create the characterization.

mention Jezebel as our mother: that she at least is recognized as such is given by Jehu's unflattering portrait of her just before he kills me (2 Kgs 9:22). Otherwise, there's no formal mention of our maternal heritage. Is it because of the writers' bias, so they neither recognize her as queen, co-ruler with our father in his lifetime, nor as biological or formal queen mother? We wonder. True, Ahab must have had many wives, as befits his status and wealth, and many (symbolically seventy! 2 Kgs 10:1) sons. None of the other wives is mentioned by name. Jezebel was his chief wife, his queen. It makes sense that she was the mother of us, his successors.

At any rate, we have no complaints about our mother: as ruler, as religious functionary, as great support for all our ventures. None whatsoever.

I, Athaliah[u], am variously described as the Judahite King J[eh]oram's wife (18:1), Ahab's paternal sister by Omri (2 Kgs 8:20; 2 Chron. 22:2) or, by implication, his daughter (2 Kgs 8:18, 27; 2 Chron. 21:6) but without mention of my mother's name. Once again: the maternal line is important: this is evident already in the Genesis Matriarchal stories. It makes no difference whether I'm Ahab's sister or daughter. But if the latter, then, as in the case of my brothers (or uncles; but it makes more sense they are my brothers, of the same generation not the older one), the name of our mother is suppressed.

My personal history is known. My son King Ahaziah[u] is killed by Jehu, together with all his royal relatives of Judah and Israel. I seize the throne, and reign for six years, until a priestly coup in favor of the child Joash deposes me (1 Kgs 11; 2 Chron. 22:10–23:15). I am accused of killing all royal descendants after my royal son dies; for your information, so did other kings in the ancient Near East (King Solomon and my own husband Jehoram are pertinent examples), which doesn't seem to be judged by the narrator as harshly as my case. At any rate, if I managed to reign in Jerusalem for six years before being liquidated, a woman and not of Davidic descent, including entry into the temple, it means that I had the knowledge and resources for that, so much so that this episode of a reigning female monarch in preexilic Judah could not be obliterated. Now, from whom did I learn statecraft, religious leadership and other skills, and from whom did I learn that a woman could reign in her own right? From Jezebel, of course; she is the shining example I followed. And it seems that I was more fortunate than Jezebel: I did manage to reign longer after my husband's death that she did after her husband's death.

With a Person from Tyre: Things Seem Different to Me from Afar

Well. I've just read the chapters where our royal princess Jezebel features, in the narratives that were included in the biblical libraries. I look at the stories and I rub my eyes in disbelief. To me, she behaved perfectly in accordance with ancient Near Eastern traditions, specifically North Semitic (including Phoenician and Ugaritic) traditions and laws. As she can tell you, royal women participated in governance, often as priestly officials (see Enheduanna daughter of Sargon, for instance): this buttressed the royal hold on economic resources and ideological control. She probably got an education, might have been literate (so could write letters, 1 Kgs 21) and interpreted the law to her advantage. Even in Israel, she must have had her financial resources and her own court: this way she could feed Baal and Asherah prophets "at her table" (18:19). It seems to me that she wanted to introduce our laws that, as in Ugarit, attributed ultimate land ownership to the local king, to her new domain. She believed Ahab is entitled to the piece of land he coveted. Yes, she must have understood that she couldn't apply her wish without some twisting of the facts. She faked a situation, but still tried to present it as legal. So what else is new? Is it the first time matters of policy have been resolved by questionable methods? Don't be naïve! Be realistic.

With the Biblical Narrator

As the narrator-in-the-text of this composite writing, 1 Kgs 16:29 to 2 Kings 10, my viewpoint is consistent. As I relate my story, I make no secret of my understanding of the characters operating within it. Yhwh's prophets are positive figures. Ahab is mainly negative, but weak rather than cruel, and at least a passable military leader. Jezebel is the villain of the piece, corrupt and corrupting. As the story unfolds, with me propelling the plot and also supplying asides, I never waiver. She is disgusting. And Jehu, who calls her a prostitute and a sorceress, expresses my opinion exactly.

Fortunately for me, most bible consumers tend to accept my viewpoint: after all, I move the plot, don't I? Hence, they also accept my judgment of the characters, consciously or otherwise, critically or otherwise.

With the Biblical Writer/Editor (an Elusive Entity), because He(!) Knows Best

I am the author or, if you wish, author/editor of this cluster of stories. When I approached my task, I first assembled a heap of sources, some from the time and some later recorded, some transmitted orally and some in writing. My sources were variegated: from prophetic stories about Elijah and Elisha to court documents to previous writers' opinions, from fact to fiction, from pious sentiments to editorial postscripts. I weaved the stories into a collage and placed the narrator-in-the-text as story teller and commentator on the action and the characters. He is my alter ego. He represents my interests. The way he tells the story shapes it as, primarily, a conflict of loyalties, one positive and one darkly negative. In that sense, the narrator is not only my voice-in-the-text, but also a character in it. A character whose *verbal* assessment of other characters in the textual passage most bible readers believe above the evidence of action and words of other characters within it.

Where Is Naboth's Wife?

It is very strange that I do not appear in the narrative where my husband, sons, property, life is summarily crushed in favor of others' desires. It seems I count even less than my menfolk. And nobody cares.

To Conclude, or, Whom to Believe?

The pericope that runs from 1 Kings 16 to 2 Kings 10 (from the ascent of the House of Omri to Jehu) is certainly complex, woven of many strands by many editors and authors, at various times and places.

As the audience, even if we take the narrative apart while critiquing it, we finally put it together again. And then we are drawn into its spectacle. The narrator, where present, fields for the author or the editor: "he" (yes, in biblical literature, mostly a "he") is a conduit for the author's view, a focalization tool, so to speak. The characters are presented as seen through "their" eyes, and according to "their" intentions and assessment. And "they" are omniscient: "their" knowledge of factors relevant to the story line is greater than the characters in the story, and the story's audience as well. As the audience, we tend to collaborate, adopt "their" positions, identify with "their" hero and so forth, then push back to discover "their" presumed intentions.

But what happens if we liberate the characters and let them talk back at us, as if that were possible? What happens if we suspend judgment and identification until they do? What happens if we demote the narrator into a non-privileged character position, hence also implicating the author's position? What if?

This is what happens if we let them tell their own partly imaginative, partly sub-textual tales, pitching them alongside and against each other. This is what happens in this MT text where Jezebel features, from foreign birth to death.

- Not all characters perceive Jezebel as a negative persona: Ahab and her sons certainly do not. Neither does Athaliah[u]. Her family members, at the very least, respect her and her abilities.
- All characters who condemn her emphasize her foreignness, as symbolized inter alia by her pagan worship.
- She is universally feared by those who hate her, like Elijah and Jehu. Even they acknowledge her power.
- Which leads us to a conclusion: Jezebel the character is a powerful and influential female figure. As such, she cannot but be judged negatively by her male adversaries, in and out of the text. And if Yhwh is considered a character in this story as well (which is obvious, I think, but has not been done above), as he is in so many biblical passages, then Jezebel dares to challenge him, so we are directed not to be on her side

Texts depend on their readers/listeners to come alive. The characters in them are certainly guided by external authors and internal narrators, but are equally created by the texts' consumers. It is up to us to be conscious of how and when we should collaborate and when to employ a resistant reading. And for what purpose.

Chapter 9

AN AMBIVALENT HERO:
ELIJAH IN NARRATIVE-CRITICAL PERSPECTIVE

Iain Provan

In the ancient Near Eastern world at large, the most important of the kings of the Omride dynasty in northern Israel was apparently Omri himself. It was he who successfully established this relatively long-lasting dynasty after the time of instability that followed the division of the kingdoms described in 1 Kings 12, and it was his name that could still be associated with the whole Northern Kingdom even in significantly later periods. Excerpts from the Assyrian annals of both Tiglath-pileser III and Sargon II refer to Israel simply as "the land of Omri."[1] In the narrative of 1–2 Kings, however, it is not Omri, but Ahab, who receives the lion's share of the authors' attention. Of Omri we learn very little, but of Ahab and his wife Jezebel we learn a great deal. This is the case, in significant measure, because Ahab and Jezebel's story is bound up so closely with Elijah's—the heroic Yahwistic prophet who so courageously opposes, in 1 Kings 17–19 and 21, the idolatrous king and his notorious queen. Yet Elijah, as we shall see, is portrayed not *only* as a hero of the faith in 1–2 Kings. He is also revealed to be, as Jas 5:17 puts it, "a human being, even as we are" (NIV)—an interestingly complicated person, who knows fear and despair, who displays incomprehension in the face of divine revelation, and who is ultimately not quite so obedient to Yahweh

---

1. Iain Provan, V. Philips Long, and Tremper Longman III, *A Biblical History of Israel*, 2nd ed. (Louisville: Westminster John Knox, 2015), 350 n. 22.

as the opening chapters of his story might have led us to expect.² As Charles Spurgeon once observed of the general case: "The best of men at best are only men."³

1. *Some Background*

The immediate background to the beginning of Elijah's prophetic activity in 1 Kings is the description of Ahab's accession to the throne of Israel in 1 Kgs 16:19-34. Here is a king who walks in the sins of Jeroboam son of Nebat (1 Kgs 12–14), but who adds to this the worship of "Baal"— properly a title ("Lord") for the ancient Semitic storm god Hadad.⁴ In the ancient myths, Baal Hadad is the son of the high god El and the consort of the goddess Anat (and, less prominently, of Astarte). His enemies are Yam ("sea") and Mot ("death"), and his weapons (appropriately, for a storm god) are thunder and lightning. According to the Old Testament, the Baal cult presented an attractive alternative or supplement to Yahweh-worship for many Israelites throughout their residency in the land of Canaan—and one can well imagine the attraction, given that this land was so entirely dependent for its fertility upon rain. All of this helps to explain what happens in 1 Kings 17 and 18. The absence of rain signified to Baal-worshippers the absence of Baal, who in their cyclical and polytheistic way of thinking was required to submit periodically to Mot (i.e., death), only to be revived at a later date so that he may once again water the earth. Elijah, on the other hand, is presented as worshipping a single God, Yahweh, whose characteristic in 1 Kgs 17:1 is that he "lives"—and

---

2. I continue to adhere, then, to the overall understanding of the characterization of Elijah developed in Iain Provan, *1 & 2 Kings*, Understanding the Bible (Grand Rapids: Baker, 1995), many aspects of which find support in the scholarly literature before and since that time. I find unpersuasive the rebuttal of "[m]odern literary readings of prophetic narratives in the book of Kings [that] have not been kind to poor Elijah" offered by Tchavdar S. Hadjiev, "Elijah's Alleged Megalomania: Reading Strategies for Composite Texts, with 1 Kings 19 as an Example," *JSOT* 39 (2015): 433–49—not least because it rests on the entirely dubious general assumption (given the nature of Hebrew narrative) that a partially negative portrayal of Elijah must necessarily involve "explicit narratorial critique of Elijah" (438), and because it simply dismisses the significance of what is admitted to be (in particular) "the impression of a disobedient and selfish prophet" in 1 Kgs 19 (439).

3. Quoted in Walter A. Maier III, "Reflections on the Ministry of Elijah," *CTQ* 80 (2016): 63–80 (77).

4. The reader interested in filling in the narrative background to the Elijah story might consult Provan, *1 & 2 Kings*, 103–31.

yet, while he lives, is able to deny both dew and rain to the land. That is, it is Yahweh, and not Baal, who brings fertility to the land, and it is Yahweh's presence in judgment that leads to infertility, rather than Baal's absence in death. The drought that persists throughout 1 Kings 17 and 18, then—along with the events that occur during the drought—reveal Yahweh to be the living and ever-present God who is sovereign over his creation.

2. *Trust and Obey: Elijah in 1 Kings 17*

This is the significance, first, of Elijah's retreat in 1 Kgs 17:2-6.[5] Having delivered his message about the drought to Ahab in the first verse, he departs to an inhospitable area east of the Jordan where, we deduce, there is no normal food supply. It is our first example of the truth that "[a]bsence hunts after life" throughout this section of 1 Kings.[6] Yet Yahweh provides for Elijah in this context, we are told—Yahweh who controls not just the rain, but the whole natural order, including the ravens (v. 4). Elijah's ancestors had once learned this same lesson as they received both bread and meat in the wilderness (Exod. 16, esp. vv. 8, 12-13). Now Elijah eats the same food, but even more of it (each sort of food twice daily).[7] It is in this short account that we begin to form an impression of his character; for it is in response to "the word of the Lord" that comes to him in v. 2 that Elijah embraces the solitude of Transjordan, in pursuit of a promise that might well be imagined to have stretched his faith (v. 4): "I have directed the ravens to supply you with food there." Elijah, we are told, is someone who obeys Yahweh to the letter in this part of his story, displaying great faith and courage in doing so. "The word of the Lord came to Elijah (v. 2)… So he did what the Lord had told him" (v. 5). We see the same pattern a few verses later: "the word of the Lord came to him: 'Go at once to Zarephath in the region of Sidon and stay there' (vv. 8-9)… So he went to Zarephath" (v. 10). It is repeated in ch. 18: "the word of the Lord came

---

5. The reading of Elijah's character offered in this essay is substantially similar to that in Provan, *1 & 2 Kings*, 132–80, informed by and modified in respect of relevant research mainly since its publication date. Readers are directed to this commentary for the more detailed exegesis that underlies the present reflections.

6. Neil Glover, "Elijah Versus the Narrative of Elijah: The Contest between the Prophet and the Word," *JSOT* 30 (2006): 449–62 (451).

7. "The motif of food and drink" is indeed "ubiquitous" throughout 1 Kgs 17–19, as the providence of Yahweh is underscored. Lissa M. Wray Beal, *1 & 2 Kings*, ApOTC 9 (Downers Grove: InterVarsity, 2014), 230.

to Elijah: 'Go and present yourself to Ahab' (v. 1)… So Elijah went to present himself to Ahab" (v. 2).

A subsequent act of obedience in ch. 17 leads Elijah out of the Promised Land and into the heartland of Baal-worship—into the region of Sidon, whence Jezebel had come, with her baneful religious influence, to marry Ahab (1 Kgs 16:31). Part of the point here may indeed be to contrast with Jezebel the widow whom Elijah meets in Zarephath: "Jezebel, the foreign queen, takes care of her own people at the expense of Israel. The Widow of Zarephath provides hospitality to the foreigner Elijah at potential risk to herself and her son."[8] Beyond this, the point is to demonstrate that Yahweh is not merely a regional god, restricted to the area within which his temples have been built. The first indication of the truth of the matter is the very fact that the region of Sidon is drought-stricken at all (1 Kgs 17:12). What happens next confirms this truth. The widow is not clearly a worshipper of Yahweh herself, but she has nevertheless been "commanded" by Yahweh to supply Elijah with food—even though the situation seems hopeless, and she herself is, in fact, preparing to die (v. 12). Elijah, however, persuades her to take a mighty step of faith with him. Against all natural odds, the word of Yahweh has come to pass once already (vv. 2-4)—and Elijah trusts it to work out in this way one more time (vv. 8-9). He prevails upon the widow to give him something to eat before feeding herself and her son from what remains (v. 13). When she complies (v. 15), she and her son are blessed, along with Elijah. The threat of death has been overcome once again, as people trust in Yahweh's word and obey it.

It is not Baal who has the power to give life—that is already clear. The final section of 1 Kings 17 goes on to establish that it is not his enemy Mot who rules over the domain of death. The widow's son dies, and both she and Elijah already seem to know that this is Yahweh's doing. The woman speaks of it obliquely, blaming Elijah for reminding Yahweh of her sin (v. 18). Elijah, for his part, speaks directly of Yahweh's action against the family (in causing her son to die, v. 20). The difference between the two is that the mother has apparently resigned herself to the death, while Elijah has not. For here is the ultimate test of Yahweh's authority. Granted that his power extends beyond the borders of Israel and into Sidon, does it also extend beyond the borders of life and into the realm of death? When faced by Mot, must Yahweh, like Baal, bow the knee? Elijah is convinced that

---

8. Stephanie Wyatt, "Jezebel, Elijah, and the Widow of Zarephath: A Ménage à Trois that Estranges the Holy and Makes the Holy the Strange," *JSOT* 36 (2012): 435–58 (451).

he knows the right answer, and this leads him to prayer. As a result, the boy's life is miraculously restored (v. 22). Even the world of the dead is not a place from which Yahweh can be excluded, as Psalm 139 will later confirm (Ps. 139:7-12)—and Elijah displays great faith in acting on this truth.

3. *The Prophets of Baal: Elijah in Kings 18*

In 1 Kings 17 Elijah is presented as operating largely in a low-key manner—in the privacy, first, of the Transjordanian wilderness and, secondly, of a Sidonian home. Now he reappears on the main stage of events within the region. Another meeting with Ahab defines the issue at hand in his kingdom: who is the "troubler" of Israel who is responsible for the great curse of the drought that has befallen the land (1 Kgs 18:16-19)? Ahab believes that Elijah is the troubler—a fundamental misunderstanding of the situation. Elijah knows that it is Ahab and his family who have abandoned Yahweh's commands and embraced the worship of the Baals (the various local manifestations of Baal). The story is designed deliberately to echo that of Achan in Joshua 7—a previous "troubler of Israel" in the biblical narrative. The issue back then had been settled in public before "all Israel," and that is how events play out also in 1 Kings 18. It is before "all Israel" (the NIV's "people from all over Israel" in v. 19), gathered on Mount Carmel, that the pressing question of the moment is to be answered: is it the worshippers of Baal or the worshippers of Yahweh who are responsible for the drought?[9] Connected with this is the question: who is really God (v. 21)? "The contest at Carmel thus is an argument between two rival perspectives on reality."[10] The god who answers by fire (i.e., lightning) will be revealed to be God (v. 24), and the people will be expected to show allegiance to him. Once again, the obedience, faith, and courage of Elijah are impressed upon us. He stands, as he believes, alone—yet he enters this contest in full confidence.

As the "ordeal by fire" gets going, the prophets of Baal make the first attempt at getting a god to "answer" them (Heb. ענה—a key word throughout the story; cf. 1 Kgs 18:26, 29, 37). They dance around the altar they have made, calling on the name of Baal (v. 26). After several hours, Elijah begins to taunt them with some disrespectful suggestions as to why

---

9. Mount Carmel "had long been used as a site sacred to Baal the slayer of the sea, god of storm and rain, and giver of abundant vegetation." Wray Beal, *1&2 Kings*, 243.

10. Walter Brueggemann, *1&2 Kings*, SHBC (Macon: Smyth & Helwys, 2000), 229.

they are receiving no "answer." Perhaps Baal is "deep in thought, or busy, or travelling"—perhaps "sleeping" (v. 27). A real god, of course, would be able to respond to shouts, no matter what he was doing. But he would in any case be unlikely to be travelling or busy (i.e., relieving himself), or sleeping. In response to the taunts, the prophets of Baal renew their efforts to get their lord to respond (vv. 28-29)—and thereby, Elijah "makes his opponents active partners in proving the nonexistence of Baal."[11] All that results from their efforts is "no voice; no answer; no attentiveness" (vv. 26, 29). Elijah then rebuilds the altar of Yahweh, using twelve stones to do so—thereby reminding the Israelites of their true identity as Yahweh's people (vv. 30-31; cf. Gen. 35:10). Having placed on this altar *his* sacrificial victim, Elijah then proceeds to saturate the whole area with water—so much water that it even filled the trench that he had dug around it (vv. 32, 35). If *this* offering is consumed by fire, the narrator implies, it *will* be a mighty miracle! Having done all this, Elijah simply prays—in marked contrast to the all-day antics of the prophets of Baal, which have been designed to force their deity into throwing his spear of lightning from the heavens and onto the pyre. Because Elijah has the ear of a *living* God, however—the God of Abraham, Isaac and Jacob—a simple prayer is sufficient, and it is "answered immediately and vigorously."[12] The fire of Yahweh falls from heaven and consumes, not only the sacrifice, but everything else associated with it, whether inflammable stones or soaking soil (v. 38). Yahweh is God! And many of the main actors among those who have truly been "troubling" Israel are duly executed, so as to remove their influence from the land (v. 40; cf. Josh. 7:25-26). Elijah then climbs to the very top of the mountain to wait for the rain that Yahweh has promised (v. 42, cf. 18:1). At last a cloud as small as a man's hand rises from the sea, assuring Elijah that the drought is over. He races Ahab to Jezreel (v. 45), where the king and his consort have a palace (1 Kgs 21:1). Clearly he thinks the war is over, and that he can enter the king's core domain territory with impunity. He is of course about to discover his mistake.

To this point in his story, Elijah is entirely a hero of Yahwistic faith, and this is how he is often remembered in later tradition. James portrays him as such in the NT (Jas 5:17-18): "He prayed earnestly that it would not rain, and it did not rain on the land for three and a half years. Again he prayed, and the heavens gave rain, and the earth produced its crops." It is precisely the two bookends of the story in 1 Kings 17–18 that allow

---

11. Uriel Simon, *Reading Prophetic Narratives*, trans. Lenn J. Schramm, Indiana Studies in Biblical Literature (Bloomington: Indiana University Press, 1997), 181.
12. Ibid., 189.

this neat NT summary of its content: Elijah was a man of faith, and a man of prayer. Thereby he won an important battle for Yahweh in the struggle with idolatry in Israel.

4. *The Word of Jezebel: Elijah in 1 Kings 19:1-4*

At this crucial juncture of the story, Elijah appears to believe that Mount Carmel has seen the decisive battle in the war against idolatry. Ahab has offered no more serious opposition than the god he worships, and the people have in fact abandoned this god. What more is there to say, or do? We deduce that this is why Elijah runs, perhaps unexpectedly, into one of the core areas of Ahab's territory. Yet the story is not yet over; and now *it* enters unexpected territory, with Elijah's running becoming one aspect of the surprise.

Jezebel has always remained in the background to this point in the story—Elijah has been dealing entirely with Ahab. Yet the reader has found some reason to think that Jezebel is the real power in the kingdom, so far as the narrator is concerned. It is Jezebel, in marked contrast to her passive and impotent husband,[13] who takes initiatives and gets things done in 1 Kings 18; it is she who kills off Yahweh's prophets (18:4) while Ahab is attempting unsuccessfully (in "a sustained parody of royal power")[14] to find both Elijah and food for his horses and mules (18:5-6, 10). So perhaps the opening lines of 1 Kings 19 are not in themselves so surprising. A bedraggled Ahab reports to Jezebel what has happened on Mount Carmel, and she offers the kind of decisive response of which Ahab has been so patently incapable. She solemnly promises Elijah that she will make his life like that of one of the Baal prophets he has executed. What follows immediately afterwards is, however, quite unexpected. Elijah becomes afraid (Heb. ירא, v. 3)—or better (and this is the understanding represented in the majority of our Hebrew manuscripts of this story), he "sees how things are" (Heb. ראה). As a result, he flees.

---

13. What one commentator has said of the portrayal of Ahab specifically on Mount Carmel rings generally true: he is "a person who has a marked tendency to yield to strong personalities." Paul J. Kissling, *Reliable Characters in the Primary History: Profiles of Moses, Joshua, Elijah, and Elisha*, JSOTSup 224 (Sheffield: Sheffield Academic, 1996), 103.

14. Peter J. Leithart, *1 & 2 Kings*, Brazos Theological Commentary on the Bible (Grand Rapids: Brazos, 2006), 125.

This development must be read against the background of what has gone before. Hitherto in this story, Elijah has been presented as a man of faith and courage, *simpliciter*—someone who trusts Yahweh for miracles. Certainly he has hidden when Yahweh has told him to (17:2-5)—when the "word of the LORD" has instructed him to hide. As this very example reminds us, however, his whole approach to life has been determined by how the "word of the LORD" has addressed him across a range of topics. Yahweh has said it, and Elijah has done it (cf. also 1 Kgs 17:7-10 and 18:1-2). Here in the opening verses of 1 Kings 19, on the other hand, the "word of the LORD" is conspicuous by its absence. It will not reappear until v. 9, where it takes the form of a question: "What are you doing here, Elijah?" Evidently, then, Elijah's flight southwards in order to escape Jezebel is not being presented as a matter of divine initiative. Indeed, the divine "word" in v. 9 is followed very shortly by a divine command in v. 15 to "go back" north. We are justified in believing, then, that Elijah's retreat as ch. 19 opens is, in the mind of the author, entirely of his own volition. Accustomed to responding to Yahweh's word, in 1 Kgs 19:2 Elijah receives Jezebel's word, and it is this *latter* word that drives him. Upon reflection, the reader may well find some sympathy for him. Here is a queen who—even after all that has happened—still swears by her gods (19:2). Here is a believer who, it seems, is impervious to evidence. In the face of this unnerving reality, then, Elijah is portrayed for the first time in this story as forgetting to think theologically, and as simply reacting to circumstances. He is, perhaps, only capable of "charisma and daring when dealing with people who are extraordinarily compliant and submissive toward him."[15]

So he runs away, with his servant—and he runs a *long* way. He travels from Jezreel in the north to Beersheba in the very south of the Promised Land (v. 3)—as far away from Jezebel as he can manage, within the borders. Having reached Beersheba, he heads alone for the desert. He seeks a lonely place in which to die, an isolated man (as he feels) under an isolated broom tree; he has had "enough" (v. 4). It is a story reminiscent of Jonah's—the great prophetic anti-hero who also travels to a far-flung place without divine permission or prompting (Jon. 1:1-3), and who also attempts to write his own contract for the job of prophet (Jon. 4).

---

15. Kissling, *Reliable Characters*, 106. It is interesting in this respect that Elijah never afterwards directly confronts the queen (e.g. in 1 Kgs 21)—indeed, "is taken up into heaven without ever having met the woman who caused him such anguish" (109).

5. *The Word of the Angel: Elijah in 1 Kings 19:5-8*

To this point in 1 Kings 19, Elijah has been responding only to Jezebel's "messenger" (Heb. מלאך, v. 2); Yahweh has been excluded from his calculations. Now it is Yahweh's turn to take the initiative with a "messenger" of his own (Heb. מלאך, vv. 5 and 7—NIV's "angel"). It is his first move in trying to lead Elijah, as he tries to lead Jonah, back on to the path of faith from which he has just strayed. Yahweh's treatment of Elijah in 1 Kings 19 is, however, noticeably gentler than his treatment of Jonah. The latter required a cataclysmic storm to get him back on track (Jon. 1–2). For the moment in 1 Kings 19, Yahweh's ways with Elijah are less spectacular—although a storm is coming later. So softly does he creep back into Elijah's life in this story, indeed, that it is not at first entirely clear to the reader that it is *Yahweh's* messenger who is leaving food beside his desert bed; we are told only of "a messenger" (v. 5). Yet the unexpectedness of the provision in such a place perhaps already suggests the identity of the donor (cf. 17:1-6). Certainly the situation is more transparent by the time we get to the second occasion upon which Elijah is awoken in order to eat (v. 7)—and now it also becomes clear that there is more to the divine plan than merely food and sleep. Elijah is presented in v. 4 as believing that his journey is over. Overwhelmed with self-loathing as he has become ("I am no better than my ancestors"), he has had enough (Heb. רב). But now in v. 7—better than his ancestors or not—he is to fortify himself for a *further* journey that will be too much for him (Heb. רב) unless he eats. Food was the divine gift when, at the end (as Elijah thought) of his journey, he cried "enough!"; now he is given food a second time so that he genuinely possesses "enough" to complete his journey.

His own destination is Horeb, the mountain of God (v. 8; cf. Exod. 3:1), although the angel may well have been thinking of Damascus (v. 15).[16] The forty days and forty nights of his travels recall Israel's own wandering in the wilderness (Num. 14:33-34) almost as much as they recall Moses' first sojourn on the same mountain (Exod. 24:18). And the narrator thereby poses the central question that confronts Elijah at this moment in his life: when he gets to his destination, will this runaway, currently self-pitying prophet be like servant Moses, or will he be like stubborn Israel? Will he indeed—like Moses—see God (Exod. 33:12-23), and will it make any difference?[17]

---

16. Wray Beal, *1&2 Kings*, 252–3.

17. See further, on the Moses/Elijah parallels in 1 Kgs 19, Thomas L. Brodie, *The Crucial Bridge: The Elijah–Elisha Narrative as an Interpretive Synthesis of*

6. In the Cave: Elijah in 1 Kings 19:9-14

If the provision of food in the wilderness is intended in context as a gentle reminder of the recent past—a past that had involved miraculous provision, resurrection, and the mighty acts of Yahweh on a mountain top (1 Kgs 17–18)—then the storyteller does not suggest in this next section of the narrative that Elijah has grasped the point. For here we encounter a prophet who is clearly still suffering a selective loss of memory. It is at least a good question to ask whether the information about his location in the "cave" (v. 9) is connected to this characterization. It is a dark place to suit a dark mood, perhaps, reminding both Elijah and the reader of the difficult times in which the story is set—times in which other prophets found themselves hiding in caves (18:4, 13). Certainly when invited by Yahweh to speak, and to explain what brings him to his cave (19:9), Elijah recounts only the negatives in the preceding history—Israelite apostasy, along with prophetic casualties (v. 10). "The Israelites have rejected (Heb. עזב) your covenant" takes us back to 1 Kgs 18:18 ("you have abandoned," Heb. עזב); they have "torn down (Heb. הרס) your altars" reminds us of the one altar that was "in ruins" (Heb. הרס) in 18:30; and they have "put your prophets to death" (Heb. הרג) recalls "Jezebel...killing the prophets" (Heb. הרג) in 18:13. Notable by their absence are any allusions to Israelites restored to faith (18:39), the altar rebuilt (18:30-32), and the prophets of *Baal* killed (Heb. הרג) with the sword (19:1).[18] The resistance of Jezebel has apparently turned massive victory into overwhelming defeat, in Elijah's mind. Indeed, the single woman currently trying to kill him has become a plurality of Israelites ("they are trying to kill me too," 19:10). It is a compelling portrayal of someone who has lost all perspective—not least about himself and his own importance. For on the one hand Elijah *has* in fact done considerably better than many of his ancestors (his statement in v. 4 notwithstanding)—as every reader of 1 Kings (and the preceding narratives) knows very well. Yet on the other hand, Elijah is in fact very far from being "the only one left" (v. 10; cf. v. 18). The truth of the matter lies somewhere between the exaggerated self-loathing and the exaggerated self-importance in which the prophet is currently indulging—and we are justified in believing that what happens next occurs in continued pursuit of the restoration of correct perspective (and proportion). Elijah has been fed, encountering once again in 1 Kings

Genesis–Kings and a Literary Model for the Gospels (Collegeville: Liturgical Press, 2000), 46–8.

18. "Curiously, Elijah's statement contradicts earlier narrative depictions." Wyatt, "Jezebel," 455.

19 the God of provision revealed in 1 Kings 17. Now he will encounter once again, on a different mountain-top, the God of fire encountered on Mount Carmel (1 Kgs 18).

The location of this second encounter is, of course, a famous one from an Israelite perspective. Horeb/Sinai is the place where the Israelites, having themselves been sustained in the wilderness by Yahweh (Exod. 16:1–17:7), met with Yahweh and discovered in some detail what sort of God they were dealing with (Exod. 19–20, along with the following chapters). It is important to register this fact about the general background against which the author of 1 Kings 19 sets his particular narrative. For it appears that Yahweh is intent here, not only on reminding Elijah of what he has learned from his own recent history, but also on teaching him something about Yahweh's ways of engaging the world *beyond* what Elijah has already understood. The emphasis at Carmel had been on God's spectacular ways, and particularly on his use of fire. The emphasis in 1 Kgs 19:11-12, on the other hand, is on God's quiet ways. He is not to be found in the spectacular elements of the storm outside the cave ("wind... earthquake...fire"). He reveals himself on this occasion (the text implies) in "a gentle whisper"—"a voice/sound, a barely audible whisper" (Heb. קול דממה דקה). Elijah needs to remember the past; but he also needs to realize that there is more to Yahweh than fire.

It is not immediately clear to the reader why it is important for Elijah to realize this, and there is nothing in text that leads us to interpret Elijah himself as understanding the point. For when Yahweh asks Elijah a second time, in v. 13, the question of v. 9 ("What are you doing here, Elijah?"), Elijah's response is exactly the same as before (vv. 10, 14). The entire point of the demonstration appears to have passed him by, just as Yahweh himself has done (v. 11): "When questioned again about the reason for his sojourn, the monotonous repetition of the prophet's earlier response corroborates the lack of any encounter...nothing has changed for Elijah, nor has Elijah changed."[19] Privileged like Moses to meet with Yahweh on the mountain-top (Exod. 33:12-23), Elijah remains steadfastly like Jonah—that is, slow to understand. There is just a suggestion in the text that he does not particularly *wish* to understand. The key here is to notice that Elijah has already characterized himself in 1 Kings 17–18 as one who "stands before Yahweh" (Heb. עמדתי לפניו, 1 Kgs 17:1; 18:15—the NIV's "whom I serve"). Yet in ch. 19, in response to the command of v. 11 that

19. Gina Hens-Piazza, *1–2 Kings*, AOTC (Nashville: Abingdon, 2006), 191; cf. John W. Olley, *The Message of Kings: God Is Present*, BST (Downers Grove: InterVarsity, 2011), who observes that Elijah "is having difficulty turning from himself to see a fresh vision of God" (180).

he should "Go out and stand on the mountain in the presence of the Lord" (Heb. צא ועמדת בהר לפני יהוה), Elijah apparently stays in the cave until the storm is over and the "whisper" is heard (v. 13). When he does go out, we notice, it is with his cloak over his face. The disobedience is once again striking in the light of previous obedience, and his apparent refusal to "see" Yahweh is directly relatable to the lack of any change in Elijah's response to his question.

7. On the Road Again: Elijah in 1 Kings 19:15-21

It is Yahweh's response to Elijah on this second occasion of questioning that suggests to the reader what the point of the "gentle whisper" really was: "anoint Hazael…Jehu…Elisha" (1 Kgs 19:15-17). A new order is to succeed the old—and it is *this* order that will bring about the final victory over Baal-worship. That is: victory will not finally arrive as a result of obviously spectacular demonstrations of divine power such as the one on Mount Carmel. In particular, it will not arrive only as a result of Elijah's own efforts. Ultimately, victory will be delivered through relatively normal political processes, as Yahweh removes certain kings and installs others, and indeed as other *prophets* are summoned to obey his word. The Carmel event is only one in a series that will stretch well beyond Elijah's lifetime (cf. 2 Kgs 8:7-15; 9–10)—and he now has an important role to play in preparing the way for the others who will shape those events. The divine strategy was always longer-term and more subtly conceived than Elijah apparently imagined. It always involved the gentle whisper—the quiet ways of God's normal providence—as well as the noisier ways of his miraculous intervention. Elijah must be content with being *part* of the plan—for he was in fact never the only one left, as he believed (1 Kgs 19:18)—and not *the plan itself.* Having run south in despair to the desert of Beersheba, he must now go north in obedience, to the Desert of Damascus (v. 15).[20]

The important things to notice in the characterization of Elijah in what remains of his story in 1–2 Kings is that he is never described as carrying through this divine plan. Disobedient and uncomprehending of God throughout 1 Kings 19 to this point, his moral and spiritual compass never truly swings "back north," as it were. We search in vain in the chapters to come for any mention of Elijah ever meeting (or trying to meet) Hazael

---

20. "By wounding Elijah ('Elijah, you are not special') the narrative is also protecting him ('Elijah, you are not alone')." Glover, "Elijah Versus the Narrative of Elijah," 459.

or Jehu. We *never* read of the former being anointed, while it is Elisha who sees to the latter (2 Kgs 9:1-13). As to Elisha himself, the story of his recruitment in 1 Kgs 19:19-21 clearly communicates a less than wholehearted commitment to Yahweh's instructions: "whereas Elisha is ready to succeed the prophet, Elijah gives no indication he is ready for a successor."[21] He does find Elisha, and he does enlist him as his "servant" (v. 21). In a narrative style that tends to deploy vocabulary very carefully and deliberately, however, it is worth noting, first of all, the nature of Elijah's verbal communication with Elisha in v. 20;[22] and secondly, that there is no mention in Elisha's case, either, of any *anointing*—any anointing of Elisha as Elijah's *prophetic replacement* ("anoint Elisha son of Shaphat from Abel Meholah to succeed you as prophet," v. 16).[23] Nor will there be any mention of this in the chapters to come. So has Elijah really adjusted himself to Yahweh's plans at all? It seems not. We shall return to this question in discussing 1 Kings 2, where Elijah takes his leave of Elisha.

8. *The Vineyard Scandal: Elijah in 1 Kings 21*

As if to underline the truth that Elijah, in spite of what he has claimed (1 Kgs 19:10, 14), is not the only servant of God remaining in Israel, the narrator of 1 Kings now inserts material pertaining to King Ahab's war against Aram (1 Kgs 20:1-43) in which Elijah does not appear at all. When we next encounter our prophet, it is in the course of a battle over a vineyard in Jezreel in 1 Kings 21—a vineyard that Ahab wants (v. 2) but that Naboth (the owner) refuses to give up because it is the inheritance of his ancestors (v. 3). He is bound by Israelite custom and law in doing so, and Ahab—in making his offer—displays disregard for this same custom and law. Indeed, the fact that it is the desire for a "vegetable garden" that prompts the offer clearly implies that this move is only one aspect of a broader agenda: to make Israel like "Egypt" (cf. Deut. 11:10, where a pointed contrast is offered between Egypt, the vegetable garden requiring human care, and Canaan, which "the LORD your God cares for"). The entirety of the succeeding narrative indeed explores the

---

21. Hens-Piazza, *1–2 Kings*, 193.
22. The Hebrew here is ambiguous: "go, return, for what have I done to you?" We *could* read Elijah here as diminishing the importance of the symbolic action with the cloak, and/or as essentially saying: "come with me or stay behind—what do I care?" It is intriguing that the Hebrew verb שוב, "return," is often used in the OT of repentance.
23. "Curiously, Elijah throws a mantle over him, but does not anoint him." Brueggemann, *1&2 Kings*, 242.

multiple ways in which this king who has abandoned Yahweh for other gods and has forgotten what it means to be Israel breaks commandment after commandment (along with his wife) in pursuit of his goals. A society given over to idol-worship and covetousness (21:1-6; cf. Exod. 20:1-6, 17) is inevitably one in which there will arise false testimony, judicial murder, and theft (1 Kgs 21:13-19; cf. Exod. 20:13, 15-16).

The word of Yahweh with which Elijah confronts Ahab in this context concerns both the immediate crime that Ahab has committed (1 Kgs 21:17-19) and the general religious context in which the vile deed has been done (vv. 20-24). Dogs feature prominently throughout—licking up Ahab's blood instead of Naboth's (v. 19), devouring Jezebel by the wall of Jezreel (v. 23), and eating Ahab's family (v. 24). Ahab's house is to suffer the same fate as the houses of Jeroboam and Baasha, Elijah tells him (v. 22; cf. 1 Kgs 14:10-11; 16:3-4), because Ahab has, like them, "provoked the LORD to anger and caused Israel to sin" (cf. 14:9, 15-16; 16:2). Yet the chapter closes in a surprising way (21:25-28). Even though Ahab was the worst of kings and deserved his fate (vv. 25-26), his immediate response to Elijah's words is one of repentance (v. 27). The consequence is that Yahweh delays the disaster which Elijah has foretold in relation to his dynasty (v. 28).

In terms of the characterization of Elijah in 1 Kings, we must read this story as a further illustration of an important biblical theme: that Yahweh continues to work in this world through his servants, in both judgment and redemption, whether or not they are always obedient. Elijah is still faithfully doing Yahweh's work, at least in some areas of his life.

9. *Hide and Seek: Elijah in 2 Kings 1–2*

It is interesting that the story of the eventual death of King Ahab does not involve Elijah (1 Kgs 22:1-40). We do not meet the prophet again until 2 Kings 1, where he is involved in a confrontation with Ahab's son Ahaziah. The occasion is an injury sustained by the king when falling out of the window of his upper room in Samaria (v. 2). This leads him to send "messengers" (Heb. מלאך) to consult one of the many local manifestations of Baal about his fate—Baal-Zebub, the god of the Philistine city of Ekron. This ongoing commitment in the house of Ahab to the worship of Baal elicits a response from Yahweh, who also sends a messenger to Elijah (Heb. מלאך, v. 3; cf. 1 Kgs 19:5-7), with the result that the prophet intercepts the king's men on the road with a prophecy about Ahaziah's death. Not for the first time in 1–2 Kings, such a negative oracle addressed to a king elicits an attempt to capture the prophet who delivered it (cf. 1 Kgs 13:1-7; 17:1-4; 18:9-10; 22:1-28)—apparently in the belief that a curse can be reversed if one can catch the curser. In 1–2 Kings, however, the prophetic word cannot be brought under human control, and this is powerfully illustrated in 2 Kings 1, as King Ahaziah is forced to come to terms with the reality of the God of Carmel, who can send fire from heaven (vv. 10 and 12; cf. 1 Kgs 18:38). Elijah may be off-track in various respects at this point in his story, but he is still a prophet of Yahweh, representing "an entire view of reality rooted in Mosaic covenantalism and linked to Yahweh, the God of prophetic insistence concerning justice and righteousness."[24] He is still called to confront a monarch who "represents [like his father] the entire royal enterprise of self-aggrandizement attached to Baalism, a strategy for security and prosperity."[25]

That Elijah is indeed still off-track, however, is strongly implied by the way in which his story ends in 2 Kings 2. Here the apparent ambivalence about Elisha's succession in 1 Kings 19 reappears. Everyone in the opening verses of this chapter seems to know that this event is imminent (2 Kgs 2:3, 5, 9)—that it is "today" that Yahweh will release Elisha from Elijah's tutelage. So why is it, at this moment, that Elijah tries to escape? As so often in Hebrew narrative, we are not explicitly told; we need to discern between the lines. From the story that follows, it seems clear that Elijah believes Elisha's presence with him at his point of departure to be necessary if the latter is to receive his "inheritance" (cf. vv. 9-12). This being the case, it is plausible to interpret Elijah's strange behavior in vv. 1-6 as further testimony to Elijah's general reluctance (observed in 19:13-21) to adopt Yahweh's plans for the future: he is trying to shake Elisha off his tail in order to subvert these plans. Only Elisha's doggedness prevents it.

Both prophets therefore arrive safely at the river Jordan, where the main action of the chapter is to take place. In a scene reminiscent of Moses at the Sea of Reeds, they cross over the Jordan on dry land (vv. 7-8; cf. Exod. 14:15-31, esp. vv. 21-22); Elijah is still Moses, even if he remains also Jonah. Elisha then requests of Elijah what an eldest son would expect of a father as his inheritance (cf. v. 12): a double portion (cf. Deut. 21:15-17). In this case, however, the inheritance is not land, but spirit. Elijah promises that Elisha will indeed receive this gift of the spirit if he sees his departure—which Elisha duly does (vv. 11-12). He is consequently

---

24. Ibid., 290.
25. Ibid.

able to repeat Elijah's action in parting the waters (vv. 13-14), proving himself to be Joshua to Elijah's Moses—for Joshua also crossed the Jordan and entered the land of Israel near Jericho, "repeating" Moses' action in parting the waters (Josh. 3).[26] Elijah, in the meantime, has been taken up into the heavens, receiving thereby "the almost unparalleled honor of being allowed to bypass death itself."[27] Truly Yahweh is the living God, and the one who gives life.

10. *Conclusion*

As we review the portrayal of Elijah in 1–2 Kings, we see clearly that the author portrays him first of all as a mighty prophet of Yahweh—very much a man for a crisis. He opposes Ahab and Jezebel and all their works, and he plays a central role in the significant victory over Baal-worship that is described in 1 Kings 17–18. In these stories, he is a man of great faith and courage, and a person who knows how to pray efficaciously. As we reach 1 Kings 19, however, we discover that he is also a flawed character—as mostly all biblical heroes of the faith ultimately turn out to be. Faced with unexpected opposition from Jezebel, he retreats from the war that he has mistakenly assumed is over. He is fearful, and he casts faith aside, looking to lay down his prophetic vocation of his own accord. A beneficiary of the kindness of Yahweh in the midst of his despair, he remains nevertheless self-focused and self-pitying as he reaches Mount Horeb, trapped in an only partially true narrative about his previous life. Faced anew with the palpable reality of God, he nevertheless declines Yahweh's invitation to leave his cave and thereby regain perspective and proportion. He remains stuck in his false narrative, apparently now unwilling to listen to the divine voice as it seeks to place his life and mission in its proper context—to define him as one servant, only, among many others. His life after Horeb is certainly one of further effective service. At those points where he has to confront the question of his own passing from the center of God's stage, however, a definite reluctance, even a disobedience, is evident. In sum, Elijah is portrayed as a person who does well when life goes in the way he expects it to go, and when he himself is apparently central to God's plans. He is indeed capable of astonishing feats when this is so. He is not so good at dealing with disappointment, and he is certainly not prepared to smooth the way for others. He "turns out to be a person who is prone to obey Yahweh's directives in such a way as to make his own role take

---

26. See further Wray Beal, *1&2 Kings*, 306–8.
27. Kissling, *Reliable Characters*, 148.

on added importance and may actually sometimes be positively resistant to obeying some of Yahweh's directives."[28] He is in so many ways similar to Moses in this narrative, even to the extent of "dying" on the other side of the Jordan (Deut. 34:1-8). However, he also has something of Jonah about him. He is a thoroughly ambivalent hero, designed by our biblical author to be helpful as such to us readers—to be our teacher, both in his successes and in his failures.

---

28. Ibid.

Chapter 10

THE CHARACTER OF ELISHA AND HIS BONES

Stuart Lasine

Introduction

Scholars often disagree dramatically in their evaluations of biblical personages, whether they are describing the personality traits of those figures or judging their moral character. Researchers on Elisha are no exception. Several factors can contribute to such variability. The narrator of a given story may withhold information needed for readers to form a single definitive interpretation or provide only ambiguous, vague, or conflicting cues. Readers may also have different assumptions about the psychological roles played by character and situation in determining human behavior.[1] Finally, readers may have differing expectations, values, and theological assumptions, all of which can influence their appraisal of a biblical figure.

After briefly indicating the spectrum of opinion concerning the basic character of the prophet Elisha, I will focus on one presentation of his character which has not received adequate attention, namely, his character *after* he has died. In 2 Kgs 13:20-21 a man's corpse[2] comes into contact with the dead prophet's bones and the corpse revives. While this brief report might seem an unlikely place to form an impression of Elisha's

---

1. See Stuart Lasine, *Weighing Hearts: Character, Judgment, and the Ethics of Reading the Bible*, LHBOTS 568 (London: T&T Clark, 2012), 3–19.

2. Aron Pinker ("Job's Perspectives on Death," *JBQ* 35, no. 2 [2007]: 84 n. 25) suggests that "the man…may not have been dead but in deep shock," but provides no evidence to support this notion. Cf. similar attempts to argue that the boys resuscitated

character, a number of commentators believe that the bones have retained the prophet's power and identity. Readers have also speculated about the identity and moral status of the corpse with whom the bones come into contact, even though the narrator supplies no information about this dead individual, either before or after his body "stands up."

I will then turn to the report of Elisha's fatal illness and his bedside conversation with King Joash earlier in ch. 13. Next I will ask what the many stories involving illness, death, and resuscitation in 2 Kings may imply about Elisha's own attitude toward his mortality. Why is no one within the story world shown to be surprised by unprecedented events such as resuscitating the dead? Is the narrator's unusual emphasis on illness, death, and human fragility in 1–2 Kings rhetorically designed to reflect or address readers' concerns and fears about their own vulnerability to illness, decay, and death? Finally, how might readers' reactions to these "death reminders" affect their evaluation of Elisha's character?

Evaluating Elisha's Character: Preliminary Issues

According to Stipp, in the parallel tales about the resuscitation of dead boys Elijah is portrayed in a "flat and one-dimensional" manner, while the "sensitive" Elisha's characterization is complex and ambiguous.[3] However, when each story is viewed in the context of all the narratives concerning each of these men of God, it is the depictions of Elisha which do not add up to a coherent and multi-dimensional portrayal of a vivid personality. This is due in part to the differences in the ways in which the narrator presents the two prophets. Elisha and Yahweh never engage in dialogue as do Elijah and Yahweh. This interaction allows readers to compare Elijah's image of himself and those around him with the "facts" given by the narrator elsewhere. It also allows readers to observe Yahweh's response to the prophet's self-presentation (1 Kgs 19:9-18). In addition, because God gives instructions to Elijah in directly quoted speech in several chapters, we are able to gauge the extent to which Elijah changes what God has told him to say when he repeats it, and to know when Elijah goes beyond what God has told him to do.[4] Readers of the

---

by Elijah and Elisha were not really or totally dead; see Stuart Lasine, "Matters of Life and Death: The Story of Elijah and the Widow's Son in Comparative Perspective," *BibInt* 12 (2004): 119–22.

3. Hermann-Josef Stipp, "Vier Gestalten einer Totenerweckungserzählung (1 Kön 17,17-24; 2 Kön 4,8-37; Apg 9,36-42; Apg 20,7-12)," *Bib* 80 (1999): 69.

4. See Lasine, *Weighing Hearts*, 67–76.

Elisha stories do not have the opportunity to learn about his personality in this fashion.⁵

In spite of this lack of information, many readers have drawn definite—and often diametrically opposed—conclusions about Elisha's character. Shemesh is the most ardent advocate for Elisha's greatness.⁶ She interprets the prophet's actions in the same way as the Shunammite in 2 Kgs 4:9. She concludes that the Elisha stories are "saints' legends" and attempts to "rebut" any reading of these stories which do not "exalt" the prophet. Scholars such as Bergen, on the other hand, criticize Elisha or his "prophetism."⁷

The same divergence of opinion can be found in reference to specific Elisha narratives. Thus, while most commentators conclude that Elisha is elevated or exalted in the story of the Shunammite and her son (2 Kgs 4:8-37), others believe that the prophet is found wanting and that his power is subverted.⁸ Similarly, many commentators believe that Elisha's behavior toward King Jehoram in 2 Kings 3, 5–6 is praiseworthy, while others are critical of the prophet's actions and sympathetic to Jehoram.⁹ And while many readers are appalled at Elisha's curse against forty-two little children/youngsters which results in their being mauled by bears (2 Kgs 2:23-25), others attempt to justify the prophet's action and put the blame entirely on the youngsters.¹⁰ Even specific statements by Elisha have been understood in diametrically opposed ways. When Naaman asks the prophet for permission to "bow down in the temple of Rimmon," Elisha replies "לך לשלום." Commentators disagree about whether this "go in/to peace" grants the requested permission, is meant ironically as a type of "go to hell!," or is expressing indifference to Naaman's plans.¹¹

---

5. See further in Stuart Lasine, "Holy Men in Space," in *Constructions of Space III: Biblical Spatiality and the Sacred*, ed. Jorunn Økland, Cor de Vos, and Karen Wennell, LHBOTS 540 (New York: Bloomsbury T&T Clark, 2016), 13–18.

6. Yael Shemesh, "The Elisha Stories as Saints' Legends," *JHS* 8, no. 5 (2008): 2–41.

7. Wesley J. Bergen, *Elisha and the End of Prophetism*, JSOTSup 286 (Sheffield: Sheffield Academic, 1999).

8. See Lasine, "Holy Men in Space," 19–20.

9. E.g., Lasine, *Weighing Hearts*, 161–70; Bergen, *Elisha and the End of Prophetism*, 138–40.

10. See, e.g., Rachelle Gilmour, *Juxtaposition and the Elisha Cycle* (London: Bloomsbury T&T Clark, 2014), 100–103; Shemesh, "The Elisha Stories," 11–13; Keith Bodner, *Elisha's Profile in the Book of Kings: The Double Agent* (Oxford: Oxford University Press, 2013), 1–5.

11. See Stuart Lasine "'Go in Peace' or 'Go to Hell?' Elisha, Naaman and the Meaning of Monotheism in 2 Kings 5," *SJOT* 25, no. 1 (2011): 3–8, 23–5.

This diversity of opinion raises the question whether the narratives have been designed to make possible different images of Elisha, in the manner of an ambiguous figure drawing in which the same configuration is seen as either an old or a young woman.[12] Stories in which Elisha deals with death could also function as a way of prompting readers to activate their own coping devices when confronted with issues related to their own mortality. For example, they might identify with the seemingly invulnerable prophet *or* recognize the ultimate futility of post-mortem survival fantasies, given the narrator's lack of interest in the people revived by Elisha.[13] If the narratives offer little reason to admire Elisha on an ethical or religious level,[14] then exalting him means bowing down to sheer amoral power.[15]

Reading Character from Corpses in 2 Kings 13:20-21

After reminding readers of the sick prophet's bodily vulnerability, the narrator of 2 Kings 13 informs us that the dead Elisha's bones are so invulnerable that they could restore another corpse to life. The same bones which had not kept Elisha alive on his deathbed now raise a stranger's corpse back to life by mere contact. In contrast, the living Elisha's resuscitation of the Shunammite's son required repeated full body contact between the living prophet and the dead boy (2 Kgs 4:34-35).

Some commentators speak as if Elisha's bones themselves had the properties of personhood, retaining the identity of the individual they propped up during his life. Sirach declares that "from where he lay buried, his body prophesied" (Sir. 48:13; NABRE).[16] Josephus notes that after Elisha's death "*he* still had divine power" (*Ant.* 9.8.6, emphasis added). Among modern scholars, Shemesh asserts that "even after his death the

---

12. Edwin G. Boring, "A New Ambiguous Figure," *The American Journal of Psychology* 42 (1930): 444–5.

13. See Lasine, "Matters of Life and Death," 120.

14. On Elisha's failure to continue the struggle against Baal worship begun by Elijah, as Yahweh commanded (1 Kgs 19:16-18), see Lasine, "'Go in Peace' or 'Go to Hell?'" 11–15. On the high regard for Elisha's powers in Baal-worshipping Aram, see, e.g., 2 Kgs 6:12; 8:7-9.

15. On scholars who view Elisha's God, the holy and powerful Yahweh, as amoral, see Stuart Lasine, "'Everything Belongs to Me': Holiness, Danger, and Divine Kingship in the Post-Genesis World," *JSOT* 35 (2010): 32–48.

16. The Hebrew has נברא, but the *rêš* is usually considered an error; see Patrick W. Skehan and Alexander A. Di Lella. *The Wisdom of Ben Sira*, AB 39 (New York: Doubleday, 1987), 532.

man of God could perform miracles."[17] Cohn concludes that "death did not totally defeat" the prophet.[18] Bodner calls this event "Elisha's encore performance."[19] For Hamilton, "Elisha dead is more effective than most people alive!"[20] Brinton claims that the bones "were still so replete with [Elisha's] miraculous individuality, that the corpse revived."[21] For all these commentators, the body of the dead prophet remains the *person* Elisha, and "his" effectiveness in performing miracles is no different in kind from that of the living prophet. To imply that Elisha "himself" resurrected the corpse is to reduce Elisha's "self" to a concentration of power stripped of all personality.[22]

While the narrator of 2 Kgs 13:20-21 shows no interest in the identity or fate of the standing revived corpse, later rabbinic commentators are interested in the personality of this minor character. According to one tradition, the corpse is the virtuous, kindly, and well-loved Shallum, the husband of Huldah the prophetess, whose son Hanamel was a cousin to Jeremiah (*Pirqe R. El.* 33[23]). According to another, it is the son of the Shunammite whom Elisha had resuscitated earlier. The son had died again, only to be revived by the bones of his former healer. However, his third and final

---

17. Shemesh, "The Elisha Stories," 34.

18. Robert L. Cohn, *2 Kings*, Berit Olam (Collegeville: Liturgical Press, 2000), 88–9.

19. Bodner, *Elisha's Profile*, 150; cf. Walter Brueggemann, *1 & 2 Kings* (Macon: Smyth & Helwys, 2000), 432.

20. Victor P. Hamilton, *Handbook on the Historical Books: Joshua, Judges, Ruth, Samuel, Kings, Chronicles, Ezra-Nehemiah, Esther* (Grand Rapids: Baker Academic, 2001), 451

21. Daniel G. Brinton, "Folk-Lore of the Bones," *The Journal of American Folklore* 3, no. 8 (1890): 19. Bergen (*Elisha*, 169) is more critical of the bones: "if Elisha's bones really wanted something to do, why did they not stop the [Moabite] raids?," as if the bones themselves had desires and were capable of feeling bored. Bergen may be asking this question with tongue in cheek, but he draws a serious conclusion from it when he takes failure to stop the raids as yet another "flawed performance" by Elisha.

22. In contrast, Thomas Overholt (*Cultural Anthropology and the Old Testament* [Minneapolis: Fortress, 1996], 57) obliquely acknowledges this weak notion of "individuality" when he appeals to Hill's study of the "local hero" in order to make sense of "this otherwise bizarre account." Overholt quotes Hill's statement that "the local hero, being dead, is completely depersonalized, and it is social forces that provide his power" (Overholt, *Cultural Anthropology*, 56; Scott D. Hill, "The Local Hero in Palestine in Comparative Perspective," in *Elijah and Elisha in Socioliterary Perspective*, ed. Robert B. Coote [Atlanta: Scholars Press, 1992], 63).

23. Gerald Friedlander, trans., *Pirḳê de Rabbi Eliezer* (London: Kegan Paul, Trench, Trubner & Co., 1916), 244.

existence was very short in duration; after standing up on his feet he died yet again and was buried in another sepulcher, because he was a sinner.[24] Yet another view is that the man was Ahab's prophet Zedekiah.[25]

What all these suggestions have in common is that they are *moralizing*. That is, they are interested in the identity of the revived corpse in so far as whether the identified individual had been a good or an evil person, who did or did not deserve this unique chance to continue living. While we are told enough about Elijah for readers to form their own opinions about whether Elijah merited ascension, 2 Kings 13 provides absolutely no information on whether this particular corpse deserves to live again— or whether Elisha did *not* merit translation.

The most surprising and intriguing of the rabbinical suggestions about the corpse in 2 Kings 13 is the notion that it was the body of the old prophet of Bethel, whose deception led to the death of the man of God from Judah in 1 Kings 13.[26] It is surprising because we know that the old prophet wanted his own bones to be laid next to the bones of the man of God after he died (1 Kgs 13:31). Much later, Josiah is informed that the two are in fact buried together (2 Kgs 23:17-18). Rashi's view seems to imply that the old prophet was first buried in Elisha's grave and only later laid to rest in the same grave as the man of God from Judah. The suggestion is intriguing because it links two cases in which there is contact between a corpse and a previously buried person's body or bones. Although 2 Kgs 13:20-21 has been used to ground the talmudic rule that an unrighteous person cannot be buried with a righteous one (*b. Sanh.* 47a), 1 Kings 13 and 2 Kings 23 report cases where this does in fact take place—if one accepts that the old prophet of Bethel was wicked and the man of God an innocent dupe.[27] In 1 Kings 13, laying one corpse's bones against another's ensures that the wicked prophet's bones will remain undisturbed even when Josiah conducts his purge hundreds of years later. It would be quite ironic if that same wicked man's corpse was expelled

---

24. *Midr. Tehillim* Bk. I, 26, 7; William G. Braude, *The Midrash on Psalms, Vol. 1*, Yale Judaica Series 13 (New Haven: Yale University Press, 1959), 363; cf. *b. Sanh.* 47a.

25. *Qoh. Rab.* 8:10; A. Cohen, "Ecclesiastes," in *The Midrash VIII: Ruth, Ecclesiastes* (London: Soncino, 1939), 222; cf. Carol A. Dray, *Studies on Translation and Interpretation in the Targum to the Books of Kings* (Leiden: Brill, 2006), 105. For Zedekiah ben Kenaanah, see 1 Kgs 22:11-24.

26. A. J. Rosenberg, trans. and ed., *Kings II*, Mikraoth Gedoloth (New York: Judaica, 1989), 341.

27. On this see Lasine, *Weighing Hearts*, 94–106.

from Elisha's grave by that true prophet's bones, only to live long enough for his bones to be placed beside those of another true prophet, one whose death had been both miraculous and bizarre![28]

Reading Character in Sickbed Scenes

In addition to offering revivification stories which explore the boundary which supposedly separates life and death, 2 Kings includes a highly unusual concentration of cases in which the bodily vulnerability of key figures is highlighted. In 2 Kings 13 King Joash visits the sick prophet Elisha. The fact that the man of God "fell sick with his sickness from which he died" (2 Kgs 13:14) led some rabbinic commentators to conclude that Elisha had been ill on previous occasions[29] and is the first person to have been ill and recovered from the illness (*b. B. Meṣiʿa* 87a; *b. Sanh.* 107b).

Three other cases in the book describe the opposite situation. In these cases the incapacitated individual is the king (Ahaziah, Ben Hadad, and Hezekiah) and the prophet's role is to announce the outcome of the disease or injury, either in person or through a messenger. None of these monarchs is said to have become ill or injured in war or as a divine punishment, although royal war wounds are also reported in 2 Kings (e.g., 2 Kgs 8:28-29; 9:14-28).

In 2 Kings 13 readers have limited information on which to base an assessment of Elisha's foil Joash. As Hobbes puts it, the very brief assessment of Joash of Israel's reign is "remarkably cryptic."[30] Immediately after this report, we encounter Joash as a visitor to Elisha's sickbed. When Elisha tells the king to strike the ground with his arrows, the king does so. Only after the fact does Elisha tell Joash that he should have done so five or six times, not three, as the king had done.[31]

---

28. While in 1 Kgs 13 the dead man of God's body is repeatedly referred to as a נבלה (carcass, corpse), the corpse in 2 Kgs 13 is consistently called the "man" (איש). Could that be due to the fact that the narrator knows that this body will soon turn out *not* to be irreversibly dead?

29. Specifically, on two former occasions, both of which were triggered by dubious behavior on Elisha's part: the cursing of the young boys with she-bears and "repulsing Gehazi with both hands" (*b. Sanh.* 107b; cf. Louis Ginzberg, *The Legends of the Jews, Vol. 4*, trans. Henrietta Szold [Philadelphia: Jewish Publication Society, 1968], 240, 245–6).

30. T. R. Hobbs, *2 Kings*, WBC 13 (Waco: Word, 1985), 165.

31. Cf. the prophet in 1 Kgs 20 who is killed by a lion because he refused to strike his colleague. Here too the condemned figure was not told the crucial information

Interpreters have denounced the king for this apparent failing. Among the milder judgments, Jones faults the king for lack of determination, spirit, and energy.³² Provan attributes Joash's failure to not obeying enthusiastically enough.³³ Similarly, Montgomery and Gehman see Joash as "remiss in forcefulness" when striking the ground.³⁴ Others go further and take the king's action as a key to his basic character. Joash exhibits timidity, lack of faith, and a tendency to think small.³⁵ Fretheim considers it likely that Elisha's "test" of Joash's confidence in God "reveals the shape" of Joash's entire life.³⁶

In contrast, Long acknowledges that shooting arrows and striking the ground are "seemingly innocent acts," for which blame is nevertheless "laid at Joash's door."³⁷ A reader who shares this view may then judge Elisha as being excessively harsh with this monarch. This would not be the first time that Elisha has been very severe with a monarch who has deferentially called him "father." I am referring to Elisha's consistently condemnatory attitude toward Jehoram of Israel.³⁸

A full analysis of the sickbed scenes in Kings is beyond the scope of this essay. However, in the final two sections I will consider two key questions. First, are the many references to illness and injury in Kings³⁹ related to the fact that these books also report cases in which the boundary separating life and death is dramatically violated? And second, what does Elisha's role in most of these scenes tell us about his character?

---

needed to save himself until after he is doomed. In this instance, he was not told that the command to strike his fellow prophet came from Yahweh until it was too late (see Lasine, *Weighing Hearts*, 104–5).

32. Gwilym H. Jones, *1 and 2 Kings, Vol. 2*, NCB (Grand Rapids: Eerdmans, 1984), 503–4.

33. Iain W. Provan, *1 and Kings*, NIBC (Peabody: Hendrickson, 1995), 228.

34. J. A. Montgomery and H. S. Gehman, *A Critical and Exegetical Commentary on the Book of Kings*, ICC (Edinburgh: T. & T. Clark, 1951), 435.

35. Hobbs, *2 Kings*, 165, 170.

36. Terence E. Fretheim, *First and Second Kings*, WBCom (Louisville: Westminster John Knox, 1999), 183–4.

37. Burke O. Long, *2 Kings with an Introduction to Historical Literature*, FOTL 10 (Grand Rapids: Eerdmans, 1991), 166.

38. See Lasine, *Weighing Hearts*, 161–70.

39. Many of these notices employ the root חלה/חלי, e.g., 1 Kgs 14:1; 15:23; 17:17; 22:34; 2 Kgs 1:2; 8:7-9, 29; 13:14; 20:1.

Elisha's Attitude Toward his Mortality

Within the story-world, Elisha shows no sign of aspiring to be another rare exception to the rule of death. Does *he* fear[40] death as had his fleeing mentor? Sirach stresses Elisha's lack of fear before royal authorities before alluding to the prophet's post-mortem wonders: "in his days he did not tremble before any ruler, and no one oppressed him" (Sir. 48:12, NETS). That Elisha exhibits no fear of death is hardly surprising. Even though Jezebel is alive during much of Elisha's career she is not said to threaten the life of *this* man of God—of course, Elisha has not attempted to annihilate Jezebel's religious establishment, as had Elijah. And when an Israelite king wishes to seize Elisha, he has no need to fear or disappear as had Elijah, since *he* has a celestial chariot army at his disposal (2 Kgs 6:16-17). Nor does Elisha need to immolate the soldiers who are sent to take him, as had Elijah; he simply blinds them, leads them to his own king, has them fed, and sends them back home to their country (2 Kgs 6:22-23).

Next Sirach reports that Elisha performed wondrous, astounding deeds both when he was alive and after death (Sir. 48:14). The narrator of Kings does not give readers enough information about Elisha's lack of fear for us to know whether the "wondrous deeds" to which Sirach alludes gave Elisha a feeling of invulnerability. Fear is not the only emotion about which readers remain uninformed. Very little is said about *any* of Elisha's emotions, although at the end of his life he *is* said to get angry at the Israelite king Joash (2 Kgs 13:19) and earlier he had seemed consistently irritable and cross with King Jehoram.[41] Nor do we learn much about Elisha's desires and wishes.

Elisha shows no sign of wanting to use his double portion of Elijah's spirit to ascend as his master had done. Nor do the "sons of the prophets" show any sign of expecting Elisha to ascend when they witness him parting the Jordan with Elijah's cloak (2 Kgs 2:13-15). When Elisha is ill, he does not pray to remind Yahweh how loyal and good he has been, as King Hezekiah does later when he is mortally ill (2 Kgs 20:2-3).[42] Finally, in Elisha's case no groups of fifty sons of the prophets are said to cluster outside the prophet's sickroom waiting for him to escape death by ascending, even though they know that Elisha is a wonder-worker who possesses miraculous powers which have been used to solve problems great and small. In short, as far as readers can tell, Elisha's many

---

40. Reading וַיִּרְא in 1 Kgs 19:3 with many manuscripts and the versions.
41. See Lasine, *Weighing Hearts*, 163–5.
42. Interestingly, in both 2 Kgs 13 and 21 it is the king who weeps, whether he is the one dying in bed or the one visiting the dying man.

experiences with human mortality have apparently not led him to dread his own demise. Nor did these encounters with death lead his followers to expect that Elisha would never die.

Our Attitude Toward our Own Mortality: Reading about Elisha and Death

Can *reading* about mortality lead one to fear one's own death? Psychologists who ascribe to "Terror Management Theory" hold that death reminders can lead some subjects to increase the rigidity of their worldviews and reinforce their other "buffers" against awareness of their mortality.[43] However, one recent study found that this effect is *not* present when the increased mortality salience is generated by literature. Van Peer and his colleagues conclude that mortality salience "in literature has as its effect not a defense mechanism,…but a psychological valve, that makes us accept our biological vulnerability."[44]

These findings suggest that literary presentations of mortality *also* function as buffers against death anxiety. Literature can function as a kind of "safe space" within which readers can explore harsh realities and feel negative emotions without reacting in the same way as they would in their daily lives, rather than being a way for readers to obscure their awareness of their vulnerability.[45] Should we expect similar results when

---

43. See, e.g., Sheldon Solomon, Jeff Greenberg, and Tom Pyszczynski, "The Cultural Animal: Twenty Years of Terror Management Theory and Research," in *Handbook of Experimental Existential Psychology*, ed. Jeff Greenberg, Sander Koole, and Tom Pyszczynski (New York: Guilford, 2004), 20–34. These individuals may also become harsher in judgments of those who disagree with their views, depending upon personality factors such as attachment style. In addition, they may attempt to bolster their self-esteem or seek closer personal relationships. 2 Kgs 13:20-21 itself is not so much reminding readers of their mortality as it is reminding them of the childhood belief that mortality may not always be inevitable or irreversible. See further in Stuart Lasine, *Jonah and the Human Condition: Life and Death in Yahweh's World*, LHBOTS 688 (London: Bloomsbury T&T Clark, 2019), 67–9.

44. Willie Van Peer, Anna Chesnokova, and Matthias Springer, "Distressful Empathy in Reading Literature: The Case for Terror Management Theory?" *Science and Education* 26, no. 1 (2017): 39. Van Peer seems to be referring to literature "making us" accept our vulnerability while we are reading the work, rather than causing a permanent attitudinal change in the reader.

45. See, e.g., Suzanne Keen (*Empathy and the Novel* [New York: Oxford University Press, 2007], 4, 131): "fictional worlds provide safe zones for readers' feeling empathy without experiencing a resultant demand on real-world action… novels can provide safe spaces within which to see through the eyes" of very negative characters.

readers respond to accounts of human fragility and mortality in biblical narratives? If the Elisha narratives increase mortality salience for readers, in what ways might different readers react to these death reminders? Could their reactions even influence their assessment of Elisha's character?

One way to address these questions is to return to the story of Elisha's life-giving bones. Several aspects of this little story raise psychological questions. First, neither the narrator nor characters within the textual world express astonishment at the corpse returning to life when it contacts Elisha's bones.[46] Nor does awe or amazement lead others to mark Elisha's burial place as unapproachably sacred or to build a shrine there,[47] in spite of the fact that such information is supplied about people's reactions to the death of Greek wonder-workers.[48]

Cohn assumes that "the reader is surprised at the resurrection of the dead man when he touches Elisha's bones."[49] This may be true of many first-time readers, but can we take for granted that this has been true of everyone who has read or heard the story? According to Meyer, surprise is elicited by unexpected events which are "discrepant with" or "contrary to" the schemata by means of which we make sense of our everyday surroundings.[50] This prompts us to focus our attention on the schema-discrepant event, and, if necessary, to revise the relevant schemata in order to increase the effectiveness of our attributions.[51] The reviving of the corpse through contacting bones is certainly "discrepant" with the reality-concept operative in the world of most modern Western readers. The same is true of the world in which biblical characters had lived prior to 1 Kings, in the sense that these books give no hint that a living prophet

---

Cf. Keith Oatley, *Such Stuff as Dreams: The Psychology of Fiction* (West Sussex, UK: Wiley-Blackwell, 2011), 125.

46. In contrast, Washington Allston's painting of 2 Kgs 13:20-21 (*The Dead Man Restored to Life*, 1811–14) directs the viewer's attention to the emotional reactions of a number of bystanders, while the prophet's bones are hardly visible in the dark background.

47. Nor is a shrine said to be erected at the location from which Elijah ascended to heaven. Shemesh dismisses the lack of reference to a shrine at Elisha's burial site by arguing that the saint legend genre is not interested in such matters. On holy sites associated with Greek wonder-workers and heroes, see Lasine, "Holy Men in Space," 13 n. 27.

48. See ibid., 12–13. In addition, the unusual number of illnesses and injuries reported in Kings is not noted by the narrator or any characters.

49. Cohn, *2 Kings*, 88.

50. Wulf-Uwe Meyer, "Die Rolle von Überraschung im Attributionsprozeß," *Psychologische Rundschau* 39 (1988): 143, 136.

51. Ibid., 136, 144–6.

could resuscitate a dead person, let alone that a dead prophet's bare bones could accomplish this feat.[52]

Elisha's wondrous acts are often described as the result of power which he himself controls, whether or not Yahweh is assumed to be the ultimate source of that power.[53] Should the prophet's deeds challenge readers to revise their "relevant schemata" about divine and human power? Phenomena similar to Elisha's "miracles" also feature prominently in other narrative genres. Tatar points out that in "wondertales…the supernatural is accepted as part and parcel of everyday reality; a figure such as a witch "never evokes the slightest degree of surprise or astonishment."[54] The same has also been said of some sophisticated literary narratives.[55] Should we readers of the Bible be equally unfazed by the reversibility of life and death in the Elisha narratives?

Characters in the Hebrew Bible—including Yahweh—do express surprise or amazement elsewhere.[56] So why not here? Is the narrator allowing readers to give full rein to their own amazement or shock? Or are readers of these narratives assumed to "expect the unexpected"? Of course, the narrator may assume the reality of these miracles and take for granted that the target audience shares those assumptions. Pinker seems to think so, arguing that "the *casual* description of a dead man's revival…

---

52. Tzvetan Todorov (*The Fantastic: A Structural Approach to a Literary Genre*, trans. Richard Howard [Ithaca: Cornell University Press, 1975], 53–7) notes another reason why readers may not experience a miraculous event as uncanny. When a text belongs to the genre of the "marvelous," characters and events are not expected to obey the laws and limitations of ordinary reality, and therefore do not elicit the feeling of tension which, for Todorov, characterizes the fantastic and the uncanny.

53. See R. W. L. Moberly "Miracles in the Hebrew Bible," in *The Cambridge Companion to Miracles*, ed. Graham H. Twelftree (Cambridge: Cambridge University Press, 2011), 64.

54. Maria Tatar, *The Hard Facts of the Grimms' Fairy Tales*, 2nd ed. (Princeton: Princeton University Press, 2003), 61. Nor do genuine *Märchen* evoke anything "uncanny," according to Sigmund Freud ("Das Unheimliche," in *Gesammelte Werke, Vol. 12*, ed. Anna Freud [London: Imago, 1947], 260).

55. Commenting on Kafka's *Metamorphosis*, Todorov (*The Fantastic*, 169) quotes Camus' comment on Gregor Samsa's lack of surprise at being transformed into a kind of enormous vermin: "we shall never be sufficiently amazed about this lack of amazement." Todorov adds that Kafka is one modern writer whose narrators also report seemingly fantastic facts without the characters sharing the readers' experience of astonishment or the uncanny (ibid., 171–4).

56. The verbs תמה, שמם and דהם convey astonishment. See, e.g., Qoh. 5:7; Hab. 1:5; Gen. 43:33; Jer. 4:9; 14:9; Ps. 48:5; Isa. 59:16; Dan. 3:24.

would be inconceivable if it were not believed that some holiness and magic are retained by the dead."[57]

One might also expect that narratives such as 2 Kgs 13:20-21 might evoke a feeling of the uncanny in some readers. According to Freud, "whatever is associated with death, corpses and the return of the dead,... appears uncanny (*unheimlich*) to the very highest degree [to many people]... our unconscious has as little room now as it did in the past for the idea of its own mortality."[58] Readers might therefore be expected to view the story of Elisha's bones as uncanny and simultaneously "realistic," in the sense that it reflects the reality of our "immortal" unconscious minds.[59] Stories about the return of the dead which generate feelings of the uncanny resonate with abandoned childhood fantasies and beliefs, and play upon any lingering doubts adults may have about the impermeability of the line separating life and death.[60] By bringing together our adult sense of reality and our childhood wishes and beliefs within the safety of a narrative world, readers need not feel threatened by this clash of realities as they would be if the same things occurred in "real life."[61]

---

57. Pinker, "Job's Perspectives," 77; emphasis added. Moberly ("Miracles," 64–5) cites the oft-noted fact that in Kings the unusual power displayed by Elijah and Elisha is envisaged as "'in their possession', 'under their control'," but adds that the narratives sometimes include something which allows readers to "make sense of what is happening in categories familiar elsewhere in the HB" (e.g., Elisha telling Gehazi that God had not informed him about the Shunammite's distress; 2 Kgs 4:27). While these stories "stand in their strangeness," such additions tend to "conform them somewhat... to the 'normal' understanding of life with YHWH as attested elsewhere in the HB."

58. Freud, "Das Unheimliche," 254–5.

59. Freud does qualify his assertions by noting exceptions to his rule, including the miracle stories about the reawakening of the dead in the New Testament. In the NT resuscitation reports, witnesses' emotions are frequently included. However, feelings of "uncanniness" are not mentioned. In the story of Jairus's daughter (Mk 5:42// Lk. 8:56) "they" or the "parents" are astounded or amazed. In the case of the widow's son at Nain (Lk. 7:16), fear seizes all of them and they glorify God. Elsewhere in the Gospels people are said to be amazed by, or wonder at, Jesus' miracles; see Mt. 8:27; 9:33; 15:31; Lk. 5:9. Acts 3:10 also reports this reaction to a healing by Peter.

60. Freud ("Das Unheimliche," 268) believes that children's anxiety is never entirely extinguished. It is usually tied to aloneness, stillness, and darkness, qualities which are all associated with childhood fears of annihilation and abandonment (cf. Jerry S. Piven, *Death and Delusion: A Freudian Analysis of Mortal Terror* [Greenwich: Information Age Publishing, 2004], 10–12).

61. The story of Elisha's bones has been called a "wonder story" (e.g., Mordechai Cogan and Hayim Tadmor, *II Kings*, AB 11 [New York: Doubleday, 1988], 150), an "anecdote...about a wonder" (Ernst Würthwein, *Die Bücher der Könige, 1. Kön. 17–2. Kön. 25,* ATD 11/2 [Göttingen: Vandenhoeck & Ruprecht, 1984], 366), and

Whether the life-giving power of Elisha's bones strikes a given reader as surprising or not, the perceived perdurance of Elisha's identity in his bones could be understood in the same way that Becker characterizes wealth as a means of symbolic immortality: it "radiates its powers even after one's death."[62] Another form of symbolic immortality recognized by Becker is transference, in the sense of participating vicariously in the apparent invulnerability of a hero or group leader.[63] Elisha certainly fits the bill for readers who view him as an exalted saint. On his own—both during his life and after his death—Elisha seems to wield power and perform גדלות (2 Kgs 8:4) which otherwise are achievable only by Yahweh himself. From this point of view, Elisha is the kind of hero with whom others might identify in order to buffer the hard facts of their lack of power and control, and especially the fact of the irreversible death which awaits each of us.

While some post-biblical traditions imagine various futures for the anonymous corpse which touched Elisha's bones, we are given no clue whether the deceased man *wanted* to return to life, or how he had felt about being dead. Several traditions *do* supply information about the continued career and feelings of a more famous revenant: Lazarus of Bethany. According to the fifteenth-century French poet Georges Chastellain, Lazarus spends his new existence burdened by "misery and every sadness in his thoughts, fearing what he must undergo."[64] Other sources tell us why. In one, the first question that Lazarus asked Jesus after his return to life was whether he would have to die again. When Jesus answers that he would, Lazarus never smiled again.[65]

---

a "saints' legend" (Shemesh, "The Elisha Stories"; see above). Even if we accept one of these genre designations, these stories have now become integrated into the body of scripture, an entirely different genre. As part of scripture they can no longer be expected to be received in the same way as typical wonder-tales and legends. On scripture as an over-arching genre designation, see Stuart Lasine, "Fiction, Falsehood, and Reality in Hebrew Scripture," *HS* 25 (1984): 24–40 (24–7).

62. Ernest Becker, *Escape from Evil* (New York: Free Press, 1975), 81.

63. Ernest Becker, *The Denial of Death* (New York: Free Press, 1973), 148–50; cf. Merlyn E. Mowrey, "The Religious Hero and the Escape from Evil: A Feminist Challenge to Ernest Becker's Religious Mystification," in *Death and Denial: Interdisciplinary Perspectives on the Legacy of Ernest Becker*, ed. Daniel Liechty (Westport: Praeger, 2002), 274–6.

64. Georges Chastellain, "Le Pas de la Mort," in *Œuvres de Georges Chastellain, Tome Sixième: Œuvres Diverses*, ed. Kervyn De Lettenhove (Brussels: F. Heussner, 1864), 59.

65. See, e.g., Raimo Hakola, "A Character Resurrected: Lazarus in the Fourth Gospel and Afterward," in *Characterization in the Gospels: Reconceiving Narrative*

Clearly, these traditions find nothing desirable about the condition of the dead *or* life after resuscitation. I would argue that the descriptions of revived individuals in the Hebrew Bible suggest the same thing, due to the narrator's lack of interest in the futures of the boys resuscitated by Elijah and Elisha, the corpse revived by Elisha's bones, and the ascended Elijah.[66] These stories might stir up abandoned childhood hopes, but only to deflate them again. In addition, while the gloomy biblical descriptions of Sheol do not necessarily "symbolize…fear of death" as Schmidt contends, they reinforce the message that all value for humans is to be found in our brief time on earth.[67]

The potency exhibited by the dead Elisha's bones is no exception, for, as discussed above, the bones lack true consciousness of self. Even though the revivifying power of the bones might weaken the impression of Elisha's vulnerability left by his ordinary illness and death, the seeming potency of his bones hardly qualifies as a conquest of death. For those who wish to live forever with their personality intact, the prospect of merely ossific immortality holds little appeal, even as a buffer against death awareness. In the end, Elisha himself remains a character who seems to accept his mortality without fear or a desire to achieve even symbolic immortality.

Criticism, ed. David Rhoads and Kari Syreeni, JSNTSup 184 (Sheffield: Sheffield Academic, 1999), 254. Some people familiar with these stories feared receiving Extreme Unction, thinking that if they recovered from their illness "they would have to live thereafter as a sort of animated corpse, as the 'stinking Lazarus' had done" (Eamon Duffy, *The Stripping of the Altars: Traditional Religion in England, C.1400–C.1580* [New Haven: Yale University Press, 2005], 313).

66. The mention of Elijah in Mal. 3:23-24 is of course significant, but his future role as a reconciler contrasts dramatically with his actions in Kings.

67. Brian Schmidt, Review of Phillip S. Johnston, 'Shades of Sheol: Death and the Afterlife in the Old Testament', *RBL* (2003): 3, https://www.bookreviews.org/pdf/2947_3084.pdf. See further in Lasine, *Jonah and the Human Condition*, 132–4.

Chapter 11

HE'S DRIVING LIKE JEHU—LIKE A MADMAN:
HUMOR AND VIOLENCE IN 2 KINGS 9–10

Mark Roncace

I find the story of Jehu amusing. But how could the brutal beheading of seventy men be funny? How could a queen trampled to death illicit a chuckle? How could a house full of priests slaughtered in cold blood be comical? It is well known that what makes something humorous is difficult to determine. You may not laugh at the same things I laugh at. While there is no agreed-upon unified theory of humor to which we can appeal, I propose that one of them—the benign violation theory—suggests that Jehu can be read as an amusing character, a joke even, because his portrayal is shot through (pun intended) with obvious verbal and social incongruities, sarcastic comments, witty dialogue, unrealistic scenarios, and cartoonish violence. The story's fantastical nature renders Jehu's brutality non-threatening, harmless, and thus entertaining. The resulting humor functions to challenge parochial ideologies.

Theories of Humor

There are many theories which try to define humor, determine what would be considered humorous, and explain its psychological, social, and spiritual functions.[1] Three well-established theories are the superi-

---

1. See, among many others, John Morreall, *The Philosophy of Laughter and Humor* (Albany: State University of New York Press, 1987); Simon Critchley, *On Humour* (London: Routledge, 2002); Jan Walsh Hokenson, *The Idea of Comedy: History, Theory, Critique* (Madison: Fairleigh Dickinson University Press, 2006);

ority theory (we laugh at the misfortunes of others), the relief theory (we laugh to relieve tension and nervous energy), and the incongruity theory (we laugh at odd juxtapositions which cause an unexpected, sudden shift in perspective). Researchers have proffered a number of other theories, many of which overlap with one another, particularly as they include some element of the incongruity theory.[2]

Another thread that runs through a number of contemporary theories is that humor is somehow connected to the dark side. Something is not funny unless it has some sort of wicked twist to it. The benign violation theory developed by A. Peter McGraw and Caleb Warren picks up on this notion.[3] They note that many theories argue that humor requires a perceived violation—something that disrupts one's sense of how the world "ought to be." Moral psychology theories, however, suggest these normative breaches cause negative emotions, such as disgust, rather than amusement. McGraw and Warren theorize that moral violations which simultaneously seem benign elicit laughter and amusement in addition to disgust. The benign violation theory, then, integrates existing theories to propose that humor occurs when three conditions are satisfied: (1) a situation violates one's sense of how the world "ought to be," (2) the threatening situation seems benign, and (3) a person sees both interpretations at the same time.

Humorous violations, from an evolutionary point of view, likely originated as apparent physical threats, such as those present in play fighting and tickling. With time, the situations that provoked amusement expanded from physical threats to other violations, including those of (a) personal dignity (e.g., slapstick, physical abuse, and deformities), (b) linguistic norms (e.g., puns, malapropisms), (c) social norms (e.g., strange behaviors, risqué jokes), and (d) moral norms (e.g., disrespectful actions, unethical conduct). The benign violation theory argues that anything that threatens one's sense of how the world "ought to be" will be humorous, as long as the threatening situation also seems benign.

John Morreall, *Comic Relief: A Comprehensive Philosophy of Humor* (Hoboken: Wiley-Blackwell, 2009); and Salvatore Attardo, *Encyclopedia of Humor Studies* (Thousand Oaks: Sage, 2014). See also *Humor: International Journal of Humor Research*.

2. There is also the question of defining terms: humor, comedy, comic, wit, funny, laughter, amusing, etc. For simplicity's sake, I am using the terms interchangeably.

3. A. Peter McGraw and Caleb Warren, "Benign Violations: Making Immoral Behavior Funny," *Psychological Science* 21 (2010): 1141–9. See also A. Peter McGraw and Joel Warner, *The Humor Code: A Global Search for What Makes Things Funny* (New York: Simon & Schuster, 2015).

Just as there are several ways in which a situation can be a violation, there is more than one way in which a violation can seem benign. A violation can seem benign if (a) one lacks a commitment to the violated norm, (b) one norm suggests the behavior is wrong but another norm suggests it is acceptable, and (c) one is psychologically distant from the violation.

For example (a), McGraw and Warren found most people disapproved of a situation in which a church raffles off a Hummer SUV to recruit new members. However, many people were also simultaneously amused, unless they attended church regularly. Churchgoers are more committed to the belief that churches are sacred and, consequently, were less likely to consider the church's actions benign; thus they were not amused.

For example (b), McGraw and Warren found that when presented with a scenario in which a man rubs his bare genitals on his pet kitten, most people judge his actions "wrong" or "disgusting." But if the kitten purrs and seems to enjoy the contact, people are more likely to be amused by the scenario as well (the amusement supplements, not replaces, the negative feelings). The man violates a moral norm related to bestiality, but because no one is harmed the behavior is acceptable according to an alternative norm. However, when presented with a different case in which the kitten does not enjoy the contact, participants were much less likely to be amused; there was no alternative norm to make the actions benign.

For example (c), McGraw and Warren found that psychological distance—whether temporal, social, spatial, or likelihood of occurring—also makes a violation seem benign. Two quotes can serve to illustrate this idea: "Comedy is tragedy plus time" (temporal distance) and Mel Brooks's "Tragedy is when I cut my finger. Comedy is when you walk into an open sewer and die" (social distance).

For the benign violation theory of humor, comedy is part darkness and part light. It takes something terrible and makes it funny. If the humor is too light-hearted, it's toothless. If it's too edgy, it makes people uncomfortable. Good humor is both violating and benign. I suggest the characterization of Jehu works in a similar way: It's part dark and violent, part light and comical. The writer (final editor) as well as the audience—from the original one (exilic? postexilic?) to contemporary readers—can find Jehu's violations benign, and thus amusing, because, first, they have psychological distance in all its forms: temporal, social, spatial, and the likelihood of it occurring. The fantastical nature of the story, the exaggerated, excessive, absurd actions of the characters from the very beginning, provides the necessary distance for readers to be amused rather than (or, in addition to) horrified. The violence is cartoonish—removed from reality—and thus benign.

Second, readers can find the violations benign depending on their own particular norms and values. Some readers lack strong commitment to the theological or religious norm that the Bible is serious, sacred literature (like those who chuckle at the raffled-off Hummer). Other readers, very differently, may find the violations benign because they have alternative norms at their disposal: Jehu's bloody massacres are a violation of a moral norm, but because they are done in accordance with Yhwh's command, they are acceptable (as when the kitten does not object to the contact).[4]

Reading 2 Kings 9–10

Finding humor in the Bible is nothing new. Many other studies have elucidated comedic elements from Genesis to Revelation.[5] The Jehu narrative has not escaped notice. Most notably, Francisco García-Treto offers a carnivalesque reading using Peter Stallybrass's morphology of carnivalesque literature and drawing on the work of Mikhail Bakhtin.[6] Following García-Treto, Helen Paynter finds seriocomic features in the Jehu narrative and throughout 1 and 2 Kings.[7] Both of these enlightening

---

4. One could also argue, perhaps more simply, that the humor in the Jehu story serves as "comic relief" whereby amusing scenes are inserted into the serious story in order to provide temporary relief from the tension. In this vein, one might see the humor as distancing the reader from the violence, providing an insulating effect. A number of recent American films (and advertisements) mix humor with violence, with seemingly the same objective—to tame or offset the violence. Scholars have done some interesting theoretical work on this combination which might also be fruitfully applied to biblical studies. See, e.g., Geoff King, "'Killingly Funny': Mixing Modalities in New Hollywood's Comedy-With-Violence," in *New Hollywood Violence*, ed. Steven Jay Schneider (New York: Manchester University Press, 2004), 126–43.

5. There are far too many such studies to name here. See Conrad Hyers, *And God Created Laughter: The Bible as Divine Comedy* (Atlanta: John Knox, 1987); Athalya Brenner and Yehuda T. Radday, eds, *On Humour and the Comic in the Hebrew Bible* (New York: Almond, 1990); William J. Whedbee, *The Bible and the Comic Vision* (New York: Cambridge University Press, 1998); Athalya Brenner, ed., *Are We Amused? Humour About Women In the Biblical World* (New York: T&T Clark, 2003); Melissa Jackson, *Comedy and Feminist Interpretation of the Hebrew Bible: A Subversive Collaboration* (Oxford: Oxford University Press, 2012); and Mark E. Biddle, *A Time to Laugh: Humor in the Bible* (Macon: Smyth & Helwys, 2013).

6. Francesco García-Treto, "The Fall of the House: A Carnivalesque Reading of 2 Kings 9 and 10," *JSOT* 15 (1990): 47–65.

7. Helen Paynter, *Reduced Laughter: Seriocomic Features and their Functions in the Book of Kings* (Leiden: Brill, 2016), 25–8, 64–7, 105–19, 149–57. Her analysis

studies open the door for the present analysis which seeks to read the characterization of Jehu as so comically ridiculous from beginning to end that it is best read as a light-hearted caricature featuring benign violations of (a) personal dignity, (b) linguistic norms, (c) social norms, and (d) moral norms.

The opening scene features a variety of incongruities which, broadly speaking, violate our expectations of how the world ought to be. Elisha instructs "one of the sons of the prophets" to go anoint Jehu (9:1-3). The reader has been introduced to Jehu back in 1 Kgs 19:15-16 where God instructed Elijah to "to anoint Jehu son of Nimshi as king over Israel." Readers who recall this passage are surprised to find Elisha, not Elijah, taking responsibility for the installation of Jehu. And even Elisha himself cannot do it, as he sends an anonymous prophet to complete the task.[8] Furthermore, we expect only one prophet to be involved in the anointing of a king, not three of them (Elijah, Elisha, and the apprentice), and we do not expect them to be anointing northern kings—Jehu is the only such one.

Elisha tells the unnamed prophet to go to Ramoth Gilead and pour oil on Jehu's head and declare, "This is what the Lord says, 'I anoint you king over Israel.'" Then the prophet is to "open the door and flee. Do not delay!" García-Treto finds "an almost comical effect" to these three verbs—open the door, run, don't wait—because it shows how "dimwitted" and "ridiculous" the novice prophet is.[9] Furthermore, maybe it explains why Elisha himself does not want to fulfill this task: It's too dangerous. Is the prophet of God being a coward? The image of the "young man" (v. 4) doing the deed and then running away in fear does not inspire confidence in this whole enterprise. If Yhwh is behind Jehu's coronation, why be afraid? The clandestine nature of the anointing by an anonymous emissary violates our socio-religious expectations of a proper Yhwh-sanctioned inauguration. Something feels "off" right from the beginning.

When the stand-in for Elisha arrives on the scene, he finds a group of army officers sitting together, and he announces, "I have a message for you, commander" (9:5). Does he even know who Jehu is? If so, why not

---

follows García-Treto in many ways. She analyzes the Jehu story as exemplifying the following "seriocomic events": inversion, masking, linguistic transgression, transgression of bodily boundaries, feasting, and profanation. These are not unlike what we are calling "incongruities" or "violations."

8. Rashi says it was Jonah, which adds another layer of intertextual comedy, given the humorous portrayal of Jonah, as many have observed.

9. García-Treto, "The Fall of the House," 55.

simply address him by name. Jehu, appropriately, asks who the message is for, since after all, each one of them is a commander. The emissary replies, "For you, commander." Still, does the young prophet even know that he is now speaking to Jehu? Only the narrator has identified him as Jehu. And how could Jehu be confident the message is for him? Did he just happen to be the one who spoke up? This exchange is a "linguistic violation" of sorts—does the student-prophet have any idea what he is doing? Where is Yhwh in all this?

Elisha had instructed the apprentice to take Jehu into an "inner room" (v. 2), but Jehu "got up and went into the house" (v. 6). Our hunch that this unnamed prophet is not following his master's commands very carefully is confirmed by the lengthy declaration he makes in vv. 6-10 which goes far beyond the simple message Elisha asked him to render in v. 3. While not discrediting the various solutions other commentators have offered to this discrepancy,[10] I would simply add that this scenario is funny. Here we have an over-eager young prophet who is on his first really big mission (he made it into the Bible!). And when he gets his chance to speak, he's not going to make some one-sentence proclamation and exit stage left. No, he's going to make the most of his fifteen seconds of fame. So he pontificates about how Jehu is to destroy everyone "who urinates on a wall" (man) in the house of Ahab, which cleverly foreshadows the urine at the end of the story (10:27). He declares that dogs will devour Jezebel and no one will bury her, an anticipation of the violation of Jezebel's personal dignity (9:32-37). His harangue is a paraphrase of a message Elijah had given to Ahab in 1 Kgs 21:21-24, although there are some differences, such as the added insult that Jezebel will not be properly interred. It's as if the young prophet wants to show off: He knows his prophetic oracles and is good enough to creatively expand and apply them as needed.

"Then he opened the door and fled" (9:10) is a comic juxtaposition to the brutal, testosterone-driven monologue he just delivered, and an example of physical (slapstick) humor. As he exits in a jiffy, we are left to conclude that "the intermediary is deliberately presented as a character of marginal, even risible status," and that Jehu has "just had kingship thrust upon him by the agency of a novice 'madman.'"[11] The entire scene is amusingly incongruous with our sense of how this important event should occur. Are we supposed to take this anointing seriously?

---

10. See Lissa M. Wray Beal, *The Deuteronomist's Prophet: Narrative Control of Approval and Disapproval in the Story of Jehu (2 Kings 9 and 10)* (New York: T&T Clark, 2007), 57.

11. García-Treto, "The Fall of the House," 55–6.

More subversions of our expectations occur in the next scene (vv. 11-13). When Jehu returns to "his master's officers" (a not-so-subtle reminder that Joram is still the king), they ask him, "Is everything alright (lit.: "is it peace," שלום)? Why did that madman come to you?" And Jehu answers, "You know the sort and how they babble." Apparently, the officers were not impressed with the unnamed prophet, calling him a "madman," which, actually, he was in his graphic, blood-thirsty babblings. But still, why assume he's mad?[12] Jehu's reluctance to apprise them of what he said is more understandable: he does not know what they will think of his coming coup. Will he have their support? So he humorously plays along with them, trying to dismiss the encounter as the incoherent ramblings of a lunatic, just as they suggested. This is the first of several instances of Jehu's lying (moral violations). But the officers are not quite buying it. Maybe they see the oil on Jehu's head (like the little boy with chocolate smeared all over his face who is denying having his hand in the cookie jar), and so they press Jehu for a better answer. He gives them the shortened version—why not the full message?—of what the madman uttered: The Lord said I anoint you king over Israel.

They immediately throw their cloaks on the floor, blow the trumpet, and herald Jehu as king (v. 13). Why the sudden and dramatic (and comic) reversal of positions? One minute, he's a madman; then the next minute, you place complete trust in the madman's words and throw your support behind Jehu's coup? Is this a farce? A parody of how a Yhwh-appointed king is to begin his reign? Can we take Jehu's coup seriously? This, it is to be noted, is the first in a series of instances in which characters are comically gullible and eager to kowtow to Jehu.

Emboldened by the support of the generals, Jehu rides to Jezreel where Joram is recovering from wounds (9:16). When the watchman in Jezreel sees Jehu and his troops coming, Joram orders that a single horseman be sent out to inquire if he comes in peace. Given that it's wartime, the king is injured, and unidentified troops are approaching, this tactic seems amusingly naïve. When the horseman reaches Jehu, he begins with a proper introduction, "Thus says the king," which is comically pretentious given the circumstances—a socio-linguistic violation. Jehu does not appear to stop or even slow his rush toward Jezreel as he responds sarcastically, "What do you have to do with peace?" Jehu may be a brutish bore, a man of the sword, but, as we see here and elsewhere, he can also be rather clever with words. He then orders the horseman to fall in behind him, which he does, unrealistically, with no protestations.

---

12. Nearly all commentators attribute this view to the ecstatic practices of the prophets.

When the sentinel reports to Joram that the lone horseman is not coming back (v. 18), one would presume the king would take this as a bad sign. Not so. Instead he simply sends out a second horseman. The watchman once more reports that the messenger is not returning—him too?!— and he explains with the titular comment: "The driving is like that of Jehu son of Nimshi; for he drives like a madman" (9:20). So Jehu, we learn, is well known for his reckless chariot driving, an entertaining bit of background information on the soon-to-be king who will indeed be reckless and excessive in just about everything he does.[13] Linguistically, of course, his style of driving echoes the madman whose message ignited the coup. A madman anointed a madman. On one hand, this is an intense scene fraught with pending violence. On the other, the preposterous innocence of Joram's actions (and irony, since we as readers know Jehu does not intend "peace"), the two laughably capitulating horsemen, and the lookout's description of Jehu's driving serve to lighten the mood and give the reader pause about just how seriously we are to read the story.

King Joram himself comes out unsuspectingly to meet the approaching cavalry (9:21). King Ahaziah of Judah, who had come to Jezreel to see the injured Joram, accompanies him. Ahaziah's presence is entertainingly curious. Why is he even in Jezreel in the first place? Since when do kings make hospital visits in the middle of war (9:16)? And why does he join Joram now in this risky venture to meet Jehu? These are two naïve kings riding straight to death—like the girl who walks into a shed of chainsaws in a spoof of a horror film.

The two monarchs meet Jehu "at the plot of ground that had belonged to Naboth" (9:22). Of all the places, it has to be in Naboth's field. A little too poetically perfect it seems. To Joram's question about peace, Jehu again answers rather eloquently, "What peace, so long as the whoring and sorceries of your mother Jezebel continue?" In this "linguistic transgression,"[14] Jehu insults his foe by cleverly denouncing his mother's cultic infidelity in terms that also impugn her sexual promiscuity—it's two slurs for the price of one. Like the hero who utters an epic one-liner in an action film, Jehu rhetorically one-ups and disrespects his opponent before killing him—a particularly enjoyable moment for the audience.

Given that Jehu has heretofore been one of Joram's loyal generals, and that Jehu has only asked a rhetorical question, even if insulting, and that Joram does not know of the anointing, his response is quite the over-reaction. He whirls his chariot around and flees. Reminiscent of the

---

13. Paynter observes that this description shows that Jehu "scarcely deports himself in a regal manner" (*Reduced Laughter*, 91).
14. Ibid., 80.

military officers who suddenly supported the words of the madman, and the two horsemen who had just come out from Jezreel, Joram makes an unquestioned and dramatic reversal of positions. He bolts the scene—another instance of physical humor—just like the madman who anointed the mad chariot driver.

After shooting Joram, Jehu instructs the heretofore unmentioned Bidkar to throw Joram's body onto Naboth's field, a violation of personal dignity. Poetic justice indeed. Jehu then becomes reflective, reminding Bidkar how the two of them were present when Elijah uttered his prophecy against Ahab (1 Kgs 21:19). The narrative in 1 Kings 21, of course, does not mention the presence of Jehu and Bidkar, so one must wonder if Jehu is making it up—an amusing possibility. Jehu, as we see in subsequent scenes, is certainly not above blatant deceit. Not surprisingly, Jehu fails to render the oracle correctly. Most notably, Elijah's word concerned Ahab, not Joram to whom Jehu is attributing it. In fact, Jehu's words are so different from Elijah's that perhaps it is not a citation of 1 Kgs 21:19, but of an oracle not previously recorded in the Ahab narrative. Or perhaps Jehu is wryly fabricating the oracle to justify his treason? Like the madman who anointed him, Jehu can be quite the orator of feigned prophecies.

Either way, the whole scene feels cartoonishly funny because while Jehu is waxing eloquent, King Ahaziah is escaping (9:27). Jehu and his troops turn and chase Ahaziah and shoot him too (a violation of personal dignity). But they only wound him and he dies later in Megiddo—an entertaining foil for all the subsequent violence: Jehu will never miss the mark again. It would make sense for Jehu to attribute his killing of Ahaziah to the fact that, even though he was king of Judah, he also belonged to the house of Ahab through his mother Athaliah, Ahab's daughter (2 Kgs 8:18, 26). But Jehu makes no such connection—a sort of linguistic incongruity by silence—so his motivation remains unclear. Is this just gratuitous, absurd violence?

Jehu then rides to Jezreel where he encounters Jezebel in a macabre scene, which also evokes a chuckle of amusement as there are benign violations across the board. Here is the scenario: Coup-leader approaches city. Queen appears in palace window, all decked out and prettied up to seduce him (social norm).[15] As he approaches, she asks if he comes in peace, knowing full well he does not. Then she sarcastically (linguistic

---

15. See Simon Parker, "Jezebel's Reception of Jehu," *Maarav* 1 (1978–79): 67–8, for a thorough and convincing interpretation of Jezebel as trying to seduce Jehu, which is followed by others (Richard D. Nelson, *First and Second Kings* [Atlanta: John Knox, 1987], 203).

norm) calls him Zimri, a witty and insulting reference to the man who had assassinated another Israelite king some forty years earlier, and who only ruled seven days before committing suicide in the royal palace, where the queen too is presumably about to meet her end (1 Kgs 16:8-20).[16] He ignores her question and stilted trash-talking and randomly calls out, "Who is on my side? Who?" Instantly, and fantastically, several eunuchs appear at the window—traitors one and all (ironically, just like the coup-leader himself). He orders the emasculated males (physical/slapstick) to push her down, which they do. She falls to the ground. The coup-leader tramples her to death with his horse (personal dignity, moral norm). Blood spatters on the wall. He then goes into the palace and parties (social norm) and sardonically orders that the "cursed woman" receive a proper burial because, after all, she was a king's daughter, not naming her as the queen she was (linguistic). When they go to bury her, they find only a few bits and pieces of her body, the rest apparently eaten by dogs (personal dignity). So, it turns out, while the usurper was inside feasting, so were the dogs on the outside. The usurper interprets her fate as the fulfillment of a divine oracle, but, as he has done before, plays fast and loose with previous prophetic pronouncements (linguistic).[17]

Chapter 10 opens with an entertaining incongruity: The madman and murderer is also characterized as a man of letters, perhaps an ironic connection to Jezebel as a woman of letters (1 Kgs 21:8-10). Jehu writes to the leaders in Samaria, the capital city which he needed to control in order to solidify his reign, pointing out how much power they have and telling them to place one of Ahab's descendants on the throne and to prepare to defend their city. This violates social (military) expectations, and it is, oddly, the complete opposite of his strategy with Jezreel, which he tried to take unawares (9:15). Here Jehu arrogantly challenges them to a duel—which feels stereotyped or stylized (perhaps a spoof of the David and Goliath story?). The leaders of Samaria are frightened, saying, "If two kings could not resist him, how can we?" (10:4), so they send word of surrender to Jehu (10:5). Really? A fortified capital with a military presence capitulates because of a letter? Jehu has bluffed his way to victory. Yes, Jehu had killed two kings, but that was in isolation, two

---

16. Zimri's assassination fulfilled the words of the prophet, ironically named Jehu (1 Kgs 16:12).

17. Jehu's words are general paraphrases of the word of Elijah (1 Kgs 21:23) and the young prophet (2 Kgs 9:10). Jehu also adds elements which are in neither previous oracle (9:37), which invites the reader to once again consider that Jehu is (wrongly, thus comically?) attempting prophetic justifications for his actions.

assassinations. His army—if he really even had one—had not defeated anyone. Samaria's automatic and complete ("we will do anything you say") submission is fantastical and thus amusing.

To test their loyalty, Jehu writes a second letter to the leaders in Samaria instructing them to "take the heads of the men, the sons of your master, and come to me at Jezreel tomorrow at this time" (10:6). As most commentators agree, Jehu's command is intentionally ambiguous, a linguistic violation.[18] Is he asking only for the "heads," that is, the "leaders" of Ahab's house to be brought to him? Or is he seeking literal decapitation? The leaders of Samaria, because of their apparent undue fear of Jehu, are "close to comical in their eagerness to accommodate a literal interpretation of his request."[19] It is about 25 miles from Samaria to Jezreel, so they must move incredibly quickly to execute the 70 men and deliver the heads within 24 hours. But they manage the feat, unrealistically. Jehu receives the deathly baskets matter-of-factly—as if he had been expecting them all along—and orders the heads to be put on display in two piles at the city gate (v. 8), a social, moral, and personal dignity violation.

The next morning, Jehu gives a "half-honest, half-impudent harangue"[20] to the people of Jezreel in which he clears them of any guilt, admits to assassinating Joram and Ahaziah, but implies he had nothing to do with the two piles of heads, which, of course, the reader knows is not true—thus a moral violation. He also, again, claims his actions fulfill the words of the prophet Elijah, although here (for the first time) he quotes no specific prophetic oracle. At best, Jehu sees his actions as a general fulfillment of prophetic judgements against Ahab. At worst, he is again using the prophetic word as a bogus justification for this own agenda. At this point, it is difficult for the reader not to lean toward the latter conclusion.

Jehu goes, once again, from slick manipulator/orator to ruthless killing machine. On his way to Samaria, he, just by chance (!), happens to run into a group of Ahaziah's family. When Jehu asks who they are (apparently he does not recognize them, suggesting the gratuitous nature of their death), they, with comic candor, identify themselves and explain that they are on their way to greet (שלום) the king and queen mother. What is it with Ahaziah and his family visiting people at the wrong time and place?

---

18. See, among others, T. R. Hobbs, *2 Kings* (Waco: Word, 1985), 120.
19. Wray Beal, *The Deuteronomist's Prophet*, 111.
20. James Montgomery, *A Critical and Exegetical Commentary on the Books of Kings* (New York: Scribner's, 1951), 409.

They ironically are unaware Joram and Jezebel are dead. Jehu orders his men to "Take them alive." So they "took them alive." Is this the end of the violence—he's not going to kill them? No, wait: "Then they slaughtered them." Jehu was just joking, toying with his victims and the audience. Once again, the narrative gives a precise body count: 42 (perhaps a clever reminder of the 42 youths mauled by bears at Elisha's curse, 2 Kgs 2:23-25). It's another absurd and sadistic violation of how the world ought to be (the same of which can be said of Elisha's curse). Yet, at the same time, this scene seems laughably "coincidental" and the grisly outcome—although teasingly and temporarily delayed—is too easily predictable, thus also benign.

The next brief scene features another chance encounter, this time with the random Jehonadab who was on his way to see Jehu (10:15-17). Jehonadab pledges his loyalty to Jehu's coup and joins him in his chariot ride to Samaria. A commoner in the royal chariot probably violates a social norm. Jehu says to him, "Come with me and see my zeal for the Lord." Given the complex and ambiguous characterization of Jehu, the reader chortles at his self-evaluation: He is hardly a pure, righteous religious figure. His "zeal" is manifested by his subsequent slaughter of Ahab's remaining family in Samaria (10:17)—the seventy sons evidently not enough.

The final scene pulls out all the stops in its characterization of Jehu (10:18-28). Jehu announces to the crowds in Samaria that he will serve Baal even more than Ahab, and he summons all the prophets and ministers of Baal for a great sacrifice. If they don't come, they "will no longer live" (wink). Presumably this is a big joke—none of these men are going to live whether they come or not—not unlike his earlier bluffing of the men in Samaria. In case there were any doubt, the narrator (comically) clarifies for the reader: "Jehu was acting deceptively in order to destroy the priests of Baal" (10:19). The deception is highlighted by the wordplay: He promises to serve (עבד) Baal, but he intends to destroy (אבד) his adherents. The reader, then, knows what Jehu has up his sleeve: The great sacrifice, ironically, will be the slaughter of the priests themselves.[21] What is funny here, though, is why the dignitaries of Baal naively believe Jehu. His earlier scam of the leaders in Samaria was clever and entertaining enough. But this ruse is ridiculous: Would any self-respecting priest of

---

21. In addition to the Hebrew wordplay, it is interesting that in English the words "slaughter" and "laughter" are so similar (etymologically, the two words are sadly not related).

Baal really fall for it?[22] Perhaps that is part of the humor: The men of Baal are in fact that dumb. But it's such a bad bluff, and their being duped by it so unbelievable, it feels like a spoof of the story of Elijah and the prophets of Baal on Mount Carmel (1 Kgs 17:16-45).

After Jehu goes to great lengths to be sure all the priests of Baal have gathered into the temple, he orders that they be given robes to wear. The image of the priests eagerly donning the garments in preparation for the(ir) slaughter is borderline hilarious, and thus a benign social and moral violation. Reminiscent of Jezebel primping for her brutal murder, Jehu dresses up his victims before they are hacked to death, a violation of personal dignity. Also similar to Jezebel, the bodies of the dead priests are disrespectfully discarded (10:25). It's at once a revolting and amusing scene.

The narrator's characterization of Jehu concludes with scatological humor, more benign violations of personal dignity and social norms. Jehu and his men destroy the temple and turn it into a latrine, or perhaps a dung heap. This description links it to the bodily remains of Jezebel which are also compared to dung on the ground (9:37).[23] The narrator has in the end yielded to toilet humor—and employed it to frame the story with a clever wordplay: Jehu was commissioned to destroy everyone "who urinates on a wall" in the house of Ahab (9:8); he did so, and now everyone urinates on the house of Baal "to this day" (10:27). It is a fittingly disgusting and amusing final image of Jehu.[24]

Just when we thought the benign violations were over, the narrative gives us an encore in the form of two different assessments of Jehu. Verses 28-29 report that Jehu destroyed Baal worship in Israel, but quickly adds that he did not turn away from the sins of Jeroboam's golden calves. Then, rather unexpectedly, Yhwh speaks directly to Jehu in v. 30 (a funny time for the deity to make his first appearance), saying he has done right by destroying the house of Ahab, and so his descendants will be on the throne for four generations. But then in v. 31, the narrator declares that Jehu did not keep the law of Yhwh with all his heart and reminds us again that Jehu continued the sins of Jeroboam. The fact that the deity and the narrator do not quite agree about Jehu is highly incongruous. While commentators

---

22. An alternate explanation is that the Baal loyalists thought that Jehu's previous appeals to Yhwh were themselves a bluff for political maneuvering, which would add another layer of irony.

23. Robert L. Cohn, *2 Kings* (Collegeville: Liturgical Press, 2000), 75.

24. Payntner (*Reduced Laughter*, 91) sums it up this way: "His two-chapter reign is characterized by recklessness, haste, non-judicial violence; excess in every regard."

have offered much insightful and serious discussion of these verses,[25] perhaps we can add that this conversation of perspectives on Jehu is amusing because the narrator seems to hold Jehu to a higher religious standard than Yhwh. The deity is just happy Jehu killed off the house of Ahab. But the narrator demands more—complete and total adherence to the law of Yhwh, and no golden calves. So while the reader grapples with the implications of Yhwh calling Jehu's numerous violations "right," the narrator essentially adds, "Yes, but it was not enough." Is this the final joke, a grand linguistic violation? Yhwh and the narrator arguing about whether Jehu was sufficiently righteous? Are they being serious? Or is each of them taking their turn at sarcasm? Are we laughing with God and the narrator? Or at them?

Reflections

The benign violation theory of humor provides a helpful heuristic device for understanding Jehu's characterization in the following ways. (1) Like our reaction to the church who raffles off the Hummer, or the man who rubs his genitals on his kitten, the theory helps us understand how feelings of disgust and amusement can be held simultaneously. Sure, we are horrified by Jehu's actions, but we can also find them funny because we deem them benign violations. The theory bridges the violent and comedic elements in the Jehu story.

(2) The theory helps us to be self-reflective. It opens space for each reader to contemplate personal and societal norms. To which ones are we strongly or weakly committed? What violates our norms? What other norms might we have which enable us to see a violation as simultaneously benign? How far are we "psychologically distant" from the story? Per the last question, I have proposed that nearly all readers of the Jehu narrative—and biblical literature as a whole—are so far removed psychologically from the story that we do not see the violations depicted in it as "real" or "likely to happen." They are hypotheticals, utterly fantastical, such that they are benign, non-threatening. I must pause, however, and recognize that not all readers have this psychological distance. Those who have witnessed or experienced genocide, war, torture, or other horrific forms of brutality are much less likely to read Jehu as a humorous figure. For them, it's not a hypothetical, the violations are not benign. Thus, the theory deepens my own self-awareness.

---

25. Wray Beal, *The Deuteronomist's Prophet*, 142–52.

(3) By offering an explanation for how we can laugh at shockingly gruesome scenes, the benign violation theory provides an avenue to explore the function of the humor. Helen Paynter concludes her analyses of the books of Kings:

> Comic elements of the text have been shown throughout. Even when the narrator is describing unspeakable events, the floridity, the hyperbole and clowning which accompany them imbue them with a certain dark humor. Are we supposed to laugh? Probably, at times… But these comedic incidents serve [to]…provoke the sophisticated reader to have an open mind, to be free to re-evaluate metanarratives, be suspicious of dogmatism, and mistrust monologic representations of truth. The seriocomic form…is a device to dig deeper into a reality which is often hidden beneath structures of power and tradition.[26]

Applied specifically to 2 Kings 9–10, I suggest the humor that results from the benign violations (i.e., the seriocomic features) serves to undermine Yhwh-alone ideology. If we cannot take Jehu and his story seriously, can we take his "zeal for Yhwh" seriously? If the whole sketch is light-hearted entertainment, marked by many fantastical elements, do we nod affirmatively, straight-faced, at Yhwh's praise for Jehu's massacres? For exilic or post-exilic readers living in a religiously pluralistic environment, the Jehu story calls them to be "suspicious of dogmatism" and to "mistrust monologic representations of truth." It is a narrative in line with the "open-minded" ideology of other stories like Joseph, Jonah, and Ruth. It is a narrative that fits with the anti-prophetic satire that threads through texts from Balaam to Jeremiah.[27] Indeed, the dialogic nature of the Hebrew Bible gives readers "alternative norms" which enable them to see Jehu's violations as benign. The resulting humor subverts narrow-minded, parochial thinking—an important and powerful "device" for the original audience. And for contemporary readers.

---

26. Paynter, *Reduced Laughter*, 193–4.
27. See, e.g., David Marcus, *From Balaam to Jonah: Anti-Prophetic Satire in the Hebrew Bible* (Atlanta: Scholars Press, 1995); Wesley Bergen, *Elisha and the End of Prophetism* (Sheffield: Sheffield Academic, 1999); and Paynter, *Reduced Laughter*, 124–48.

Chapter 12

ATHALIAH: THE QUEEN WHO WAS NOT*

Patricia Dutcher-Walls

The story of Athaliah, the only queen of Judah, presents an apparently powerful ruler who overthrows the royal house of David and controls the throne for six years. However, the story is written to repudiate her at every turn, and ultimately to erase her character from the ongoing story of the Davidic monarchy. The character study in this essay will detail how the narrative and rhetorical strategies of the story accomplish this amazing disappearing act on her behalf.

This study takes as one of its premises that biblical narratives such as the Athaliah story serve purposes other than that of historically accurate reporting, despite the general historical style of the writing. That said, there are interesting and significant historical issues behind the narrative. Scholars have explored how to place the events narrated into their ninth-century BCE context,[1] focusing particularly on the international and national political machinations and connections behind Athaliah's seizure of the throne. Issues of historical reconstruction include Athaliah's remaining associations with Phoenicia after the massacre of the Omride dynasty by Jehu[2] and the conflicts between the urban elites, who supported

---

* I am thankful for my colleague, Dr. Maryann Amor, for her careful editing of this chapter.

1. For example, J. Maxwell Miller and John H. Hayes, *A History of Ancient Israel and Judah*, 2nd ed. (Philadelphia: Westminster John Knox, 2006), 327–52.

2. For example, Marvin A. Sweeney, *I & II Kings: A Commentary*, OTL (Louisville: Westminster John Knox, 2007), 343–4; Stuart Cohen, "How to Mount a Successful Coup d'Etat: Lessons from the Bible (II Kings 11, II Chronicles 23)," *Diplomacy and Statecraft* 11 (2000): 9.

the queen's northern and Phoenician connections, and those associated with a rural power base, who supported the return of a Davidide to the throne.³

While my study will make some reference to probable historical situations and sociological analysis, that is not my primary interest. Rather, my attention is focused on the way the story is shaped as a narrative, which aligns with others who adopt a similar approach. Although numerous commentators accept that authorial interests have shaped the Athaliah narrative, their descriptions of the nature of these interests vary. Many scholars recognize that a principal concern of the story is "to de-legitimate Athaliah."⁴ Others develop arguments that the story serves larger ideological or political purposes in the way it is told.⁵ This essay will neither explore nor endorse any particular view on this but it holds that narratives in biblical historiography are shaped to convey a variety of interests.⁶

Within the variety of views on 2 Kings 11, my particular purpose is to examine the shaping of the character of Athaliah. My method examines the narrative and rhetorical artistry of the passage, with reference on occasion to the storyteller's probable historical and sociological context

---

3. For example, Robin Gallagher Branch, "Athaliah, a Treacherous Queen: A Careful Analysis of her Story in 2 Kings 11 and 2 Chronicles 22:10–23:21," *In die Skriflig* 38 (2004): 546; Kyung Sook Lee, "1 and 2 Kings," in *Global Bible Commentary*, ed. Daniel Patte, José Severino Croatto, and Teresa Okure (Nashville: Abingdon, 2004), 115; Claudia V. Camp, "1 and 2 Kings," in *The Women's Bible Commentary*, ed. Carol A. Newsom and Sharon H. Ringe (London: SPCK, 1998), 111.

4. For example, among others, Branch, "Athaliah, a Treacherous Queen," 539; Camp, "1 and 2 Kings," 111; Mordechai Cogan and Hayim Tadmor, *II Kings*, AB 11 (New York: Doubleday, 1988), 133; Richard D. Nelson, *First and Second Kings*, Interpretation (Louisville: John Knox, 1987), 207.

5. For example, see Wabayanga Robert Kuloba, "Athaliah of Judah (2 Kings 11): A Political Anomaly or an Ideological Victim?" in *Looking through a Glass Bible: Postdisciplinary Biblical Interpretations from the Glasgow School*, ed. A. K. M. Adam and Samuel Tongue (Leiden: Brill, 2014), 151; E. Theodore Mullen, *Narrative History and Ethnic Boundaries: The Deuteronomistic Historian and the Creation of Israelite National Identity*, SBL Semeia Studies (Atlanta: Scholars Press, 1993), 40–1; Lloyd M. Barré, *The Rhetoric of Political Persuasion*, CBQMS 20 (Washington, DC: Catholic Biblical Association, 1988), 140; L. K. Handy, "Speaking of Babies in the Temple," *Proceedings of the Eastern Great Lakes and Midwest Biblical Societies* 8 (1988): 163; Cogan and Tadmor, *II Kings*, 131.

6. Patricia Dutcher-Walls, *Reading the Historical Books: A Student's Guide to Engaging the Biblical Text* (Grand Rapids: Baker Academic, 2014).

to make sense of an ancient text.⁷ My purpose is not to make historical or redactional decisions about the composition of this text, which I will leave to others, but I will assume that this story was shaped as part of a stream of Deuteronomistic traditions developing around the time of the exile.⁸ This story fits within the themes, theology, and vocabulary often associated with a purported Deuteronomistic school, and no matter how one labels it, that shaping is visible in the books of Kings and impinges on Athaliah's characterization. My manner of proceeding will be to consider several contextual and structural issues around and in ch. 11, and then to follow the order of the narrative in looking at how the story conveys a portrait of the queen that intends her erasure.

A first examination of the literary context of Athaliah's story reveals that her initial characterization begins well before the story in ch. 11 starts. She was introduced in the regnal formula of her husband King Jehoram of Judah by being blamed for Jehoram's doing evil and "walking in the way of the kings of Israel as the house of Ahab had done, for the daughter of Ahab was his wife" (2 Kgs 8:18). She is re-introduced when her son Ahaziah comes to the throne. Here her contagious association with the evil of the house of Ahab as a "daughter of King Omri of Israel" (2 Kgs 8:26) is stated even more directly: "He (Ahaziah) also walked in the way of the house of Ahab, doing what was evil in the sight of the Lord, as the house of Ahab had done, for he was son-in-law to the house of Ahab" (v. 27).⁹ This initial portrait accomplished by direct narratorial description rates as a "positive" characterization because, even though it provides a negative rating of Athaliah as "evil," she is given attention by the narrator rather than simply being ignored or dismissed from consideration. Compared to her erasure in her own story, this evaluative comment gives her narrative presence. However, the rhetoric about the evil of the House of Omri and Athaliah's Omride connections functions as a prelude to the queen's own story that already establishes her contagious evil nature and her delegitimate origins as a foreigner.¹⁰ These connections with the evil of the Northern Kingdom may help account for why the story aims to erase her.

---

7. See the explanation of my multi-disciplinary method in my *Narrative Art and Political Rhetoric: The Case of Athaliah and Joash*, JSOTSup 209 (Sheffield: Sheffield Academic, 1996), 16–22 and passim.

8. I will take the MT as my text; my initial study of ch. 11 considered text-critical issues in the narrative analysis chapter; see *Narrative Art*, 23–63. Translations in this chapter are my own unless otherwise noted as NRSV.

9. For a discussion of the relationship of Athaliah to the house of Ahab, see ibid., 27–8, and commentaries on the chapter.

10. Ibid., 30, 70.

In an earlier study of this queen, I noted, "Evident in the Deuteronomistic author's reality is a strongly held and expressed ideology which condemns all of the dynasties of the Northern Kingdom, with special attention to the House of Ahab and particular focus on the women of the royal house... Thus its direct incursion into Judah's monarchic line through Athaliah had to be and was delegitimated and condemned in the strongest possible terms."[11]

Secondly, it is also important to pay attention to the literary context of ch. 11. Athaliah's reign as queen over Judah is initiated by a coup in which she destroys "all the heirs of the kingdom" (v. 1); after which she rules for six years (v. 3). The story quickly turns to a counter-coup made possible by the survival of a royal heir (vv. 2-3), which is carefully prepared and carried out by the priest Jehoiada, who installs that heir on the throne and has Athaliah killed (vv. 4-20). But ch. 11 is also immediately preceded by the story of the prophetically initiated overthrow of the Omride dynasty by Jehu in 2 Kings 9–10. This means that the narrative of Athaliah's coup is framed by two others—that of Jehu and that of Jehoiada.

The shaping and juxtaposition of chs. 9–11 create comparisons among the coups. Jehu's coup is a thoroughly violent overthrow that stretches over 64 verses (2 Kgs 9:1-37 and 10:1-27) in which he kills a lot of people: Joram, king of Israel and the entire royal line of Ahab along with other royal retainers; the queen mother Jezebel; King Ahaziah of Judah and 42 royal kin of Ahaziah; and all the worshippers, prophets, and priests of Baal in Israel. Jehoiada's coup against Athaliah is portrayed as a measured, controlled affair related in 17 verses which is equally successful in transferring power to a new ruler but in which just two people die—Athaliah and the Baal priest Mattan. Athaliah's coup is given only one verse (11:1) but that verse focuses on the violence of her destruction of the heirs of the kingdom.

Scholars have noted and studied the comparisons among the three coups presented in chs. 9–11, particularly contrasts between Jehu's and Jehoiada's coups.[12] The point for my study is that framing Athaliah's take-over against a coup on either side of her story rhetorically shapes the portrayal of her action through analogy. She uses the violence of Jehu, but shows none of the astute planning of Jehoiada, and her action warrants

---

11. Ibid., 112–13.
12. See especially Barré, *Rhetoric of Political Persuasion*, as well as Robert L. Cohn, *2 Kings*, Berit Olam (Collegeville: Liturgical Press, 1999), 80; Terrence E. Fretheim, *First and Second Kings*, WBCom (Louisville: Westminster John Knox, 1999), 176. Branch compares Athaliah and Jezebel (Branch, "Athaliah, a Treacherous Queen," 554–5).

only the shortest narrative space possible. She comes to power and reigns for six years, but we know already from the literary context that the establishment of her power is judged by the stories about elite royal males on either side of her story.

A structural issue emerges when we turn to the story within ch. 11. In the books of Kings, each ruler is given a longer or shorter "window" between their introductory and concluding regnal formulas in which the story of their rule is related.[13] In Athaliah's case, not only are the regnal formulas omitted (see below), but also the story of her rule is not about her. It is striking how little narrative space the queen is given.[14] In a passage of 21 verses concerning her "ruling over the land" (v. 3), this queen is the subject of only 11 verbs in five verses. For two of those verbs in v. 16, she is either a passive subject or under the control of others. This leaves the story of her "rule" with only nine active verbs in four verses [she "saw," "arose," and "destroyed" in v. 1; she "was ruling" in v. 3; she "heard" and "went" in v. 13; and she "saw," "tore," and "cried out" in v. 14]. The other 17 verses of the chapter focus on the plot against her, the protection, coronation, and enthronement of her replacement, and her overthrow and death. In these verses too, Athaliah is barely mentioned directly; only in one verse does the priest Jehoiada speak about her and then only to direct how and where she is to be killed (v. 15). Athaliah has no voice in her story; she speaks only two words, the repeated "Treason!" in v. 14.[15] Death (מות) frames her story, moving from her seeing that her son was dead in v. 1 to her own death, accomplished in v. 16 and reprised in v. 20.

Even from these initial observations about the story of Athaliah a theme becomes clear: her characterization is accomplished by her erasure. Her coup is minimized by those of the male elites on either side of her, she is not actively involved in "her" story, she does not have a voice. Overall, her rule is discounted, her narrative presence diminished. The rest of this essay will examine the ways Athaliah's story succeeds in "dissing" her, narratively and rhetorically. Many commentators have noticed aspects of this repudiation;[16] I will gather key insights from them as I assemble a fuller chronicle of the ways her character is diminished. She was a queen of Judah who ruled for six years—but you would barely know it from the way her story is told.

13. Dutcher-Walls, *Narrative Art*, 88.
14. Ibid., 41, 76.
15. See for example Branch, "A Treacherous Queen," 543; Kuloba, "Athaliah," 144.
16. See particularly Branch, "A Treacherous Queen," 544; Kuloba, "Athaliah," 150.

Athaliah is introduced as an active character in v. 1. When she saw that her son was dead, she "arose and destroyed (or "set about to destroy," NRSV) all the heirs of the kingdom." Using dramatic action as a technique, her characterization immediately conveys that she is a powerful and violent actor because she "acts decisively and directly to kill all the legitimate heirs to the throne of Judah."[17] At this point, the rhetorical strategy of analogy to Jehu's "bloodbath" helps portray her as violent.[18] As Kuloba notes, "The story obscures Athaliah's political merit and interests by accentuating the act of killing of the royal seed."[19] Helping her character's obliteration in the story at this point are her limited narrative role and lack of rhetorical presence—her coup merits only one violent verse and the story moves on to describe resistance to her actions immediately in v. 2. One heir within the royal family is saved from being killed by the action of Jehosheba, described as the sister of the dead king Ahaziah, and the child is raised in secret in the temple compound (11:2).

However, this single verse uses other techniques to shape aspects of her characterization. First, as many scholars have noted, Athaliah's rule is neither introduced nor summarized by the standard regnal formulas used throughout Kings. This rhetorical technique of omitting an expected pattern[20] makes the point that, "…Athaliah's reign is not granted full legitimacy, for neither an opening nor closing formula is given for her six years."[21] Not only does this omission deny Athaliah any legitimacy in the Davidic dynasty,[22] but also it denies her the evaluative attention given to other rulers in their regnal formulas. In particular, the fact that her husband and son receive a disapproving evaluation highlights how she does not even warrant the negative attention those two rulers receive from the storyteller.

The techniques supporting Athaliah's narrative and rhetorical obliteration continue in this same verse. While the quickness of Athaliah's actions adds to her decisive character, the brevity of the account denies

---

17. Dutcher-Walls, *Narrative Art*, 30. Kuloba characterizes Athaliah as "heartless" because she contravenes the normal, "affectionate" expectations of mothers and grandmothers in the Bible (Kubola, "Athaliah of Judah," 144).

18. Camp, "1 and 2 Kings," 110.

19. Kuloba, "Athaliah of Judah," 141.

20. Dutcher-Walls, *Narrative Art*, 70; Branch, "Athaliah, a Treacherous Queen," 544.

21. Cogan and Tadmor, *II Kings*, 133. See similarly, for example, Sweeney, *I & II Kings*, 342; Fretheim, *First and Second Kings*, 178; Mullen, *Narrative History*, 24.

22. Branch, "Athaliah, a Treacherous Queen," 542; Ken Stone, "1 and 2 Kings," in *The Queer Bible Commentary*, ed. Deryn Guest (London: SCM, 2006), 244.

her narrative presence because no details are given for how she accomplishes her task of acquiring the throne. Further, narrative brevity also denies her a fuller characterization that could have been given by portraying her inner thoughts as she acts. Particularly, no reason is given for why she kills all the heirs to the throne.[23] This omission has led some scholars to wonder about why she murders the heirs, which would have included her own grandchildren;[24] although such historical speculations are not in any case provable. The characteristic reticence of the biblical narrator refuses us any inner view, which further expunges her character. With any interior view denied, the action of murdering the heirs works narratively to introduce abruptly the queen's incursion into royal power and rhetorically to portray a reprehensible but powerful actor.

The denial of Athaliah through the brevity of the account is reinforced by an analogy to both Jehu's and Jehoiada's coups, referenced above, which are given exquisite, detailed attention, although of a gruesome nature in Jehu's case.[25] A further repudiation of Athaliah is accomplished in these analogies. Athaliah's coup has no type of authorization beyond her own power; her action lacks both the prophetic initiation of Jehu (2 Kgs 9:1-10) and the priestly authority of Jehoiada (2 Kgs 11:4).

It is also significant that Athaliah accomplishes her coup on her own, a detail that impacts her characterization.[26] Even though it would have been highly unlikely or even impossible in an ancient agrarian monarchy for a ruler to seize the throne without a powerful elite faction or factions at her back, here no one is visible in support of her.[27] Some scholars recognize that in reality she would have to have had supporters;[28] however, the point here is that the rhetorical shaping of the story denies her all support. This depiction is also reinforced by looking once more at the coups that frame her story. In Jehu's coup, not only are his own supporters visible (2 Kgs 9:2, 5, 11-13) but even the soon-to-be-eliminated supporters of his rivals are noted. These include Ahab's sons and all his "leaders, close friends and priests" (2 Kgs 10:1-11); relatives of Amaziah (2 Kgs 10:12-14); and

23. Dutcher-Walls, *Narrative Art*, 30; Cohn, *2 Kings*, 77.
24. See for example, Gina Hens-Piazza, *1–2 Kings*, AOTC (Nashville: Abingdon, 2006), 307; Lee, "1 and 2 Kings," 115; cf. Volkmar Fritz who claims she did not in fact murder the royal family (Volkmar Fritz, *1 & 2 Kings*, Continental Commentary [Minneapolis: Fortress, 2003], 298).
25. See Branch, "Athaliah, a Treacherous Queen," 550–1.
26. Mullen, *Narrative History*, 23, 28.
27. Dutcher-Walls, *Narrative Art*, 154.
28. For example, Branch, "Athaliah, a Treacherous Queen," 546; Camp, "1 and 2 Kings," 111.

the priests and worshippers of Baal. In the rendering of Jehoiada's coup, there is a careful accounting of those who support the priest by protecting the child heir, by attending the coronation and acclaiming him as king, and by destroying the temple of Baal (2 Kgs 11:4-9, 11, 17-20). Even the portrayal of Jezebel creates an analogous situation. Jezebel clearly has supporters under her authority when she schemes against Naboth in 1 Kings 21.[29] By contrast to all these characters, Athaliah is completely alone.

The play of perspectives between vv. 1 and 2 also contributes towards the dismissal of Athaliah in this narrative. Athaliah can see (v. 1) that her son is dead, but she is blind to the fact that another of the heirs is alive, a child rescued by Jehosheba from among those being killed (v. 2). This lack of perception portrays her as unaware and politically obtuse. Mullen notes her "unbelievable stupidity"; as he says, "she apparently failed due to her inability to count"[30] how many dead heirs there were and did not notice one was missing from the body count.

When we examine the half verse that covers the entire account of Athaliah's actual reign as monarch in Judah, we see that she is accorded just a brief phrase of four words in the Hebrew text, "Athaliah was ruling over the land" (v. 3b). The story apparently cannot completely suppress the fact that the queen did hold power in Jerusalem for six years. The narrative and rhetorical strategies already established in v. 1 come into play. However, as Stone remarks,

> It is important to note...that in spite of her negative representation in the text, Athaliah is able to hold the throne of Judah for six years. This length of time surpasses the duration of the reigns of several other kings of Israel and Judah, including that of her own son, Ahaziah. It is clear, then, that Athaliah's rule must have had supporters; and that she was, in certain respects at least, a successful sovereign.[31]

The narrative of Athaliah's reign is dedicated to her overthrow, which stands in stark contrast to the narratives of other rulers, who are associated with building projects, international relations, and military accounts. As Fritz notes, Athaliah "remains largely at the edge of events."[32] In line with the opening scene, numerous, overlapping narrative and rhetorical

---

29. See Branch, "Athaliah, a Treacherous Queen," 555, who notes other instances of Jezebel's "network of spies."
30. Mullen, *Narrative History*, 28.
31. Stone, "1 and 2 Kings," 244.
32. Fritz, *1 & 2 Kings*, 296.

techniques shape her characterization. Of course, the plot itself at this point shifts to Jehoiada, describing in detail his successful overthrow of her rule and reinstatement of a legitimate Davidic monarch. Although one could focus on how the story positively characterizes Jehoiada and legitimates the child king Joash, here I will consider how it discounts and obliterates Athaliah's character. This is accomplished by rhetorical strategies of contrast and absence or omission—what is attributed positively to Jehoiada's plot reflects negatively on Athaliah.

I have already noted how the detail given to Jehoiada's coup denies narrative presence to Athaliah and reflects poorly on her lack of detailed planning for her coup. However, the details of Jehoiada's plot go further. The story dwells on specifics about his careful commandeering of the guards from both the temple and palace to create a protective ring for the presentation and acclamation of the young heir. In this way, the story shows how the priest's power claims all the available armed forces for the coalition of military and priestly factions associated with the restoration of a true Davidic ruler. The possibility that Athaliah might be able to stage a defense is referenced by Jehoiada: in v. 8, he warns that "anyone coming toward the ranks [of guards around the king] will be killed." Yet, with all the weight of the military personnel on Jehoiada's side, any possible protection is denied to Athaliah. She has lost all military support from what should have been her own guards in the palace and temple—the new king has "maximum security";[33] she has none.[34] However, the story also uses symbolic associations in building the details of Jehoiada's plot. The story conveys how Jehoiada claims and uses the huge symbolic power of both the temple and the palace to support his conspiracy against the queen who usurped the throne. The priest and the new king carry all the symbolic weight of the royal house and the house of the Lord; Athaliah has none.

The weapons presented to the guards by the priest add to the shaping of the political associations of Jehoiada's actions and the disavowal of any legitimacy for Athaliah. The priest brought to the officers of the guard the "spears and shields which were King David's which were in the House of Yahweh" and the guards, weapons in hand, stood across the whole space of the temple "about the king all around" (vv. 10-11). Likely weapons this old would have not been a practical choice,[35] but the story uses the symbolic association of both David and the temple to convey the authority

---

33. Kuloba, "Athaliah of Judah," 141.
34. Fretheim, *First and Second Kings*, 178.
35. Sweeney, *I & II Kings*, 346; Kuloba, "Athaliah of Judah," 148.

of the priest and the Davidic military might of the guards. The priest and the guards bear all the symbolic weight of David; Athaliah is presented as the one against whom the might of David is arrayed.[36]

This section of the story culminates in the presentation and acclamation of the rescued child as king (v. 12). The story uses a set of royal symbols and actions to communicate the legitimacy of the coronation of the new king as a Davidic ruler. The priest places on "the son of the king" the נזר (crown) and the עדות (testimony or decree); they proclaim him king (מלך), anoint him (משח), and then clap their hands and say, "May the king live!" the equivalent of "long live the king." All of these objects and actions use the rhetorical technique of an "associational cluster" of terms that convey the authenticity of the coronation as a proper ceremony and the new king as a true heir of the Davidic dynasty.[37] The amount of detail provided to describe the coronation establishes another contrast aimed at diminishing Athaliah, who had no coronation or acclamation when she came to the throne. The child king bears all the symbolic weight of the royal house and true kingship; Athaliah has none.[38]

In the next dramatic scene of the story (vv. 13-16), Athaliah literally re-enters the picture with only enough time to perceive accurately that she has been overthrown before she is killed. Those proclaiming the new king in the temple make so much noise that the queen comes to see what is happening. This is the second and final point in the story where we have a glimpse of Athaliah's point of view, when "there!" (הנה), the marker for an abrupt change in perspective, allows us to see through the queen's eyes. She "saw" her son was dead (v. 1) and here she "sees" a coup. "The powerful play of perspectives (between Athaliah and the forces arrayed against her) reaches its inevitable confrontation."[39] The story gives the queen only enough visibility and viewpoint to heighten the drama of her downfall, as she enters the temple and perceives the whole of the plot against her in one moment.

What she sees is portrayed by the story with another associational cluster of royal symbols: the king "standing by the pillar, according to the custom," surrounded by the officers and trumpeters around the king, and all the "people of the land rejoicing and blowing the trumpets" (v. 14). The narrator's aside in the phrase "according to the custom" communicates

---

36. Kuloba, "Athaliah of Judah," 149.
37. See Dutcher-Walls, *Narrative Art*, 77–80, for a detailed analysis of the rhetoric of this section of the story.
38. Branch, "Athaliah, a Treacherous Queen," 542.
39. Dutcher-Walls, *Narrative Art*, 80.

the ineluctable meaning of the scene; "[t]he honour accorded to Joash repudiates Athaliah in all aspects, and renders her credibility to the throne of Judah illegitimate."[40] Like the symbols associated with David in the previous scene, this symbolization of a coronation disassociates Athaliah from royalty, dynasty, and legitimacy; she is an onlooker and outsider only.

Again, narrative and rhetorical artistry add layers to Athaliah's characterization in this scene. That she is portrayed as completely surprised by the coronation scene before her in the temple conveys that Jehoiada's plot had successfully been kept secret. This implies again that she did not have any supporters, particularly informants, guards, or officials who could keep her aware of what was happening in the temple,[41] the royal sanctuary right next to the palace, for which she as monarch was ostensibly the patron and head. That she enters the temple alone conveys again that she had no supporters and no bodyguards,[42] a point historically unprovable, sociologically untenable, but narratively powerful. Jehoiada cautions his military force, the officers of the army, that anyone coming after her is to be killed (v. 15). Again, he mentions possible support for the queen, but no one shows up in the story to come after her in support. Further, in the *realpolitik* of the ancient world, a ruler such as Athaliah who claimed the throne likely would have watched elite political institutions carefully for potential disloyalty or otherwise destroyed the political power of rival elites.[43] Jehoiada and Joash are portrayed as having all the cunning, political astuteness, and military power to pull off a coup; Athaliah has none and discovers too late that her rule has been eclipsed.

In addition to the exclusive control of political and military forces associated with Jehoiada and Joash in the narrative's shaping, another key set of characters line up with the new king. In the scene that confronts Athaliah as she enters the temple, she hears the noise of the guards "and the people," the latter group not previously mentioned in the story. In response, she "came to the people in the House of Yahweh" (v. 13), and upon entering, she sees not only the officers and trumpeters, but also "all the people of the land" (v. 14). Whatever the historical and sociological implications of this phrase,[44] the repetition of the terms "people" and

---

40. Kuloba, "Athaliah of Judah," 142.
41. Branch, "Athaliah, a Treacherous Queen," 548.
42. Ibid., 549.
43. Cohen, "How to Mount a Successful Coup," 11.
44. I will not discuss the historical import of this term in this essay; see the commentaries and Dutcher-Walls, *Narrative Art*, 149–51.

"all the people of the land" functions rhetorically to align this collective character with the plot against Athaliah. While these terms may not indicate what we would consider "popular" support, what is clear is that all the narrative weight of this group is used to provide another layer of authentication to Jehoiada's coup and thereby deny it to the queen. Whether or not there is a distinction underlying the story between an urban elite and a more rural aristocracy, a distinction the ancient audience might have understood, it is evident that both sides of that distinction are fully lined up behind Joash and against Athaliah.[45]

With all the characters arrayed against Athaliah, and the irrefutable symbolism of a proper Davidic and dynastic coronation and acclamation right in front of her, the queen is given her only speech of the story. And she speaks truth; this is indeed "conspiracy" or "treason" (v. 14). The story has so shaped the scene that this queen's dramatic words gain her no sympathy, no support, and no assistance in holding on to her position. Jehoiada's more powerful words intervene, and they are effective. As previously noted, the only time another character talks about Athaliah directly is here, when Jehoiada commands her manner and place of death in the immediate aftermath of her cry of "conspiracy!" She will die as violently as she acted against the royal heirs.

As a character Athaliah has one remaining active verb. As she had "entered into" (בוש) the temple (v. 13), she now "enters into" the palace by way of the horses' entrance, only this time she is on a forced march to her death; the army sets their force against her (v. 16). The palace where she had been while ruling over the land is now denied to her, becoming the place of her death. By having her enter through the space between the palace and the temple that was used by the horses, the narrator rhetorically associates her with dishonor.[46] Again the story conveys that she is alone, even in death—no one has come to her aid; no one mourns her.[47] Noting the analogies to the coups on either side of this story, the brevity of her actual death scene in v. 16 rhetorically denies her a narrative presence in death. Even Jezebel is granted a full, dramatic scene for her final swan song.[48]

---

45. Branch, "Athaliah, a Treacherous Queen," 553.
46. Hens-Piazza, *1–2 Kings*, 308.
47. Branch, "Athaliah, a Treacherous Queen," 553; Cohen, "How to Mount a Successful Coup," 19.
48. Branch, "Athaliah, a Treacherous Queen," 555.

The final scene of Athaliah's story (vv. 17-21) continues the tale and the dismissal of Athaliah, even though she is already dead. More loaded language communicates the righteousness of the actions of Jehoiada and disapproval for the queen. Verse 17 reports that Jehoiada "made the covenant (ברית) between Yahweh and the king and the people to be the people of Yahweh, and between the king and the people." The term "covenant" is also found in v. 4, where Jehoiada made a covenant with the captains and guards when he began planning his coup. That the term in v. 4 uses the preposition ל instead of the usual אים indicates that in this covenant Jehoiada was the authoritative party putting the guards under agreement.[49] The covenants made in v. 17 among the parties of the king, the Lord, and the people create a connection with the wider implications of covenant language. "In the context of the Book of Kings, this must be understood as the covenant set forth in Deuteronomy. Its pivotal consequence is that Judah is to be the 'people of Yahweh.'"[50] Commentators debate the historical circumstances and referents of the covenant-making scene in v. 17, as well as whether one or two covenants are intended.[51] However those arguments are decided, the rhetorical point in the story is clear. The positive associations of covenant-making all line up on the side of Jehoiada on behalf of the new king. In vv. 4 and 17, the priest makes three (or two, depending on how v. 17 is read) covenants on the way to creating a legitimate kingship for Joash; Athaliah has no covenants associated with her rule.

As soon as the covenants are made, "all the people of the land" proceed to the temple of Baal to tear it down and kill its priest (v. 18). Both the priest and his temple are "discovered" in the narrative only late in the tale, which add skepticism to any arguments concerning historical validity, but the scene still functions to corroborate the interests of the story. There is consistent disapproval of Baal worship throughout Kings. The most immediate analogy for this theme framing the Athaliah story is the brutally thorough destruction of the Baal sect in Israel by Jehu (2 Kgs 10:18-28). The description of the action of the people in destroying the vestiges of Baal worship now in Jerusalem picks up and uses that image on behalf of Jehoiada's intentions and the narrative's interests. The immediacy of the people's action against Baal illustrates that the action is a response to the covenant-making, at least narratively if not

---

49. Cogan and Tadmor, *II Kings*, 127; Kuloba, "Athaliah of Judah," 141.
50. Nelson, *First and Second Kings*, 210.
51. See for example Cogan and Tadmor, *II Kings*, 132–3; Nelson, *First and Second Kings*, 210.

historically.⁵² The destruction of the house of Baal and the murder of its priest rhetorically provide covenant-based approval for all the events surrounding the installation of the new king, which in turn delegitimates Athaliah.

Furthermore, "all the people of the land" contribute to the destruction of the temple and priest of Baal, and they appear throughout this scene (vv. 17, 18, 19, and 20). The partisanship of this collective character for all things associated with the Davidic king, the temple of Yahweh, and covenant-making is again reinforced; Athaliah is left out of all of it. In addition, the story has finally found one supporter, or at least, associate for Athaliah—the Baal priest Mattan. That finally late in the game one political associate appears but only in time to be killed, and that this sole associate is a priest of a apostate cult, further reinforce the shaping of the solitary and illegitimate nature of her rule.

Another negative association against the queen is communicated by the triumphant procession of everyone in the story to bring the young king from the house of the Lord to the house of the king (v. 19). Commentators note how the processional scene functions as a part of Jehoiada's and the story's communication that this is a "restoration, not a revolution."⁵³ The creation of an image of a restoration of what *should* have been in place all along, that is, a Davidic, legitimate king, further dissuades any audience of the story from sympathy with Athaliah. The description that "all the people of the land rejoiced, and the city was quiet" in v. 20 reports reactions to Jehoiada's coup that reiterate the acceptability of his action. Commentators theorize underlying tensions between the two social groups (rural/urban)⁵⁴ but the argumentative force within the narrative is that everyone is glad that Athaliah is gone. The introduction of an element of a standard regnal formula for Joash in v. 21 conveys that, finally, all is again right with the monarchy in Judah.

I have chronicled a whole series of narrative and rhetorical moves in the story of Athaliah that work together to deny all legitimacy to her, her actions, and her rule in Judah. The characterization of this queen works against her for the entire narrative, from obvious omissions to subtle comparisons that undermine her. While a number of scholars have noted some of the ways the story works, one scholar has grasped key elements of this consistent "dissing" of Athaliah.

---

52. Hens-Piazza, *1–2 Kings*, 309; Nelson, *First and Second Kings*, 210.
53. Cohen, "How to Mount a Successful Coup," 19; see also Cohn, *2 Kings*, 80, and Hens-Piazza, *1–2 Kings*, 309.
54. See for example Fritz, *1 & 2 Kings*, 300; Camp, "1 and 2 Kings," 111.

Although Athaliah is acknowledged as ruling the land the "Dtr redactor" tactfully omitted details regarding her coronation and enthronement. Athaliah is presented as a leader without the support and the will of the people. There is no information about her seven year reign. Her rule is not granted full legitimacy. There is neither an opening nor closing formula give as is the case with all the other heads of the Crown either in Judah or Israel.[55]

However, the study conducted here has added detail and new insights into how the story works so that the characterization of the queen does everything possible to obliterate her from the story.

1. One striking quality of the story is how little narrative space is given to the queen; she has only a limited narrative role and rhetorical presence. Athaliah is barely mentioned directly; only in one verse is she named by another character. She has a limited voice in her story; she speaks only two words. Her coup merits only one violent verse in which no details are given for how she accomplishes her task of acquiring the throne. Her reign is given the briefest possible narrative time; there are no details of her six years of rule. The brevity of her reign is reinforced by an analogy to both Jehu's and Jehoiada's coups, which are given exquisite, detailed attention. She has no narrative presence even in death.
2. She is always cast as a solitary actor. She acts completely alone in accomplishing her coup. This is reinforced by the rhetorical technique of analogy to the two coups on either side where supporters are evident. No one appears in the story as part of an administration or coalition of supporters during her reign. When she discovers the plot against her, she does not have any supporters, particularly informants, guards, or officials. She is alone, even in death. Too late to do any good, one political associate appears but only in time to be killed, and this sole associate is a priest of an apostate cult.
3. Her character is repudiated repeatedly by comparisons to male elites who stage coups on either side of hers, particularly Jehoiada in his establishment of Joash as king in her stead. Her coup has no type of authorization, not prophetic like Jehu's or priestly like Joash's. She had no coronation or acclamation when she came to the throne. All the cunning, political astuteness, and military power to pull off a coup belong to Jehoiada; Athaliah has none. All

---

55. Kuloba, "Athaliah of Judah," 150.

the weight of the military personnel is on Jehoiada's side and any possible protection is denied to Athaliah. All the symbolic weight of the royal house and the house of the Lord lines up behind Joash; Athaliah has none. All the symbolic weight of David is wielded by Jehoiada; Athaliah is presented as the one against whom the might of David is arrayed. The symbolization of a coronation for Joash leaves Athaliah outside any connection with royalty, dynasty and legitimacy; she is an onlooker and outsider only. All the narrative weight of the "people of the land" is used to provide a layer of authentication to Jehoiada's coup and thereby deny it to the queen. All the positive associations of covenant-making line up on the side of Jehoiada on behalf of the new king—Athaliah has no covenants associated with her rule. The destruction of the house of Baal and the murder of its priest rhetorically provide covenant-based approval for all the events surrounding the installation of the new king, which in turn delegitimates Athaliah. All things associated with the Davidic king and dynasty, the temple of Yahweh, and covenant-making are again reinforced as belonging to Jehoiada on behalf of Joash; Athaliah is left out of all of it.

Other strategies occur only in limited verses of her story; however, cumulatively they are no less powerful in presenting Athaliah as a queen who can and should be denied legitimacy.

4. She is a powerful and violent actor, a characterization made more intense by analogy to Jehu's "bloodbath."
5. She is neither introduced nor summarized by the standard regnal formulas. This denies her any dynastic legitimacy and denies her the evaluative attention given to other rulers so that direct narratorial valuation of her reign is lacking.
6. Resistance to her rule begins immediately, even while Athaliah is in the act of seizing the throne.
7. The story of her reign is dedicated to the narrative of her overthrow.
8. The play of perspectives achieved between v. 1 and v. 2 casts her as unaware and politically obtuse.
9. Her dramatic words when she discovers the treason against her gain her no sympathy, no support, and no assistance in holding on to her position.
10. The place of her death associates her with dishonor.
11. Everyone is glad that Athaliah is gone.

She is characterized by what is not said, overlooked, denied, erased, avoided, and misconstrued; she suffers from comparison to both Jehu's violent coup and Jehoiada's controlled coup. Unless we grant recognition to the one reality that the writers could not evade, Athaliah's seizure of power and six-year rule in Judah, we have acceded in their attempt to erase this queen.

Chapter 13

ARTIFACTS OF SCENERY OR AGENTS OF CHANGE? A SUBALTERN CHARACTER IN 2 KINGS 4:1-7

Gina Hens-Piazza

Subaltern Studies

Grounded in Marxist principles of social analysis and guided by the work of Antonio Gramsci, subaltern studies began in fascist Italy in the early twentieth century. Known for his theory of cultural hegemony, Gramsci argued that the state or ruling class uses ideology—rather than violence, economic force, or coercion—to promote its values so that they become the status quo. This hegemonic culture, maintained and promoted by the dominant class, forces consent of the masses through the institutions that form the superstructure. Hence, the experiences and needs of those controlled social groups, who reside outside the dominant class, never receive representation. Gramsci referred to these silent and invisible populations as the subaltern.

In academic circles, subaltern studies has become an area of concentration within the disciplines of social, historical, and cultural studies, investigating the theoretical and social dimensions of subordinate/dominant relationships. Some think of it as a secular version of liberation theology's "preferential option for the poor."[1] However, its scope encompasses more than an economic disparity between the "haves" and the "have-nots." As originally coined by Gramsci, the term *subaltern* designated groups of people who are socially, politically, and geographically

---

1. John Beverley, *Subalternity and Representation: Arguments in Cultural Theory* (Durham: Duke University Press, 1999), 38.

excluded from the power base of the ruling hegemony. Initially, this focused primarily upon politically colonized groups. For example, in Indian society, subaltern studies analyzed the caste system and identified the subaltern as confined to the Dalit and Adivasi communities because they fell outside the Hindu-based caste framework.[2] However, as the dynamics constituting the binary relationship between dominant/subordinate gained exposition, the terrain of subaltern studies expanded. Today, it takes into account persons ranked inferior because of race, gender, social class, ethnicity, religion, or sexual orientation. Thus, subordination has become the constitutive characteristic defining the subaltern, exceeding the original focus upon the politically colonized.

A group of south Asian scholars that would later include groups of Latin American colleagues became known as the Subaltern Studies Collective. These working groups, who originally formalized the study of the subaltern, demonstrate in their writings the variety of considerations that come under this disciplinary umbrella. In her widely recognized essay, "Can the Subaltern Speak?" Gayatri Chakravorty Spivak, a longtime member of the group, crafted one of the most formative expositions on the subaltern, giving definition to who constitutes the group.[3] Spivak argued that silence was the fundamental characteristic of the subaltern. Hannah Arendt refers to a life without speech as a life that is "literally dead to the world: it has ceased to be a human life…"[4] Along with being silent and thus inaudible, the subaltern's societal marginality renders them almost invisible. Low visibility makes them unrepresented or "always sliding away from or under representation…"[5]

As research continues, the aim of subaltern studies eclipses merely identifying and documenting the case against such groups. Instead, it seeks to bring about a sea change in the academy and society as a whole. It promotes a new kind of history, a history from below. Such an interpretative narrative of the past would not only replace the typical state-centered discourses but include the stories of a society's excluded members, whose pasts had been disregarded in previous accounts. In addition, the liminal space that the subaltern occupy needs not be thought of as a location

---

2. Sathianathan Clarke, "Viewing the Bible Through the Eyes and Ears of Subalterns in India," *BibInt* 10, no. 3 (2002): 248.

3. Gayatri Chakravorty Spivak, "Can the Subaltern Speak?" in *Colonial Discourse and Post-Colonial Theory: A Reader*, ed. Patrick Williams and Laura Chrisman (New York: Columbia University Press, 1994), 66–111.

4. Hannah Arendt, *The Human Condition* (Chicago: Chicago University Press, 1998), 176–7.

5. Beverley, *Subalternity and Representation*, 101.

where only acquiescence and conformity exist; Homi Bhabha observes that invisibility and marginalization of the subaltern also makes possible resistance and subversion.[6] Hence, the subaltern are not fixed in a position lacking agency or weakness. They actually have a certain kind of quiet subversive and political power to undercut hegemonic values and turn things upside down.

Further, subaltern studies diagnoses the disparities between the dominant and the subordinate wherever they exist in an effort to incite "a radical change in direction toward a more democratic and non-hierarchical social order."[7] Such transformation requires massive alterations in how people live together and define themselves in relationship to one another. But even prior to such shifts, they also warrant other preliminary changes in how we think and how we read.

How We Read Matters

Research in the area of sociology of reading practices suggests that a dynamic relationship exists between our reading and interpretation habits when it comes to texts and our practices of engagement and interpretation when it comes to our world.[8] How we read important cultural texts influences how we read our world. At the same time, how we read and interpret our world influences how we read and understand important cultural texts, including the Bible.[9] Fixing attention only upon dominant characters (also referred to as major characters) in stories does more than cooperate with the hierarchy of the narrative or support the caste system of a story. It may reinforce and validate a similar perception of our own

6. Homi Bhabha, *The Location of Culture* (New York: Routledge, 1994), 90.
7. Beverely, *Subalternity and Representation*, 38.
8. Among those contributing to the current field of study are Peter Smagorinsky, "If Meaning Is Constructed, What Is It Made From? Toward a Cultural Theory of Reading," *Review of Educational Research* 71, no. 1 (2001): 133–69; R. J. Tierney and P. D. Pearson, "Towards a Composing Model of Reading," *Language Arts* 60 (1983): 568–80; and J. Wertsch, *Voices of the Mind: A Sociocultural Approach to Mediated Action* (Cambridge: Harvard University Press, 1993).
9. In "Negotiating What Counts: Roles and Relationships, Texts and Contexts, Content and Meaning," in *Linguistics and Education* 5 (1993): 241–74, Ana Floriani discusses how reading itself is a constructive act, carried out in conjunction with all kinds of texts. Specifically, Floriani notes the interactive relationships between how one reads a text and how one reads that same reader's context, which she calls "intercontext." Similarly, Smagorinsky notes that reading is a constructive act, lived through a process of association into a response in a reader's context ("If Meaning Is Constructed," 149).

social world. By contrast, enlisting a more inclusive approach to reading, which attends not only to protagonists but also to characters who might qualify as subaltern in the story, may shift attention, or even cultivate a sensitivity, to their counterparts in our surroundings. Hence, the analysis of these marginal and silent characters invites readers to reflect upon whether the hierarchy embedded in the narrative world (which privileges some characters over others) and even the hierarchy of our literary designations (major vs. minor) may be related to classism, hierarchies, or "caste" categories that often order the perception of the world in which we live. Moreover, analysis of these marginal figures may disclose new gains in interpretation resulting from more democratized reading practices, as well as highlight what would be lost if this group continued to be overlooked. Hence, new insights about these often ignored characters may not only enhance our understanding of these biblical stories but may also subtly challenge readers to further considerations. What other histories are embedded here? Can more than one dominant story reside in a narrative? What might these silent characters disclose in the course of a biblical tale? And does how we read an important cultural and religious text, such as the Bible, actually contribute to the build up of a more non-hierarchical and democratic social order?

Granted a one-time reference to "laborers," "virgin daughters," "servants," "the crowd," etc., who are not described and are silent, may fall outside the taxonomy of what even constitutes a character. The subaltern of the narrative world are typically viewed as literary props in the service of highlighting the role of the protagonist or as human scenery filling in the implied backdrop of the tale. Adele Berlin refers to such characters as either a *type* or an *agent*. Designation as *a type* lacks elaboration and comes off less as a real person and more of a blueprint of a trait or category, such as a "wife," "mother," "king," etc. An *agent* achieves significance only in so far as he or she performs a function for the narrative or in the service of the plot. Hence, *types* and *agents* may be contrasted to *full-fledged* characters who speak and are granted representation by the narrator and others characters in the story "like real persons."[10] A *type* plays a typified role or stand-in that, at the same time, brackets the person their character might represent.[11] Being designated a *type* sidelines a character's particularity, which would emerge if his or her unique story was recognized in the narrative. *Agents*, "who are not important in their own right," are further disqualified as they exist only to perform a function in

---

10. Adele Berlin, *Poetics and Interpretation of Biblical Narrative* (Winona Lake: Eisenbrauns, 1994), 31–2.
11. Ibid., 32.

the service of the narrative construction or in the service of other characters in the plot.[12] Such a hierarchy of character analysis renders *agents* or *types* outside the categories of *full-fledged* characters, and thus qualifies them as analogues to the subaltern.

Of course, these subaltern characters' status as subordinates is not necessarily analogous to the subaltern of hegemonic regimes or societal conditions that so marginalizes them that they cannot be seen or heard. But like their real life counterparts, the subaltern in the biblical literary context are those "laborers," "servants," "elders," "harvesters," etc., who are rendered silent, lack any description, are referenced only once in a narrative, and have a story or a history to tell but it never gets aired. Thus, they rarely attract interpretive representation and so are thought of as almost invisible.

In her monumental work *The Poetics of Postmodernism*, Linda Hutchinson summarizes it well. She writes, "How we read is not unrelated to how we see at least from the point of view of subjectivity."[13] In other words, how we read and interpret texts, especially important cultural or religious texts such as the Bible, has a great deal of influence upon how we read and interpret the texts of our world. Who we attend to, who we ask questions about, or who we study in depth within a given text seeds a similar interest in terms of who we see, who we inquire about, and who we seek to better understand in our own world. Thus, if acknowledging and giving interpretive space to the subaltern of biblical narrative could set us on a path to "a more democratic and non-hierarchical social order," then even our reading practices may actually contribute to the establishment of a more equitable society.[14]

---

12. Ibid., 85.

13. Linda Hutcheon, *The Poetics of Postmodernism: History, Theory, Fiction* (New York: Routledge, 1988), 168.

14. The "subaltern" can be thought of as a class of the most powerless existing among those already once labeled the colonized. Their existence is often hardly visible and they typically don't possess a voice. Within Biblical Studies the use of subaltern has been limited to defining the reader response of those from postcolonial cultural groups who can claim this position. See, for example, Sathlanathan Clarke, "Viewing the Bible through the Eyes and Ears of Subalterns in India," available as an on-line publication at www.brill.nl or https://www.religion-online.org/article/viewing-the-bible-through-the-eyes-and-ears-of-subalterns-in-india/. See also the 25th Anniversary Edition of R. S. Sugirtharajah's *Voices from the Margins: Interpreting the Bible in the Third World* (Maryknoll: Orbis, 2016) where Part Two features six essays under the heading "Subaltern Readings" representing subaltern perspectives within postcolonial groups from various locations around the world.

The Subaltern in 2 Kings 4:1-7

2 Kings 4:1-7 registers as the first of four stories, featuring five miracles and illustrating the power of Elisha, the prophet, across this chapter. In the previous chapter, Elisha displayed his miraculous activities in a very public and national sphere, assisting the armies of Israel, Edom, and Judah in their military conflict against Moab. By contrast, in this chapter, he acts in more domestic and local settings, including the households of an unnamed widow (vv. 1-7) and the Shunnamite woman (vv. 8-37), the assembly of the brotherhood of prophets for a meal (vv. 38-41), and a village stricken with famine (vv. 42-44). Moreover, these four stories are not only united by the persistent intervention of Elisha, they all manifest the thematic shift of life rescued from death.

Despite its brevity and simplicity, the first story (vv. 1-7) introduces and illustrates this dramatic movement from threat of death to the promise of life that governs all these accounts. This uncomplicated tale (2 Kgs 4:1-7) begins with an encounter between a woman and Elisha. While most commentaries and Bibles label this brief story with a focus upon the prophet, i.e., "Elisha and the Miraculous Jug of Oil" or "Elisha Helps a Poor Widow," the woman is the first to speak in the narrative. The wife of one of the followers of Elisha, she has lost her husband. She addresses the prophet and, without explicitly asking for his help, sets before him the crisis she faces. Her husband has died, leaving her a widow with dependents. Now a creditor is threatening to take her two children as slaves if she does not settle some outstanding debts (v. 1).[15] Initially, the prophet asks her what he can do about this. Then he asks what she has in her house. At first, the widow reports that she has nothing of value in her house. And then, almost as an afterthought, she adds that she does have one thing. She still has "one pouring of oil" (v. 2).[16] The prophet instructs her to gather jars from all her neighbors and, with her two children, shut

---

15. Yael Shemesh, "Elisha and the Miraculous Jug of Oil," *JHS* 8, no. 4 (2008): 9, notes that the woman does not provide details of her destitute poverty. It is unclear whether the debt stems from her deceased husband or from an unpaid loan for which her husband was responsible. It may also stem from her own transaction since his death for capital. As an impoverished widow who has nothing in her house, she still has two dependents that she now supports. No doubt, her husband's death has played a role in the worsening of her circumstances.

16. Reading with John Gray, *I & II Kings A Commentary*, 2nd ed. (Philadelphia: John Knox, 1970), who notes the MT *'āsūk* is a hapax legomenon, the meaning "pot" being unattested. The connection with *nāsak* ("to pour") suggests that *'āsuk* may be a corruption of *massāk*, in the proto-Hebraic script, 491,b.

the door of her house and start pouring her oil into all the jars that she and her children have gathered (vv. 3-4). She does as the prophet instructs. Next we learn that she shuts the door behind herself and her children, and she starts pouring (v. 5). She fills jars with oil until one of her children announces that there are no more jars (v. 6). Finally, she goes back to the prophet and reports what has occurred. In turn, he tells her to sell the oil and pay off her debts. As a final note, he adds that she and her sons can live on the surplus that is left (v. 7).

The structure of the story mirrors the simplicity of the narrative itself. An encounter between the woman and the prophet at both the beginning and end of the story (vv. 1-4, 7) encloses a narrative featuring the actions by the widow and the miracle unfolding in her house (vv. 5-6). Despite its brevity, this simple tale hosts not only several subaltern characters but an array of other characters, all of whom play essential and important roles. The widow and her dialogue with the prophet, along with the narrative focus upon her actions, cast her in a key role as a supporting cast member. She has real staying power in the story. She not only initiates the dialogue with the prophet at the opening of the story but also their second and final encounter, which closes the tale. Further, because she takes the lead in approaching the prophet and exhibits a clear willingness to carry out his instructions, she has a significant influence in determining the outcome of the plot. She participates in a good deal of direct discourse, despite the very abbreviated nature of this story. The plot turns on the woman's obedience to the prophet's instructions. Her willingness to approach the prophet and subsequently follow his directives implies a faith in Yahweh, the God for whom the prophet is agent. Finally, the crisis of the story resolves, in part, because the actions of the widowed woman bring about her own change of destiny.

Her two children are briefly referenced in the opening encounter between their mother and the prophet. That they are the children whom a creditor has threatened to take as slaves from their mother provides the brief but requisite description of them. Their fate is not only desperate but central to the multilayered nature and depth of the crisis. The threat to their well-being intensifies the gravity of their widowed mother's fate. Moreover, the story reveals that not only has the woman lost her husband, but the children suffered the loss of a father. They now must depend upon a widowed woman in a man's world. They are residents in a society whose laws do not protect them. Instead, they become commodities by means of which debts are settled. In the process, they not only endure the loss of a father, but they also might be stripped of the little security to which they could cling. They are about to be taken from their mother and made slaves.

When the prophet issues directives to the woman, he includes the children in his instructions. He directs that she and her children gather vessels and shut the door of their house behind them. Later, the narrative reveals more about the children. Their identities are specified as two sons, who assist their mother gathering jars and passing them to her as she pours oil. In addition, as the miracle unfolds, one of the sons has a brief speaking role. When his mother requests that they pass another jug to her, it falls to him to announce that "there are no more." The recognition and announcement that the miracle is complete falls from the lips of one of these two children. He gives witness to the conclusion of their effort, which will reverse both he and his brother's fate, as well as will restore both the widow and her sons to life. At the end of this short account, the children are referenced again. The prophet instructs the widow that she is to sell the oil, pay off the debt, and then she and her two children can live on the remaining income. Not only the widow, but her two young children have become the recipients of a renewed future. Restored to the assurance of safety and security of their mother's care, the conclusion bears witness to the scope of the miracle's effect. Though playing only minor roles, the children, as important characters in the story, reside at the heart of the crisis that eventually yields to a life-giving resolution.

Next another character, "a creditor," registers in the woman's opening plea to Elisha. Mentioned only once (v. 1), the creditor constitutes the central threat that prompts the woman's pursuit of the prophet for assistance. He instigates her predicament. Despite the one time reference to the creditor and his lack of speech, his character receives description. The direct discourse of the woman's explanation to Elisha describes the creditor's character. He has come to her house and threatened to take her children as slaves. His role as creditor gives way to his plan of action. In fact, report of the existence of this creditor and what he intends gives reason for this story. Were there no creditor, there would be no crisis. Hence, because the story stems from this sole mention of a creditor and of his claim on her children, his role in the story achieves a dominance and significance even though he is mentioned only briefly.

Who is this creditor? The Elijah/Elisha narratives, in which this story resides, presume the monarchic era of the Omrides, known for their development of extensive trade routes and building projects. "The Omride building program, which required the citizens to serve in corvées, and the extensive military campaign of Ahab put extreme economic pressure on the citizens of Israel."[17] The status of small free landowners

---

17. Gregory C. Chirichigno, *Debt Slavery in Israel and the Ancient Near East*, JSOTSup 141 (Sheffield: Sheffield Academic, 1993), 123.

probably deteriorated in the face of creditors, and a drought that occurred during Ahab's kingship may have forced many of them to go into debt or even lose their land.[18] Ahab, the successor to his father's Omri kingship, so heavily burdened the peasants working on the land in order to accomplish these projects that he is often referred to as the Solomon of the North.[19] Taxation, the monopoly of resources and services among the state and private elite, and high interest loans financed these projects while, at the same time, it led to the collapse of control by local kinship groups. Peasants would be forced to seek frequent survival loans from creditors privileged with economic means or surplus. The rise of debt slavery can be attributed to the insolvency among free citizens caused by these shifts in both economic factors and social stratification tied to this monarchy. Moreover, debt instruments, such as confiscating children as slaves to repay loans, became the means of a second and escalating round of surplus extraction by creditors.[20] As evidenced in the prophetic writings of the ninth and eighth centuries, the relationship between Israel's elite and peasant citizens on the land was one of exploitation. The prophets in Israel made it clear that during this period the peasantry and small farmers were particularly vulnerable to wealthy private and state elite and landowners who readily took them in as debt slaves (1 Kgs 21; Amos 2:6-8; 5:8-12; Hos. 4:2; 5:10; 12:7-8 [Heb. 8-9]). That these sociopolitical circumstances form the backdrop of this tale begins to tarnish the character of the creditor, who has come to take the widow's children as slaves.

In what, at first glance, appears as a simple tale about a local private matter, the study of "a creditor" in the presumed context of the Omride dynasty discloses much more. The sociopolitical consequences of the Omride hegemony and its accomplishments are not confined to the level of the state but trickle down and are made pitifully tangible by this creditor's presence in a woman's domestic sphere.[21] What the text

---

18. Ibid.

19. Marvin L. Chaney, "Debt Easement in Israelite History and Tradition," in *The Bible and the Politics of Exegesis: Essays in Honor of Norman K. Gottwald on His Sixty-fifth Birthday*, ed. David Jobling, Peggy L. Day, and Gerald T. Sheppard (Cleveland, OH: Pilgrim, 1991), 136.

20. Marvin L. Chaney, *Peasants, Prophets and Political Economy: The Hebrew Bible and Social Analysis* (Eugene: Cascade, 2017), 106.

21. Because the widow appeals to the prophet instead of a royal official or the king himself, Keith Bodner's suggestion that "the creditor is configured as a *cipher* for the king" is especially plausible. See Keith Bodner, *Elisha's Profile in the Book of Kings: The Double Agent* (Oxford: Oxford University Press, 2013), 74.

does not narrate is also revealing. There is no room for negotiation or leniency in a socially stratified world of haves and have-nots. This creditor's loyalties are aligned with the state, and his pockets are likely lined with the growing wealth of the state's elite, to which he belongs. The care of the orphan and widow, or even the basic human sentiment that later becomes formal legislation to refrain from harming them, seems not to bind this individual. The profit yielded from acquiring two children as slaves defines and governs his fidelities. Defaulted loans and the subsequent loss of land or even children are the capital that contributes to the build-up of his class. The wealth of the elite identified with the state stems from the increasing impoverishment of the larger peasant population. That a widowed woman will be deprived of her children, incur incalculable maternal anguish because of such a loss, as well as be deprived of the future that two sons could offer her, seems inconsequential to the creditor when compared to his larger economic gain. A prolonged focus upon the creditor in conjunction with the sociopolitical milieu in which this story resides, occasions a close-up glance of these transactions and the devastation visited upon those who are powerless to resist them.

Subaltern as Invisible Silent Changemakers

At the level of the story world, the creditor has created the crisis warranting resolution. Commentaries have suggested a variety of agents essential to the rescue of this widow and her children. Some point out how the "prophetic word" becomes the source of rescue here and elsewhere in the Elisha tradition.[22] Some interpretations note how the prophets themselves use their agency to reverse the fate of the destitute.[23] Still others interpret how the initiative of the widow and her insistence before the

---

22. A. Graeme Auld, *I & II Kings* (Louisville: John Knox, 1986), 162–3; Burke O. Long, *2 Kings*, FOTL 10 (Grand Rapids: Eerdmans, 1991), 48–51; G. H. Jones, *1 and 2 Kings, Vol. 2*, NCB (Grand Rapids: Eerdmans, 1984), 400–404; Iain Provan, *1 and 2 Kings*, NIBC (Peabody: Hendrickson, 1995), 187–90; Richard Nelson, *First and Second Kings*, Interpretation Commentary (Louisville: John Knox, 1987), 170–2.

23. Terence E. Fretheim, *First and Second Kings*, WBCom (Louisville: Westminster John Knox, 1999), 144–50; Robert Cohn, *2 Kings*, Berit Olam: Studies in Hebrew Narrative & Poetry (Collegeville: Liturgical Press, 2000), 25–6; Tamis Renteria Hoover, "The Elijah/Elisha Stories: A Sociocultural Analysis of Prophets and People in Ninth Century B.C.E. Israel," in *Elijah and Elisha in Socioliterary Perspective*, ed. Robert Coote (Atlanta: Scholars Press, 1992), 75–136.

prophet became a means to her own salvation.[24] But if we train our reading practice to be more inclusive, we further discover who also should be numbered among the agents of change and restoration in this tale.

Out of the shadows of the story's margins, and mentioned only once, emerges the subaltern. And though remaining completely silent in the narrative, when their story is excavated, their potential as change agents, who present an alternative to a stratified society, begins to be recognized. As part of the prophet's instructions to the woman (v. 3), "the neighbors" are mentioned only once in passing, have no speaking part, and remain anonymous. The prophet commands her to go "gather jars from all your neighbors, and not only a few" (v. 3), and then she is to shut the door behind herself and her children and start pouring. The neighbors are so obscured in the story that when the woman follows the prophet's instructions, we only read, "So she left him, and she shut the door behind herself and her children" (v. 5).

Who are "the neighbors" in Israelite society that the woman is supposed to approach? Neighbors make up community. The original meaning of neighbor was "associate" (Heb. *rea*). Its frequent occurrence across the Covenant Code indicates these laws were intended to legislate on behalf of the members of the Israelite community (Exod. 20:16-17; 21:14, 18, 35; 22:7-10, 14, 26; 32:27; 33:11). In Lev. 19:18, the term clearly referred to a fellow Hebrew: "Do not take revenge or bear a grudge against members of your community, but love your *neighbor* as yourself; I am Yahweh." Here members of the community are synonymous with neighbors. Moreover, how one treated a neighbor determined one's righteousness. In fact, the ill treatment of one's neighbor was both a sign and cause of a community or nation's disintegration (Isa. 3:5; Jer. 9:4-9; Mic. 7:5-6).

Across the Old Testament, the word *neighbor* is most frequently used to describe fellow Israelites in particular. The notion of neighbor as fellow Israelites or associates coincided well with the communal framework that characterized pre-monarchic Israel's self-governance in local kinship groups. In fact, it was the rejection of monarchy and its oppressions, and the desire to return to this more egalitarian self-understanding that instigated the north's break away from the south after Solomon's death. The later mandate, "to love your neighbor as yourself," in Deuteronomy seemed to formalize and underscore the consideration and care for another that was to characterize this community and even override what the law required.

---

24. Gina Hens-Piazza, *1–2 Kings*, AOTC (Nashville: Abingdon, 2006), 250–7.

The prophet's instructions to the woman regarding the request to the neighbors is notably specific. The woman is to gather jars from "all your neighbors." That the instructions specify "all (*kol*) your neighbors" indicates not only a sizable number of neighbors but that all of them are needed for the success of this plan. The instruction requires an encounter between the widow and all her neighbors, in which she will have to ask them for something they can give her. Moreover, implied here is the fact that neighbors will have a decision to make: whether to say "yes" or "no." The woman has no choice. So much is at stake. This may be her only chance to find a solution that may rescue her and her two children from the consequences of the law regarding outstanding debts. By contrast, the neighbors, if they cooperate, do so freely. They have nothing to gain if they do and nothing to lose if they don't.

The prophet's instruction to the widow also insists upon the secrecy of what is to take place.[25] Upon gathering jars, she and her children are to go into her house and shut the door behind them. The drama of what unfolds bars the neighbors from witnessing what she does with the jars. Evidently, the neighbors have to trust for what purpose she needs so many of these containers. Shrouded in secrecy, what occurs behind closed doors excludes the neighbors who have lent the woman what she needed.

Despite the nature of her request for jars, and the secrecy surrounding their purpose, there must have been a clear certainty that the neighbors would provide. The narrative simply skips over the complicated task of the widow and children going to and from each house of their neighbors and gathering jugs. Instead, we hear that the family shut the door behind themselves and, as the children handed their mother the jars, she kept pouring. The Hebrew here makes use of participle forms to demonstrate continuous action, not only suggesting their participation but also the very large number of jars continuing to be filled. And how many jars did she fill? Well, we don't have a number; but the oil filled enough jars for her to pay off her debts and more. The surplus was enough to support her children and herself. That allows us to imagine a great number of jars supplied by neighbors to hold a great amount oil.

The neighbors and their cooperation were essential to the fulfillment of the prophet's instruction. The neighbors and their generosity were the means to the social change that took place in the life of that widow and her two children. The transition from the threat of loss of her children,

---

25. Cohn, *2 Kings*, 25.

her own marginalization, and a further level of economic impoverishment are all reversed by what the story skips over but implies: the neighbors were willing to give. That they said yes to her request for jugs became the means to the renewal of life that took place not only because of the prophet's word and the woman's initiative. This transition to life and a future also rested upon the participation of this anonymous group, who have no voice and are mentioned only once in the story. We hardly see them. The narrator acknowledges them only once as a nameless collective group. They are given no details or social definition other than the one-time reference as "neighbors."

Though the subaltern of the literary world, the neighbors were the agents of change and restoration through their unacknowledged but implied cooperation and generosity. They provided the resources the widow lacked. Their generosity made it possible for the woman to have jugs to fill. Their jugs became vessels of hope at a time when she was surrounded by hallmarks of despair. They became grassroots agents of social transformation and empowerment by handing over what they had so that the miracle could unfold. We don't know what it cost them. We don't know if they had to go without as the result of what they gave. We don't know who they were. That they said yes is not even narrated. As the subaltern of the narrative, their presence qualifies as only a slight thread in this larger story in which their role and importance can be easily missed. Still, the story's successful outcome hinges upon their generosity. It bears evidence of their virtue, their unacknowledged giving, and their willingness to be a community for this widow and her children. bell hooks talks about community as "keepers of hope."[26] And hope becomes a means of empowerment for those for whom all else seems hopeless. Thus, the neighbors also disclose the potential of the subaltern to exercise a subversive power in the face of dominant forces in hegemonic circumstances. They represent a notion of the subaltern about which Bhabha invites us to think differently.[27] They become a quiet source of subversive power and offer a notion of an alternate reality that opposed the consequences of stratified society.

But the neighbors are more than community for the widow. They become formatters of their own ongoing character. Virtue, when practiced on behalf of another, not only forms an individual's character but also

---

26. See bell hooks, "Keepers of Hope," in *Teaching Community* (New York: Routledge, 2007), 105–16.

27. See the preceding introductory discussion on Subaltern Studies.

becomes a means to the formation of what a community becomes when it is practiced by the community.[28] It fashions "not simply the particular, historical and diverse communities but, more importantly, moral communities for moral characters are an inherent and constitutive element of a community."[29] Hence, such behavior, when practiced by a communal group such as "all the neighbors," generates and sustains not just a member, like the widow, but the community by shaping its identity and its moral formation.

Conclusion

The creditor and the neighbors form two opposing poles of the story. One constitutes a threat that dominates and subordinates. The other offers an alternative reality grounded in community. Their occurrence in the same story may also reveal the tension between two competing societal configurations. The creditor and his role in the story represent the increasing build-up of a socially stratified society, in which the few wealthy powerful at the top control and even take advantage of the ever-increasing and impoverished population at the bottom. The neighbors, as the subaltern, narrate an alternative society of a more egalitarian self-governing kinship group of earlier days, before monarchy. Though supported by Israelite law, the creditor gives no evidence of any human concern that would be moved by the dire straits of a poor widow whose only hope resides in her two sons. Over and against the creditor, the neighbors represent a kind of social configuration that is communal rather than hierarchically stratified. It is possible to think of them operating out of an ethic of care, rather than an economics of personal gain or self-enhancement.

The creditor and the neighbors play key antithetical roles in the story world. The creditor and his plan create the crisis needing resolution. The neighbors and their implied generosity provide the tangible means for the woman to bring about a changed fate for herself and her two children. Faced with the plight of the most vulnerable in ancient Israelite society, they represent two courses of action, one grounded in self-interest defended by legalities and the other of self-giving grounded in a communal ethic. In the process, both the creditor, who receives description, and the neighbors, about whom nothing is narrated, are not only key to the crisis and resolution in this story. They also summon readers to

---

28. Lúcás Chan S.J., *Biblical Ethics in the 21st Century: Developments, Emerging Consensus, and Future Directions* (New York: Paulist Press, 2013), 90–2.
29. Ibid., 111.

dual considerations. Who are the tyrants that wield legalities that further disable the already disenfranchized in our society? And who are the anonymous changemakers, whose small collective acts lift up as worthy the least amongst us?

Cooperating with hierarchy of the narrative and even the hierarchical categories of literary analysis, the challenge and insights that the subaltern offer in this tale would be lost. While the neighbors are mentioned only once, lack any description, and are rendered silent in the narrative, they do have a story to tell. Moreover, as Bhabha observes, their invisibility does not necessarily render them weak and without political influence. Rather, it enables them to quietly exercise a kind power that can undercut hegemonic values and turn things upside down. Such disruptions of the status quo fuel radical change, the kind of change in which we too can participate if we alter the ways we read and think.

Chapter 14

THE TRUST OF HEZEKIAH: IN YHWH ... AND ASSYRIA, EGYPT, AND BABYLON (2 KINGS 18–20)

David T. Lamb

1. *Introduction*

The empires of Egypt, Assyria, and Babylon had a dramatic impact on Israel and Judah over the course of the Hebrew Bible.[1] Moses the deliverer is the character most frequently associated with Egypt,[2] Jeremiah the prophet, with Babylon,[3] and Hezekiah the king, with Assyria as his extended interactions with Sennacherib are recorded in detail in three locations (2 Kgs 18–19; Isa. 36–37; 2 Chron. 32).[4]

---

1. For extended recent discussions of each of these empires and how they interacted with the nations of Israel and Judah, see the following three essays: Christopher B. Hays with Peter Machinist, "Assyria and the Assyrians," in *The World around the Old Testament: The People and Places of the Ancient Near East*, ed. Bill T. Arnold and Brent A. Strawn (Grand Rapids: Baker Academic, 2016), 31–105; and in the same volume David S. Vanderhooft, "Babylonia and the Babylonians," 107–37, and Joel M. LeMon, "Egypt and the Egyptians," 169–96.

2. The book of Exodus has far more repetitions of "Egypt" (*miṣrayim*; 175) than any other biblical book.

3. The book of Jeremiah has far more repetitions of "Babylon" (*bābel*; 169) than any other biblical book.

4. The highest concentrations of repetitions of "Assyria" (*'aššûr*) in Scripture appear in the chapters recording the Hezekiah narratives (2 Kgs 18; 19; Isa. 37; 2 Chron. 32).

But Hezekiah, the ruler praised for his incomparable trust in YHWH (2 Kgs 18:5), also placed his trust in each of these three other empires during times of crisis. Why is this ruler who reformed religion and practiced prayer, also characterized in the book of Kings as relying not only on YHWH, but also on Assyria, Egypt, and Babylon?

This character study of Hezekiah will primarily take a synchronic approach to 2 Kings 18–20. Interaction with the many diachronic studies on this material will be limited here to insights relevant to the textual portrayal of Hezekiah in Kings.[5] While some scholars perceive that the Assyrian narrative includes two discrete sources, "A" (18:13-16) and "B" (18:17–19:37),[6] and that the events of 2 Kings 20 took place before the conclusion of the Assyrian crisis (see §7 below), here Hezekiah's narrative will be discussed in the progression suggested by the text. His narrative will be shown to have been shaped intentionally, both recalling the Assyrian threat (2 Kgs 17; 18:9-12), and anticipating the Babylonian threat (2 Kgs 20:12-19; 24:1–25:21), to make a point about the danger of involvement with foreign empires.

2. *Hezekiah in Kings, Chronicles, and Isaiah*

Typically, the reigns of northern rulers are only recorded in Kings (e.g., Jehu: 2 Kgs 9–10), while those of their southern counterparts are recorded in both Kings and Chronicles (e.g., Josiah: 2 Kgs 22:1–23:30; 2 Chron. 34–35). Hezekiah, however, is unusual as a third account of his reign appears in Isaiah, and all three Hezekiah narratives are extended, involving multiple chapters. To the three-chapter version in 2 Kings (18–20), we can add the four-chapter accounts in both 2 Chronicles (29–32) and Isaiah (36–39).[7] The biblical authors took a great interest in Hezekiah, but not equally so in all aspects of his reign. Because Kings is the focus of this volume, I will not primarily be discussing Hezekiah's characterization in Isaiah and 2 Chronicles, but will merely make a few comments about the most significant differences in these accounts.

---

5. I discuss my views on the Deuteronomistic redaction of the book of Kings in *Righteous Jehu and his Evil Heirs: The Deuteronomist's Negative Perspective on Dynastic Succession* (Oxford: Oxford University Press, 2007), 2–8.

6. For a survey, see Mordecai Cogan and Hayim Tadmor, *II Kings: A New Translation with Introduction and Commentary* (New York: Doubleday, 1988), 240–4.

7. The total number of verses focusing on Hezekiah in these three books is 302 (95 verses in 2 Kings + 117 verses in 2 Chronicles + 90 verses in Isaiah).

Chronicles is more interested in Hezekiah the reformer, while Kings focuses on his engagement with Assyria. Chronicles narrates Hezekiah's reformation over three chapters (2 Chron. 29–31), while Kings only briefly mentions his reforms in one verse (2 Kgs 18:4).[8] Kings devotes sixty-seven verses to the Assyrian threat (2 Kgs 18:7–19:37), while Chronicles limits it to only twenty-three verses, about a third of the Kings' version (2 Chron. 32:1-23). Since Hezekiah's reforms are perceived highly favorably in both books, while his interaction with Assyria is mixed, Hezekiah's portrayal in Kings is less positive.

The accounts of Hezekiah's Assyrian crisis is very similar in 2 Kings (67 verses) and Isaiah (60 verses), except in one significant respect.[9] It appears that Isaiah has attempted to diminish the negative perspective on Hezekiah in Kings.[10] Both books include a comment positioning the Assyrian invasion in the fourteenth year of Hezekiah's reign (2 Kgs 18:13; Isa. 36:1)—identical, except Isaiah includes a *wayĕhi* (left untranslated in many English translations) at the beginning of the verse. But then Isaiah omits Hezekiah's obsequious message to Sennacherib and the details of his enormous tribute (2 Kgs 18:14-16). While one cannot completely discount Child's theory that Isaiah's omission of 2 Kgs 18:14-16 was due to haplography, it is more reasonable to assume that Isaiah's omission was intentional, to redeem the portrayal of a righteous ruler by removing material that characterizes him so negatively.[11] After the omission, Isaiah picks up the story with the arrival of the Rabshakeh and generally follows 2 Kings closely (2 Kgs 18:17; Isa. 36:2). Thus, vis-à-vis Isaiah, in Kings, Hezekiah's involvement with Assyria is cast in a much more negative light. Since this discussion focuses on Hezekiah's interactions with foreign empires, this material unique to Kings recording his submission and tribute to Assyria (2 Kgs 18:14-16) will be a primary focus (see §§5.2, 5.3 below).

---

8. Scholars generally perceive that the Chronicler used Samuel-Kings as a source, not vice versa; see H. G. M. Williamson, *1 and 2 Chronicles* (Grand Rapids: Eerdmans, 1982), 19.

9. As the text is laid out, after the Assyrian crisis has been resolved (Isa. 37:36-38), Isaiah also includes Hezekiah's psalm (Isa. 38:9-20), which is not present in 2 Kings.

10. Since Gesenius's commentary on Isaiah (1821), most scholars think that Isaiah used Kings as a source. For a recent survey of scholarly views on this issue, see Joel Edmund Anderson, "The Rise, Fall, and Renovation of the House Gesenius: Diachronic Methods, Synchronic Readings, and the Debate over Isaiah 36–39 and 2 Kings 18–20," *CBR* 11, no. 2 (2013): 147–67.

11. Brevard Childs, *Isaiah and the Assyrian Crisis* (London: SCM, 1967), 69–70.

3. *Characterization in 2 Kings 18–20*

The book of Kings specifically brings the issue of characterization to the fore by repeatedly acknowledging its use of sources. The book informs readers that it relies on three sources: the royal annals of Solomon, Israel, and Judah (e.g., 1 Kgs 11:41; 14:19, 29; 15:23, 31). In each of the thirty-three references to these royal annals in Kings, the text records that additional information about the rulers of Israel and Judah is available in these sources. Thus, the author acknowledges that certain material from the reigns of these rulers was intentionally omitted (or selected) in order to make a point.

For Hezekiah, the southern annals included details regarding the construction of his conduit to bring water into Jerusalem that were omitted from the book of Kings (20:20). This information was deemed unnecessary for the ruler's primary narrative, but worth a brief mention in his concluding regnal formula.[12] Solomon the builder's projects are narrated over the course of 107 verses (1 Kgs 5–7), but Hezekiah the builder's projects are limited to a fraction of a verse. Ironically, his tunnel into Jerusalem has survived twenty-seven centuries, outlasting the temples of Solomon, Zerubbabel, and Herod.

Perhaps more so than in any other biblical book, the readers of Kings are therefore left to ask, why was certain information included and other information excluded? How is the characterization of Hezekiah affected by the fact that the text focuses on his interactions with Assyria, Egypt, and Babylon, and not on his building projects?

While not interested in his tunnel, the author of Kings is, however, interested in Hezekiah himself. Hezekiah's narrative in Kings is longer than that of any other king of Judah (95 verses).[13] His unusually long narrative cannot be merely attributed to his long reign (29 years; 18:2), since five Judean rulers reigned longer than he did (Manasseh, Azariah, Asa, Jehoash, and Josiah; Amaziah also reigned 29 years). Hezekiah's name also appears more often than any other Judean ruler (45 times in

---

12. Keith Bodner observes the irony that while the text is not primarily interested in Hezekiah's tunnel, it needs to be mentioned in his concluding regnal formula because the water will be desperately needed during the Babylonian siege of Jerusalem; see "Isaiah's Interview," in *Tzedek, Tzedek Tirdof: Poetry, Prophecy, and Justice in Hebrew Scripture*, ed. Andrew Colin Gow and Peter Sabo (Leiden: Brill, 2018), 37–49.

13. Based on his initial and final regnal formulas (18:1; 20:21). See also William H. Barnes, *1–2 Kings* (Carol Stream: Tyndale House, 2012), 349.

the book). Hezekiah's incomparably righteous counterpart Josiah is only mentioned fourteen times in Kings. Why is Hezekiah so important in the book of Kings?

4. *Hezekiah and Trust*

Hezekiah is viewed favorably in the text for his reforms (18:4), and his prayers (19:15-19; 20:2-3). But other rulers in Kings also actively engaged in reforms (e.g., Asa: 1 Kgs 15:12-13; Jehoram: 2 Kgs 3:2; Jehu: 2 Kgs 10:18-27; Josiah: 2 Kgs 23:1-20), or prayers (e.g., Solomon: 1 Kgs 8:22-53; Jehoahaz: 2 Kgs 13:4; Josiah: 2 Kgs 22:13, 19). Reform and prayer therefore do not distinguish Hezekiah from his royal peers.

According to the text, what made Hezekiah unique was his trust. Solomon was uniquely wealthy and wise (1 Kgs 3:12-13).[14] Jeroboam, Omri, Ahab, and Manasseh were uniquely evil (1 Kgs 14:9; 16:25, 30; 21:25; 2 Kgs 21:11).[15] Josiah was unique in his turning to YHWH (2 Kgs 23:25). But Hezekiah trusted (*bāṭaḥ*) in YHWH the God of Israel more so than any other ruler (18:5).

Before analyzing how the narrative characterizes the trust of Hezekiah, we need to make a few observations about how the word appears in the text. The verb "trust" (*bāṭaḥ*) appears nine times in the book of Kings, all within the context of Hezekiah's narrative (2 Kgs 18:5, 19, 20, 21 [×2], 22, 24, 30; 19:10).[16] Trust is therefore a major theme of Hezekiah's narrative. Other kings may have displayed trust, but no other ruler in the book is described with the word *bāṭaḥ*.

Curiously, only once does *bāṭaḥ* appear in narrative contexts where Hezekiah is characterized as trusting in YHWH. Immediately after recording his reforms of worship practices (18:4; removing high places, destroying Moses' bronze snake, and cutting up Asherah poles), the text speaks of his incomparable trust (*bāṭaḥ*; 18:5). Then the text describes his obedience and rebellion against Assyria (18:6-7). Thus, all of these initial actions of Hezekiah are linked to his trust in YHWH. The two other

---

14. On the positive incomparability formulas of Kings (Solomon, Hezekiah, and Josiah), see Gary N. Knoppers, "'There Was None Like Him': Incomparability in the Book of Kings," *CBQ* 54 (1992): 411–31. Knoppers does not discuss the negative incomparability formulas (Jeroboam, Omri, Ahab, and Manasseh).

15. Jeroboam, Omri, and Ahab were each compared to those before them, so if one assumes an increasing level of depravity (or simply, hyperbole), there is no conflict. Manasseh is compared to the Amorites who were before him.

16. Nominal forms of the root also appear in 1 Kgs 5:5 (*bāṭaḥ*; ET 4:25), and in 2 Kgs 18:19 (*biṭāḥôn*).

instances where Hezekiah displayed trust in YHWH involve prayer, but neither context mentions *bāṭaḥ*.[17] He prayed after receiving the threatening message from Sennacherib (19:14-19), and after receiving the message from Isaiah that he would die (20:2-3). Hezekiah's trust manifested itself not only in his reforms and obedience, but also in his prayers, even though the text does not connect these later actions to trust.

The majority of the occurrences of *bāṭaḥ* are concentrated where Hezekiah is the least trusting of YHWH (giving tribute to Assyria, relying on Egypt, and avoiding the Rabshakeh). After the initial reference (18:5), the other eight occurrences of this verb all come from the mouth of a curious individual—the Rabshakeh of Assyria, one of Sennacherib's officials (18:19 [×2], 20, 21, 22, 24, 30; 19:10).[18]

In most of the *bāṭaḥ* references in Kings, Hezekiah is the one doing the trusting. The subject of the verb for six of the nine *bāṭaḥ* references is Hezekiah (18:5, 19, 20, 21, 24; 19:10).[19] Thus, the text emphasizes the trust of Hezekiah.

The contexts of the six Hezekiah subject references are three statements (18:5, 21; 19:10) and three questions (18:19, 20, 24). When Hezekiah is the subject of *bāṭaḥ*, twice the object is YHWH (18:5; 19:10), twice it is Egypt (18:21, 24), and twice it is indeterminate because the Rabshakeh is asking a question ("On what do you rest this trust [*bāṭaḥ*] of yours?": 18:19; "In whom do you now trust [*bāṭaḥ*]?": 18:20).

The question that the Rabshakeh raises here is one that the text is raising for its readers—where does Hezekiah place his trust? Based merely upon these *bāṭaḥ* repetitions, Hezekiah's trust appears evenly divided between YHWH and Egypt.

Hezekiah is described as uniquely trusting in YHWH, but to assume that means he never places his trust in other objects can lead to not taking problematic aspects of his narrative seriously, resulting in a flat characterization of the ruler. In his interactions with foreign powers, Hezekiah's narrative suggests his loyalty is divided. In order to achieve a more rounded, more accurate characterization of Hezekiah, these problematic incidents cannot be ignored. We will therefore next discuss how Hezekiah is characterized as trusting in each of these three empires in the order they appear in the text (Assyria, Egypt, and Babylon).

---

17. Hezekiah's request for Isaiah to pray is more accurately characterized as lament, than trust (19:2-4).

18. The issue of the Rabshakeh's trustworthiness regarding Hezekiah's trust in Egypt will be discussed below (see §6).

19. Twice the subject is Judah (18:22, 30), and once anyone who trusts in Egypt (18:21).

5. Hezekiah and Assyria

5.1. Hezekiah's Rebellion (18:7)

Hezekiah's narrative includes twenty-six references to Assyria (18:7, 9, 11 [×2], 13, 14 [×2], 16, 17, 19, 23, 28, 30, 31, 33; 19:4, 6, 8, 10, 11, 17, 20, 32, 35, 36; 20:6). The first of these references describes how he rebelled (*mārad*) against Assyria and did not serve him (18:7).[20] Hezekiah's rebellion is listed in the midst of many other positively perceived attributes about him (his reforms, trust, and obedience) suggesting that the text viewed his rebellion highly favorably.[21] The independence of Hezekiah toward Assyria is thus contrasted with the subservience of his father Ahaz toward Assyria (2 Kgs 16:7). The rebellion of Hezekiah here, while viewed positively, is not highlighted or emphasized. It is described in a terse, perfunctory manner, with no narrative elaboration—only five words in Hebrew (*wayyimrōd bemelek-'aššûr welō' 'ăbādô*, 18:7).

Even though the previous chapter recorded the Assyrian conquest of the Northern Kingdom (17:3-7), a four-verse reiteration is included here (18:9-12), sandwiched between Hezekiah's Assyrian rebellion (18:7) and his Assyrian capitulation (18:14-16). This redundant insertion serves as a warning about the danger of either rebelling against, or capitulating to Assyria without consulting YHWH.[22] Hezekiah's subsequent actions provide a stark contrast to his initial rebellion.

5.2. Hezekiah's Message (18:14a)

When Hoshea of Israel conspired against Sennacherib's predecessors, they retaliated by besieging Samaria and conquering the Northern Kingdom (17:3-6). In response to Hezekiah's rebellion here, Sennacherib captured the fortified cities of the Southern Kingdom (18:13). Hezekiah's immediate response to this threat evidenced no trust in YHWH. In his initial moment of crisis he does not pray, or seek out the prophet Isaiah; those actions come later (19:2, 15). The text records no Assyrian demands from the Judean ruler, but Hezekiah initiates and offers total submission.

---

20. Some scholars (e.g., Barnes, *1 & 2 Kings*, 324), perceive that Hezekiah's rebellion occurred late in his reign, but in his speech the Rabshakeh uses the same verb (*mārad*; 18:20) in the perfect tense to describe Hezekiah's action, implying that, from his perspective, Hezekiah's rebellion had already taken place.

21. For scholars who perceive Hezekiah's rebellion positively, see Cogan and Tadmor, *II Kings*, 217; Barnes, *1 & 2 Kings*, 324.

22. Marvin Sweeney states about 18:9-12, "This narrative warns the reader of the futility of attempted revolt against the Assyrians without divine support"; *I & II Kings* (Louisville: Westminster John Knox, 2007), 410.

A few scholars perceive Hezekiah's actions here positively. Evans views Hezekiah's words and tribute in 18:14-16 very favorably, portraying him "as a valorous king."[23] Similarly, Knoppers considers the portrayal of Hezekiah as "uniformly positive in 18:1–20:11."[24] However, a close examination of these verses reveals that the actions of Hezekiah in 18:14-16 should be perceived highly negatively.

Hezekiah's first words (18:14) contribute significantly to his negative characterization here. Alter observes, "In any given narrative event, and especially at the beginning of a new story, the point at which dialogue first emerges will be worthy of special attention, and in most instances, the initial words spoken by a personage will be revelatory, perhaps more in manner than in matter, constituting an important moment in the exposition of character."[25]

Hezekiah's initial speech reveals a ruler who does not trust exclusively in YHWH. Hezekiah's message to Sennacherib (18:14) can be divided into three components: a confession ("I have done wrong"; *ḥāṭāʾtî*), a request ("Withdraw from me"; *šûb mēʿālay*), and a submission ("Whatever you impose on me I will bear"; *ʾēt ʾăšer-tittēn ʿālay ʾeśśāʾ*). At this moment, Hezekiah is characterized as obsequious, fearful, and relying on a tribute to bribe his way out of this crisis.

In the preceding verses, the text has had nothing but positives to say about Hezekiah. But in his own first recorded words he confesses to Sennacherib that he has done wrong. Hezekiah's language here is shockingly religious, particularly in light of the question Sennacherib poses about where Hezekiah places his trust (18:19). The verb Hezekiah uses to describe his actions (*ḥāṭāʾ*) is usually translated as "sin" (e.g., 1 Kgs 8:31; 14:22; 15:26; 16:19; 18:9), often used in contexts of confession to YHWH (e.g., 1 Sam. 15:25, 30; 2 Sam. 12:13; 24:10, 17). In the book of Kings, *ḥāṭāʾ* has highly negative connotations, associated with the altars of Jeroboam (e.g., 1 Kgs 14:16; 15:30, 34; 16:2, 19; 2 Kgs 3:3; 10:29), and the downfall of both kingdoms. The verb was last used in the previous chapter describing Israel's rebellion, justifying their destruction by Assyria (17:7, 21), and it is used next in Manasseh's narrative describing his many crimes, explaining Judah's eventual destruction

---

23. Paul S. Evans, *The Invasion of Sennacherib in the Book of Kings: A Source-critical and Rhetorical Study of 2 Kings 18–19* (Leiden: Brill, 2009), 124–30 (quote from 126).

24. Knoppers perceives a more critical attitude toward Hezekiah at the end of his narrative (20:12-19); see "Incomparability," 418–25 (quote from 423).

25. Robert Alter, *The Art of Biblical Narrative* (New York: Basic Books, 1981), 74.

by Babylon (21:11, 16, 17). Hezekiah's own description of himself as sinning (*ḥāṭā'*) here should be perceived highly negatively. Even if he is merely saying that he did wrong (*ḥāṭā'*) to appease Sennacherib, he appears deceptive. He is certainly not relying on divine assistance.

The context suggests that his rebellion, viewed favorably above (18:7), was the act he was repenting of here. Hezekiah is clearly desperate to get relief. If Sennacherib withdraws, Hezekiah will essentially write a blank check, giving the Assyrian whatever he asks (18:14). Just as Hezekiah's rebellion against Assyria was perceived positively, his subservience to Assyria should be perceived negatively.

Bostock wonders how such a negative view of Hezekiah could remain in the text (18:14-16), after such a positive portrayal a few verses earlier (18:3-8).[26] Similarly, Mullen finds Hezekiah's statement "remarkable in light of the evaluation given by the historian."[27] But neither of these scholars offers rationale for why the text included something that characterized Hezekiah so negatively.

Josiah delivers two long addresses in the first thirteen verses of his narrative to instigate his reforms (2 Kgs 22:4-7, 12-13). In contrast, Hezekiah is silent in Kings during his reforms (18:3-6). Hezekiah's message to Sennacherib in 18:14 are his only words for the first forty verses of his narrative, until 19:3. He is thus characterized from his own mouth as obsequious, looking for salvation during this time of crisis, not from his God, but from his enemy.

5.3. *Hezekiah's Tribute (18:14b-16)*

Hezekiah's foreign tribute did not make him unique among kings.[28] Twelve rulers in the book of Kings gave tribute to foreign nations, two from Israel (Menahem and Hoshea) and ten from Judah (Rehoboam, Asa, Jehoash, Amaziah, Ahab, Hezekiah, Jehoahaz, Jehoiakim, Jehoiachin, and Zedekiah).[29] Over half of the southern rulers of the Divided Monarchy gave tribute (10 of 19). Like Hezekiah, most of these Judean tributaries (8

---

26. David Bostock, *A Portrayal of Trust: The Theme of Faith in the Hezekiah Narratives* (Milton Keynes: Paternoster, 2006), 46.

27. E. Theodore Mullen, "Crime and Punishment: The Sins of the King and the Despoliation of the Treasuries," *CBQ* 54 (1992): 231–48.

28. For a longer discussion of foreign tribute in the ancient Near East and in the book of Kings, see Lamb, *Righteous Jehu*, 120–4. Table 2.7A (p. 122) lists rulers of Israel and Judah who gave tribute or were plundered.

29. Here I call "tribute" exchanges of valuable goods involving both voluntary gifts to foreign powers (e.g., 1 Kgs 15:18; 2 Kgs 16:8), and involuntary seizures by

of 10), used the temple treasuries as one of the sources for the tribute (all except Jehoahaz and Jehoiakim).[30]

What made Hezekiah's tribute unusual was its size and its detailed description. Most of the tributes in Kings (9 of 12) are recorded in less than a verse (1 Kgs 14:26; 15:18; 2 Kgs 12:19 [ET 12:18]; 14:14; 16:8; 17:3; 23:33, 35; 24:13), but the description of Hezekiah's tribute requires two and half verses (18:14b-16).[31]

Often the text of Kings merely records vague information about the tributes, ten mention gold, eight mention silver, but usually (9 of 12 instances) there are no quantities recorded (e.g., 1 Kgs 15:18; 2 Kgs 14:14; 16:8; 23:35). In three instances specific numbers of talents are stated, all from the later period of the Divided Monarchy. Menahem of Israel gave 1,000 talents of silver (37 tons) to Tiglath-pileser III of Assyria (2 Kgs 15:19).[32] Here, Hezekiah gave 300 talents of silver (11 tons) and 30 talents of gold (1 ton) to Sennacherib (2 Kgs 18:14).[33] Jehoahaz of Judah gave 100 talents of silver (3.75 tons) and 1 talent of gold (75 pounds) to Neco of Egypt (2 Kgs 23:33).

It is impossible to be certain about precise relative values of gold and silver during the period of the Divided Monarchy, but gold was typically about fifteen times more valuable by weight than silver.[34] Using a 15:1 conversion ratio, we can convert each of these three tributes into purely silver talent equivalents for comparison. Hezekiah's tribute would be worth 750 silver talents.[35] Thus Hezekiah's equivalent 750 silver

---

foreign powers (e.g., 1 Kgs 14:26; 2 Kgs 14:14). Assyrian sources record tributes from two other Israelite rulers (Jehu and Jehoash) not recorded in Kings (see *COS* 2:270, 276).

30. Presumably, the treasuries were replenished by offerings between these numerous temple despoliations (see 2 Kgs 12:4-16).

31. Other longer descriptions include Menahem's tribute to Tiglath-pileser III (2 Kgs 15:19-20) and the final Babylonian plundering of the temple after Zedekiah has been deported (2 Kgs 25:13-16).

32. He is referred to by his hypercorism "Pul" in this context, but a few verses later he is called "Tiglath-pileser" (2 Kgs 15:29; see also 16:7, 10).

33. Sennacherib's inscription agrees with the biblical texts on the number of gold talents (30) but has a much larger number of silver talents (800, instead of 300; *COS* 2:303).

34. In the context of discussing money in the Hebrew Bible, John W. Betlyon states, "One gold shekel was the equivalent of 15 silver shekels," in "Coinage," *ABD* 1:1078.

35. For Hezekiah, 750 silver talent equivalents = 300 silver talents + 450 silver talents (= 30 gold talents).

talent tribute was less than, but comparable to, Menahem's 1,000 silver talent tribute (depending upon the actual conversion ratio). However, Jehoahaz's tribute is most easily comparable to Hezekiah's since both include a specific number of talents of gold and silver, and Jehoahaz is also a Judean ruler. Jehoahaz's tribute would be worth 115 silver talents.[36] Hezekiah gave three times more silver than Jehoahaz and thirty times more gold. Therefore, Hezekiah's tribute was almost seven times larger than Jehoahaz (750 to 115 silver talent equivalents). If we assume that the tribute accounts that include specific amounts were larger than those that did not, it would suggest that Hezekiah's tribute was by far the largest among southern rulers.[37]

Jehu of Israel's enormous tribute of silver and gold to Assyria was recorded in four distinct royal inscriptions of Shalmaneser III (*COS* 2:267, 268, 270). According to its four-panel depiction on Shalmaneser's Black Obelisk, Jehu's tribute required thirteen individuals to transport (*ANEP*, 120-122, #351-355).[38] But Jehu's tribute was not recorded in the book of Kings. Jehu and Hezekiah were both righteous rulers (2 Kgs 10:30; 18:3), who gave large tributes to Assyria, that were recorded in Assyrian sources (for Hezekiah's, see *COS* 2:303). But only Hezekiah's was recorded in Kings.

Like many Judean rulers before him, Hezekiah paid his tribute from the temple. The silver came from the temple and the royal treasuries (18:15), and the gold came from the doors and doorposts of the temple (18:16).[39] David and Solomon are honored for bringing dedicated gifts of gold and silver to YHWH (1 Kgs 7:51). Rulers who loot the temple to pay off foreign rulers, like Hezekiah, are not explicitly condemned for it, but these acts cannot be viewed favorably, as valuables are essentially stolen from YHWH and offered to foreign powers. Just as Hezekiah's rebellion

---

36. For Jehoahaz, 115 silver talent equivalents = 100 silver talents + 15 silver talents (= 1 gold talent).

37. A variety of reasons could explain why these amounts were not recorded in Kings.

38. For an extended discussion of Jehu's tribute, and the Black Obelisk specifically, see Lamb, *Righteous Jehu*, 124–8. The first four individuals behind the prostrate Jehu on the panels are Assyrians; the remaining thirteen (with tasseled caps and pointed shoes) are probably meant to be Israelites carrying the tribute.

39. While the word "gold" (*zāhāb*) appears in the MT of 18:14, it does not appear in 18:16. Most English translations (e.g., ESV, NRSV, NAS, NIV) add the word "gold" in 18:16 since the text records that Solomon covered the doors and doorposts with gold (1 Kgs 6:31-35), and there is no record that this gold had already been removed. Thus, 18:15 records the source of the silver, and 18:16 records the source of the gold for Hezekiah's tribute.

is viewed positively (18:7), his obsequious message and massive tribute should be viewed negatively.

Na'aman addresses the problem of righteous rulers like Hezekiah who are plundered or give tribute.[40] He concludes that the Deuteronomist's polemic is focused on voluntary servitude, thus Menahem, Ahaz, and Jehoiakim are viewed negatively since they initiated the transaction. While Na'aman's thesis is generally valid, it does not work for Hezekiah. He mentions Hezekiah's rebellion (18:7), but he avoids Hezekiah's problematic tribute by relegating it to a footnote, and he ignores two other righteous rulers who give tribute (Jehoash and Amaziah of Judah).[41] Na'aman concludes reasonably that taking gold and silver from the temple treasuries has clearly unfavorable connotations and is viewed critically, but does not explain how righteous Hezekiah escapes explicit condemnation for perpetrating this action.

Mullen argues that the Deuteronomist viewed the despoliation of the temple treasuries as a judgment on rulers for not removing high places or not trusting in YHWH.[42] He addresses the problem of Hezekiah's tribute, concluding that he failed to remain firm and trust YHWH so was punished with the loss of this massive tribute. Wray Beal also perceives Hezekiah's actions in 18:14-16 negatively: "they reveal his lack of trust in YHWH to deliver Jerusalem."[43] Bostock observes that the text does not directly criticize Hezekiah, but he appears to betray his trust in YHWH by "kow-towing" to the Assyrian ruler.[44] Bostock also perceives an emphasis on the "fruitlessness of foreign rapprochement generally."[45]

While Hezekiah does not rely on Assyria in the same way he relies on Egypt and Babylon, he trusts that his submission and his gift of tribute to Assyria should cause Sennacherib to withdraw from Judah (18:14), thus removing the threat. But as the narrative is constructed (ignoring the possibility that 18:14-16 was once a separate account) his gift has no impact. Instead of departing, Sennacherib immediately sends his messengers to demand unconditional surrender (18:17). The crisis has not been averted. The only difference from before is that Hezekiah is now a lot poorer. Assyria did not prove trustworthy.

---

40. Nadav Na'aman, "The Deuteronomist and Voluntary Servitude to Foreign Powers," *JSOT* 65 (1997): 37–53. For a longer discussion of Na'aman, see Lamb, *Righteous Jehu*, 123–4.
41. Na'aman, "Voluntary Servitude," 44.
42. Mullen, "Crime and Punishment," 231–48.
43. Lissa M. Wray Beal, *1 & 2 Kings* (Downers Grove: InterVarsity, 2014), 466.
44. Bostock, *Portrayal of Trust*, 48–9.
45. Ibid., 50.

5.4. *Hezekiah's Disappearance (18:18)*

When Sennacherib's three officials arrive at Jerusalem, they asked to speak with Hezekiah, but the text observes that Hezekiah sent three officials instead (18:18). While it might seem normal for Hezekiah's officials to speak to Sennacherib's officials, the narrative records that the Assyrians specifically requested Hezekiah. We cannot be sure why Hezekiah did not interact with them himself, but the fact the text mentions their request makes it appear that Hezekiah is intentionally avoiding them. Bostock wonders if Hezekiah's decision to remain inside was an intentional act of non-compliance.[46] Josephus, however, provides a more compelling reason for Hezekiah's no show, explaining that it was cowardice (*deilias*) that prompted him to send three friends instead (*Ant.* 10.1.2).[47] Josephus' perspective on the ruler is supported by the observation that in this long initial Assyrian narrative (18:8-37), Hezekiah is absent as an active participant, except to acquiesce to Assyria (18:14-16). Just as Hezekiah's obsequious message and massive tribute were omitted in Isaiah, so also Isaiah omits the comment that Sennacherib's officials explicitly called for Hezekiah (Isa. 36:3). Thus in Isaiah once again, Hezekiah appears less cowardly than he does in Kings. Sweeney describes how the "virtual whitewash of his character in the Isaiah version" supports "his presentation as an ideal model for piety to readers of the book."[48] While in his rebellion Hezekiah displayed faith in YHWH (18:7), in his submission, his tribute, and his disappearance (18:13-18) he displayed a lack of faith in YHWH and an abundance of fear of Assyria.

6. *Hezekiah and Egypt (18:21, 24)*

Assyria was not the only foreign power that Hezekiah relied upon. Egypt is mentioned four times in the Hezekiah narrative (18:21 [×2], 24; 19:24). Three of these are from the mouth of the Rabshakeh, who sends two messages to Hezekiah about trusting in Egypt:

> Behold, you are trusting (*bāṭaḥ*) now in Egypt, that broken reed of a staff, which will pierce the hand of any man who leans on it. Such is Pharaoh king of Egypt to all who trust (*bāṭaḥ*) in him. (18:21)

---

46. Ibid., 51.
47. See also Louis H. Feldman, "Josephus's Portrait of Hezekiah," *JBL* 111, no. 4 (1992): 603.
48. Sweeney, *I & II Kings*, 411.

> How then can you repulse a single captain among the least of my master's servants, when you trust (*bāṭaḥ*) in Egypt for chariots and for horsemen? (18:24)

The inclusion of the Rabshakeh's repeated comments about Hezekiah's trust (*bāṭaḥ*) in Egypt serves to characterize Judah's ruler as having divided loyalties.

In his discussion of the parallel text in Isaiah, Seitz argues that the Rabshakeh is not a reliable witness, so one should not necessarily conclude that Hezekiah had made an agreement with Egypt.[49] However, it is more reasonable to assume the Judean-Egyptian alliance the Rabshakeh refers to here was a reality. If Hezekiah did not in fact have an alliance with Egypt, the Rabshakeh's logic makes no sense. In his discussion of the Rabshakeh's message here, Bostock observes, "The most cunning deception is that which is close to the truth."[50]

The truthfulness of the rest of the Rabshakeh's initial speech is supported by the context of the chapter. The Rabshakeh speaks of Hezekiah's reforms and his reliance on YHWH (18:21, 22), both of which the narrative has already recorded (18:4, 5). The Rabshakeh seems to know that the Judean ruler trusts both in YHWH and Egypt. Darr states it boldly, "Hezekiah is guilty of resorting to Egypt."[51]

Janzen points out the tension here in the king's actions, "Hezekiah was depending on Egypt's help in order to rescue Judah…and he refused to rely solely on divine power to save, no matter how perfect his cultic actions had been."[52] The text never states Hezekiah was allied with Egypt, but it also never states he was not allied with them. The text does not correct the Rabshakeh's words here. Hezekiah trusted not only in YHWH, but also in Egypt, presumably for assistance against Assyria.

---

49. Christopher R. Seitz, *Zion's Final Destiny: The Development of the Book of Isaiah: A Reassessment of Isaiah 36–39* (Minneapolis: Fortress, 1991), 73. Seitz, however, admits that many scholars conclude Hezekiah did make an alliance with Egypt (see pp. 76–8). See also Bostock's discussion of Seitz, *Portrayal of Trust*, 53–4.

50. Bostock, *Portrayal of Trust*, 53.

51. Katheryn Pfisterer Darr, "No Strength to Deliver: A Contextual Analysis of Hezekiah's Proverb in Isaiah 37.3b," in *New Visions of Isaiah*, ed. Roy F. Melugin and Marvin A. Sweeney (Sheffield: Sheffield Academic, 1996), 219–56.

52. David Janzen, "The Sins of Josiah and Hezekiah: A Synchronic Reading of the Final Chapters of Kings," *JSOT* 37 (2013): 349–70 (358). T. R. Hobbs also states, "It is clearly implied here that Hezekiah had opened negotiations with Egypt," in *2 Kings* (Waco, TX: Word, 1985), 257.

Further support for the reliability of the Rabshakeh's statement about Judean trust in Egypt is seen in prophetic texts expressing similar ideas. Like the Rabshakeh, Isaiah warned against looking to Egypt for help (Isa. 30:1-5; 31:1-3). Seitz observes that Hezekiah is not explicitly criticized in these texts by Isaiah,[53] but neither is any other ruler, so it is reasonable to assume the context of Isaiah's oracles is the reign of Hezekiah. The language used by the Rabshakeh to describe dependence upon Egypt (a broken reed that pierces the hand of those who lean on it) is also strikingly similar to the language used by Ezekiel for Egypt (Ezek. 29:6-7; see also Isa. 42:3). Thus, the text here includes a prophetic warning to Hezekiah from the lips of Judah's enemy about the foolishness of relying on Egypt. Just as Assyria proved unreliable, Egypt will shatter and injure if Hezekiah continues to trust in them

7. Hezekiah and Babylon (20:12-19).

At this point, we move through the middle section of Hezekiah's long narrative, where he most clearly displays his trust in YHWH (see §4 above), to the end of his narrative, the visit of the Babylonian embassy from Merodach-baladan (20:12-19).[54] Babylon is mentioned four times in the Hezekiah narrative, all in this section (20:12, 14, 17, 18). While individuals from Babylon were mentioned briefly in the context of Assyrian deportations (17:24, 30), this incident is the first time that Babylon, eventual destroyer of Judah, plays a significant role.

The Babylonian embassy comes to deliver letters and a get-well gift to Hezekiah (20:12). Hezekiah shows the Babylonians all the silver, gold, spices, precious oils, and armor in his treasuries (20:13). Isaiah and Hezekiah interact over the prophet's questions (20:14-15). Isaiah pronounces a judgment (20:16-18), and Hezekiah gives a deeply ambivalent (at best) response (20:19).

Many scholars reasonably assume Hezekiah's interaction with the Babylonian embassy occurred before the completion of the Assyrian

---

53. Seitz, *Zion's Final Destiny*, 73.

54. The name of the Babylonian ruler in 20:12 is transliterated into English in a variety of ways: Berodach-baladan (NAS, KJV, based on the MT of 20:12), Merodach-baladan (ESV, NRSV, based on the MT of Isa. 39:1), Marduk-apla-iddin (based on cuneiform sources), and Marduk-Baladan (NIV, following Isa. 39:1, but using the more familiar Marduk). See also Shmuel Vargon's discussion of Merodach-baladan, in "The Time of Hezekiah's Illness and the Visit of the Babylonian Delegation," *Maarav* 21, no. 1-2 (2014): 39–40.

crisis.⁵⁵ The most compelling textual reason for this conclusion is that Hezekiah's treasuries are still full (20:13), which would not have been the case after his massive tribute to Sennacherib (18:14-16). The Hezekiah narrative's apparent intentional dischronology, inserting his trust in YHWH (19:14-19; 20:2-3) between his trust in Assyria and Egypt (18:14-16, 21, 24) and his trust in Babylon (20:12-19), prevents perceiving a character progression toward greater trust in God, but suggests a complex characterization of a king with divided loyalties.

A lack of textual clarity regarding Hezekiah's motivation for his treasury display has prompted numerous scholarly examinations of Hezekiah's motives.⁵⁶ There is no explicit condemnation of Hezekiah's actions here, prompting scholars like Bostock to perceive Hezekiah's behavior as neutral, even hospitable.⁵⁷ However, many scholars perceive the actions of this righteous ruler critically at this point. Both Brueggemann and Wray Beal view Hezekiah's actions negatively, calling them foolish.⁵⁸ Cogan and Tadmor think 20:17-19 view Hezekiah critically and place the blame for the plundering of Jerusalem and the exile on the king.⁵⁹ Similarly, Jang states that Isaiah condemns Hezekiah for his engagement with Babylon, and that the Babylonian exile was partly caused by it.⁶⁰

There are at least three strong textual reasons to conclude that Hezekiah's actions were viewed negatively both by the prophet and the narrator. First, the simple ordering of the narrative suggests causality.⁶¹ Hezekiah shows his treasures to Babylon. Isaiah asks what the Babylonians saw. Then Isaiah announces a judgment involving Babylon taking away

---

55. E.g., Janzen, "Josiah and Hezekiah," 358; Wray Beal, *1 & 2 Kings*, 482. Similarly, Vargon argues Hezekiah's sickness and prayer (20:1-6) preceded the end of the Assyrian crisis because Isaiah's oracle speaks of the king being rescued from the king of Assyria (20:6).

56. See the extended discussion of various scholarly views on this incident in Bostock, *Portrayal of Trust*, 121–47. For a recent discussion focused on the Isaianic accounts, see Sehoon Jang, "Is Hezekiah a Success or a Failure? The Literary Function of Isaiah's Prediction at the End of the Royal Narratives in the Book of Isaiah," *JSOT* 42 (2017): 117–35.

57. Bostock, *Portrayal of Trust*, 126, 131, 133.

58. Walter Brueggemann, *1 & 2 Kings* (Macon: Smyth & Helwys, 2000), 525; Wray Beal, *1 & 2 Kings*, 482.

59. Cogan and Tadmor, *II Kings*, 262.

60. Jang, "Is Hezekiah a Success?," 131.

61. Brueggemann acknowledges that the text is not clear, but that the arrangement of the narrative suggests Isaiah's oracle was prompted by Hezekiah's actions; *1 & 2 Kings*, 525.

his treasures. The action, the questions, and the judgment all involve Babylon. The causality is clearly implied by the way the narrative is constructed. When a sixteen-year-old son arrives home several hours after his curfew and the father is waiting at the door and announces, "You are grounded!" he does not need to provide a reason for the punishment. To expect an explanation would be ridiculous ("Because you were late, I am now going to ground you"). The context makes the reason obvious, as it does in this prophet–king interaction. The punishment announced by Isaiah was prompted by Hezekiah's actions. The link between Hezekiah's display and Isaiah's judgment is further strengthened by the placement of this scene at the end of Hezekiah's narrative, ominously foreshadowing the Babylonian exile. While Hezekiah's initial words (18:14) revealed his trust in Assyria, his final words (20:19) suggests he only cares for himself, and has no regard for the fate of his descendants. Scholars who argue for a neutral or positive view of Hezekiah here ignore the straightforward manner in which the narrative is constructed.

Second, Isaiah's address makes it clear that his words are targeting the ruler specifically, and not the nation generally. Isaiah speaks directly "to Hezekiah" (*'el-ḥizqiyyāhû*), and then uses a string of four second person *singular* pronouns ("your house," "your fathers," "your sons," and "born to you"; 20:16-18). Even Bostock (who views Hezekiah neutrally here) refers to Isaiah's barrage of questions to Hezekiah as an interrogation.[62] There are no other examples in the book of Kings where a prophet pronounces judgment directly to a ruler but the ruler is not somehow responsible for the condemnation. When Micaiah pronounced judgment, like Isaiah here, he gives no explicit reason for why Ahab was being punished (1 Kgs 22:17, 19-23; but see 21:17-26). Isaiah's judgment is focused exclusively on Hezekiah, suggesting the ruler was culpable.[63]

Third, the distinctive language used by Isaiah in this passage has negative connotations elsewhere in the book of Kings. The phrase "hear the word of YHWH" (*šemaʿ debar-yhwh*; 2 Kgs 20:16) only appears elsewhere in Kings when Micaiah pronounces the coming judgment to Ahab (1 Kgs 22:19). The only other time a prophet asks someone about a location in Kings ("from where"; *mēʾayin*; 2 Kgs 20:14) is when Elisha interrogates Gehazi after his deception with Naaman the Aramean

---

62. Bostock, *Portrayal of Trust*, 121, 128.
63. Christopher T. Begg describes how throughout Israel's history prophets speak directly to the king with generally negative announcements concerning the future; in "2 Kings 20:12-19 as an Element of the Deuteronomistic History," *CBQ* 48 (1986): 34.

general (2 Kgs 5:25). Unlike Gehazi, Hezekiah was honest with the prophet, but Ahab valued honesty in his interaction with Micaiah (1 Kgs 22:16) and he was still punished.

Why is Hezekiah characterized so negatively here? Several scholars observe that Hezekiah does not pray in response to the judgment oracle.[64] But a lack of prayer afterwards does not explain why the oracle was necessary. Other scholars believe Hezekiah may have been guilty of pride as he displayed his wealth and possessions to his guests.[65]

However, the most compelling explanation for Isaiah's harsh condemnation here is that Hezekiah was hoping to establish an alliance with Babylon. Josephus states the purpose of the Babylonian embassy was to secure an alliance with Judah (*Ant.* 10.2.2), which is a reasonable assumption anytime two nations meet and exchange goods. Schipper thinks that Dtr faults Hezekiah here for desiring to enter into an alliance with Babylon.[66] Janzen states, "Hezekiah displays his royal treasury to envoys from Babylon, which suggest the king was assuring a foreign power that he had the resources to pay for their aid in driving the Assyrians out of Judah."[67] Vargon similarly concludes that Hezekiah was attempting to forge a military alliance against Assyria.[68] Sweeney also sees the Judean ruler's display as a preparation for alliance and revolt.[69]

If there were no other examples of Hezekiah relying on other foreign powers, we might assume he would not look to Babylon here for support since he trusted incomparably in YHWH. But since he has already (as the narrative is laid out) depended upon both Assyria and Egypt, it is not surprising, and perhaps even expected, that he would look for assistance from another imperial power.

The fact that Hezekiah showed the Babylonians all of his silver and gold suggests he was willing to offer some, or even all of it to them as part of an agreement. Begg argues that Hezekiah here is "placing his

---

64. See for example, Begg, "2 Kings 20:12-19," 35–8; Barnes, *1–2 Kings*, 348; Bostock, *Portrayal of Trust*, 144–5.

65. See, for example, Walter Brueggemann, *Isaiah 1–39* (Louisville: Westminster John Knox, 1998), 311; Wray Beal, *1 & 2 Kings*, 482.

66. Jeremy Schipper, "Hezekiah, Manasseh, and Dynastic or Transgenerational Punishment," in *Soundings in Kings: Perspectives and Methods in Contemporary Scholarship*, ed. Mark Leuchter and Klaus-Peter Adam (Minneapolis: Fortress, 2010), 85.

67. Janzen, "Josiah and Hezekiah," 358.

68. Vargon, "The Babylonian Delegation," 37–56.

69. Sweeney, *I & II Kings*, 424.

property at the Babylonian king's disposal."[70] During the period of the Divided Monarchy in Kings, most of the instances where silver and gold are mentioned together appear in contexts of tribute to foreign nations, including the three immediately before this incident (2 Kgs 14:14; 16:8; 18:14), and the three that immediately follow it (2 Kgs 23:33, 35; 25:4).

Schipper thinks Isaiah is critical of Hezekiah for his potential agreement with Babylon, a violation of a central tenet of so-called "Zion theology," which forbids rulers from entering into foreign alliances.[71] Prophetic texts condemn reliance on foreign empires (Isa. 31:1-3; Jer. 2:36-37; Hos. 7:11). Assyria, Egypt, and Babylon were the most powerful nations in the region, and Hezekiah trusted in each of them. According to the prophet Isaiah, Babylon, just like Assyrian and Egypt before, will not prove trustworthy.

8. Conclusion: The Complicated Trust of Hezekiah

Hezekiah's trust in YHWH was unique among southern rulers, but that was not the only aspect of his character that made him unusual. No other ruler of Israel or Judah interacted directly with each of the three surrounding empires (Assyria, Egypt, and Babylon). While Hezekiah prayed in the middle of the Assyrian crisis (19:15-19; 20:3), at the beginning and end of his narrative he looked to political power and alliances for support. His loyalties were divided among YHWH, Assyria, Egypt, and Babylon. The temptation to rely on these three foreign powers was great because they had had such a dramatic impact on Israel and Judah throughout their history. The most common way Judean rulers expressed dependence in Kings was to give tribute, just as Hezekiah did to Assyria and he offered to do to Babylon.[72]

However, each of the foreign empires Hezekiah relied upon are portrayed in 2 Kings 18–20 as untrustworthy. Assyria did not withdraw after an enormous tribute. Egypt would collapse and injure any nation that relied on them. Babylon would return and take Judah's treasures and royal children. Just as Solomon's marriage alliances led to his downfall and the division of the monarchy (1 Kgs 11:1-13, 29-39), Hezekiah's dependence upon these empires contributed to the downfall of Judah.

---

70. Begg, "2 Kings 20:12-19," 32.
71. Schipper, "Hezekiah, Manasseh," 85–8.
72. In terms of the details of Hezekiah's alliance with Egypt, the text provides few clues.

Thus, readers of Hezekiah's story are warned against any type of foreign reliance. Ultimately, it was not Hezekiah's alliances with Assyria, Egypt, or Babylon that delivered him, but his prayers.

Why would righteous Hezekiah be portrayed so negatively in his interactions with foreign empires? Perhaps this is the wrong question to ask because it assumes a flat characterization. A few of the character studies discussed earlier seem to view Hezekiah's portrayal as needing to be uniformly or consistently positive based on 18:3-8. But this inclination can lead to glossing over, downplaying, or ignoring the negative aspects of his interactions with foreign powers. The characterization of Hezekiah in 2 Kings 18–20, however, is quite rounded and complex, and not as righteous as he may appear based purely on his regnal evaluation and incomparability formula. Thus, his complexity—the ruler who trusted not only in YHWH, but also in Assyria, Egypt, and Babylon—is what makes his characterization more real.

Chapter 15

MANASSEH THE BORING:
LACK OF CHARACTER IN 2 KINGS 21

Alison L. Joseph

In the book of Kings, Manasseh is held responsible for the destruction of Jerusalem and Judah, because he "did...[more] evil than all that the Amorites who were before him did and also caused Judah to sin with his idols" (2 Kgs 21). The ramifications of the fall of Judah and the end of the Judean monarchy—with a Davidic king on the throne—are immense. Among other effects, the event calls into question the entire theology that the biblical books leading up to Kings have established: the promise of the land, the importance of centralized worship in the Jerusalem temple, and the eternal dynastic promise to David. Given the momentous consequences attributed to Manasseh's actions, the reader might well expect an extraordinary literary presentation of this king's reign. The reader, however, would not find it. Instead, Manasseh is portrayed as an ordinary bad king about whom we do not know much more than we do about many thoroughly inconsequential kings.

The account of Manasseh's reign is brief: a mere eighteen verses long,[1] of which likely nine or ten are secondary additions. It consists of the standard regnal formula (vv. 1-2) evaluating his cultic behavior,[2] a list of

---

1. Compare this to the 208 verses of Ahab's account (1 Kgs 16:29–22:40) or 95 verses devoted to Manasseh's father, Hezekiah (2 Kgs 18–20). Solomon features in eleven chapters.

2. The regnal formula is a primary organizing feature of the book of Kings. Almost every reign begins with a notice that X became king and reigned for Y years over either Israel or Judah, contextualizing this king with the contemporaneous king of the other kingdom, and finishes with a judgment that the king did what was

his transgressions (vv. 3-7), and then the pronouncement of the impending doom of Judah (vv. 8-15). Manasseh's reign ends with the notice that he slept with his fathers and that his son succeeded him—i.e., the usual closing death and burial formula (vv. 17-18).[3]

The account is also strikingly bare of detail and color. Manasseh becomes king after the death of his father Hezekiah. He reinstitutes the cultic sites and symbols that Hezekiah destroyed and then inaugurates and/or restores a host of other cultic practices, including the worship of Baal, Asherah, and the host of heaven, and a variety of divination practices. He also embarks on building projects to support those practices. But Manasseh does not speak to or interact with prophets, foreign nations, or even the people. There are no specific events mentioned at all.

Scholars have noticed this puzzling flatness[4] of character; they have described Manasseh as a "cardboard" cutout[5] and a "faceless portrait... set against a blank background."[6] The account is "dull" and "lacking" in narrative interest; Manasseh has no emotions or backstory as some of the other kings do.[7] Of course, in the book of Kings, the narrative in general evinces little interest in the kings as people, in their lives, or personalities. Manasseh is not the only king in the book who functions solely as an

---

right or evil in YHWH's eyes. Style varies a little, but the regnal formula is used to synchronize the narrative about the kings of Israel and Judah, to make the chronology of events and reigns clear, to create segues and uniformity in the presentation of the information about each king, and to judge each king by the standards of deuteronomistic theology. See Alison L. Joseph, *Portrait of the Kings: The Davidic Prototype in Deuteronomistic Poetics* (Minneapolis: Fortress, 2015), 79–83. For full bibliography on regnal formulae, see ibid., 80 n. 6.

3. Baruch Halpern and David S. Vanderhooft, "The Editions of Kings in the 7th–6th Centuries BCE," *HUCA* 62 (1991): 179–244.

4. In literary studies, characters are sometimes described as flat: "flat characters, or types, are built around a single quality or trait. They do not stand out as individuals"—or round: "round characters...are much more complex, manifesting a multitude of traits, and appearing as 'real people'" (Adele Berlin, *Poetics and Interpretation of Biblical Narrative* [Winona Lake: Eisenbrauns, 1994], 23).

5. Richard D. Nelson, *The Double Redaction of the Deuteronomistic History* (Sheffield: JSOT Press, 1981), 164.

6. Stuart Lasine, "Manasseh as Villain and Scapegoat," in *New Literary Criticism and the Hebrew Bible*, edited by J. Cheryl Exum and David J. A. Clines (Sheffield: JSOT Press, 1993), 164.

7. Klaas A. D. Smelik, "The Portrayal of King Manasseh: A Literary Analysis of II Kings Xxi and II Chronicles Xxiii," in *Converting the Past: Studies in Ancient Israelite and Moabite Historiography*, Oudtestamentische Studiën (Leiden: Brill, 1992), 132.

agent of the plot, who, in other words, is someone "about whom nothing is known except for what is necessary for the plot."[8] But he is by far the most important of them to receive this kind of literary treatment. Francesca Stavrakopoulou has clearly articulated our confusion: "Given the fact that Manasseh plays what is arguably the most crucial role within Kings in causing the destruction of Judah and the exile of her people, this brief and flimsy characterization is surprising, presenting Manasseh as little more than a man of straw."[9]

To repeat, given the Deuteronomistic Historian's (Dtr) penchant for developing his important royal characters proleptically, the portrayal of Manasseh is baffling. The narrative explicitly blames Manasseh for the fate of Judah (2 Kgs 21:11-15) and yet makes no attempt to develop or enhance his characterization so as to parallel the accounts of the other important kings. Why *is* Manasseh so boring? I suggest below that this was done in order to reduce the impact of the king's responsibility and that this strategy may adumbrate a theological shift: no longer will the king's behavior serve to determine the fate of the people, as was the case for the narratives of Solomon, Jeroboam, and Ahab. Instead, the behavior of the people will determine their fate. This shift reflects a theological difference between the preexilic and exilic editions of Kings.

Characterization of the Kings

The history of the monarchy in the books of Samuel and Kings is organized roughly chronologically; it tells the stories of the kings who ruled Israel and Judah for the greater part of 450 years, beginning around the tenth century BCE. Some of these kings were important, others less so. Some kings were good, but more frequently they were bad. Some kings did what was right in YHWH's eyes, some did what was evil in YHWH's eyes, and most did what was bad in the eyes of the Deuteronomist. What ties them all—over forty of them—together is the continuity of the position; until the destruction of the Northern Kingdom of Israel in 721 BCE by the Assyrians and the destruction of the Southern Kingdom of Judah by the Babylonians in 586 BCE, Israel and Judah were ruled by a native monarch.

---

8. Berlin, *Poetics and Interpretation of Biblical Narrative*, 32.
9. Francesca Stavrakopoulou, "The Blackballing of Manasseh," in *Good Kings and Bad Kings: The Kingdom of Judah in the Seventh Century BCE*, ed. Lester L. Grabbe (London: T&T Clark International, 2005), 22.

While the book of Kings purports to be about the kings themselves (hence the title of the book), the accounts of their reigns serve primarily to promote the theology of the Deuteronomistic School. Much of this theology is built around the ideal of fidelity to the covenant, which will guarantee prosperity and continued habitation in the land of Israel.[10] Continuous infidelity by the kings and the people leads to the destructions of both Israel and Judah. Proffering this theologically grounded view of the world, Dtr strategically deploys his literary skill to paint portraits of the kings that promote his theology. Each king offers an instructive example: good kings are like David—at least they are like David as he was re-imagined as one who adhered faithfully to the covenant—and bad kings are like the anti-David, Jeroboam.[11]

A significant feature of deuteronomistic historiography is thus the attribution of theological cause to historico-political events. It is the lens through which Dtr tells the story of the monarchy.[12] As such, the kingdom split not (just) because of Rehoboam's unfair demand for increased corvée labor, as in 1 Kings 12, but, more significantly for Dtr, as punishment for Solomon's apostasy in 1 Kings 11. This didactic purpose shapes Dtr's literary choices as well; the royal characters who are fleshed out in the narrative receive this treatment in order to promote deuteronomistic theology and to explain *why* what happens to the kingdoms happens. For example, the portrait of Jeroboam functions in order to elevate David, depict a royal anti-type, and explain much of the fate of the Northern Kingdom, yet, unlike Manasseh, the character of Jeroboam is fully developed. He has ups and downs, finds opportunities to interact with the people and with prophets, and has a family: a wife who inquires of the prophet and a sick son who dies. Initially, he has the prophet's and YHWH's favor, but then is viewed as unfaithful to the covenant, and will be harshly punished. While his triumphs and trials are largely explained through theological values in promotion of deuteronomistic ideals, he is more like a "real" person.

---

10. See Moshe Weinfeld, *Deuteronomy and the Deuteronomic School* (Winona Lake: Eisenbrauns, 1992), 1–9.

11. See my explication of the model of the Davidic prototype and its application in the portraits of Solomon, Jeroboam, Josiah, and Manasseh in *Portrait of the Kings*.

12. Ibid., 50–3; Yairah Amit, "The Dual Causality Principle and Its Effects on Biblical Literature," *VT* 37 (1987): 385–400; Gerhard von Rad, *Theologie des Alten Testaments* (Munich: Kaiser, 1957), vol. 1; *Old Testament Theology* (Edinburgh: T. & T. Clark, 1962), 1:334–6.

Similar to Jeroboam, Ahab is also a round character and gets full treatment; his reign runs over six chapters (1 Kgs 16:29–22:40). Ahab is seen as having done what is evil in YHWH's eyes, "more than all who preceded him" (2 Kgs 16:30). He and the rest of the Omrides have the inimitable ability to cause YHWH to anger (Hiphil of כעס), beyond the sins of the other kings of Israel. Ahab's punishment for introducing Baal worship, persecuting Yahwistic prophets, listening to his Phoenician wife, and abusing his power is the annihilation of his house (1 Kgs 21:20-24; 2 Kgs 9:8-9). Despite all the evil, Ahab is given an opportunity for repentance and his punishment is delayed (1 Kgs 21:27-29). He is a complex character and the reader even feels something close to sympathy for him at times.

While portrayed as either flat or round, deuteronomistic theology sets up the potential for king characters as agents. As many scholars have noted, the fates of the kingdoms are dependent on their behavior, specifically their cultic obedience.[13] The kings lead the people to sin and destruction. Bad things happen when the kings are bad. For example, YHWH will forsake Israel because of the sins of Jeroboam (1 Kgs 14:15-16); also, David's census taking brings a seven-year famine on the people (2 Sam. 24:10-17).

Characterization in Redaction

The lack of events in the narrative is one of the factors that makes the portrait of Manasseh's reign like that of the other ordinary bad kings. (It may have originally only included five to six verses.) In those accounts, the ordinary bad kings ascend to the throne, are evaluated as having done what is evil in YHWH's eyes, commit a number of sins, and then die and are buried. The remainder of the things that presumably must have happened during their reigns is relegated to the annals of the kings (as in the accounts of Joash of Israel, 2 Kgs 13:10-13; and Jotham of Judah, 2 Kgs 15:32-38). The account of Manasseh began as one of an ordinary bad king with the regnal formula that he did evil in the eyes of YHWH,

---

13. In my survey of the literature, it seems almost as if this tendency is taken for granted, without much discussion of the evidence, as in the brief mention by Mordechai Cogan and Hayim Tadmor, *II Kings: A New Translation*, AB 11 (Garden City: Doubleday, 1988), 206–7. For ancient Near Eastern parallels of this phenomenon, see Isabel Cranz, "Royal Illness in Dynastic and National Crises: The Illness of Abijah and Hezekiah in Light of Israelite and Judean History," in *Sick Kings: Royal Illness in the Hebrew Bible*, forthcoming.

like other bad kings. Only the additions of an exilic Dtr make Manasseh particularly noteworthy as a bad king.

I read the compositional history of the book of Kings as a double redaction. A preexilic Dtr compiled existing sources, writing them together and adding original composition, so that his interpretation of history reflected his deuteronomistic, theological outlook. This version of the history is largely optimistic, written during the reign of Josiah (640–609) and builds to his cultic reform in 2 Kings 22–23. A secondary, exilic update is made to the history to allow historical reality (the destruction of Judah and exile) to be fitted into the theological perspective. The rewriting of the history makes its focus largely pessimistic.[14]

It is worthwhile to consider the characterization of Manasseh separately in the preexilic and exilic editions. Some of the redactional seams in 2 Kings 21 are apparent.[15] While we will never definitively know which verses are from the preexilic edition and which from the exilic, I am confident identifying as preexilic vv. 1, 2a, 3a, and 17-18. These verses roughly correspond to the typical regnal formulae found in DtrH.

---

14. Frank Moore Cross, "The Themes of the Book of Kings and the Structure of the Deuteronomic History," in *Canaanite Myth and Hebrew Epic: Essays in the History of the Religion of Israel* (Cambridge: Harvard University Press, 1973), 274–89.

15. Early on, Driver, Kuenen, and Wellhausen all identified vv. 10-15 as intrusive (Cogan and Tadmor, *II Kings*, 270). There is a lack of agreement on the extent of that intrusion and on further additions. Some of the major positions include the following—Cross, vv. 7-9 and 10-15: exilic (Cross, "Themes," 285–6); Cogan and Tadmor, vv. 10-15: exilic, vv. 7-9: preexilic (*II Kings*, 270); John Gray, vv. 8-15: a late deuteronomistic addition (*I & II Kings: A Commentary*, 2nd ed., OTL [Philadelphia: Westminster, 1970], 644–5); Richard Friedman, vv. 8-15: exilic (*The Exile and Biblical Narrative: The Formation of the Deuteronomistic and Priestly Works* (Chico, CA: Scholars Press, 1981), 11); Erik Eynikel, vv. 4, 6, 7b-16: exilic ("The Portrait of Manasseh and the Deuteronomistic History," in *Deuteronomy and Deuteronomic Literature* [Louvain: Peeters, 1997], 241); Nelson, vv. 3-7 and 8-15: exilic, but also incorporate several predeuteronomistic annalistic notices (vv. 4a, 6a, and perhaps 7a) "floating somewhere in between" the exilic composition (*Double Redaction*, 43, 65–7). It is interesting to note that even those who do not subscribe to the double redaction model see multiple hands at work in these verses. For example, Ehud Ben Zvi similarly breaks up the sections and identifies vv. 4, 7b, 8-9 (DtrN) and 10-14 (DtrP) as secondary additions to DtrH(G) ("The Account of the Reign of Manasseh in II Reg 21:1-18 and the Redactional History of the Book of Kings," *ZAW* 103 [1991]: 365, 370, 373). A major difference is that the Göttingen school views all three of these redactions as exilic.

Verse 16 is also probably preexilic.[16] Many scholars are convinced that the doom oracle blaming Manasseh in vv. 10-15 is definitely exilic. Blaming the exile on Manasseh extends beyond these verses. It appears also in vv. 3, 6, and 9. Therefore, if blame of Manasseh is exilic, these verses need to be reconsidered. I would thus attribute 3b, 6c, and 7b-9 to an exilic redaction. Verse 5 is probably exilic as well. The host of heaven is mentioned only five times in DtrH; all of these are likely secondary.[17] For its heuristic value, I present the following as my best guess at the original, preexilic account of the reign of Manasseh in 2 Kings 21:

> Manasseh was twelve years old when he became king. And he reigned fifty-five years in Jerusalem. And his mother's name was Hephzibah. (2a) He did what was evil in the eyes of YHWH. (3a) He rebuilt the high places that Hezekiah his father had destroyed. (4) And he built altars in the house of Yahweh of which Yahweh said, "In Jerusalem I will set my name"...(16) the innocent blood Manasseh spilled was very great until it filled Jerusalem

---

16. While some scholars see the sin of spilling innocent blood in v. 16 as a later addition, (Volkmar Fritz, *1 & 2 Kings: A Continental Commentary*, trans. Anselm Hagedorn, Continental Commentaries (Minneapolis: Fortress, 2003), 392; Eynikel, "Portrait of Manasseh," 241), it is quite out of place in the exilic version of the narrative. Manasseh is evaluated as doing what is evil in YHWH's eyes. His sins are enumerated in the first verses (vv. 2-7) of the account; they are then followed by the oracle against Judah. The sin of spilling innocent blood is not mentioned until after the verdict of Judah and just before the concluding formula of the regnal account. The strange placement of this accusation points to the verse being separated from its original context in the list of sins in the preexilic account. Verse 16 seems to continue the list of the sins from the beginning of the chapter, and the oracle is inserted in the middle of the list. Also, this verse appears more closely related to the preexilic use of Jeroboam as the prototype of the evil king, rather than Ahab in the exilic addition, using the sinning verb, Hiphil of חטא. In the preexilic version, this verse functions as the close of the regnal formula and connects Manasseh's sins with those of Jeroboam. This is in contrast with the exilic account, which breaks the regnal formula in order to expand the narrative. Just as Jeroboam caused Israel to sin (החטא), so too does Manasseh. In the close of this verse, Manasseh is like Jeroboam (not Ahab). Causing Judah to sin has as its consequence the destruction of Judah, but the causation is not made here as in v. 11. This is because v. 16 was composed by the preexilic Dtr, who, while viewing Manasseh as an evil king, does not blame him for the exile. Also, the verse begins with גם, which functions as a redactional juncture, connecting two redactional levels of the text, showing the seams of redaction.

17. Deut. 4:19; 2 Kgs 17:16; 21:3, 5; 23:4, 5; also in Jer. 8:2; 19:13; Zeph. 1:5. Nelson, *Double Redaction*, 65.

from end to end, apart from his sin which he caused Judah to sin, doing evil in the eyes of YHWH. (17) The rest of the deeds of Manasseh and all that he did and the sin he committed, are they not written in the book of the chronicles of the kings of Judah? (18) And Manasseh slept with his fathers and was buried in the garden of his house, in the garden of Uzzah; and Amon his son became king in his place.

Beyond the sin of spilling innocent blood in 2 Kgs 21:16, there is nothing noteworthy about Manasseh. In overturning the progress of his father's reform, he is in some ways reestablishing the status quo, in which the *bāmôt*, high places, since the reign of Jeroboam I almost 300 years prior, feature prominently in the evaluations of the bad kings. This behavior, while not positive, is commonplace and does not seem to justify the great punishment of Judah.

One might say that the preexilic Manasseh looks much like the other bad kings, except that his reign is so long. Manasseh has the longest reign of any king of Israel or Judah, an unprecedented fifty-five years. For Dtr, length of reign and prosperity are a reward for fidelity (as in 1 Kgs 3:14), but he must deal with the realities of history.[18] Historically, Manasseh may in fact have been one of Judah's most successful monarchs. Beginning his reign in the late seventh century BCE, he recovered from the Assyrian siege of 701 BCE, and during his long, peaceful reign, the kingdom flourished.[19]

In the exilic revision of the history of the monarchy, this relatively unremarkable reign is rewritten. Its significance is transformed, the account is provided with more details, and the list of transgressions expands from three verses to seven (vv. 2-7, 16). The sins of every king are attributed to him. In addition to the high places, Manasseh erects altars to Baal, makes an Asherah, worships all the host of heaven, builds altars to the host of heaven in the temple, passes his son through fire, seeks omens and conjures spirits, and puts an Asherah in the temple. And yet, strikingly, the character of Manasseh is left just as flat as before. Nothing is added to the account that would make him more three dimensional, no additional characterization, no mention of specific events or any personal interactions.

---

18. The Chronicler offers an exegetical solution to the problem of the long reign by including a picture of a repentant Manasseh (2 Chron. 33:18-19).

19. Stavrakopoulou, "The Blackballing of Manasseh," 248.

On the other hand, the enhanced list of sins creates a caricature of a villain, an unreal scapegoat.[20] Like Josiah, the best of kings, who surpasses the good deeds of the few good kings, Manasseh exceeds the bad kings in wickedness, committing all the sins of the bad kings and more, making him the one "who did [more] evil than all...who were before him" (2 Kgs 21:11).[21] Scholars have frequently speculated on why Manasseh is given this exceptional (dis)honor. Perhaps it was his name, shared with the northern tribe, that allowed the historian to equate Manasseh with both the sinful Northern Kingdom of Israel and Israel's sin of worshiping at the *bāmôt*, high places.[22]

Perhaps, however, it was his "spilling of innocent blood." No other king is accused of this. Other notably evil kings, namely, Jeroboam and Ahab, have their own "transgression-innovations." Jeroboam establishes the countercult at Dan and Bethel, while Ahab, "thinking it light" to follow the sins of Jeroboam, adds Baal worship to Israelite practice. In contrast, ordinary bad kings do not commit "new" sins. They tend to commit the same sins as (primarily) Jeroboam and (some) Ahab. But Manasseh does contribute a new sin to the repertoire of Judah's transgressions: the spilling of innocent blood.[23] Perhaps the exilic Dtr picked up on this sin and expanded the narrative because of it.[24]

Why does any king need to be blamed for the destruction of the temple and the exile? Alternative options are presented in Chronicles, where it is not the king's cultic behavior, but his inability to humble himself (2 Chron. 36:12), and the ongoing transgressions of the people of Judah that cause YHWH to bring Nebuchadnezzar against Jerusalem (2 Chron. 36:14-19). But the historical reality of the destruction of Judah must be explained in a way that conforms to Dtr's system of attribution of theological meaning to historico-political events.

---

20. Lasine, "Manasseh as Villain and Scapegoat," 163.
21. Smelik, "The Portrayal of King Manasseh," 139–40; Joseph, *Portrait of the Kings*, 187–223.
22. Francesca Stavrakopoulou, *King Manasseh and Child Sacrifice: Biblical Distortions of Historical Realities* (Berlin/New York: de Gruyter, 2004), 63–7; Stavrakopoulou, "The Blackballing of Manasseh," 253.
23. The term נקי דם is often used in prophetic lists of Judah's sins (see Isa. 59:7; Jer. 7:6; 19:4; 22:3, 17; 26:15). It is related to a prohibition in Deut. 19:10: "Don't spill innocent blood (דם נקי) within your land." The term is also used twice more during the reign of Jehoiakim in the report of the exile, referring to Manasseh and the reminder that he is to blame for the destruction of Judah (2 Kgs 24:4).
24. Joseph, *Portrait of the Kings*, 217.

It is Dtr's literary *modus operandi* to choose one figure to highlight as a didactic exemplar to convey his theological beliefs. This is done with the portrayals of David, Solomon, and Jeroboam.[25] The preexilic Dtr portrays David as the paradigm of the good king, comparing other kings to the Davidic standard and depicting Jeroboam and Josiah in ways that illustrate the importance of obedience (and the consequences of disobedience) to the deuteronomic law, including the stipulations for centralized and nonsyncretistic worship. Similarly, the exilic Dtr chooses the figure of Manasseh as a counter-example to convey his warnings against idolatry, especially Baal worship and the practices of the other nations, and the severe consequences of disobedience.

Martin Noth has argued convincingly that Dtr "inevitably concluded that the monarchy had led the Israelite nations to destruction."[26] Solomon, Jeroboam, and subsequent kings lead the people to their demise. In this way, Dtr represents "the monarchy, responsible only to itself, as a burden on the people (vv. 9-18), even if the people have yet to recognize it as such."[27] The text illustrates over and over the role of the king in determining the fate of the people; the bad kings continue the sin of Jeroboam, worshiping at his shrines and causing Israel to sin (the Hiphil of חטא).[28] In the regnal formulae of fifteen of the nineteen kings of Israel, they are said to have done what is evil in YHWH's eyes. Only Jehu is said to "do what is right" (2 Kgs 10:30 [and not even in the regnal formula, but in the narrative proper]), and the other three, whose reigns are particularly brief, do not have a regnal formula.[29] In almost every instance, the report of having done evil in YHWH's eyes continues with a qualifying statement that the king "follows the way of Jeroboam and his sin, which he caused Israel to sin." Jeroboam "caused" the people to sin by establishing his countercult in Dan and Bethel, and subsequent kings follow this model.

Borrowing the style of the preexilic judgments on the kings of Israel, Manasseh is similarly blamed for leading the people to ruin. 2 Kings 21:9 charges that the people "did not listen [to the torah commanded by

---

25. Ibid., especially Chapters 2–3.
26. Martin Noth, *The Deuteronomistic History* (Sheffield: JSOT Press, 1981), 77; *Überlieferungsgeschichtliche Studien. Die Sammelnden und Bearbeitenden Geschischtswerke im Alten Testement* (Tübingen: Max Niemeyer, 1957).
27. Noth, *The Deuteronomistic History*, 80.
28. See Nadab (1 Kgs 15:26); Baasha (1 Kgs 15:34); Omri (1 Kgs 16:25-26); Ahaziah (1 Kgs 22:53); Jehoash (2 Kgs 13:11); Jeroboam II (2 Kgs 14:24); Zechariah (2 Kgs 15:9); Menahem (2 Kgs 15:18); Pekahiah (2 Kgs 15:24); Pekah (2 Kgs 15:28); Jehoahaz (2 Kgs 13:2).
29. Elah (1 Kgs 16:8-14), Tibni (1 Kgs 16:21-22), and Shallum (2 Kgs 15:13-15).

Moses] and Manasseh caused them to err doing the evil of the nations…'"[30] It is made utterly clear that it is because of Manasseh's sin that Judah is destroyed: "Because of what Manasseh king of Judah did, these transgressions, he did [more] evil than all that the Amorites who were before him did and also caused Judah to sin with his idols. Therefore, thus said YHWH God of Israel: 'Behold I am bringing evil on Jerusalem and Judah…'" (2 Kgs 21:11-12).

It is not evident precisely why the account of Manasseh is rewritten for him to take the blame. For Stavrakopoulou, it is because Manasseh as a scapegoat distances Judah from direct responsibility for exile, shifting blame from Judah to the king. Manasseh is like the foreign nations, like the northern kings.[31] Similarly, Lasine argues, as "a royal scapegoat-villain [Manasseh] provides a more comforting explanation for their plight than one based on the assumption that they and their ancestors are fundamentally corrupt."[32] Shifting the blame from the people to the king leaves room for the potential of the continuing promise and maintaining the covenant. In this view, Dtr is theologically comfortable with attributing responsibility to the king over the people. Another possibility, Halpern suggests, is that Manasseh's sin explains Josiah's premature death by casting his reform as futile. "Manasseh's irreversible provocation of Yhwh precipitated the failure of Josiah's reform to save a Judah and Samaria now wholly purified of cultic pollution."[33] Manasseh's sin explains "why Josiah was killed by Necho rather than dying a natural death, an ideal to which Kings repeatedly adverts."[34] In this way, Manasseh fore-dooms Josiah.[35]

But it is important to notice how poorly integrated vv. 8-15 are in the already sparse characterization of Manasseh, causing us to wonder whether the text is entirely committed to shifting the blame to this king? Elsewhere, I have argued that the reason the Manasseh account seems halfhearted or ineffective is because it is not the literary production of the preexilic Dtr who uses the Davidic prototype strategy to fill out the

---

30. It is noticeable that while here Manasseh causes the people to do wrong, again the Hiphil, the verb is ויתעם, rather than the ויחטא of Jeroboam and in v. 11.

31. Stavrakopoulou, "The Blackballing of Manasseh," 252.

32. Lasine, "Manasseh as Villain and Scapegoat," 166–7.

33. Baruch Halpern, "Why Manasseh Is Blamed for the Babylonian Exile: The Evolution of a Biblical Tradition," *VT* 48 (1998): 492.

34. Ibid., 493.

35. Halpern argues that this also allows Huldah's oracle in 2 Kgs 22:16-17 to stand. The scapegoating of Manasseh "rescues the prophetess's prediction of a 'peaceful' death, almost surgically, without overt reference to the rest of the oracle" (ibid., 510).

portraits of the kings who are theologically meaningful to him. Instead, it is the exilic Dtr who tries, with limited success, to apply preexilic poetics.[36] The final version of the Manasseh account looks somewhat like the preexilic style, but it uses Ahab as the model for the evil king, rather than Jeroboam. Ahab is not used elsewhere as a comparative, except for three kings who are directly related to his house.[37] Manasseh outdoes the sins of Ahab, much as Josiah outdoes the good deeds of David (2 Kgs 21:2, 7).

Yet another complication is that Manasseh is not himself punished; instead punishment is meted out on Judah as a whole, some ninety years after the end of Manasseh's reign. Unlike in the case of Solomon, whose punishment—that the kingdoms will split—is delayed until after his death, for the sake of his father David (1 Kgs 11:11-12), no explanation for the delay is mentioned here. Even in the case of Ahab, whose punishment—the destruction of his house—is also delayed, an excuse is made: Ahab is said to humble himself in the face of disaster (1 Kgs 21:29).

Excuses like these, even if somewhat transparent, are necessary to maintaining the historical accuracy of the history, despite its theological cast. The historian, whether he likes it or not, feels beholden to historical fact.[38] The readers of the book of Kings may well have known that the united monarchy did not split during the reign of Solomon, but only after his death, that the House of Ahab was destroyed later, and that Judah was destroyed decades after the reign of Manasseh. Much as he might have wanted to, Dtr may have considered himself free to take liberties only with historical causation, not with the historical reality that was his framework. As Noth has commented, and I would agree, Dtr was an "honest broker," one who "had no intention of fabricating the history of the Israelite people. He wished to…base it upon the material to which he had access."[39]

I would like to suggest that the spectacularly boring portrayal of Manasseh is an intentional strategy in the promotion of deuteronomistic theology. The colorless portrait of Manasseh taken together with his

---

36. Joseph, *Portrait of the Kings*, 187–233.

37. Other comparisons to Ahab are only made in the cases of relatives, both kings of Israel and Judah. Ahaziah, son of Ahab and Jezebel, followed in the "way of his father and mother" (1 Kgs 22:53). Joram, son of Jehoshaphat of Judah, who marries Ahab's daughter Athaliah, "followed in the ways of all the kings of Israel, like the house of Ahab did…" (2 Kgs 8:18). Their son, Ahaziah, son of Joram of Judah (Ahab's grandson), "followed the ways of the House of Ahab" (2 Kgs 8:27-29).

38. Baruch Halpern, *The First Historians: The Hebrew Bible and History* (San Francisco: Harper & Row, 1988), 76–99.

39. Noth, *The Deuteronomistic History*, 128.

important role in "history" both highlight and undermine what appears to be the prevailing view—that the fates of Israel and Judah are determined by the behaviors of the kings. In this case, the fate of the nation is explicitly said to be determined by the king's behavior, but he is so poorly developed as a character and so bland and dull, even as a bad king, the result is to undercut the apparent message. The shift in focus away from the king may even suggest that it is really the actions of the people that determine their fate, by leaving the reader with the sense that one should not pin the immense importance of the exile on a character this unconvincing.[40]

This intentional undermining through the sparse portrayal of Manasseh to shift the focus of the text is similar to the text's approach to the equally sparse reign of Athaliah (2 Kgs 11). Athaliah, the daughter of Ahab and Jezebel, seizes the throne of Judah when her son Ahaziah dies. Her parentage and actions tell us everything we need to know about her character and her reign. Upon taking the throne, she murders any competitors to her reign, namely her sons and grandsons (2 Kgs 11:1). Jehoash escapes, hidden in the temple, until he appears dramatically six years later, when the priest Jehoiada installs him on the throne. While Athaliah is certainly more colorful than Manasseh, her characterization is intentionally flat and sparse; the text refuses to fully recognize her reign (she has no regnal formula) and shifts the focus from Athaliah to the priest Jehoiada, his investiture of Jehoash, his affirmation of the covenant, and subsequent reform, parallel to the future covenant and reform of Josiah (2 Kgs 22–23). The goal is to highlight deuteronomistic theology.

The People's Control of their Fate

The underlying shift in blame from the king to the people is not unique to Manasseh's account. In contrast to widespread understanding, from the very beginning of the monarchy, the view that the people control their own fate is implicit in the narrative. In 1 Samuel 12, the people share the blame for the actions of the kings, because they requested the king in the first place. Samuel responds to the people's request for a king and warns

---

40. Similarly, the characterization of Josiah, one of the best kings, is also strikingly thin. While his reign is covered in two chapters (2 Kgs 22–23), and many things happen, the narrative does not focus on Josiah himself. In this case, despite Josiah's best efforts at reform, Judah is still destroyed, and the people are still exiled. Here, the lack of characterization shifts the focus to his acts; the book of instruction becomes the main character, rather than the king himself, in line with the deuteronomistic focus on the law.

them how they must behave. After briefly outlining the history of the Judges, Samuel makes clear that YHWH's favor is conditional:

> Now here is the king whom you have chosen, whom you have requested; see, YHWH has set a king over you. If you will fear YHWH and serve him and heed his voice and not rebel against the commandment of YHWH, and if both you and the king who reigns over you will follow YHWH your God, then he will rescue you; but if you will not heed the voice of YHWH and rebel against YHWH's command, then the hand of YHWH will be upon you and your king. (1 Sam. 12:13-15)

Here, the condition of prosperity requires that both the king and the people be obedient to YHWH. Continuing, Samuel further warns the people:

> Do not be afraid; you have done all this evil, yet do not turn away from YHWH, but serve YHWH with all your heart; and do not turn towards nothingness, which cannot help or save, for they are nothing. For YHWH will not abandon his people... Yet fear YHWH and serve him faithfully with all your heart; for you have seen the great things he has done for you. But if you act wickedly, both you and your king will be swept away. (1 Sam. 12:20-25)

These are deuteronomistic words, similar to the injunction of Deut. 6:5 and the positive judgments on David (2 Kgs 2:3-4) and Josiah (2 Kgs 23:25) in Kings. Like many of the kings of Israel who do not turn away from the sins of Jeroboam,[41] in 1 Samuel 12, the people's behavior is not only the condition for success, but also determines the fate of the king, as in v. 25. This text makes clear that the fate of the people is determined by their own actions. The people will always ultimately be responsible, even when the king is nominally blamed, as they are the ones who demanded a king.

The doom pronouncement against Israel demonstrates this same tendency. Throughout the history leading up to the destruction of the North, Jeroboam is blamed for the fate of the people. He is held responsible for Israel's bad cultic behavior, its eventual fate, and the evil deeds of the subsequent kings, and yet, the final doom oracle in 2 Kgs 17:7-23 is largely focused on the role of the people themselves in determining their fate:

---

41. "He did not turn from (all) the sins of Jeroboam son of Nebat which he caused Israel to sin" is repeated in the regnal formulae of six of the kings: Jehoash (2 Kgs 13:11); Jeroboam II (2 Kgs 14:24); Zechariah (2 Kgs 15:9); Menahem (2 Kgs 15:18); Pekahiah (2 Kgs 15:24); Pekah (2 Kgs 15:28). See Joseph, *Portrait of the Kings*, 128.

> And it was because the children of Israel sinned against YHWH their God, who brought them up from the land of Egypt... And they followed the statutes of the nations... And the children of Israel ascribed things that were not so upon YHWH... And they installed *massebot*... And they made offerings there, at all the high places like the nations, which YHWH exiled before them: and they did evil things, causing YHWH to anger. And they worshipped the idols... (2 Kgs 17:7-12)

The point is very clear: Israel's evil deeds are the reason they will be destroyed. When they are charged with making and worshipping the two calves, it is their own action that incurs YHWH's wrath: "And they abandoned all the commandments of YHWH their God and they made for themselves molten images—two calves; and they made an Asherah..." (2 Kgs 17:16). The rest of Kings blames Jeroboam and Ahab for the fact that the people worship the calves and Asherah and Baal, but here the sins are cast as the actions of the people alone.[42]

While the blame on Jeroboam for the downfall of the kingdom is consistent throughout Kings, in 2 Kings 17, Jeroboam is not even mentioned until v. 21, and there the charge is against Israel—they made Jeroboam king over them, rejecting the house of David. Furthermore, the sins that Jeroboam "caused them to sin" are generic, and not connected to the calf shrines: because "they made Jeroboam son of Nebat king and Jeroboam led Israel away from following YHWH and he caused them to sin greatly. And the children of Israel followed in every sin of Jeroboam that he did and they did not stray from it" (2 Kgs 17:21-22).[43]

Scholars have long seen the indictment against Israel as two discrete units. Verses 21-23 reflect the theology of most of Kings, focusing more on Jeroboam and his role as king in the fate of the people. The beginning of the homily against Judah, vv. 7-18, is concerned with the sins of the people.[44] Verses 21-23, which pick up the phraseology of the preexilic regnal formulae, as discussed above, are the product of the preexilic Dtr, while vv. 7-18, assigning the blame to the people themselves, appear to

---

42. Marvin A. Sweeney, "King Manasseh of Judah and the Problem of Theodicy in the Deuteronomistic History," in Grabbe, ed., *Good Kings and Bad Kings*, 268.

43. Responsibility for the split of the kingdom is ambiguous in the text, but Israel's role in setting Jeroboam as king over them is clear. 2 Kgs 17:21 begins, כי קרע ישראל מעל בית דוד, "For *he* tore Israel from the House of David." The masculine, singular verb does not have an explicit subject. It is possible to read the charge both with Israel as subject, as do NJPS and LXX, or YHWH as subject and Israel as the direct object, as do NRSV, KJV, NJB, Gray (*I & II Kings*, 592), and Cogan and Tadmor (*II Kings*, 206), similar to 1 Kgs 11:11, 31; 14:8.

44. Cogan and Tadmor, *II Kings*, 206–7.

be exilic. (Verses 19-20 are not the continuation of the previous verses and probably derive from a third, also exilic, source, unimportant to our discussion here.[45]) In the doom proclamation against Israel in 2 Kings 17, we see two types of blame. The first part—the later, exilic addition—blames the people and holds them responsible for determining their fate. The second, which is akin to the preexilic version of Kings, blames Jeroboam for the downfall of Israel. The theological tension reflected in this passage can be read as reflecting the different stages of redaction.

The same tension is present in the account of Manasseh, but here it can be seen in the stark difference between Manasseh's responsibility for the downfall of the temple, Jerusalem, Judah, the entire institution of kingship, and exile and his thin characterization. Manasseh is but a shadow of a character and the thin characterization of Manasseh is, I would suggest, a subversive transfiguration of the preexilic reflex of blaming the king for the fate of the people. Like 2 Kgs 21:7-18, the narrative is instead blaming the people. The dissonance is a result of the competing perspectives of the preexilic and exilic historians.

---

45. Ibid., 207 n. 1.

Chapter 16

To Reform or Not to Reform: Characterization and Ethical Reading of Josiah in Kings*

S. Min Chun

Introduction

This is a study of the character of Josiah by the means of an ethical reading of his narrative as found in 2 Kgs 22:1–23:30.[1] The story of Josiah begins with an overall evaluation of Josiah, which is very positive (2 Kgs 22:2). Another very positive evaluation is given near the end the story (2 Kgs 23:25). Because these are global evaluations that cover the entire story,[2] Josiah seems to be a flat character that does not change throughout the narrative.[3]

---

* This essay is adapted from Chapter 8 of S. M. Chun, *Ethics and Biblical Narrative* (Oxford: Oxford University Press, 2014) and supplements it with further interactions with additional literature.

1. As to the meaning of "ethical reading," see ibid., 84–6. Lasine's reading of biblical narratives with focus on characters' dilemmas, deliberation, choices, judgments, and conception of their situations resembles my ethical reading of Josiah's story in this essay. S. Lasine, *Weighing Hearts: Character, Judgment, and the Ethics of Reading the Bible*, LHBOTS 568 (New York: T&T Clark, 2012), 9.

2. As to the linguistic concept of evaluation, see Chun, *Ethics*, 136–49, esp. 144 regarding the scope of evaluation.

3. While flat characters can be used as *exempla* for ethical admonitions, flattening out round characters in order to deduce ethical teachings impoverishes the "existential

Lohfink's description of Josiah as "a cult reformer, nothing more"[4] reinforces such an impression. Recently, Joseph argues that Josiah is "the reformer who out-reforms others"[5] but states "the character of Josiah is literally flat."[6] However, a careful reading of the story as a unified whole[7] yields a rather complex characterization of Josiah, which has ethical implications. His character develops as the story unfolds: Josiah is not the reforming hero at the beginning; rather, the book of the law triggers the change in Josiah's character, and he eventually becomes a person who puts his concern for the fate of the nation before that of his own personal fortune. In this development of Josiah's character, two elements are particularly important: the book of the law and the oracle of the prophetess Huldah.[8] Ethically significant is the fact that these elements emerge unexpectedly, driving the plot into crisis and calling for responses from the characters, most notably from Josiah. I am particularly interested in how Josiah responds to the contingent crises that those two elements bring out because ethics is not only about principles but also about practical wisdom for ever-changing situations in complex life.

Act I: Josiah, Not-Yet-Reformer (22:1-11)

At the outset of the story, the narrator characterizes Josiah through a global evaluation, employing evaluative devices:[9] "He did what was *upright in the eyes of YHWH*"; "He walked *all* the way of David, his father"; and "And he did *not* turn right or left." Josiah is the only king who is evaluated using the last two statements. The metaphor of "walking" and "not turning

---

force" that Old Testament narratives can release. See J. Barton, *Ethics and the Old Testament* (London: SCM, 2002), 32, and his essay on characterization and ethics in the present volume.

4. N. Lohfink, "The Cult Reform of Josiah of Judah: 2 Kings 22–23 as a Source for the History of Israelite Religion," in *Ancient Israelite Religion: Essays in Honor of Frank Moore Cross*, ed. P. D. Miller, Jr., P. D. Hanson and S. D. McBride (Philadelphia: Fortress, 1987), 460.

5. A. L. Joseph, *Portrait of the Kings* (Minneapolis: Fortress, 2015), 183.

6. Ibid., 152.

7. On whether the story can be read as a unified story, see Chun, *Ethics*, 179–87.

8. Joseph does not acknowledge any role of Huldah's oracle in the development of Josiah while emphasizing the significance of the book finding. Joseph, *Portrait of the Kings*, 149 n. 3. In fact, Joseph represents most scholars' understanding of the role of Huldah's oracle regarding the characterization of Josiah.

9. As to evaluative devices, see Chun, *Ethics*, 139–42.

right or left" insinuates that Josiah is the king who meets the condition of enduring dynasty (1 Kgs 2:4; 8:25; 9:4-5; Deut. 17:20). These statements certainly set up the basic tenets as to the way the reader is to understand the character of Josiah. He must be the one who can bring a bright future to Judah even after the despairing time of Manasseh. The unfolding story, however, gives a more nuanced picture of Josiah.

First of all, the actions begin in the eighteenth year of Josiah's reign. This silence for eighteen years raises suspicion that Josiah might have been in the sin of Manasseh until now.[10] Furthermore, while Josiah is mostly known as "the reformer," he is not yet a particularly reforming hero. Such a characterization is based on three grounds: (1) the discourse feature of Josiah's first "command," that is, "send" (the verb is not a mainline verb); (2) the nature of temple repair (it is not reforming activity in itself); (3) discourse features of Josiah's speech and the socio-linguistic relationship between Josiah and Hilkiah (the king was not particularly superior to the high priest in cultic matters; thus the jussives in Josiah's speech are not orders but requests). We will look at each of these in turn.[11]

First, "send" in v. 3 is not a mainline verb. Lohfink analyzes the structure of Josiah's story based on Josiah's five "commands" expressing royal initiative and sees the verb "send" in v. 3 as the first verb among them (22:3, 12; 23:1, 4, 21).[12] It is noteworthy, however, that while the other four verbs are mainline verbs in *wayyiqtol*, the one in v. 3 is *qatal* in the temporal apodosis and functions as the quotative frame, making the royal initiative less strong. Cohn even suggests that vv. 3-7 are the backdrop of the main verb "said," of which the subject is Hilkiah, in v. 8.[13]

Secondly, temple repair itself is not a cultic reform[14] but "a continuous necessity" in Judah's history,[15] and could be a normal aspect of a king's

---

10. D. Janzen, "The Sins of Josiah and Hezekiah: A Synchronic Reading of the Final Chapters of Kings," *JSOT* 37 (2013): 355–6.

11. The main interpretative method I employ for this reading is "synchronic literary criticism anchored in discourse analysis" (Chun, *Ethics*, 93–113). I will pay particular attention to discourse functions of various verbal constructions and participant references in relation to the literary and linguistic features of their surrounding verses. See Chun, ibid., Part II, for more extensive discussion regarding how to use discourse analysis for synchronic literary reading of Old Testament narrative.

12. Lohfink, "The Cult Reform of Josiah of Judah," 460.

13. R. L. Cohn, *2 Kings* (Collegeville: Liturgical Press, 2000), 153.

14. Cf. Lowery's comments on Joash: "Joash was not a cult reformer." R. H. Lowery, *The Reforming Kings* (Sheffield: JSOT Press, 1991), 109.

15. A. H. Konkel, *1 & 2 Kings*, NIVAC (Grand Rapids, Zondervan, 2006), 634.

duty. In addition, Josiah expresses no concern about the cultic activities or objects at this point. It is just the physical condition of the temple that is in his view.[16] This will change only after he hears the content of the book of the law. At this stage, Josiah is not concerned with cultic matters.

Lastly, Josiah's first speech is not necessarily an order. It is the longest speech in the story and its length may give the impression that he is very attentive to the work. However, its discourse features, especially the use of jussives to express his wishes to the third parties, do not characterize him as an active reformer of the cult. The speeches in 2 Sam. 25:5-8 and 2 Kgs 19:9b-13 have similarities to Josiah's speech in terms of their syntactic and discourse structure: those who are sent by the speaker bear the message to the third party.[17] David sent ten young men with a message to Nabal (1 Sam. 25:6-8). The Assyrian king sent the messengers with the message directed to Hezekiah (2 Kgs 19:10b-13). Likewise, Josiah sent Shaphan with the messages to Hilkiah and the overseers of the temple. At the same time, Josiah's speech differs from other cases in that it expresses his desire not in the embedded direct speech but in jussives ("let him sum up,"[18] v. 4b; "let them give,"[19] v. 5b). Thus the use of jussives is a particular feature of this speech.

How strong, then, is the force of desire conveyed in the jussives? Is it an order or a wish? This is related to the sociolinguistic relationship between the speaker and the addressees, i.e., the subjects of the jussives. If the speaker has power over the addressees, it may have the "force of a command" (e.g., Judg. 7:3; Deut. 20:5-8);[20] if not, "the speaker's desire must be interpreted as a wish."[21] One may assume that Josiah is superior because he is the king, but the issue is more complex.

---

16. This may be suggested to reveal Josiah's piety in YHWH worship (M. Cogan and H. Tadmor, *II Kings* [New York: Doubleday, 1988], 293), but this does not necessarily characterize him as a reformer.

17. For a detailed discussion, see Chun, *Ethics*, 193–4.

18. This is to read וְיַתֵּם as Hiphil jussive of תמם. E.g., I. W. Slotki, *Kings: Hebrew Text & English Translation with an Introduction and Commentary* (London: Soncino, 195), 298. Some translations understand the form as *w-yiqtol* which denotes the purpose of the preceding imperative. E.g. NASB. For other possible readings, see, e.g., Sweeney who proposes to understand it as Hiphil of נתן with 3mp objective suffix. M. A. Sweeney, *I & II Kings* (Louisville: Westminster John Knox, 2007), 437 n. a-a.

19. וְיִתְּנוּ can be understood as *w-yiqtol* that states the purpose of the preceding volitional form, which is jussive here. E.g., NJB.

20. A. Shulman, "The Function of the 'Jussive' and 'Indicative' Imperfect Forms in Biblical Hebrew Prose," *ZAH* 13 (2000): 177–8.

21. Ibid., 178.

1. The superiority of the speaker over the ultimate addressees is not as clear as in the cases of 2 Samuel 15 and 2 Kings 19 where an embedded direct speech was used to relate what the ultimate addressee should do. The use of jussives in Josiah's speech opens up another possibility.
2. Josiah designates Hilkiah as "the high priest" in his speech to Shaphan (v. 4a) and the narrator also shares Josiah's perspective by using the same designation (v. 8a). The designation of "high priest" is rare in Kings (2 Kgs 12:11; 22:4, 8; 23:4).[22] Even within the story of Josiah, not only "the high priest" but also "the priest" is used to refer to Hilkiah (22:10, 12, 14). Such a mixed use of the designations has implications for characterizations of Hilkiah and thus ultimately of Josiah.[23] Designating Hilkiah as "the high priest" can imply Josiah's respect for Hilkiah's role in the temple repair. Handy observes: "Josiah never enters the temple and, indeed, deals with the temple through his subordinates and the high priest."[24] Once Josiah takes the stronger initiative later in the story, Hilkiah is referred to as "the priest" by the narrator (22:12, 14).[25]
3. Josiah's respect for Hilikah's status can be inferred from the relationship between Joash and the priests over the temple repair portrayed in 2 Kings 12, "a kind of type-scene."[26] In 2 Kings 12, when Joash suggests a new procedure for the temple repair, the priests are said to "agree" (v. 9). Beside this passage, the verb אות appears only in Gen. 34:15, 22, 23 and the participants of the agreement seems to be of equal status. In 2 Kings 12, the priests did not begin the temple repair immediately after Joash's first speech (v. 6) and it is Jehoiada who actually instigates a new repair procedure after Joash's second speech. Joash's royal authority, and Josiah's authority by analogy, may not be strong at least in cultic affairs, the temple repair in particular.

---

22. See Chun, *Ethics*, 195–6, for a short discussion on whether or not הגדול is a postexilic gloss.

23. As to the significance of the designation for the characterization, see E. J. Revell, *The Designation of the Individual* (Kampen: Kok Pharos, 1996).

24. L. K. Handy, "The Role of Huldah in Josiah's Cult Reform," *ZAW* 106 (1994): 47.

25. Hilkiah is referred as "the high priest" again in 23:4. This may be explained by the fact that he appears with the priests of another rank.

26. Cohn, *2 Kings*, 152.

These three sub-points (1) through (3) lead to the conclusion that the sociolinguistic relationship between Josiah and Hilkiah is quite equal and thus the force of jussives is likely a request not an order. To sum up the discussion thus far, Josiah is not portrayed as a reforming king taking initiative at the beginning of the story but rather is portrayed as a king who performs his ordinary duty with no particular royal authority, perhaps remaining in the sin of Manasseh for eighteen years.

As the story continues, the book of the law rather than Josiah drives the reform. In fact, the book is found independently of Josiah's request. The sequence of the events does not necessarily imply a causal relation between Josiah's request and the discovery of the book. Hilkiah's speech in v. 8 suggests no link between the book and the repair: he simply reports the discovery of the book and gives it to Shaphan (contra 2 Chron. 34:14). Moreover, the full nominal participant references in 22:8, "Hilkiah, the great priest" and "Shaphan, the scribe" mark a new literary unit, and thus separate the actions in v. 8 from the preceding unit about the temple repair.[27]

Weak connection between the temple repair and the discovery of the book continues in vv. 9-10. Each speech of Shaphan in vv. 9-10 reports on the temple repair (v. 9) and Hilkiah's delivery of the book (v. 10), but they are in the different literary units. Both vv. 9 and 10 begins with the compound participant reference, "Shaphan, the scribe," which marks the beginning of a new unit. Note that the object סֵפֶר is fronted in Shaphan's speech in v. 10, as it was in Hilkiah's speech in v. 8: the book of the law remains the key player. Thus, it is not Josiah but the book to which the reform should not be credited. Eslinger reaches a similar conclusion regarding the non-heroic characterization of Josiah:

> Without the guidance of the book of the law…Josiah was simply one of a line of kings who did right in the eyes of the Lord, as demonstrated by his pre-law book continuation of Jehoash's Temple restorations, in which the Kings presentation shows nothing that goes beyond his predecessor.[28]

In v. 10, Shaphan reads the book before the king and by now all three characters know what the book says. Their responses are, however, narrated differently. While neither Hilkiah nor Shaphan's emotion is told (cf. 2 Kgs 18:26, 37), that of Josiah is: "he tore his clothes" (v. 11).

---

27. As to the full nominals as the boundary markers, see Chun, *Ethics*, 120–1.
28. L. Eslinger, "Josiah and the Torah Book: Comparison of 2 Kgs 22:1–23:28 and 2 Chr 34:1–35:19," *HAR* 10 (1986): 59.

Contrary to Hilkiah and Shaphan's emotionless response, Josiah's emotional reaction depicts how seriously he takes the situation. Their different responses to the crisis will lead to a different approach to the crisis in the following Act.

Act II: Josiah, the Inquirer (22:12-20)

Upon the unexpected hearing of the words of the book of the law, Josiah's character develops into one who takes initiatives. The verb צוה in v. 12a, being a mainline verb, implies Josiah's initiative. Here the designation of Hilkiah is also changed from "the great priest" to "priest" as Josiah's initiative becomes clearer.

Josiah's first action with initiative is to command an inquiry. He is now the inquirer who is concerned about the fate of not only himself but also the people and the nation. He realizes that he faces a crisis resulting from disobedience to "the words of this book." After Josiah's command to inquire, the narrator relates that the delegates went to Huldah. Nearly all scholars presume that it is Josiah who sent the delegates to Huldah[29] but the text itself does not explicitly state this. The name "Huldah" is absent in Josiah's command. No particular person or place is mentioned after the first imperative לכו, which is likely an introductory word before the main imperative. "Inquire" rather than "go" is the core of Josiah's command. The name "Huldah" first appears in v. 14 where the delegates' move is narrated. Provan is probably the only one who pays attention to this issue. He comments: "The prophet chosen *by Josiah's official* for consultation was…Huldah."[30] Thus the following questions emerge: Who really chose Huldah? And why Huldah? The answers to these questions can be sought based on the structure and the purpose of Huldah's double prophecy in vv. 15-20 as well as on the information about her family and residence in v. 14. We will see that the answers have ethical implication in relation to the characterization of Josiah.

Huldah's double prophecy consists of two oracles: a woe oracle (vv. 15-17) and a weal oracle (vv. 18-20).[31] Each oracle has the distinctive designation for the addressee at least in its literal form: "the man who sent you [the delegates] to me [Huldah]" (v. 15) and "the king of Judah who sent you [the delegates] to inquire of YHWH" (v. 18). While

---

29. E.g., M. A. Sweeney, *King Josiah of Judah* (Oxford: Oxford University Press, 2001), 42.
30. I. W. Provan, *1 and 2 Kings* (Peabody: Hendrickson, 1995), 271, my italics.
31. I have argued for the unity and simultaneity of the final form of Hudah's prophecy elsewhere. Chun, *Ethics*, 201–3.

nearly all scholars assume that both refer to Josiah,[32] the differences between them should be analyzed more carefully.

The most significant difference is the propositional phrases in the relative clauses: "to me [Huldah]" (v. 15) versus "to inquire of YHWH" (v. 18). While the phrase in v. 18 has a clear connection to Josiah (דרש את־יהוה is identical to Josiah's wording in v. 13), the phrase in v. 15 does not because the text is not explicit regarding who sent the delegates to Huldah. Another decisive observation is that Josiah is mentioned in third person in the first oracle ("the king of Judah," v. 16). This is unusual, though not entirely impossible, if Josiah is the actual addressee (the addressee of the second oracle is referred to in second person throughout the oracle). In fact, the designation of the addressee ("the man") has no linguistic and literary link to Josiah unless one presumes, despite the lack of textual support, that Josiah sent the delegates to Huldah. There is linguistic difference as well. The phrase in v. 15 is syntactically unmarked and the one in v. 18 is a focus marker, which is referred to by the resumptive pronominal suffix in אליו. These differences can be vividly marked if one translates the conjunction *waw* prefixed to the phrase in v. 18 as an adversative ("Say to the man who sent you to me… *But*, as to the king of Judah who sent you to inquire of YHWH, thus shall you say to him").

Four examples will suffice to look at how scholars have explained the differences. First, Sweeney sees "the king of Judah" in v. 18 as a specification of "man" in v. 15, and asserts "the initial anonymity" is an aid for "building up the mystique of an oracular consultation."[33] Secondly, Nelson explains that the first expression "puts emotional distance between God and the king" because it leads to "the complicating counter theme of irrevocable doom."[34] Thirdly, Revell proposes that the reference "the king of Judah" represents "deliberate distancing," stating that such a reference seems to treat him as if he is a foreign king and such a distancing is already seen in "the man."[35] Fourthly, Leuchter questions whether it is possible that the designation "the man" is "an attempt to diminish royal status," which is in agreement with "the ideology of Deuteronomy…as well as the book of Kings."[36]

---

32. E.g. B. Halpern and D. Vanderhooft, "The Editions of Kings in the 7th–6th Centuries," *HUCA* 62 (1991): 221.

33. Sweeney, *I & II Kings*, 445.

34. R. D. Nelson, *First and Second Kings* (Louisville: John Knox, 1987), 256.

35. Revell, *Designation of the Individual*, 131, §9.3.3.

36. M. Leuchter, review of *Ethics and Biblical Narrative* by S. Min Chun, *JTS* 66 (2015): 297–8. I am thankful for Leuchter's careful and keen reading of my work

Against these explanations, it is also possible that such differences are meant to signify different senders. The four explanations above are based on the assumption, for various (good) reasons, that it is Josiah who chose Huldah. Such an assumption, however, has no explicit textual support, as pointed out earlier. When this weakness is acknowledged, this new suggestion can gain plausibility and have ethical implications for the characterization of Josiah.

Given the new suggestion, the different core interests of the addressees are of significance: while "the king of Judah" is interested in *inquiring of YHWH* concerning the fate of the country including himself, it is the message from *Huldah* that "the man" is interested in. Why Huldah then? The most common suggestion is that she is consulted in the hope of an optimistic and comforting response. The Talmud suggests that she was

---

in general and his suggestion in particular. I would like to take this opportunity to respond to his suggestion here. While the suggestion is worth considering, it still requires explaining the flow of the oracles and the relationship between the two oracles. If the term "the man" is employed to diminish Josiah's royal status in the first oracle, why is his royal status reinstated in the second oracle? Even if such a reinstatement suits the positive mood of the second oracle (cf. Nelson, *First and Second Kings*, 256), the reinstatement itself undermines the validity of the suggestion. How plausible is it that Josiah's royal status is intended to be diminished when he is not culpable for the judgment as the second oracle implies? Why should Josiah be criticized (through the diminishment of his royal status) and "rewarded" (Lasine, *Weighing Hearts*, 208; contra M. Avioz, "Josiah's Death in the Book of Kings: A New Solution to an Old Theological Conundrum," *ETL* 83 [2007]: 362–5) at the same time when the oracles are read as a unified whole? Furthermore, how does the reinstatement fit the "ideology of Deuteronomy" and the book of Kings? Is Josiah even susceptible to such an anti-monarchical ideology given the overall positive evaluations of him in the story? These questions hardly emerge if the two addressees can be distinguished.

My proposal attempts to explain the different addressees in terms of their relationship with the purposes of each oracle. As long as the first oracle is regarded as a criticism of the motivation to choose Huldah, and the second oracle is regarded as praise for the sincere motivation behind the desire for a divine consultation—these are the purposes of using different designations for each addressee—the actual identities of the addressees are not a primary interest of mine or the text. It would be in line with my proposal if one says the first oracle is against *Josiah*'s hidden *motive to seek false comfort* from Huldah. This is why I stated "identifying who chooses Huldah is not critical for understanding the function of Huldah's oracles" (Chun, *Ethics*, 205). In a sense, "the man" can be argued to be a symbolic and psychological figure that is used as a literary device to unmask the hidden desire to maintain the *status quo* even at a time of national crisis.

chosen because "women are tender-hearted";[37] Edelman argues that she is consulted in order to avoid further wrath of Yahweh because, she suggests, Huldah is a prophet of Asherah, the female partner of Yahweh.[38] The names of her family members also have optimistic connotations: Shallum (related to "peace") and Tikvah (meaning "hope"). In the seventh-century BCE neo-Assyrian context, "woman prophets…often delivered messages concerning the safety of the king and the granting of divine protection against his enemies."[39]

In addition, Huldah's social status raises the expectation of an optimistic response. In v. 14, she is commented to live in המשנה of Jerusalem. This information in a non-*wayyiqtol* comment line gives a particular perspective on Huldah's character, especially regarding her social status. As to the socio-geographical significance of המשנה, Mazar states:

> In the *Mishneh* ("New Quarter," or "Secondary Quarter"), the prophetess Huldah is known to have lived (2 Kgs 22:14). The term most probably refers to the Western Hill, the newer residential area of the city, *where the upper class lived.*[40]

Although this is still a speculation,[41] it fits well with the text: Huldah is the wife of a temple official ("the keeper of the clothes")[42] who likely belongs to the upper class. In addition, in ancient Israel, class was an important factor in making a woman's social role preeminent.[43] From these observations, one can make a reasonable inference as to why Huldah was chosen: Huldah was a suitable choice if "the man" wanted to hear an optimistic or comforting message because high social status tends to makes people pro-power to maintain the *status quo*. Thus, the phrase "to Huldah" is a

---

37. *b. Meg.* 14b.

38. D. Edelman, "Huldah the Prophet—Of Yahweh or Asherah?" in *A Feminist Companion to Samuel and Kings*, ed. A. Brenner (Sheffield: Sheffield Academic, 1994), 247–8.

39. Cogan and Tadmor, *II Kings*, 284.

40. A. Mazar, *Archaeology of the Land of the Bible: 10,000–586 B.C.E* (New York: Doubleday, 1992), 424, my italics.

41. Cf. R. J. Weems, "Huldah, the Prophet: Reading a (Deuteronomistic) Woman's Identity," in *A God So Near*, ed. B. A. Strawn and N. R. Bowen (Winona Lake: Eisenbrauns, 2003), 321–39. Weems too suggests some type of preeminence of Huldah though arguing for her "marginality."

42. J. Gray, *I & II Kings*, 3rd ed. (London: SCM, 1977), 726.

43. J. A. Hackett, "Women's Studies and the Hebrew Bible," in *The Future of Biblical Studies*, ed. R. E. Friedman and H. G. M. Williamson (Atlanta: Scholars Press, 1987), 149.

clue for the first sender's motive: having faced the crisis, "the man" was interested in receiving a message of comfort. This is in contrast to "the king of Judah," who sought the divine message to cope with the crisis.

Here we sense the ethical implication of Huldah's double prophecy. The first judgment oracle not only confirms the book of the law but also implies a criticism of how "the man" deals with the crisis—seeking false comfort without facing it properly. In contrast to him, Josiah, "the king of Judah," who humbled himself (v. 19) and inquired of YHWH, receives a comforting, though limited, message on a personal level. While the second weal oracle does not revoke the judgment—it is silent about it—Josiah himself is promised a death "in peace": he will not experience the disaster that will fall upon Judah. The precise connotation of בשלום—whether it refers to "the manner of Josiah's death" ("a peaceful death") or the circumstance of Josiah's burial ("in time of peace")[44]—matters little. Whichever connotation it may have, Josiah will certainly escape the evil fate of Judah.

Now the delegates brought back word to the king. Is the promise for personal weal good enough for him, or is the future woe of the nation still of concern to him? In the case of Hezekiah, he did not seem to care about national judgment in the future when he could have peace during his lifetime (2 Kgs 20:19).[45] How will Josiah, then, respond to Huldah's oracles? What kind of character is Josiah? The story continues with these questions in mind.

Act III: Josiah, the Reformer (23:1-15)

Act III begins the verse with *wayyiqtol*, "And the king sent," which shows Josiah's initiative. As to the question that emerged in the last Act—how Josiah will respond to Huldah's oracles?—he now proves himself to be the reformer who cares for the covenantal relationship with YHWH. He is not content with his personal comfort and goes beyond the personal horizon. Now a new series of questions emerges. Why does he make such sweeping reforms? What is the use in reforming after the judgment has been announced? What is his motive for the reforms?

---

44. I. W. Provan, *Hezekiah and the Books of Kings* (Berlin: de Gruyter, 1988), 149. See also P. S. F. van Keulen, "The Meaning of the Phrase *WN'SPT 'L-QBRTYK BŠLWM* in 2 Kings XXII 20," *VT* 46 (1996): 259, endnotes 1 and 2.

45. This is an irony in that Hezekiah, having experienced the possibility of changing the divine announcement on a personal level (2 Kgs 20:1-7), does not attempt to change the national fate at all.

Broadly speaking, there have been three types of explanations of Josiah's motive for the reforms.[46] The first one is that Josiah carries out the reforms without knowing the "full version" of Huldah's prophecy that seals the fate of Judah.[47] It argues that if Josiah had known the sealed future of the nation, he would have had no motive to carry out reforms that would have had no effect at all.[48] This view is held by those who tend to deny the unity of Huldah's prophecy. However, while the second part of the prophecy (vv. 18-20) does not confirm the fate of Judah, it does not annul it either. If that is the case, then Josiah knows that divine wrath is still effective, if not actively confirmed, even if he is not aware of the whole prophecy: hence, the second and third views. The second view is that Josiah simply obeys the law and is not interested in the possibility of averting the judgment.[49] The third view is that the reform is Josiah's effort to alter the future of his nation against the pending judgement.

The first and the third views are similar in that Josiah aspires to change the fate of Judah, but they differ in their understandings of divine–human interaction. Whereas the first view (and the second view as well) has a "mechanistic view of prophecy"[50] (a prophecy once declared cannot be averted), the third view believes that the divine–human interaction is genuine. The wider literary contexts of the story of Josiah, and the story of Hezekiah in particular, fit well with the third view. Fretheim states:

> It is clear from various texts (most closely, 20:1-7…) that the response of people can deflect the trajectory of a prophetic word… The threat was real and prophecies were known to be deflected in view of human response; these motivations were sufficient for Josiah and the nation to make every effort to counteract the threat and seek to shape a different future.[51]

---

46. This discussion is about the motives "in the text." It involves "psychologizing," which some biblical scholars may shun, but it is "a fact of reading" (Lasine, *Weighing Hearts*, 11). As to the motives "behind the text," four views can be delineated: political, religious, fiscal, and cultural. See Chun, *Ethics*, 210 n. 123.

47. E.g. G. N. Knoppers, *Two Nations Under God: The Deuteronomistic History of Solomon and the Dual Monarchies, Vol. 2* (Atlanta: Scholars Press, 1993), 149.

48. E.g. Joseph, *Portrait of the Kings*, 140–50.

49. E.g. Provan, *1 and 2 Kings*, 272.

50. T. E. Fretheim, *First and Second Kings* (Louisville: Westminster John Knox, 1999), 218.

51. Ibid., 218–9.

Therefore, Josiah is motivated to change the nation's fate despite the divine decree. Josiah answers "Reform!" to the question, "To reform or not to reform," through his actions. Josiah has been transformed from "not-yet-reformer" to "the sincere inquirer," and now he is the decisive leader who undertakes the comprehensive reform, going beyond his personal weal.

Josiah is pictured as a decisive leader in several ways. (1) The nominal subject is repeated three times in a relatively short narrative ("the king"; 23:1, 2, 3). This repetition marks each stage, as it were, of covenant-making ritual and keeps the reader's attention focused on the royal initiative. (2) The expression in v. 3, "and the king stood by the pillar," conveys a decisive atmosphere. The expression עמד על-(ו)(ה)עמוד appears three times in the Old Testament in two contexts (2 Kgs 11:14//2 Chron. 23:13; 2 Kgs 23:3). In 2 Kgs 11:14, the narrator describes the legitimacy of the enthronement of Joash by stating that עמד על-העמוד is "according to the custom" (כמשפט).[52] Moreover, while the expression is in a phrase employing *qotel* describing the circumstance in 2 Kgs 11:14 (and 2 Chron. 23:13), it is in a *wayyiqtol* phrase with an explicit nominal subject in 2 Kgs 23:3, which presents the action as the thread of the story, thus adding more weight to it. (3) The report of the covenant-making ritual and the subsequent reforms is all in narration: there is no speech in vv. 1-15. As to this discourse feature, Cohn suggests: "[W]atching Josiah at work is like viewing a silent film clip of a pogrom. The lack of dialogue conveys the speed and efficiency with which Josiah wrecks the nativist cult without meeting a shred of resistance."[53] This suggestion reinforces the picture of Josiah being a decisive and determined leader.

Josiah's covenant-making is not only decisive but also comprehensive. Verses 1-3 abound with the intensifier "all" (כל), which particularly emphasizes the totality of the participants of the covenant. All are liable to the covenant. Josiah is indeed the leader of all the people. The scope of Josiah's reform is also exhaustive in terms of time and space. The overall structure of 23:4-15, where the demolitions of the idolatrous institutions are narrated, can be analyzed in terms of space and time.[54] In the midst of a series of *wayyiqtol*s, there are two *w-qatal*s ("and he carried their ashes to Bethel," v. 4; "and he removed the idol-priests whom the kings of Judah

---

52. Provan, *1 and 2 Kings*, 272 and 222.
53. Cohn, *II Kings*, 157.
54. Analysis of this section is certainly challenging. See Nelson, *First and Second Kings*, 254, 257.

had appointed," v. 5) that can be recognized as pivotal events,[55] and they deal with the spatial and temporal dimensions of the narrative. In terms of space, Josiah's reforming activities extend to Bethel (v. 4b). In terms of time, the reforms reach back to Josiah's predecessors' apostasy (v. 5a). The next section also concerns these two dimensions: the references to various spaces abound in 23:4-10 and the references to the previous kings as well as spatial references permeate 23:11-15. After the generic designation "the kings of Judah," relatively recent kings (Ahaz and Manasseh; vv. 11-12) and kings in the early history (Solomon and Jeroboam, vv. 13-15) are mentioned. Josiah is abrogating the embodiments of his predecessors' sin. Josiah is the all-embracing reformer in terms of time and space. The following anecdote in vv. 16-20, which relates the fulfillment of prophecy concerning Josiah uttered at Bethel in the time of Jeroboam, instances that the reform is far-reaching in terms of space and time. At the same time, it ironically reveals the paradox of Josiah's reform in particular and the paradox permeating life in general.

As Josiah carries out the reforms of which the purpose is to avert the fate of Judah, he burns the bones from the graves on the hill of Bethel. The narrator states that this is the fulfillment of an old prophecy (v. 16; cf. v. 20). By designating Josiah with his personal name "Josiah," rather than "the king," the narrator reinforces the connection between this event and the prophecy in 1 Kgs 13:2 which mentions the name "Josiah" (see also v. 19; cf. 23:13 and 21). It is noteworthy here that Josiah defiles the altar, thereby fulfilling the prophecy without being aware of it. He comes to know of it only after he defiled the altar (v. 17).[56] Josiah carries out the reforms in order to make a difference in Judah's fate, that is, to annul Huldah's prophecy against Judah. As he does so, however, he comes

---

55. R. E. Longacre, "*Weqatal* Forms in Biblical Hebrew Prose," in *Biblical Hebrew and Discourse Linguistics*, ed. R. D. Bergen (Dallas: Summer Institute of Linguistics, 1994), 80–2.

56. This prophetic naming of Josiah adds the dimension of "providence" to Josiah's reforms: they are done according to the divine words. Such a dimension, however, should not cancel out the dimension of contingency in ethical reflection. It is rare, if not impossible, for *the characters in the story* to comprehend such a privileged dimension of divine providence; in most cases it is betrayed by *the narrator*'s comment. While one can say that the narrator's comment in v. 16 characterizes Josiah as a vehicle of the divine judgement, such a characterization should not override the fact that the ethical choices he makes when encountering contingencies are genuinely "free choices" at least according to his perception, and thus he is responsible for them (cf. 1 Kgs 12:15).

to confirm the efficacy of prophetic utterances.[57] This is the paradox of Josiah's reform. Josiah is the character who embodies such a paradoxical reality of life that what is pursued is occasionally, if not often, undermined by the pursuit itself.

In this respect, that this anecdote is a flashback is significant.[58] As the timeline regresses and its speed slows down, the reader is given an opportunity to do a reality check regarding the enduring effect of Josiah's reforms before the story goes on to the celebration of the passover, the pinnacle of the reform. The checked reality indeed becomes an actuality in the following Act: Josiah's reform goes in vain and he becomes an unfortunate hero.

Act IV: Josiah, the Unfortunate Hero (23:21-30)

The first part of this Act relates the limit of Josiah's reform (vv. 21-27) and its second part is the epilogue of the whole story (vv. 28-30). The first part begins and ends with speeches that are in conflict with each other. The effect of the reform anticipated by the first speech of the king (v. 21) is countered by the judgment speech of YHWH (v. 27). Such a limit to Josiah's reform, however, is not on the horizon at the outset of the Act. Until the story reaches v. 26, the atmosphere is highly encouraging.

As the Act begins, Josiah's royal initiative resumes. The Act starts with a verb of royal initiative, "command," and the designation of Josiah changes back to "the king" from his personal name "Josiah." The following report of the Passover celebration is supposed to be the climax of the story, and the final summary of the reforms in v. 24 wraps up the whole story as it re-mentions the discovery of the law book. Moreover, such an uplifting conclusion to the reform leads to a highly positive evaluation of Josiah, the scope of which is global. These features characterize Josiah as the successful hero who "established" the words of the law. Simply, he is the best (v. 25).[59] However, what makes the characterization of Josiah complex is that v. 25 does not represent the whole story and is not its end.

When read along with the rest of the Act (vv. 26-27), the positive characterization of Josiah functions ominously. While some regard the

---

57. Knoppers makes the same observations. *Two Nations*, 209.
58. The time regresses as v. 16 begins; the altars at Bethel are demolished in v. 15 but they exist in vv. 16-20.
59. G. N. Knoppers, "'There Was None Like Him': Incomparability in the Books of Kings," *CBQ* 54 (1992): 411–31.

tenets of vv. 21-25 and 26-27 as contradictory,[60] they are not necessarily so. The statements that (1) Josiah has the incomparable merit in v. 25 and (2) the divine judgement will not be revoked in v. 26 are not logically incompatible antitheses. As the fulfillment of prophecy is not mechanical, the divine–human interaction is not so either. Human actions cannot manipulate the divine response. God is sovereign and free as much as divine–human interaction is genuine. Thus, it is reasonable to read v. 25 as a backdrop to v. 26. When they are read in this way, the shock created by v. 26 is even more intensified. The wordplay on "return" (שוב) also binds these two verses together (YHWH did not "return" in spite of Josiah's "return") and reinforces the shock.

In fact, the phrase "return to YHWH" in the positive evaluation of Josiah in v. 25 is already ominous. While the expression בכל־לבבו ובכל־נפשו ובכל־מאדו echoes Deut. 6:4, it is preceded by not אהב but שוב אל, which is found in Solomon's temple dedication prayer in 1 Kgs 8:48-50. In the prayer, "returning to YHWH" happens "in the land of their enemies." Thus, even the positive evaluation of Josiah in v. 25 characterizes him as being in exile as it were. Josiah, the reformer, is certainly a hero, or even the hero, in Judah's history, but his reforms are limited. The more positively Josiah is understood, the more unfortunate becomes Josiah's character and the more pessimistic becomes the future of Judah. In addition to this irony, contingency defines the last moment of his personal life.

Between a typical closing formula and the report of the next king's enthronement, the death and the burial of Josiah are narrated in a very terse manner. After Pharaoh Neco's military movement is told in an *x-qatal* construction as background information, the death and burial of Josiah are narrated in a series of five consecutive *wayyiqtol* constructions: there is no comment line or speech. This terse style gives an impression that Josiah's death itself is abrupt and surprising.

Although his death itself may be anticipated since Huldah's oracle, the manner in which he died and was buried raises an ethical problem. Josiah was killed away from Jerusalem and his corpse remained in the chariot while being brought to Jerusalem to be buried. This scene echoes the death of Ahab, whose corpse also supposedly remained in his chariot

---

60. For the survey of various double redaction theories in general, see R. D. Nelson, *The Double Redaction of the Deuteronomistic History* (Sheffield: JSOT Press, 1981), 13–28. Lasine argues for the priority of careful literary analysis in psychological terms over redactional explanation when facing "seemingly incoherent characters" (Lasine, *Weighing Hearts*, 18).

while being brought to his capital for burial (1 Kgs 22:35-38). Is it appropriate for one of the best kings of Judah to encounter such an abrupt and disrespectful death that echoes the death of the most evil king of Israel? Moreover, from the verset that narrates Neco's killing of Josiah in v. 29 ("when Pharaoh Neco met *him* at Megiddo, he killed *him*"), Josiah is belittled as he continues to be referred to only with the pronominal suffix in v. 30 ("And *his* servants carried *him* dead in a chariot from Megiddo and brought *him* to Jerusalem and buried *him* in *his* tomb").

There are two main traditions to address this "problem of evil." The first one is to regard Josiah himself as culpable (i.e. Chronicles' resolution); the second one is to see Josiah's death as the first judgement due to Manasseh's sin (i.e. Kings' implication).[61] No matter how one attempts to resolve the issue, however, the surprising and abrupt death of Josiah is given an undeniable reality in the text of Kings.[62] The situation of Josiah's death is beyond full comprehension; the reason for and the course of Josiah's death are ambiguous and it is even unclear whether it is the fulfillment of Huldah's oracle. Such an incomprehensible situation tends to be regarded as an ethical *problem* but it may need to be acknowledged as an ethical *reality* of life.

The story of Josiah may be not so much interested in resolving ethical problems as representing ethical reality faithfully. In this respect, Kings' account of Josiah's death makes readers perceptive to the reality of life so that they might become capable of coping with those contingencies in their own life that may perplex them ethically.[63] Josiah demonstrated what is called for in the world of contingencies and ambiguities. One cannot defer the action until everything is comprehended and its outcome is guaranteed. Faithful actions are indeed regarded as faithful because they are done without the desired outcome being guaranteed (cf. Dan. 3:18; Est. 4:16; Job 1:9). In this respect, the abrupt death of Josiah, along with his reform that failed to make a difference to the fate of the nation, makes his character even more faithful and demonstrates how one should live.[64]

---

61. Cf. S. Delamarter, "The Death of Josiah in Scripture and Tradition: Wrestling with the Problem of Evil?" *VT* 54 (2004): 58–60. Avioz argues that even Kings' account presents his death as the result of his sin, i.e., not consulting "with the prophets before going to war" ("Josiah's Death," 362).

62. For a brief summary of various interpretations, see Chun, *Ethics*, 222–3, and Avioz, "Josiah's Death," 360–2.

63. Cf. J. Barton, *Ethics in Ancient Israel* (Oxford: Oxford University Press, 2014), 171.

64. If Josiah can function as an ethical example, his character would be a model for the virtue of faithfulness rather than law-keeping obedience. In other words,

Conclusion

Despite the impression that the character of Josiah remains the same throughout the whole story, given by the positive evaluations of him both at the beginning and the end of the story, the character of Josiah develops as he encounters contingencies. The discovery of the book and hearing the words of it was such a contingency. It changed him from a king carrying out a mundane duty to one commanding his officials to inquire of YHWH regarding the impending divine wrath, which he had become unexpectedly aware of through the book.

It was noteworthy that Josiah did not explicitly name Huldah as the one to consult. Two different designations for the addressees of Huldah's double oracle could actually refer to two distinctive addressees: one who wanted to consult Huldah and the other who wanted to inquire of YHWH. Huldah, a resident of the Second District and a temple official's wife, was likely expected to be a safe source for a comforting message, which seems to be the reason for choosing her.

Characters continued to face contingencies. Huldah confirmed the divine wrath to the officials against expectation, whereas she talked of peace to Josiah who had a genuine concern for the nation's fate. How should Josiah respond to such a mixed situation? Should he carry out reform to revoke the judgment? Could it really make any difference? At this juncture, he acted as the reformer for the nation's sake, despite the promise of peace on a personal level.

Josiah's demolition of the altar at Bethel betrayed the paradox of his reform. His attempt to nullify the judgement oracle by carrying out the reform ironically confirmed the prophetic fulfillment. In a similar vein, his character created an irony in relation to Judah's fate. The better king he was, the more hopeless the fate of Judah was. If the reform of the best king turned out to be in vain, nothing could do good for the nation.

The story ended with contingency as well. Josiah died unexpectedly. Josiah's wholehearted and thorough obedience to the law of Moses did not save his nation nor prevent contingency from affecting his life. This may pose an ethical problem but it certainly represents an ethical reality that the readers must deal with in their lives. Ethical reading appropriate to the nature of narratives is not about distilling principles from the story

---

characterization of Josiah in the story as a whole contributes to virtue ethics rather than to the ethics of obeying God the lawgiver. Though he is certainly praised for his obedience to the law of Moses (23:25), his choice, judgment, conception of situations, and emotions exhibited throughout the whole story demonstrate the virtue of faithfulness. Cf. Barton, *Ethics in Ancient Israel*, 170.

and applying them to moral dilemmas, but about cultivating the practical wisdom and virtue of the readers so that they can live authentically in the world where contingencies prevail. This is how the story of Josiah in Kings and its characterization of him as one who became a reformer and acted out such an identity in the midst of contingencies contributes to the ethical life of the reader.[65]

---

65. This conclusion resonates with the thesis of Barton's introductory essay in the present volume. He argues that round characters who have the "capacity to surprise" the reader should not be made into flattened *exempla*. Round characters reflect the complexity of life out of which practical wisdom can be fostered and that is how they contribute to ethical appropriation of Old Testament narrative. While Barton's list of round characters does not include Josiah, I hope I have made a good case to lengthen the list. When Josiah is understood as an ordinary king who initially remained in the sin of Manasseh, his responses to the book of the law and to Huldah's oracle can surprise or challenge those readers who tend to remain in their *status quo*. I believe there are many other characters waiting for their complexity to be appreciated as their stories are read as a whole without being separated into redactional layers.

Afterword

We have now journeyed through the book of Kings giving sustained attention to some of the most important—and in some cases some of the less important—characters in this work. We have seen that even characters which on the surface may seem one-dimensional are capable of surprising the reader. John Barton gave us a survey of the way that complex characterization often coincides with complex ethical issues, undermining the idea that biblical ethics is either simple or crude, but is rather more sophisticated and rich than may sometimes be assumed. If the complexity of the text that we have is not rich enough, A. Graeme Auld has highlighted the way that the potential growth of the text over time may make for even more complex engagement with characterization.

Although her story is one of the most famous in all the Bible, Sara Koenig has highlighted the ambiguity that is involved in the characterization of Bathsheba and shown how that has resulted in various interpretations of her over the years. Amos Frisch has given us a reading of Solomon that highlights the slow decline of his character arc from light towards dark. Solomon's son, who is usually seen as a simple caricature of a petulant king, is, in Rachelle Gilmour's reading, more nuanced than that, and while one would not mistake him for a character to emulate, he is given a little rehabilitation.

Paul Hedley Jones has highlighted for us the significant way that the characterization of the man of God from Judah and the old prophet from Bethel foreshadow the events of the rest of the book. Lissa Wray Beal has given us another look at Ahab that shows that there may be more to this arch-villain than meets the eye. Athalya Brenner-Idan has shown that even a character like Jezebel is capable of being seen from multiple perspectives. Iain Provan, on the other hand, has highlighted that even the great hero Elijah is characterized more ambivalently than his Mt. Carmel reputation may suggest.

Although most studies focus on the life of the characters under examination, Stuart Lasine offered an analysis of the significant characterization of Elisha after his death, confronting us with significant reflection on mortality. Mark Roncace, on the other hand, focused on life rather than death in that his analysis of the death-filled story of Jehu was focused on the comedic rather than the tragic.

Patricia Dutcher-Walls has offered an analysis of Athaliah, the one queen of Judah, and allowed us space to focus on her even though the text does a fair job of erasing her. Gina Hens-Piazza turns our gaze to other characters who most often do not receive it as she draws on subaltern studies to highlight the significance of the "neighbors" in 2 Kgs 4:1-7 in carrying out the prophetic mission.

In a study of Hezekiah's character, David Lamb found that Hezekiah is portrayed as round and complex and yet is a character who is marked by trust in Yhwh. Alison Joseph has looked at the lack of characterization of Manasseh, the king who shoulders the blame for the exile, and suggested that in this flat character we see the tension of various historical voices. Finally, S. Min Chun brings our study full circle by giving a sustained reading of the character of Josiah and showing what the contingencies in the portrayal of his life can offer us for ethical engagement with this story.

Hopefully in the course of this journey with the various characters of the book of Kings we have been surprised, informed, and engaged with what this kind of study has to offer. A volume like this, however, is never intended to be the final word. It is hopefully a contribution to the appreciation of what character study within this literature has to offer and is but one part of a conversation on character that we hope will continue.

Keith Bodner
Benjamin J. M. Johnson

Bibliography

Ababi, Ionel. *Natan et la succession de David: Une étude synchronique de 2 Samuel 7 et et 12 et 1 Rois 1*. BTS 32. Leuven: Peeters, 2017.
Aberbach, Moses and Leivy Smolar. "Aaron, Jeroboam & the Golden Calves." *JBL* 86 (1967): 129–40.
Ackerman, Susan. "On Queen Mothers." In *Warrior, Dancer, Seductress, Queen: Women in Judges and Biblical Israel*, 128–80. ABRL. New York: Doubleday, 1998.
Adelman, Rachel. *The Female Ruse: Women's Deception and Divine Sanction in the Hebrew Bible*. Sheffield: Sheffield Phoenix, 2015.
Alter, Robert. *The Art of Biblical Narrative*. New York: Basic Books, 1981.
Alter, Robert. *The David Story*. New York/London: W. W. Norton, 1999.
Amit, Yairah. "Design and Meaning in the Story of Naboth'. *Beit Miqra'* (2015): 19–36 (Hebrew).
Amit, Yairah. "The Dual Causality Principle and Its Effects on Biblical Literature." *VT* 37 (1987): 385–400.
Amit, Yairah. *Hidden Polemics in Biblical Narrative*. BibInt 25. Leiden: Brill, 2000.
Amit, Yairah. *Reading Biblical Narratives: Literary Criticism and the Hebrew Bible*. Minneapolis: Fortress, 2001.
Anderson, Joel Edmund. "The Rise, Fall, and Renovation of the House Gesenius: Diachronic Methods, Synchronic Readings, and the Debate over Isaiah 36–39 and 2 Kings 18–20." *CBR* 11, no. 2 (2013): 147–67.
Angel, Hayyim. "Hopping Between Two Opinions: Understanding the Biblical Portrait of Ahab." *JBQ* 35 (2007): 3–10.
Appler, Deborah A. "From Queen to Cuisine: Food Imagery in the Jezebel Narrative." *Semeia* 86 (1999): 55–71.
Arendt, Hannah. *The Human Condition*. Chicago, IL: Chicago University Press, 1998.
Arnold, Bill T. and Brent A. Strawn, eds. *The World around the Old Testament: The People and Places of the Ancient Near East*. Grand Rapids: Baker Academic, 2016.
Ashkenasy, Nehama. *Woman at the Window: Biblical Tales of Oppression and Escape*. Detroit: Wayne State University Press, 1998.
Attardo, Salvatore. *Encyclopedia of Humor Studies*. Thousand Oaks, CA: Sage, 2014.
Auld, A. Graeme. *I & II Kings*. Louisville: John Knox, 1986.
Auld, A. Graeme. *Life in Kings. Reshaping the Royal Story in the Hebrew Bible*. Ancient Israel and its Literature 30. Atlanta: SBL, 2017.
Avioz, Michael. "Josiah's Death in the Book of Kings: A New Solution to an Old Theological Conundrum." *ETL* 83 (2007): 359–66.
Bal, Mieke. "Narration and Focalization." In *Narrative Theory: Critical Concepts in Literary and Cultural Studies, Vol. 1*, edited by M. Bal, 263–96. London/New York: Routledge, 2004.

Bal, Mieke. *Narratology: Introduction to the Theory of Narrative*. 2nd ed. Toronto: University of Toronto Press, 1997; 4th ed. Toronto: University of Toronto Press, 2017.

Bar-Efrat, Shimon *Narrative Art in the Bible*. Sheffield: Sheffield Academic, 1989.

Barnes, William H. *1–2 Kings*. Carol Stream, IL: Tyndale House, 2012.

Barré, Lloyd M. *The Rhetoric of Political Persuasion*. CBQMS 20. Washington, DC: Catholic Biblical Association, 1988.

Barth, Karl. *Church Dogmatics II.2: The Doctrine of God*, translated by G. W. Bromiley et al. Edinburgh: T. & T. Clark, 1957.

Barton, John. *Ethics and the Old Testament*. London: SCM, 2002.

Barton, John. *Ethics in Ancient Israel*. Oxford: Oxford University Press, 2014.

Barton, John. "Prophecy and Theodicy." In *Thus Says the Lord: Essays on the Former and Latter Prophets in Honor of Robert R. Wilson*, edited by J. J. Ahn and S. L. Cook, 73–86. New York/London: T&T Clark, 2011.

Barton, John. "Reading for Life: The Use of the Bible in Ethics." In *The Bible in Ethics: The Second Sheffield Colloquium*, edited by J. W. Rogerson, M. Davies, and M. D. Carroll R., 66–76. JSOTSup 207. Sheffield: Sheffield Academic, 1996.

Barton, John. *Understanding Old Testament Ethics: Approaches and Explorations*. Louisville: Westminster John Knox, 2003.

Beach, Eleanor Ferris. *The Jezebel Letters: Religion and Politics in Ninth-Century Israel*. Minneapolis: Fortress, 2005.

Becker, Ernest. *The Denial of Death*. New York: Free Press, 1973.

Becker, Ernest. *Escape from Evil*. New York: Free Press, 1975.

Begg, Christopher T. "2 Kings 20:12–19 as an Element of the Deuteronomistic History." *CBQ* 48 (1986): 27–38.

Ben Barak, Zafrira. "The Status and Right of the *Gebîrâ*." In *A Feminist Companion to Samuel and Kings*, edited by Athalya Brenner, 170–85. Sheffield: Sheffield Academic, 1994.

Benson, Joseph. *Critical and Explanatory Notes, Vol 1: Genesis to the Second Book of Samuel*. New York: T. Mason and G. Lane, 1841.

Ben Zvi, Ehud. "The Account of the Reign of Manasseh in II Reg 21:1–18 and the Redactional History of the Book of Kings." *ZAW* 103, no. 3 (1991): 355–74.

Bergen, Wesley J. *Elisha and the End of Prophetism*. JSOTSup 286. Sheffield: Sheffield Academic, 1999.

Berlin, Adele. *Poetics and Interpretation of Biblical Narrative*. Winona Lake: Eisenbrauns, 1994.

Berman, Joshua. *Narrative Analogy in the Hebrew Bible: Battle Stories and their Equivalent Non-battle Narratives*. VTSup 103. Leiden: Brill, 2004.

Betlyon, John W. "Coinage." *ABD* 1:1076–89.

Beverley, John. *Subalternity and Representation: Arguments in Cultural Theory*. Durham, NC: Duke University Press, 1999.

Biddle, Mark E. *A Time to Laugh: Humor in the Bible*. Macon, GA: Smyth & Helwys, 2013.

Birch, Bruce C. "Old Testament Narrative and Moral Address." In *Canon, Theology, and Old Testament Interpretation: Essays in Honor of Brevard S. Childs*, edited by G. M. Tucker, 75–91. Philadelphia: Fortress, 1988.

Bodner, Keith. *David Observed: A King in the Eyes of His Court*. Sheffield: Sheffield Phoenix, 2005.

Bodner, Keith. *Elisha's Profile in the Book of Kings: The Double Agent*. Oxford: Oxford University Press, 2013.

Bodner, Keith. *Jeroboam's Royal Drama*. Biblical Refigurations. Oxford: Oxford University Press, 2012.
Bodner, Keith. "Nathan: Prophet, Politician, and Novelist?" *JSOT* 26 (2001): 43–54.
Bodner, Keith and Benjamin J. M. Johnson, eds. *Characters and Characterization in the Book of Samuel*. LHBOTS 669. London: Bloomsbury T&T Clark, 2020.
Boer, Roland. *The Earthy Nature of the Bible: Fleshly Readings of Sex, Masculinity, and Carnality*. Houndsmill: Palgrave Macmillan, 2012.
Boer, Roland. *Jameson and Jeroboam*. Semeia. Atlanta: Scholars Press, 1996.
Boer, Roland. "National Allegory in the Hebrew Bible." *JSOT* 74 (1997): 95–116.
Boer, Roland. "Rehoboam Meets Machiavelli." In *Rewriting Biblical History: Essays on Chronicles and Ben Sira in Honor of Pancratius C. Beentjes*, edited by Jeremy Corley and Harm van Grol, 159–72. Berlin: de Gruyter, 2011.
Booth, Wayne C. *The Rhetoric of Fiction*. 2nd ed. Chicago: University of Chicago Press, 1983.
Boring, Edwin G. "A New Ambiguous Figure." *The American Journal of Psychology* 42 (1930): 444–5.
Bostock, David. *A Portrayal of Trust: The Theme of Faith in the Hezekiah Narratives*. Milton Keynes: Paternoster, 2006.
Bosworth, David A. "Revisiting Karl Barth's Exegesis of 1 Kings 13" *BibInt* 10 (2002): 360–83.
Bosworth, David A. *The Story within a Story in Biblical Hebrew Narrative*. CBQMS 45. Washington: Catholic Biblical Association of America, 2008.
Bowen, Nancy. "The Quest for the Historical *Gĕbîrâ*." *CBQ* 63 (2001): 597–618.
Branch, Robin Gallagher. "Athaliah, a Treacherous Queen: A Careful Analysis of her Story in 2 Kings 11 and 2 Chronicles 22:10–23:21." *In die Skriflig* 38 (2004): 537–59.
Brandes, Yochi. *The Secret Book of Kings: A Novel*, translated by Yardenne Greenspan. New York: St. Martins, 2016.
Braude, William G. *The Midrash on Psalms, Vol 1*. Yale Judaica Series, 13. New Haven, CT: Yale University Press, 1959.
Brenner, Athalya, ed. *Are We Amused? Humour About Women in the Biblical World*. New York: T&T Clark, 2003.
Brenner, Athalya. *I Am*: *Biblical Woman Tell their Own Stories*. Minneapolis: Fortress, 2004.
Brenner, Athalya. *The Israelite Woman: Social Role and Literary Type in Biblical Narrative*. BibSem 2. Sheffield: JSOT Press, 1985. Reprinted by Bloomsbury T&T Clark, 2014, under Brenner-Idan.
Brenner, Athalya. "Jezebel." *Shnaton* 5, no. 6 (1981–82): 27–39 (Hebrew).
Brenner, Athalya. "Michal and David: Love between Enemies?" In *The Fate of King David: The Past and Present of a Biblical Icon*, edited by T. Linafelt, C. Camp, and T. Beal, 260–70. New York/London: Continuum, 2010.
Brenner, Athalya and Yehuda T. Radday, eds. *On Humour and the Comic in the Hebrew Bible*. Bible and Literature Series 23. New York: Almond Press, 1990.
Brenner-Idan, Athalya. "On Scholarship and Related Animals: A Personal View from and for the Here and Now." *JBL* 135, no. 1 (2016): 6–17.
Brettler, Marc. "The Structure of 1 Kings 1–11." *JSOT* 49 (1991): 87–97.
Brichto, Herbert Chanan. *Toward a Grammar of Biblical Poetics: Tales of the Prophets*. Oxford: Oxford University Press, 1992.
Brinton, Daniel G. "Folk-Lore of the Bones." *The Journal of American Folklore* 3, no. 8 (1890): 17–22.

Brodie, Thomas L. *The Crucial Bridge: The Elijah–Elisha Narrative as an Interpretive Synthesis of Genesis–Kings and a Literary Model for the Gospels.* Collegeville, MN: Liturgical Press, 2000.

Brooks, Geraldine. *The Secret Chord.* New York: Viking, 2015.

Brooks, Simcha Shalom. *Saul and the Monarchy: A New Look.* Aldershot: Ashgate, 2005.

Brosh, B.-Sh. "Complex Royal Characters in the Book of Kings." PhD diss., Tel Aviv University, 2005 (Hebrew).

Brueggemann, Walter. *1 & 2 Kings.* Macon, GA: Smyth & Helwys, 2000.

Brueggemann, Walter. *Isaiah 1–39.* Louisville: Westminster John Knox, 1998.

Brueggemann, Walter. *Power, Providence, and Personality: Biblical Insight into Life and Ministry.* Louisville: Westminster John Knox, 1990.

Brueggemann, Walter. *Solomon: Israel's Ironic Icon of Human Achievement.* Studies on Personalities of the Old Testament. Columbia: University of South Carolina Press, 2005.

Calvin, John. *Sermons on 2 Samuel: Chapters 1–13.* Edinburgh: The Banner of Truth Trust, 1992.

Camp, Claudia V. "1 and 2 Kings." In *The Women's Bible Commentary*, edited by Carol A. Newsom and Sharon H. Ringe, 102–16. London: SPCK, 1998.

Candido da Silva, Fernando. "To Whom Do Jezebel's Remains Belong?" In *Texts@Contexts: Samuel, Kings and Chronicles, Vol. 1*, edited by Athalya Brenner-Idan and Archie C. C. Lee, 24–45. London: Bloomsbury T&T Clark, 2017.

Carroll R., M. Daniel and Jacqueline E. Lapsley, eds. *Character Ethics and the Old Testament: Moral Dimensions of Scripture.* Louisville: Westminster John Knox, 2007.

Chan, Lúcán, S.J. *Biblical Ethics in the 21st Century: Developments, Emerging Consensus, and Future Directions.* New York: Paulist Press, 2013.

Chapman, Stephen B. *1 Samuel as Christian Scripture: A Theological Commentary.* Grand Rapids: Eerdmans, 2016.

Chastellain, Georges. "Le Pas de la Mort." In *Œuvres de Georges Chastellain, Tome Sixième: Œuvres Diverses*, edited by Kervyn De Lettenhove, 49–65. Brussels: F. Heussner, 1864.

Childs, Brevard. *Isaiah and the Assyrian Crisis.* London: SCM, 1967.

Chirichigno, Gregory C. *Debt Slavery in Israel and the Ancient Near East.* JSOTSup 141. Sheffield: Sheffield Academic, 1993.

Chun, S. M. *Ethics and Biblical Narrative: A Literary and Discourse-Analytical Approach to the Story of Josiah.* Oxford: Oxford University Press, 2014.

Clarke, Sathianathan. "Viewing the Bible Through the Eyes and Ears of Subalterns in India." *BibInt* 10, no. 3 (2002): 245–66.

Cogan, Mordechai. *1 Kings.* AB 10. New York: Doubleday, 2001.

Cogan, Mordechai and Hayim Tadmor. *II Kings.* AB 11. New York: Doubleday, 1988.

Cohen, A. "Ecclesiastes." In *The Midrash VIII: Ruth, Ecclesiastes*, i–318. London: Soncino, 1939.

Cohen, Stuart. "How to Mount a Successful Coup d'Etat; Lessons from the Bible (II Kings 11, II Chronicles 23)." *Diplomacy and Statecraft* 11 (2000): 1–28.

Cohn, Robert L. *2 Kings.* Berit Olam. Collegeville, MN: Liturgical Press, 2000.

Cohn, Robert L. "The Literary Structure of Kings." In *The Books of Kings: Sources, Composition, Historiography and Reception*, edited by A. Lemaire and B. Halpern, 107–22. Leiden: Brill, 2010.

Cranz, Isabel. "Royal Illness in Dynastic and National Crises: The Illness of Abijah and Hezekiah in Light of Israelite and Judean History." *Sick Kings: Royal Illness in the Hebrew Bible*, forthcoming.

Critchley, Simon, *On Humour*. London: Routledge, 2002.

Cronauer, Patrick T. *The Stories about Naboth the Jezreelite: A Source, Composition, and Redaction Investigation of 1 Kings 21 and Passages in 2 Kings 9*. LHBOTS 424. New York: T&T Clark, 2005.

Cross, Frank Moore. *Canaanite Myth and Hebrew Epic: Essays in the History of the Religion of Israel*. Cambridge, MA: Harvard University Press, 1973.

Cushman, Beverly. "The Politics of the Royal Harem and the Case of Bat-Sheba." *JSOT* 30 (2006): 327–43.

Darr, Katheryn Pfisterer. "No Strength to Deliver: A Contextual Analysis of Hezekiah's Proverb in Isaiah 37.3b." In *New Visions of Isaiah*, edited by Roy F. Melugin and Marvin A. Sweeney, 219–56. Sheffield: Sheffield Academic, 1996.

Daube, David. "Absalom and the Ideal King." *VT* 48 (1998): 315–25.

DeVries, Simon J. *1 Kings*. 2nd ed. WBC 12. Nashville: Thomas Nelson, 2003.

Dietrich, Walter. *The Early Monarchy in Israel: The Tenth Century B.C.E.*, translated by Joachim Vette. BibEncycl 3. Atlanta: SBL, 2007.

Dorp, Jaap van. "Wat is die steenhoop daar? Het graf van de man Gods in 2 Koningen 23." [What Is that Pile of Stone There? The Grave of the Man of God in 2 Kings 23] In *Amsterdamse Cahiers voor Exegese en Bijbelse Theologie* 8, edited by K. A. Deurloo et al., 64–97. Kampen: Kok, 1987.

Dozeman, Thomas B. "The Way of the Man of God from Judah: True and False Prophecy in the Pre-Deuteronomic Legend of 1 Kings 13." *CBQ* 44, no. 3 (1982): 379–93.

Dray, Carol A. *Studies on Translation and Interpretation in the Targum to the Books of Kings*. Leiden: Brill, 2006.

Driver, S. R. *Notes on the Hebrew Text of the Books of Samuel*. Oxford: Clarendon, 1890.

Duffy, Eamon. *The Stripping of the Altars: Traditional Religion in England, C.1400–C.1580*. New Haven, CT: Yale University Press, 2005.

Dutcher-Walls, Patricia. *Jezebel: Portraits of a Queen*. Collegeville: Liturgical Press, 2004.

Dutcher-Walls, Patricia. *Narrative Art and Political Rhetoric: The Case of Athaliah and Joash*. JSOTSup 209. Sheffield: Sheffield Academic, 1996.

Dutcher-Walls, Patricia. *Reading the Historical Books: A Student's Guide to Engaging the Biblical Text*. Grand Rapids: Baker Academic, 2014.

Edelman, Diana. "Huldah the Prophet—Of Yahweh or Asherah?" In *A Feminist Companion to Samuel and Kings*, edited by A. Brenner, 231–50. Sheffield: Sheffield Academic, 1994.

Elliot, John H. "Deuteronomy—Shameful Encroachment on Shameful Parts." In *Ancient Israel: The Old Testament in its Social Context*, edited by Philip F. Esler, 161–90. London: SCM, 2005.

Eslinger, Lyle. *House of God or House of David: The Rhetoric of 2 Samuel 7*. JSOTSup 164. Sheffield: Sheffield Academic, 1994.

Eslinger, Lyle. "Josiah and the Torah Book: Comparison of 2 Kgs 22:1–23:28 and 2 Chr 34:1–35:19." *HAR* 10 (1986): 37–62.

Evans, Paul S. *The Invasion of Sennacherib in the Book of Kings: A Source-critical and Rhetorical Study of 2 Kings 18–19*. Leiden: Brill, 2009.

Exum, J. Cheryl. *Fragmented Women: Feminist (Sub)versions of Biblical Narratives*. Sheffield: JSOT Press, 1993.

Exum, J. Cheryl. *Plotted, Shot and Painted: Cultural Representations of Biblical Women.* Sheffield: Sheffield Academic, 1996.
Eynikel, Erik. "The Portrait of Manasseh and the Deuteronomistic History." In *Deuteronomy and Deuteronomic Literature*, 233–61. Louvain: Peeters, 1997.
Eynikel, Erik. "Prophecy and Fulfillment in the Deuteronomistic History: 1 Kgs 13; 2 Kgs 23, 16–18." In *Pentateuchal and Deuteronomistic Studies*, edited by C. Brekelmans and J. Lust, 227–37. BETL 94. Leuven: Leuven University Press, 1990.
Feldman, Louis H. "Josephus's Portrait of Hezekiah." *JBL* 111, no. 4 (1992): 597–610.
Feldman, Louis H. *Studies in Josephus' Rewritten Bible.* JSJSup 58. Leiden: Brill, 1998.
Firth, David G. *1 & 2 Samuel: An Introduction and Study Guide: A Kingdom Comes.* T&T Clark Study Guides to the Old Testament. London: Bloomsbury T&T Clark, 2017.
Firth, David G. "Shining the Lamp: The Rhetoric of 2 Samuel 5–24." *TynBul* 52 (2001): 203–24.
Fleishman, Y. "Ahab's Request and Naboth's Response." *Beit Miqra'* (2015): 92–116 (Hebrew).
Floriani, Ana. "Negotiating What Counts: Roles and Relationships, Texts and Contexts, Content and Meaning." *Linguistics and Education* 5 (1993): 241–74.
Forster, E. M. *Aspects of the Novel.* London: Penguin, 2005 (original publication 1927).
Franklin, Norma. "Jezreel before and after Jezebel." In *Israel in Transition: From Late Bronze II to Iron IIa (c. 1250–850 B.C.E.), Volume 1: The Archaeology*, edited by Lester L. Grabbe, 45–53. LHBOTS 491. London: Bloomsbury T&T Clark, 2010.
Franklin, N., J. Ebeling, and P. Guillaume. "An Ancient Winery in Jezreel." *Beit Miqra'* (2015): 9–18 (Hebrew).
Freedman, David Noel. "Dinah and Shechem: Tamar and Amnon." *Austin Seminary Bulletin Faculty Edition* 105 (1990): 51–63.
Fretheim, Terence E. *First and Second Kings.* WBCom. Louisville: Westminster John Knox, 1999.
Freud, Sigmund. "Das Unheimliche." In *Gesammelte Werke.* Vol. 12, edited by Anna Freud, 229–68. London: Imago, 1947.
Friedlander, Gerald, trans. *Pirḳê de Rabbi Eliezer.* London: Kegan Paul, Trench, Trubner & Co., 1916.
Friedman, Richard E. *The Exile and Biblical Narrative: The Formation of the Deuteronomistic and Priestly Works.* Chico, CA: Scholars Press, 1981.
Frisch, Amos. "The Exodus Motif in 1 Kings 1–14." *JSOT* 87 (2000): 3–21.
Frisch, Amos. "A Literary and Theological Analysis of the Account of Solomon's Sins (1 Kings 11:1–8)." *Shnaton* 11 (1997): 167–79 (Hebrew).
Frisch, Amos. "Midrashic Derivations of Solomon's Name in the Book of Kings." *Beit Mikra* 45 (1999): 84–96.
Frisch, Amos. "The Narrative of Solomon's Reign in the Book of Kings." PhD diss., Bar-Ilan University, 1986 (Hebrew).
Frisch, Amos. "Structure and its Significance: The Narrative of Solomon's Reign (1 Kings 1–12.24)." *JSOT* 51 (1991): 3–14.
Frisch, Amos. *Torn Asunder: The Division of the Kingdom Narrative in the Book of Kings.* Beer Sheva: Ben-Gurion University of the Negev Press, 2013 (Hebrew).
Fritz, Volkmar. *1 & 2 Kings*, translated by Anselm Hagedorn. A Continental Commentary. Minneapolis: Fortress, 2003.
Frolov, Serge. "Succession Narrative: A Document or a Phantom?" *JBL* 121 (2002): 81–124.

Frymer-Kensky, Tikvah. *Reading the Women of the Bible*. New York: Schocken Books, 2002.

Gaines, Janet Howe. "How Bad Was Jezebel?" *Bible History Daily* (2010). Reprinted in *BRev* October 2000 and June 2013, http://www.biblicalarchaeology.org/daily/people-cultures- in-the-bible/people-in-the-bible/how-bad-was-jezebel/2013.

Gaines, Janet Howe. *Music in the Old Bones: Jezebel through the Ages*. Carbondale: Southern Illinois University Press, 1999.

García-Treto, Francisco O. "The Fall of the House: A Carnivalesque Reading of 2 Kings 9 and 10." *JSOT* 15 (1990): 47–65. Reprinted in *Reading Between Texts: Intertextuality and the Hebrew Bible*, edited by Danna Nolan Fewell, 153–71. Louisville: Westminster John Knox, 1992.

Garsiel, Moshe. *The First Book of Samuel: A Literary Study of Comparative Structures, Analogies and Parallels*. Ramat-Gan: Revivim, 1985.

Garsiel, Moshe. "'King Solomon's Trip to Gibeon and His Dream." In *Ben-Yehudah Jubilee Volume*, edited by B. Lurie, 191–271. Tel Aviv: Israel Society for Biblical Research, 1981 (Hebrew).

Garsiel, Moshe. "A Literary Analysis of the Sinners and Their Punishment." *Beit Miqra'* (2015): 37–64 (Hebrew).

Garsiel, Moshe. "Puns upon Names as a Literary Device in 1 Kings 1–2." *Bib* 72 (1991): 378–86.

Gericke, Jaco. "Rethinking the 'Dual Causality Principle' in Old Testament Research—a Philosophical Perspective." *OTE* 28 (2015): 86–112.

Gesenius, Wilhelm. *Gesenius' Hebrew Grammar*. 2nd ed, edited and translated by E. Kautzsch. Oxford: Clarendon, 1910.

Gilmour, Rachelle. *Juxtaposition and the Elisha Cycle*. London: Bloomsbury T&T Clark, 2014.

Ginzberg, Louis. *The Legends of the Jews*. Vol. 4, translated by Henrietta Szold. Philadelphia: Jewish Publication Society, 1968.

Glover, Neil. "Elijah Versus the Narrative of Elijah: The Contest between the Prophet and the Word." *JSOT* 30 (2006): 449–62.

Goldingay, John. *1 and 2 Samuel for Everyone*. Louisville: Westminster John Knox, 2011.

Goldingay, John. *An Introduction to the Old Testament: Exploring Text, Approaches and Issues*. London: SPCK, 2016.

Gordon, Robert P. "David's Rise and Saul's Demise: Narrative Analogy in 1 Samuel 24–26." *TynBul* 31 (1980): 37–64.

Gravett, Sandie. "Reading 'Rape' in the Hebrew Bible: A Consideration of Language." *JSOT* 28 (2004): 279–99.

Gray, John. *I & II Kings*. OTL. 3rd ed. London: SCM, 1977.

Gray, Mark. "Amnon: A Chip off the Old Block? Rhetorical Strategy in 2 Samuel 13.7-15: The Rape of Tamar and the Humiliation of the Poor." *JSOT* 77 (1993): 39–54.

Greenberg, M. "תפלה." *Encyclopaedia Biblica*, vol. 8, cols. 896–922. Jerusalem: Bialik Institute, 1982 (Hebrew).

Gross, Walter. "Lying Prophet and Disobedient Man of God in 1 Kings 13: Role Analysis as an Instrument of Theological Interpretation of an OT Narrative Text" (translated by Robert Robinson). *Semeia* 15 (1979): 97–129.

Guillaume, Phillippe. "Naboth the Nabob: A View from Assyrian Jezreel." *UF* 46 (2015): 161–82.

Guillaume, Phillippe. "Naboth's Vineyard." *Bible Odyssey* (cited 1 January 19), http://www.bibleodyssey.org/en/passages/main-articles/naboths-vineyard-1-kgs-21.aspx.

Gunn, David M. "Bathsheba Goes Bathing in Hollywood: Words, Images and Social Locations." *Semeia* 74 (1996): 75–101.
Gunn, David M. *The Story of King David*. Sheffield: JSOT Press, 1978.
Hackett, J. A. "Women's Studies and the Hebrew Bible." In *The Future of Biblical Studies*, edited by R. E. Friedman and H. G. M. Williamson, 141–64. Atlanta: Scholars Press, 1987.
Hadjiev, Tchavdar. S. "Elijah's Alleged Megalomania: Reading Strategies for Composite Texts, with 1 Kings 19 as an Example." *JSOT* 39 (2015): 433–49.
Hadjiev, Tchavdar. S. "The King and the Reader: Hermeneutical Reflections on 1 Kings 20–21." *TynBul* 66 (2015): 63–74.
Hakola, Raimo. "A Character Resurrected: Lazarus in the Fourth Gospel and Afterward." In *Characterization in the Gospels: Reconceiving Narrative Criticism*, edited by David Rhoads and Kari Syreeni, 223–63. JSNTSup 184. Sheffield: Sheffield Academic, 1999.
Halpern, Baruch. *The First Historians: The Hebrew Bible and History*. San Francisco: Harper & Row, 1988.
Halpern, Baruch. "Why Manasseh Is Blamed for the Babylonian Exile: The Evolution of a Biblical Tradition." *VT* 48, no. 4 (1998): 473–514.
Halpern, Baruch and David S. Vanderhooft. "The Editions of Kings in the 7th–6th Centuries BCE." *HUCA* 62 (1991): 179–244.
Hamilton, Victor P. *Handbook on the Historical Books: Joshua, Judges, Ruth, Samuel, Kings, Chronicles, Ezra–Nehemiah, Esther*. Grand Rapids: Baker Academic, 2001.
Handy, L. K. "The Role of Huldah in Josiah's Cult Reform." *ZAW* 106 (1994): 40–53.
Handy, L. K. "Speaking of Babies in the Temple." *Proceedings of the Eastern Great Lakes and Midwest Biblical Societies* 8 (1988): 155–65.
Hays, Christopher B. with Peter Machinist. "Assyria and the Assyrians." In *The World around the Old Testament: The People and Places of the Ancient Near East*, edited by Bill T. Arnold and Brent A. Strawn, 31–105. Grand Rapids: Baker Academic, 2016.
Hazleton, Lesley. *Jezebel: The Untold Story of the Bible's Harlot Queen*. New York: Doubleday, 2007.
Henry, Matthew. *An Exposition of the Old and New Testaments*. Philadelphia: Alexander Towar, and Hogan & Thompson, 1833.
Hens-Piazza, Gina. *1–2 Kings*. AOTC. Nashville: Abingdon, 2006.
Herrmann, W. "Baal." *DDD*, 132–9.
Hill, Scott D. "The Local Hero in Palestine in Comparative Perspective." In *Elijah and Elisha in Socioliterary Perspective*, edited by Robert B. Coote, 37–73. Atlanta: Scholars Press, 1992.
Hobbs, T. R. *2 Kings*. WBC 13. Waco, TX, Word, 1985.
Holstein, Jay A. "The Case of *'îš hā'ĕlōhîm* Reconsidered: Philological Analysis versus Historical Reconstruction." *HUCA* 48 (1977): 69–81.
hooks, bell. "Keepers of Hope." In *Teaching Community*, 105–16. New York: Routledge, 2007.
Hoover, Tamis Renteria. "The Elijah/Elisha Stories: A Sociocultural Analysis of Prophets and People in Ninth Century B.C.E. Israel." In *Elijah and Elisha in Socioliterary Perspective*, edited by Robert Coote, 75–136. Atlanta, GA: Scholars Press, 1992.
Hoppe, L. J. "The Death of Josiah and the Meaning of Deuteronomy." *Liber Annuus* 48 (1998): 31–47.
Hutcheon, Linda. *The Poetics of Postmodernism: History, Theory, Fiction*. New York: Routledge, 1988.

Hyers, Conrad. *And God Created Laughter: The Bible as Divine Comedy.* Atlanta: John Knox, 1987.
Iser, Wolfgang. "The Reading Process: A Phenomenological Approach." *New Literary History* 3 (1972): 279–99.
Jackson, Melissa. *Comedy and Feminist Interpretation of the Hebrew Bible: A Subversive Collaboration.* Oxford: Oxford University Press, 2012.
Jang, Sehoon. "Is Hezekiah a Success or a Failure? The Literary Function of Isaiah's Prediction at the End of the Royal Narratives in the Book of Isaiah." *JSOT* 42, no. 1 (2017): 117–35.
Janzen, David. "The Sins of Josiah and Hezekiah: A Synchronic Reading of the Final Chapters of Kings." *JSOT* 37 (2013): 349–70.
Japheth, Sara. *I & II Chronicles.* OTL. Louisville: John Knox, 1993.
Jeon, Yong Ho. "The Retroactive Re-evaluation Technique with Pharaoh's Daughter and the Nature of Solomon's Corruption in 1 Kings 1–12." *TynBul* 62 (2011): 15–40.
Jobling, David. *The Sense of Biblical Narrative, II. Structural Analyses in the Hebrew Bible.* JSOTSup 39. Sheffield: JSOT Press 1986.
Jones, Gwilym H. *1 and 2 Kings.* Vol. 2. NCB. Grand Rapids: Eerdmans, 1984.
Jones, Gwilym H. *The Nathan Narratives.* JSOTSup, 80; Sheffield: Sheffield Academic, 1990.
Jones, Paul Hedley. "Anonymous Prophets and Archetypal Kings: Reading 1 Kings 13." PhD diss., University of Durham, 2016.
Jones, Paul Hedley. Review of *Portrait of the Kings: The Davidic Prototype in Deuteronomistic Poetics*, by Alison L. Joseph. *VT* 67, no. 1 (2017): 153–7.
Joseph, Alison L. *Portrait of the Kings: The Davidic Prototype in Deuteronomistic Poetics.* Minneapolis: Fortress, 2015.
Kaufmann, Yehezkel. *From the Secrets of the Biblical Art: A Collection of Essays.* Tel Aviv: Dvir, 1966 Hebrew.
Keen, Suzanne. *Empathy and the Novel.* New York: Oxford University Press, 2007.
Keil, Carl Friedrich. *The Book of the Kings, Biblical Commentary on the Old Testament*, translated by J. Martin. Grand Rapids: Eerdmans, 1950.
Keil, Carl Friedrich and F. Delitzsch. *Biblical Commentary on the Books of Samuel*, translated by James Martin. Edinburgh: T. & T. Clark, 1868.
Kermode, Frank. "New Ways with Biblical Stories." In *Parable and Story in Judaism and Christianity*, edited by Clemens Thoma and Michael Wyschogrod, 121–35. Mahwah, NJ: Paulist Press, 1989.
Keulen, P. S. F. van. "The Meaning of the Phrase *WN'SPT 'L-QBRTYK BŠLWM* in 2 Kings XXII 20." *VT* 46 (1996): 256–9.
Keys, Gillian. *The Wages of Sin: A Reappraisal of the "Succession Narrative."* JSOTSup, 221. Sheffield: Sheffield Academic, 1996.
Kim, Uriah. "Uriah the Hittite: A (Con)Text of Struggle for Identity." *Semeia* 90/91 (2002): 69–85.
King, Geoff. "'Killingly Funny': Mixing Modalities in New Hollywood's Comedy-With-Violence." In *New Hollywood Violence*, edited by Steven Jay Schneider, 126–43. New York: Manchester University Press, 2004.
Kirk-Duggan, Cheryl. "Slingshots, Ships, and Personal Psychosis: Murder, Sexual Intrigue, and Power in the Lives of David and Othello." In *Pregnant Passion: Gender, Sex and Violence in the Bible*, edited by Cheryl Kirk-Duggan, 37–70. Leiden: Brill, 2004.
Kissling, Paul J. *Reliable Characters in the Primary History: Profiles of Moses, Joshua, Elijah, and Elisha.* JSOTSup 224. Sheffield: Sheffield Academic, 1996.

Kitz, Anne Marie. "Naboth's Vineyard after Mari and Amarna." *JBL* 134 (2015): 529–45.
Klement, Herbert H. *II Samuel 21–24: Context, Structure and Meaning in the Samuel Conclusion*. EUS, XXIII/682. Frankfurt am Main: Peter Lang, 2000.
Klopfenstein, Martin. "1. Könige 13." In *ΠAPPHΣIA: K. Barth zum achtzigsten Geburtstag*, edited by E. Busch, J. Fangmeier, and M. Geiger, 639–72. Zurich: EVZ-Verlag Zurich, 1966.
Knight, Douglas A. "Moral Values and Literary Traditions: The Case of the Succession Narrative (2 Kings 9–20; 1 Kings 1–2)." *Semeia* 34 (1985): 7–23.
Knoppers, Gary N. "Theories of the Redaction(s) of Kings." In *The Books of Kings: Sources, Composition, Historiography and Reception*, edited by A. Lemaire and B. Halpern, 69–88. Leiden: Brill, 2010.
Knoppers, Gary N. "'There Was None Like Him': Incomparability in the Book of Kings." *CBQ* 54 (1992): 411–31.
Knoppers, Gary N. *Two Nations Under God: The Deuteronomistic History of Solomon and the Dual Monarchies; Volume 2: The Reign of Jeroboam, the Fall of Israel, and the Reign of Josiah*. Atlanta: Scholars Press, 1993.
Koenig, Sara. *Bathsheba Survives*. Columbia: University of South Carolina Press, 2018.
Koenig, Sara. *Isn't This Bathsheba? A Study in Characterization*. Eugene, OR: Pickwick, 2011.
Konkel, A. H. *1 & 2 Kings*. Grand Rapids: Zondervan, 2006.
Koosed, Jennifer L. "Death of Jezebel." *Bible Odyssey*. (cited 1 January 2019), http://www.bibleodyssey.org/people/related-articles/death-of-jezebel.aspx.
Kuhl, Curt. "Die 'Wiederaufnahme'—ein literarkritisches Prinzip?" *ZAW* 64, no. 1 (2009): 1–11.
Kren, Thomas. "Looking at Louis XII's Bathsheba." In *A Masterpiece Constructed: The Hours of Louis XII*, edited by Thomas Kren and Mark Evans, 43–61. Los Angeles: The J. Paul Getty Museum, 2005.
Kuloba, Wabayanga Robert. "Athaliah of Judah (2 Kings 11): A Political Anomaly or an Ideological Victim?" In *Looking through a Glass Bible: Postdisciplinary Biblical Interpretations from the Glasgow School*, edited by A. K. M. Adam and Samuel Tongue, 139–52. Leiden: Brill, 2014.
Lamb, David T. *Prostitutes and Polygamists: A Look at Love, Old Testament Style*. Grand Rapids: Zondervan, 2015.
Lamb, David T. *Righteous Jehu and his Evil Heirs: The Deuteronomist's Negative Perspective on Dynastic Succession*. Oxford: Oxford University Press, 2007.
Lange, John Peter. *Commentary on the Holy Scriptures: Critical, Doctrinal and Homiletical: Samuel*, translated by Philip Schaff. Grand Rapids: Zondervan, 1877.
Lasine, Stuart. "'Everything Belongs To Me': Holiness, Danger, and Divine Kingship in the Post-Genesis World." *JSOT* 35 (2010): 31–62.
Lasine, Stuart. "Fiction, Falsehood, and Reality in Hebrew Scripture." *HS* 25 (1984): 24–40.
Lasine, Stuart. "'Go in peace' or 'Go to Hell'? Elisha, Naaman and the Meaning of Monotheism in 2 Kings 5." *SJOT* 25, no. 1 (2011): 3–28.
Lasine, Stuart. "Holy Men in Space." In *Constructions of Space III: Biblical Spatiality and the Sacred*, edited by Jorunn Økland, Cor de Vos, and Karen Wennell, 3–22. LHBOTS 540. New York: Bloomsbury T&T Clark, 2016.
Lasine, Stuart. *Jonah and the Human Condition: Life and Death in Yahweh's World*. LHBOTS. London: Bloomsbury T&T Clark, forthcoming.

Lasine, Stuart. "Manasseh as Villain and Scapegoat." In *New Literary Criticism and the Hebrew Bible*, edited by J. Cheryl Exum and David J. A. Clines, 163–83. Sheffield: JSOT Press, 1993.

Lasine, Stuart. "Matters of Life and Death: The Story of Elijah and the Widow's Son in Comparative Perspective." *BibInt* 12 (2004): 117–44.

Lasine, Stuart. *Weighing Hearts: Character, Judgment, and the Ethics of Reading the Bible*. LHBOTS 568. London: T&T Clark, 2012.

Lee, Kyung Sook. "1 and 2 Kings." In *Global Bible Commentary*, edited by Daniel Patte, José Severino Croatto, and Teresa Okure, 105–18. Nashville, TN: Abingdon, 2004.

Leithart, Peter J. *1 & 2 Kings*. Grand Rapids: Brazos, 2006.

Lemaire, A. "Wisdom in Solomonic Historiography." In *Wisdom in Ancient Israel: Essays in Honour of J. A. Emerton*, edited by J. Day et al., 106–18. Cambridge: Cambridge University Press, 1995.

Lemke, Werner E. "The Way of Obedience: I Kings 13 and the Structure of the Deuteronomistic History." In *Magnalia Dei: The Mighty Acts of God. Festschrift for G. E. Wright*, edited by F. M. Cross, W. E. Lemke, and P. D. Miller, Jr., 301–26. Garden City: Doubleday, 1976.

LeMon, Joel M. "Egypt and the Egyptians." In *The World around the Old Testament: The People and Places of the Ancient Near East*, edited by Bill T. Arnold and Brent A. Strawn, 169–96. Grand Rapids: Baker Academic, 2016.

Leneman, Helen. *Love, Lust and Lunacy: The Stories of David and Saul in Music*. Sheffield: Sheffield Phoenix, 2010.

Leneman, Helen. "Portrayals of Power in the Stories of Delilah and Bathsheba: Seduction in Song." In *Culture, Entertainment and the Bible*, edited by George Aichele, 139–55. Sheffield: Sheffield Academic, 2000.

Létourneau, Anne. "Bathing Beauty: Concealment of Bathsheba's Rape and Counter-Power in 2 Sam 11:1–5." Paper presented at Society of Biblical Literature Meeting, Atlanta, GA, November 21, 2015.

Liddon, H. P. *Sermons on Old Testament Subjects*. London: Longmans, Green & Co., 1891.

Lifton, Robert Jay. *Thought Reform and the Psychology of Totalism: A Study of "Brainwashing" in China*. New York: Norton, 1961.

Lipka, Hilary. "Shaved Beards and Bared Buttocks: Shame and the Undermining of Masculine Performance in Biblical Texts." In *Being a Man: Negotiating Ancient Constructs of Masculinity*, edited by Ilona Zsolnay, 176–97. London: Routledge, 2017.

Liver, J. "The Book of the Acts of Solomon." *Bib* 48 (1967): 75–101.

Lohfink, N. "The Cult Reform of Josiah of Judah: 2 Kings 22–23 as a Source for the History of Israelite Religion." In *Ancient Israelite Religion: Essays in Honor of Frank Moore Cross*, edited by P. D. Miller, Jr., P. D. Hanson and S. D. McBride, 459–75. Philadelphia: Fortress, 1987.

Long, Burke O. *1 Kings with an Introduction to the Historical Literature*. FOTL 9. Grand Rapids: Eerdmans, 1984.

Long, Burke O. *2 Kings with an Introduction to Historical Literature*. FOTL 10. Grand Rapids: Eerdmans, 1991.

Löwenclau, Ilse von. "Der Prophet Nathan im Zwielicht von theologischer Deutung und Historie." In *Werden und Wirken des Alten Testaments: FS Westermann*, edited by Rainer Albertz et al., 202–15. Göttingen: Vandenhoeck & Ruprecht, 1980.

Lowery, R. H. *The Reforming Kings: Cult and Society in First Temple Judah*. Sheffield: JSOT Press, 1991.

Lumby, J. Rawson. *The First Book of the Kings.* Cambridge: Cambridge University Press, 1898.
Luther, Martin. *Luther's Works: Lectures on Genesis, Chapters 38–44*, edited by Jaroslav Pelikan and Walter Hansen. St. Louis: Concordia, 1965.
Maier, Walter A. "Reflections on the Ministry of Elijah." *CTQ* 80 (2016): 63–80.
Marcus, David. "David the Deceiver and David the Dupe." *Prooftexts* 6 (1986): 163–71.
Marcus, David. *From Balaam to Jonah: Anti-Prophetic Satire in the Hebrew Bible.* Brown Judaic Studies 301. Atlanta: Scholars Press, 1995.
Mazar, A. *Archaeology of the Land of the Bible. 10,000–586 B.C.E.* New York: Doubleday, 1992.
McCarter, P. Kyle, Jr. *2 Samuel.* AB 9. Garden City, NY: Doubleday, 1984.
McCarthy, Dennis. "II Samuel 7 and the Structure of the Deuteronomistic History." *JBL* 84 (1965): 131–8.
McGraw, Peter A. and Caleb Warren. "Benign Violations: Making Immoral Behavior Funny." *Psychological Science* 21 (2010): 1141–9.
McGraw, Peter A. and Joel Warner. *The Humor Code: A Global Search for What Makes Things Funny.* New York: Simon & Schuster, 2015.
McKay, J. *Religion in Judah under the Assyrians: 732–609 BC.* London: SCM, 1973.
McKenzie, Steven L. *The Chronicler's Use of the Deuteronomistic History.* HSM 33. Atlanta: Scholars Press, 1985.
McKenzie, Steven L. *King David: A Biography.* New York: Oxford University Press, 2000.
McKenzie, Steven L. *The Trouble with Kings: The Composition of the Book of Kings in the Deuteronomistic History.* VTSup 42. Leiden: Brill, 1991.
McKinlay, Judith E. *Reframing Her: Biblical Women in Postcolonial Focus.* Bible in the Modern World 1. Sheffield: Sheffield Phoenix, 2004.
Meyer, Wulf-Uwe. "Die Rolle von Überraschung im Attributionsprozeß." *Psychologische Rundschau* 39 (1988): 136–47.
Miller, J. Maxwell, and John H. Hayes. *A History of Ancient Israel and Judah.* 2nd ed. Philadelphia: Westminster John Knox, 2006.
Miscall, Peter. "The Jacob and Joseph Stories as Analogies." *JSOT* 6 (1978): 28–40.
Miscall, Peter. *The Workings of Old Testament Narrative.* Semeia Studies. Chico, CA: Scholars Press, 1983.
Moberly, R. W. L. *The Bible in a Disenchanted Age: The Enduring Possibility of Christian Faith.* Grand Rapids: Baker Academic, 2018.
Moberly, R. W. L. *The Bible, Theology, and Faith: A Study of Abraham and Jesus.* Cambridge: Cambridge University Press, 2000.
Moberly, R. W. L. "Miracles in the Hebrew Bible." In *The Cambridge Companion to Miracles*, edited by Graham H. Twelftree, 57–74. Cambridge: Cambridge University Press, 2011.
Montgomery, J. A. and H. S. Gehman. *A Critical and Exegetical Commentary on the Book of Kings.* ICC. Edinburgh: T. & T. Clark, 1951.
Morreall, John. *Comic Relief: A Comprehensive Philosophy of Humor.* Hoboken, NJ: Wiley Blackwell, 2009.
Morreall, John. *The Philosophy of Laughter and Humor.* Albany, NY: State University of New York Press, 1987.

Mowrey, Merlyn E. "The Religious Hero and the Escape from Evil: A Feminist Challenge to Ernest Becker's Religious Mystification." In *Death and Denial: Interdisciplinary Perspectives on the Legacy of Ernest Becker*, edited by Daniel Liechty, 269–80. Westport, CT: Praeger, 2002.
Mullen, E. Theodore. "Crime and Punishment: The Sins of the King and the Despoliation of the Treasuries." *CBQ* 54 (1992): 231–48.
Mullen, E. Theodore. *Narrative History and Ethnic Boundaries: The Deuteronomistic Historian and the Creation of Israelite National Identity*. SBL Semeia Studies. Atlanta, GA: Scholars Press, 1993.
Na'aman, Nadav. "The Deuteronomist and Voluntary Servitude to Foreign Powers." *JSOT* 65 (1997): 37–53.
Nahkola, Aulikki. *Double Narratives in the Old Testament: The Foundations of Method in Biblical Criticism*. Berlin: de Gruyter, 2001.
Nell, Victor. "Mythic Structures in Narrative: The Domestication of Immortality." In *Narrative Impact: Social and Cognitive Foundations*, edited by Melanie C. Green, Jeffrey Strange, and Timothy Brock, 17–37. Mahwah, NJ: Erlbaum, 2002.
Nelson, R. D. *The Double Redaction of the Deuteronomistic History*. Sheffield: JSOT Press, 1981.
Nelson, R. D. *First and Second Kings*. Interpretation. Louisville: John Knox, 1987.
Newkirk, Matthew. "Reconsidering the Role of Deception in Solomon's Ascent to the Throne." *JETS* 57, no. 4 (2014): 703–13.
Newsom, Carol A. "Narrative Ethics, Character, and the Prose Tale of Job." In *Character and Scripture: Moral Formation, Community, and Biblical Interpretation*, edited by W. P. Brown, 121–34. Grand Rapids: Eerdmans, 2002.
Nicol, George. "The Alleged Rape of Bathsheba: Some Observations On Ambiguity in Biblical Narrative." *JSOT* 73 (1997): 43–54.
Nicol, George. "Bathsheba: A Clever Woman?" *ExpTim* 99 (1988): 360–3.
Noth, Martin. *The Deuteronomistic History*. Sheffield: JSOT Press, 1981.
Noth, Martin. *Könige 1. 1. Könige 1–16*. BKAT. Neukirchen-Vluyn: Neukirchener Verlag, 1968.
Noth, Martin. *Überlieferungsgeschichtliche Studien. Die Sammelnden und Bearbeitenden Geschischtswerke im Alten Testement*. Tübingen: Max Niemeyer, 1957.
Oatley, Keith. *Such Stuff as Dreams: The Psychology of Fiction*. West Sussex, UK: Wiley-Blackwell, 2011.
Okuro Ojwang, Gilbert. "Juridical Impotence in the Naboth Story in the Context of Kenya's New Land Laws." In *Texts@Contexts: Samuel, Kings and Chronicles, Vol. 1*, edited by Athalya Brenner-Idan and Archie C. C. Lee, 65–94. London: Bloomsbury T&T Clark, 2017.
Okyere, Kojo. "An Empowered People: A Literary Reading of 1 Kings 12:1-20." *MJTM* 14 (2012–2013): 124–47.
Olley, John W. *The Message of Kings: God Is Present*. BST. Downers Grove: InterVarsity, 2011.
Organ, Barbara E. "'The Man Who Would Be King': Irony in the Story of Rehoboam." In *From Babel to Babylon: Essays on Biblical History and Literature in Honour of Brian Peckham*, edited by Joyce Rilett Wood, John E. Harvey, and Mark Leuchter, 124–32. New York: T&T Clark, 2006.
Oswald, Wolfgang. *Nathan der Prophet: Ein Untersuchung zu 2 Samuel 7 und 12 und 1 Könige 1*. AThANT 94. Zurich: Theologischer Verlag, 2008.
Otto, Eckart. *Theologische Ethik des Alten Testaments*. Stuttgart: Kohlhammer, 1994.

Overholt, Thomas. *Cultural Anthropology and the Old Testament.* Minneapolis: Fortress, 1996.
Parker, Simon. "Jezebel's Reception of Jehu." *Maarav* 1 (1978–79): 67–78.
Paynter, Helen. "Ahab—Heedless Father, Sullen Son: Humour and Intertextuality in 1 Kings 21." *JSOT* 41 (2017): 451–74.
Paynter, Helen. *Reduced Laughter: Seriocomic Features and their Functions in the Book of Kings.* BibInt 142. Leiden: Brill, 2016.
Person, Raymond F. Jr. "A Reassessment of *Wiederaufnahme* from the Perspective of Conversation Analysis." *BZ* 43, no. 2 (1999): 239–48.
Pinker, Aron. "Job's Perspectives on Death." *JBQ* 35, no. 2 (2007): 73–85.
Pippin, Tina. "Jezebel Re-Vamped." In *A Feminist Companion to Samuel and Kings*, ed. A. Brenner, 196–206. Sheffield: Sheffield Academic, 1994.
Piven, Jerry S. *Death and Delusion: A Freudian Analysis of Mortal Terror.* Greenwich, CT: Information Age Publishing, 2004.
Plein, Ina. "Erwägungen zur Überlieferung von 1Reg. 11,26–14,20." *ZAW* 78 (1966): 8–24.
Porten, Bezalel. "The Structure and Theme of the Solomon Narrative (1 Kings 3–11)." *HUCA* 38 (1967): 93–128.
Provan, Iain W. *1 and Kings.* NIBC. Peabody: Hendrickson, 1995.
Provan, Iain W. *Hezekiah and the Books of Kings: A Contribution to the Debate about the Composition of the Deuteronomistic History.* Berlin: de Gruyter, 1988.
Provan, Iain, V. Philips Long, and Tremper Longman III. *A Biblical History of Israel.* 2nd ed. Louisville: Westminster John Knox, 2015.
Pruin, Dagmar. *Geschichten und Geschichte: Isebel als literarische und historische Gestalt.* OBO 222. Fribourg: Academic Press; Göttingen: Vandenhoeck & Ruprecht, 2006.
Rad, Gerhard von. "The Deuteronomistic Theology of History in the Books of Kings', *Studies in Deuteronomy*, 74–91. SBT 1/9. Translated by David Stalker. London: SCM, 1953.
Rad, Gerhard von. *Old Testament Theology.* Edinburgh: T. & T. Clark, 1962.
Rad, Gerhard von. *Theologie des Alten Testaments.* Vol. 1. Munich, 1957.
Revell, E. J. *The Designation of the Individual: Expressive Usage in Biblical Narrative.* Kampen: Kok Pharos, 1996.
Rice, Gene. *1 Kings: Nations Under God.* ITC. Grand Rapids: Eerdmans, 1990.
Rimmon-Kenan, Shlomith. *Narrative Fiction.* 2nd ed. London: Routledge, 2002.
Robinson, Joseph. *The First Book of Kings.* The Cambridge Bible Commentary. Cambridge: Cambridge University, 1972.
Rofé, Alexander. "Elders or Youngsters? Critical Remarks on 1 Kings 12." In *One God–One Cult–One Nation: Archaeological and Biblical Perspectives*, edited by Reinhard G. Kratz, Hermann Spieckermann, 79–89. Berlin: de Gruyter, 2010.
Rofé, Alexander. "Naboth's Vineyard: The Story's Origin and Its Purpose." *Mishpatim* 14 (1985): 521–6 (Hebrew).
Rofé, Alexander. *The Prophetical Stories: The Narratives about the Prophets in the Hebrew Bible, their Literary Types and History*, translated by D. Levy. Jerusalem: Magnes, 1988.
Rofé, Alexander. "The Vineyard of Naboth: The Origin and Message of the Story." *VT* 38 (1988): 104–89.
Römer, Thomas. *The So-called Deuteronomistic History: A Sociological, Historical and Literary Introduction.* London: T&T Clark, 2005.

Rosenberg, A. J., trans. and ed. *Kings II*. Mikraoth Gedoloth. New York: Judaica Press, 1989.
Russell, Stephen C. "Ideologies of Attachment in the Story of Naboth's Vineyard." *BTB* 44 (2014): 29–39.
Schenker, Adrian. "Jeroboam and the Division of the Kingdom in the Ancient Septuagint." In *Israel Constructs its History*, edited by Albert de Pury, Thomas Römer, and Jean-Daniel Macchi, 193–236. JSOTSup 34. Sheffield: Sheffield Academic, 2000.
Schenker, Adrian. "Jeroboam's Rise and Fall in the Hebrew and Greek Bible. Methodological Reflections on a Recent Article…" *JSJ* 38 (2008): 367–73.
Schiff, R. "The Stylistic Means for the Ethical Evaluation of the Characters in the Narratives of the Book of II Samuel." M. A. thesis, Bar-Ilan University, 1977 (Hebrew).
Schipper, Jeremy. "Hezekiah, Manasseh, and Dynastic or Transgenerational Punishment." In *Soundings in Kings: Perspectives and Methods in Contemporary Scholarship*, edited by Mark Leuchter and Klaus-Peter Adam, 81–105. Minneapolis: Fortress, 2010.
Schmidt, Brian. Review of Phillip S. Johnston, *Shades of Sheol: Death and the Afterlife in the Old Testament*. RBL (2003). Online: https://www.bookreviews.org/pdf/2947_3084.pdf.
Scholz, Suzanne. *Sacred Witness: Rape in the Hebrew Bible*. Minneapolis: Fortress, 2010.
Seibert, Eric. *Subversive Scribes and the Solomonic Narrative: A Rereading of 1 Kings 1–11*. New York: T&T Clark, 2006.
Seitz, Christopher R. *Zion's Final Destiny: The Development of the Book of Isaiah: A Reassessment of Isaiah 36–39*. Minneapolis: Fortress, 1991.
Seow, Choon-Leong. "The First and Second Book of Kings." In *The New Interpreter's Bible*, Volume 3, 1–295. Nashville: Abingdon, 1999.
Sergi, Omer. "The Composition of Nathan's Oracle to David (2 Samuel 7:1–17) as a Reflection of Royal Judahite Ideology." *JBL* 129, no. 2 (2010): 261–79.
Shaw, Charles S. "The Sins of Rehoboam: The Purpose of 3 Kingdoms 12.24a-z." *JSOT* 73 (1997): 55–64.
Shemesh, Yael. "Elisha and the Miraculous Jug of Oil." *JHS* 8, no. 4 (2008): 1–18.
Shemesh, Yael. "The Elisha Stories as Saints' Legends." *JHS* 8, no. 5 (2008): 2–41.
Shemesh, Yael. "A Gendered View." *Beit Miqra'* (2015): 117–40 (Hebrew).
Shulman, A. "The Function of the 'Jussive' and 'Indicative' Imperfect Forms in Biblical Hebrew Prose." *ZAH* 13 (2000): 168–80.
Simon, Uriel. "I Kings 13: A Prophetic Sign—Denial and Persistence." *HUCA* 47 (1976): 81–117.
Simon, Uriel. "A Prophetic Sign Overcomes Those Who Would Defy It: The King of Israel, the Prophet from Bethel, and the Man of God from Judah." In *Reading Prophetic Narratives*, translated by Lenn. J. Schramm, 130–54. Bloomington: Indiana University Press, 1997.
Simon, Uriel. *Reading Prophetic Narratives*, translated by Lenn J. Schramm. Indiana Studies in Biblical Literature. Indianapolis: Indiana University Press, 1997.
Skehan, Patrick W. and Alexander A. Di Lella. *The Wisdom of Ben Sira*. AB 39. New York: Doubleday, 1987.
Slotki, I. W. *Kings: Hebrew Text & English Translation with an Introduction and Commentary*. London: Soncino, 1950.
Smagorinsky, Peter. "If Meaning Is Constructed, What Is It Made From? Toward a Cultural Theory of Reading." *Review of Educational Research* 71, no. 1 (2001): 133–69
Small, Brian C. *The Characterization of Jesus in the Book of Hebrews*. Leiden: Brill, 2014.

Smelik, Klaas A. D. "The Portrayal of King Manasseh: A Literary Analysis of II Kings Xxi and II Chronicles Xxiii." In *Converting the Past: Studies in Ancient Israelite and Moabite Historiography*, 129–89. Oudtestamentische Studiën. Leiden: Brill, 1992.

Smith, Richard G. *The Fate of Justice and Righteousness During David's Reign: Rereading the Court History and Its Ethics according to 2 Samuel 8:15b–20:26*. LHBOTS 508. New York/London: T&T Clark, 2009.

Solomon, Sheldon, Jeff Greenberg, and Tom Pyszczynski. "The Cultural Animal: Twenty Years of Terror Management Theory and Research." In *Handbook of Experimental Existential Psychology*, edited by Jeff Greenberg, Sander Koole, and Tom Pyszczynski, 13–34. New York: Guilford Press, 2004.

Solvang, Elna. *A Woman's Place is in the House: Royal Women of Judah and their Involvement in the House of David*. Sheffield: Sheffield Academic, 2003.

Spieckermann, Hermann. *Juda unter Assur in der Sargonidenzeit*. Göttingen: Vandenhoeck & Ruprecht, 1982.

Spivak, Gayatri Chakravorty. "Can the Subaltern Speak?" In *Colonial Discourse and Post-Colonial Theory: A Reader*, edited by Patrick Williams and Laura Chrisman, 66–111. New York: Columbia University Press, 1994.

Stamm, J. J. "Der Name des Königs Salomo." *ThZ* 16 (1960): 285–97.

Stanton, Cady. *The Woman's Bible*. Seattle: Coalition Task Force on Women and Religion, 1974.

Stavrakopoulou, Francesca. "The Blackballing of Manasseh." In *Good Kings and Bad Kings: The Kingdom of Judah in the Seventh Century BCE*, edited by Lester L. Grabbe, 248–63. London: T&T Clark, 2005.

Stavrakopoulou, Francesca. *King Manasseh and Child Sacrifice: Biblical Distortions of Historical Realities*. Berlin: de Gruyter, 2004.

Sternberg, Meir. *The Poetics of Biblical Narrative: Ideological Literature and the Drama of Reading*. Bloomington: Indiana University Press, 1985.

Steussy, Marti. *David: Biblical Portraits of Power*. Columbia: University of South Carolina Press, 1999.

Stipp, Hermann-Josef. "Vier Gestalten einer Totenerweckungserzählung (1 Kön 17,17-24; 2 Kön 4,8-37; Apg 9,36-42; Apg 20,7-12)." *Bib* 80 (1999): 43–77.

Stone, Ken. "1 and 2 Kings." In *The Queer Bible Commentary*, edited by Deryn Guest, 222–50. London: SCM, 2006.

Sun, Chloe. "Bathsheba Transformed: From Silence to Voice." In *Mirrored Reflections: Reframing Biblical Characters*, edited by Young Lee Hertig and Chloe Sun, 30–42. Eugene: Wipf & Stock, 2010.

Sweeney, Marvin A. *I & II Kings*. OTL. Louisville: Westminster John Knox, 2007.

Sweeney, Marvin A. *King Josiah of Judah: The Lost Messiah of Israel*. Oxford: Oxford University Press, 2001.

Sweeney, Marvin A. "King Manasseh of Judah and the Problem of Theodicy in the Deuteronomistic History." In *Good Kings and Bad Kings: The Kingdom of Judah in the Seventh Century BCE*, edited by Lester L. Grabbe, 264–78. London: T&T Clark, 2005.

Sweeney, Marvin A. "A Reassessment of the Masoretic and Septuagint Versions of the Jeroboam Narratives in 1 Kings/3 Kingdoms 11–14." *JSJ* 38 (2007): 165–95.

Talshir, Zipora. *The Alternative Story. 3 Kingdoms 12:24 A–Z*. Jerusalem Biblical Studies 6. Jerusalem: Simor, 1993.

Tatar, Maria. *The Hard Facts of the Grimms' Fairy Tales*. 2nd ed. Princeton: Princeton University Press, 2003.

Tierney, R. J. and P. D. Pearson. "Towards a Composing Model of Reading." *Language Arts* 60 (1983): 568–80.
Todorov, Tzvetan. *The Fantastic: A Structural Approach to a Literary Genre*, translated by Richard Howard. Ithaca, NY: Cornell University Press, 1975.
Trible, Phyllis. "Exegesis for Storytellers and Other Strangers." *JBL* 114 (1995): 3–19.
Tsumura, David Toshio. *The First Book of Samuel*. NICOT. Grand Rapids: Eerdmans, 2007.
Vail, Kenneth E., III, Zachary Rothschild, Dave R. Weise, Sheldon Solomon, Tom Pyszczynski, and Jeff Greenberg. "A Terror Management Analysis of the Psychological Functions of Religion." *Personality and Social Psychology Review* 14, no. 1 (2010): 84–94.
Vanderhooft, David S. "Babylonia and the Babylonians." In *The World around the Old Testament: The People and Places of the Ancient Near East*, edited by Bill T. Arnold and Brent A. Strawn, 107–37. Grand Rapids: Baker Academic, 2016.
Van Peer, Willie, Anna Chesnokova, and Matthias Springer. "Distressful Empathy in Reading Literature: The Case For Terror Management Theory?" *Science and Education* 26, no. 1 (2017): 33–41.
Van Seters, John. "The Deuteronomistic History: Can it Avoid Death by Redaction?" In *The Future of the Deuteronomistic History*, edited by Thomas Römer, 213–22. BETL 147. Leuven: Leuven University Press, 2000.
Van Seters, John. "On Reading the Story of the Man of God from Judah in 1 Kings 13." In *The Labour of Reading: Desire, Alienation, and Biblical Interpretation*, edited by Robert C. Culley et al., 225–34. Atlanta: Scholars Press, 1999.
Van Winkle, D. W. "1 Kings XII 25–XIII 34: Jeroboam's Cultic Innovations and the Man of God from Judah." *VT* 46 (1996): 101–14.
Van Winkle, D. W. "1 Kings XIII: True and False Prophecy." *VT* 39, no. 1 (1989): 31–43.
Vargon, Shmuel. "The Time of Hezekiah's Illness and the Visit of the Babylonian Delegation." *Maarav* 21, no. 1–2 (2014): 37–56.
Viviano, Pauline A. "Ethbaal." *ABD* 2:645.
Walsh Hokenson, Jan. *The Idea of Comedy: History, Theory, Critique*. Madison, NJ: Fairleigh Dickinson University Press, 2006.
Walsh, Jerome T. *1 Kings*. Berit Olam. Collegeville, MN: Liturgical Press, 1996.
Walsh, Jerome T. *Ahab: The Construction of a King*. Collegeville: Liturgical Press, 2006.
Walsh, Jerome T. "The Contexts of 1 Kings xiii." *VT* 39 (1989): 355–70.
Walsh, Jerome T. "Methods and Meanings: Multiple Studies of 1 Kings 21." *JBL* 111, no. 2 (1992): 193–211.
Waltke, Bruce K. and M. O'Connor. *Introduction to Biblical Hebrew Syntax*. Winona Lake: Eisenbrauns, 1990.
Weems, R. J. "Huldah, the Prophet: Reading a (Deuteronomistic) Woman's Identity." In *A God So Near: Essays on Old Testament Theology in Honor of Patrick D. Miller*, edited by B. A. Strawn and N. R. Bowen, 321–39. Winona Lake: Eisenbrauns, 2003.
Weinfeld, Moshe. *Deuteronomy and the Deuteronomic School*. Oxford: Clarendon, 1972.
Weinfeld, Moshe. "The King as the Servant of the people: The Source of the Idea." *JJS* 33 (1982): 27–53.
Weisman, Ze'ev. *Political Satire in the Bible*. Semeia Studies. Atlanta: Scholars Press, 1998.
Weiss, Meir. *The Bible from Within: The Method of Total Interpretation*. Jerusalem: Magnes, 1984.

Weitzman, Steven. *Solomon: The Lure of Wisdom*. New Haven: Yale University Press, 2011.
Wenham, Gordon. *Story as Torah: Reading Old Testament Narrative Ethically*. Edinburgh: T. & T. Clark, 2000.
Wertsch, J. *Voices of the Mind: A Sociocultural Approach to Mediated Action*. Cambridge, MA: Harvard University Press, 1993.
Whedbee, J. William. *The Bible and the Comic Vision*. Cambridge: Cambridge University Press, 1998.
Whybray, R. N. *The Succession Narrative; A Study of II Samuel 9–20, [and] I Kings 1 and 2*. Naperville: A. R. Allenson, 1968.
Williams, James G. "The Beautiful and the Barren: Conventions in Biblical Type-scenes." *JSOT* 17 (1980): 107–19.
Williamson, H. G. M. *1 and 2 Chronicles*. Grand Rapids: Eerdmans, 1982.
Witte, Markus. "'What Share Do We Have in David…?' Ben Sira's Perspectives on 1 Kings 12." In *One God–One Cult–One Nation: Archaeological and Biblical Perspective*, edited by Reinhard G. Kratz and Hermann Spieckermann, 91–117. Berlin: de Gruyter, 2010.
Wray Beal, Lissa M. *The Deuteronomist's Prophet: Narrative Control of Approval and Disapproval in the Story of Jehu (2 Kings 9 and 10)*. LHBOTS 478. New York: T&T Clark, 2007.
Wray Beal, Lissa M. *1 & 2 Kings*. ApOTC 9. Downers Grove: InterVarsity, 2014.
Würthwein, Ernst. *Die Bücher der Könige, 1. Kön. 17–2. Kön. 25*. ATD 11/2. Göttingen: Vandenhoeck & Ruprecht, 1984.
Wyatt, Stephanie. "Jezebel, Elijah, and the Widow of Zarephath: A Ménage à Trois that Estranges the Holy and Makes the Holy the Strange." *JSOT* 36 (2012): 435–58.
Yamada, Frank. C*onfigurations of Rape in the Hebrew Bible: A Literary Analysis of Three Rape Narratives.* New York: Lang, 2008.
Yee, Gale A. "Coveting the Vineyard: An Asian American Reading of 1 Kings 21." In *Texts@Contexts: Samuel, Kings and Chronicles, Vol. 1*, edited by Athalya Brenner-Idan and Archie C. C. Lee, 46–64. London: Bloomsbury T&T Clark, 2017.
Yee, Gale A. "Fraught with Background: Literary Ambiguity in II Samuel 11." *Int* 42, no. 3 (1988): 240–53.
Yee, Gale A. "Jezebel," *ABD* 3:848–9.
Zakovitch, Y. "The Synonymous Word and Synonymous Name in Name Midrashim." *Shnaton* 2 (1977): 100–115 (Hebrew).
Zalewski, S. *Solomon's Ascension to Throne: Studies in the Books of Kings and Chronicles*. Jerusalem: Y. Markus, 1981 (Hebrew).
Zevit, Ziony. "First Kings." In *The Jewish Study Bible*. 2nd ed, edited by A. Berlin and M.Z. Brettler, 668–725. New York: Oxford University Press, 2014.

Index of References

Old Testament/Hebrew Bible

Genesis
2–3	94
20:11	59
22	6
24:16	36
28	27
32	27
33	27
34	38
34:15	254
34:22	254
34:23	254
35:10	140
37:17	88
37:34	117
38	94
42:7	29
43:33	163
50:20	8

Exodus
1:11	57
2:11	57
3:1	143
5:5	57
5:9	57
6:6	57
6:7	57
7:14	57
8:11	57
14:4	57
14:15-31	149
14:17	57
14:18	57
14:21-22	149
14:25	57
16	137
16:1–17:7	145
16:8	137
16:12-13	137
20:1-6	148
20:3	104
20:13	116, 148
20:15-16	148
20:16-17	209
20:17	148
21:14	209
21:18	209
21:35	209
22:7-10	209
22:14	209
22:26	209
22:28	14
24:18	143
32	27
32:11	28
32:27	209
33:11	209
33:12-23	143, 145

Leviticus
14:5	35
15:28	35
19:18	209
20:10	39
24:10-12	24
25:8-34	114

Numbers
14:33-34	143

Deuteronomy
1:26	99
1:43	99
4:6	59
4:19	107, 240
5:7	104
5:17	116
6:4	265
6:5	247
7:1-6	106
7:5	107
8:19	107
9	27
9:23	99
11:10	114, 147
11:11	107
11:116-17	107
11:15	107
11:17	107
12	86
12:2-7	107
12:3	107
12:11-14	107
13:6	116
16:21-22	104
16:21	107
17	11, 62
17:14-20	75
17:15	111
17:18-19	103
17:20	252
18:21-22	87
19:10	242
20:5-8	253
21:15-17	149
22:22	39
22:23-27	38
26:6	57
28:12	107
28:15-68	104
28:24	107

Index of References

Deuteronomy (cont.)		12	97, 246, 247	11:17	43
29:26	107			11:21	36
30:15-18	103, 119	12:2	75	11:24	62
30:17-18	107	12:13-15	247	11:25	45
33:28	107	12:14-15	99	11:26-27	42
34:1-8	151	12:20-25	247	11:26	42
		12:25	247	11:27	43
Joshua		14:29	110	12	43, 44, 52
1:11	115	15	5, 25	12:1-23	43
1:18	99	15:24	74, 80	12:1-6	94
3	150	15:25	221	12:9	43
6:8	88	15:30-31	31	12:10	43
6:9	88	15:30	221	12:13	118, 221
6:13	88	16:12	36	12:15	43
6:18	110	16:14-23	6	12:24	43
6:26	107	19:8-10	5	12:25	52
7	139	20:30-45	5	13–19	8
7:25-26	140	23	9	13	38, 39
7:25	110	24	9	15	254
13–21	115	25	8, 94, 101	15:1	24
13:1	115	25:6-8	253	15:2-6	54
13:6-7	114	28:6	29	15:12	37
13:6	115	28:19	5	16–17	74
23:5	115	29:11-17	12	16:20-22	37
23:7	107			19:18-23	8
23:16	107	*2 Samuel*		19:41 MT	77
24:4	115	1:19-27	6	19:42	77
		2:2	25	19:42 MT	77
Judges		3:15-16	9	19:43	77
2:11	94	3:21	26	19:43 MT	77
3:2	59	6	4	19:44	77
7:3	253	6:20-23	9	20	77–9
9:7-15	94	6:23	12	20:1	78
11:1-11	24	7	46, 97	20:2-3	78
13:6	87	7:15	20	20:4	78
19	38	7:16	31	20:22	78
19:20	59	8:15	62	20:24	78
		11–12	32, 34, 41	23	37, 157
1 Samuel		11	7, 32, 33, 35, 39, 40, 43, 48	23:34	37
1:20	44			24	76
2:27	87			24:10-17	238
4:21	44	11:1	34	24:10	28, 221
6:12	88	11:2	35, 36, 41	24:17	221
8:22	74	11:3	36	24:25	28
9:6	87	11:4	33, 35–8, 40, 41, 43	25:5-8	253
10:9-12	4				
10:23	5	11:5	41, 42		

Index of References

1 Kings
1–11	50	3:9-12	53	7:14	52
1–2	32, 34, 41, 46	3:9	81	7:51	224
		3:10	55, 58	8	96, 97
		3:11	53	8:1-3	56
1	33, 50, 60	3:12-13	218	8:5	19
1:4	44	3:12	52, 53	8:9	96
1:5	24, 44, 60	3:14	241	8:13	56
1:11-14	44	3:16-28	10	8:19	58
1:11	44	3:16	80, 81	8:20	56
1:12	44	3:28	52, 54	8:23-24	56
1:13	36, 45	4:1	54	8:23	55
1:17	45	4:2-6	54	8:25	252
1:21	45	4:6	78	8:27	56
1:28-30	46	4:7-19	54	8:31-32	56
1:31	46	4:7	85	8:31	221
1:32–2:12	46	4:20	54, 55	8:33-34	56
1:35	54	4:25	218	8:35-36	56
1:40	55	4:25 MT	54, 55	8:39	56
1:45	55	4:29 MT	52	8:43	56
2	47, 60, 147	4:29-34 MT	53	8:46-48	56
2:1	52	4:30 MT	52	8:48-50	265
2:4	252	4:31 MT	52, 53	8:56	56
2:6	54	4:32 MT	53	8:60	56
2:7-8	149	4:34 MT	52, 54	8:66	55
2:8-9	8	5–7	217	9:1-9	61
2:9	52, 54	5:3-4 MT	55	9:1	85
2:13-46	60	5:5	54, 55	9:4-5	61, 252
2:13	46, 47	5:5 MT	58, 218	9:6-9	56, 61
2:14	47	5:7 MT	52, 53, 55	9:6	61
2:15	54	5:9-14	53	9:7	56
2:17	47	5:9	52	9:10-28	11
2:18	48	5:10-11 MT	62	9:10-14	62
2:19-25	11	5:10	52	9:15-25	58
2:20	47, 48, 54	5:11	52, 53	9:17-19	57
2:22-24	48	5:12	53	10:1-13	62
2:22	54	5:12 MT	52, 54, 55	10:4	52
2:45	60	5:14	52, 54	10:6	52
2:46	61	5:17-18	55	10:7	52
3	59, 74, 80	5:19	58	10:8	52
3:1-3	59	5:21	52, 53, 55	10:9	53, 62
3:2-3	59	5:24-25	62	10:10-29	62
3:3	28, 30, 31, 51, 52, 60	5:26	52, 54, 55	10:15	81
		6–8	61	10:16-17	81
3:4-15	53	6–7	4	10:23	52
3:4	19, 30, 56	6:11-13	61	10:24	52
3:5	52	6:31-35	224	11–14	17, 22, 25, 94–6, 98
3:6-9	55	7:7	53		

1 Kings (cont.)

11	58, 59, 61, 63, 131, 237	12:2-3	27, 72	13:1-7	149
		12:2	26	13:1	86, 87
		12:3	26	13:2	28, 86, 87, 95, 263
		12:4-14	24		
11:1-13	232	12:4	57, 69, 73, 74, 77	13:3-6	87
11:1-8	31			13:3	28, 86
11:4	51	12:6	29, 67, 68, 73, 80, 81	13:4	87
11:5	81			13:5	28
11:6	51, 60	12:7	73, 74	13:6	28, 87
11:7-8	56, 58, 81	12:8	80	13:8-9	88
11:8	28, 51, 81	12:9	57, 67, 77, 80	13:8	87
11:11-13	80			13:9	87
11:11-12	245	12:10	57, 67, 77, 81	13:11-32	90, 94
11:11	56, 248			13:11-20	89
11:12-13	56	12:11	57, 69	13:11	85, 87, 90
11:14-22	25	12:12	27	13:12	88
11:17	28	12:13	77	13:13	88
11:18	52	12:14	57	13:14	88
11:26–14:20	63	12:15	26, 66, 72, 73, 75, 81, 263	13:15	88
11:26	27			13:17	88
11:28	25, 57			13:18	84, 85, 87, 89, 97, 99
11:29-39	25, 232	12:16	78		
11:29-31	31	12:17	72	13:19	89
11:29	245	12:18	26, 78	13:20-23	84
11:31-39	27	12:19-20	78	13:20	99, 100
11:31-35	96	12:19	93	13:21	99
11:31-33	26	12:21-24	24, 65, 69, 70, 72	13:26	90, 99, 102
11:31-32	56			13:30-31	100
11:31	248	12:21	81, 98	13:30	85
11:33	31	12:22-24	77	13:31	157
11:34-36	56	12:22	87	13:32	90
11:35	118	12:24	22, 50, 70, 71	14	98
11:37	26			14:1-20	26
11:38	31, 58	12:25-33	26	14:1-18	22, 26
11:40	25	12:25	22, 27	14:1	159
11:41-43	26	12:26-30	27	14:2	28
11:41	52, 217	12:27	79	14:6	71
12–14	65, 70, 71, 136	12:28-33	107	14:7-14	106
		12:28	80	14:7-9	27
12	73, 77, 78, 82, 135, 237	12:30-33	28	14:8-11	116
		12:30	95, 106	14:8	248
		12:33–13:34	86	14:9	106, 107, 148, 218
12:1-24	50, 65, 77	12:33	107		
12:1-20	66, 67, 72	13	26, 83–6, 90, 92–102, 157, 158	14:10-11	148
12:1-19	72			14:15-16	148, 238
12:1-15	73, 80			14:15	79
12:1	26	13:1-10	85	14:16	106, 221

14:19-20	26	16:25-26	106, 243	18:3	109
14:19	217	16:25	218	18:4	108, 115,
14:21-34	70	16:26	107		130, 141,
14:21-31	65	16:29–22:40	234, 238		144
14:21	79, 81	16:29-34	105, 107,	18:5-6	141
14:22-24	71, 79		116, 119	18:5	109
14:22	65, 70–2,	16:29	132	18:7	110
	221	16:30	106, 218	18:8	110
14:23-24	81	16:31-33	125	18:9-10	110, 149
14:25-28	79	16:31	117, 138	18:9	110, 221
14:25-26	24, 81	17–19	135	18:10	109, 141
14:26	223	17–18	140, 144,	18:12-13	108, 110
14:29	217		145, 150	18:12	109, 110
14:30	93, 98	17	107, 136–9,	18:13	108, 110,
15:1-7	63		145		144
15:2	81	17:1-6	143	18:14	110
15:3	71	17:1-4	149	18:15	109, 112,
15:6	98	17:1	12, 105,		145
15:12-13	218		107, 110,	18:16-19	139
15:16-17	98		136, 138,	18:16	110
15:18	222, 223		145	18:17	112, 116
15:23	159, 217	17:2-6	109, 137	18:18	109, 144
15:25	26	17:2-5	142	18:19	107, 108,
15:26	71, 221,	17:2-4	138		111, 132,
	243	17:2	137, 138		139
15:30	71, 107,	17:4	108, 137	18:20	111
	221	17:5	137	18:21	139
15:31	217	17:7-10	142	18:22	85
15:34	71, 221,	17:8-9	137, 138	18:24	139
	243	17:9	108	18:26	139, 140
16–19	104	17:10	137	18:27	140
16	105, 133	17:12	138	18:28-29	140
16:2-4	116	17:13	138	18:29	139, 140
16:2	107, 148,	17:16-45	179	18:30-32	144
	221	17:17	159	18:30-31	140
16:3-4	148	17:18	85, 138	18:30	144
16:7	107, 116	17:20	138	18:32	140
16:8-20	176	17:22	139	18:35	140
16:8-14	243	17:24	107	18:37	139
16:12	176	18	129, 136,	18:38	140, 149
16:13	107		137, 139,	18:39	111
16:19-34	136		141, 145	18:40	12, 140
16:19	221	18:1-20	108	18:41-46	12, 111
16:21-23	124	18:1-2	142	18:41	112
16:21-22	243	18:1	109, 110,	18:42	140
16:21	124		112, 140	18:44	112
16:24	113	18:3-4	108, 110	18:46	112

1 Kings (cont.)		20:1-43	147		21:23	115, 130,
19	104, 105,	20:42	113			148, 176
	113, 136,	20:43	113, 114		21:24-26	115
	141-43,	21	14, 76,		21:24	148
	145, 146,		104–6, 111,		21:25-28	148
	149, 150		113, 124,		21:25-26	76, 116,
19:1-4	141		126, 132,			148
19:1-2	124, 130		135, 142,		21:25	59, 129,
19:1	112, 115,		147, 175,			130, 218
	144		189, 207		21:27-29	238
19:2	115, 142,	21:1-29	113		21:27	148
	143	21:1-6	148		21:28	148
19:3	130, 141,	21:1	113, 140		22	98, 104,
	142, 160	21:2	114, 147			105, 108
19:4	142, 144	21:3-4	114		22:1-40	148
19:5-8	143	21:3	147		22:1-28	149
19:5-7	148	21:4-10	115		22:4	98
19:5	143	21:4	113		22:5-28	129
19:7	143	21:5	114		22:6	111
19:8	143	21:6-7	114		22:11-24	157
19:9-18	153	21:8-10	176		22:16	231
19:9-14	144	21:8-9	126		22:17	230
19:9	142, 144,	21:8	115		22:19-23	230
	145	21:10	128		22:19	230
19:10	12, 144,	21:11-14	115		22:34	159
	145, 147	21:13-19	148		22:35-38	266
19:11-12	145	21:13-14	128		22:41	130
19:11	145	21:14	115		22:52	130
19:12	13	21:15-16	114, 115		22:53	243, 245
19:13-21	149	21:15	115		33:34	95
19:13	145, 146	21:16	115, 126			
19:14	12, 145,	21:17-26	230		*2 Kings*	
	147	21:17-22	115		1–2	148
19:15-21	146	21:17-19	116, 148		1	148, 149
19:15-17	146	21:17	113, 116		1:2	148, 159
19:15-16	171	21:18-22	129		1:3	148
19:15	142, 143,	21:18-19	115		1:10	149
	146	21:18	113, 116		1:12	149
19:16	147	21:19-27	126		1:52	126
19:17	14	21:19	115, 116,		2	149
19:18	12, 144,		175		2:1-6	149
	146	21:20-24	116, 119,		2:3-4	247
19:19-21	147		148, 238		2:3	149
19:20	147	21:20-22	114		2:5	149
19:21	147	21:20	76, 113		2:9-12	149
20	104, 108,	21:21-24	172		2:9	149
	113, 158	21:22	76, 148		2:10	13

2:11-12	149	9–11	99, 185	10:1-11	188
2:12	149	9–10	117, 118,	10:1-8	119
2:13-15	160		146, 167,	10:1	131
2:13-14	150		170, 181,	10:4	176
2:23-25	154, 178		185, 215	10:5	176
3	98, 154	9	105, 124	10:6	177
3:1	126, 130	9:1-37	185	10:8	177
3:2	218	9:1-14	128	10:10	119
3:3	221	9:1-13	147	10:11	119
3:7	98	9:1-10	188	10:12-14	188
4:1-7	199, 204,	9:1-3	119, 171	10:15-28	118
	267	9:1	129	10:15-17	178
4:1-4	205	9:2	172, 188	10:16	119
4:1	204, 206	9:3	172	10:17	119, 178
4:2	204	9:4	171	10:18-28	178, 194
4:3-4	205	9:5	171, 188	10:19	178
4:3	209	9:6-10	119, 172	10:22-53	218
4:5-6	205	9:6	172	10:25	179
4:5	205, 209	9:7	119	10:27	118, 172,
4:6	205	9:8-9	238		179
4:7	205	9:8	119, 179	10:28-29	179
4:8-37	154, 204	9:9	119	10:29	221
4:9	154	9:10	172, 176	10:30	119, 179,
4:27	164	9:11-13	173, 188		224, 243
4:34-35	155	9:13	173	10:31	179
4:38-41	204	9:14-28	158	11	183–6, 246
4:42-44	204	9:15	176	11:1	185, 187,
5–6	154	9:16	173, 174		189, 191,
5:25	231	9:18	174		197, 246
6:12	155	9:20	174	11:2-3	185
6:16-17	160	9:21	174	11:2	187, 189,
6:22-23	160	9:22	118, 129,		197
6:22	6		131, 174	11:3	99, 185,
8:4	165	9:24-27	119		186, 189
8:7-15	146	9:25-26	119	11:4-20	185
8:7-9	155, 159	9:27	175	11:4-9	189
8:18	18, 98, 105,	9:30-37	14, 118	11:4	188, 194
	119, 131,	9:30-32	129	11:8	190
	175, 184,	9:32-37	172	11:10-11	190
	245	9:32-33	129	11:11	189
8:20	131	9:34-37	129	11:12	191
8:26	175, 184	9:34	124	11:13-16	191
8:27-29	245	9:36-37	119, 130	11:13	186, 192,
8:27	18, 98, 119,	9:37	176, 179		193
	131, 184	10	129, 132,	11:14	186, 191–3,
8:28-29	158		133, 176		262
8:29	159	10:1-27	185	11:15	186, 192

2 Kings (cont.)		15:32-38	238	18–19	214		
11:16	186, 193	16	17, 19–21	18	214		
11:17-21	194	16:2	18	18:1–20:11	221		
11:17-20	189	16:3	19	18:1-8	15		
11:17	194, 195	16:4	19	18:1	217		
11:18	105, 194, 195	16:5	20	18:2	217		
		16:6	20	18:3-8	222, 233		
11:19	195	16:7	20–2, 220, 223	18:3-6	222		
11:20	186, 195			18:3	224		
11:21	195	16:8	20, 222, 223, 232	18:4	105, 216, 218, 227		
12	254						
12:3-9	76	16:9	20	18:5	215, 218, 219, 227		
12:6	254	16:10-16	20				
12:8	255	16:10	223	18:6-7	218		
12:9-10	255	16:13	21, 28	18:7–19:37	216		
12:9	76, 254, 255	16:15	22, 28	18:7	220, 222, 226		
		16:17-18	19, 21				
12:10-15	76	16:17	20, 21	18:8-37	226		
12:10	255	16:18	20	18:9–19:37	15		
12:11	254, 255	16:20	20	18:9-12	215, 220		
12:16	76	16:29-34	103	18:9	220		
12:18 ET	223	16:30	238	18:11	220		
12:19	223	17–20	63	18:13-18	226		
12:24	86	17	71, 96, 98, 99, 215, 248, 249	18:13-16	215		
13	153, 155, 157, 158, 160			18:13	216, 220		
				18:14-16	216, 220–2, 225, 226, 229		
		17:3-7	220				
13:2	88, 243	17:3-6	220				
13:4	218	17:3	223	18:14	220–5, 230, 232		
13:11	243, 247	17:7-23	247				
13:14	158, 159	17:7-20	97	18:15	224		
13:19	160	17:7-18	248	18:16	220, 224		
13:20-21	152, 155–7, 161, 162, 164	17:7-12	248	18:17–19:37	215		
		17:7	221	18:17	216, 220, 225		
		17:16	240, 248				
14:11-14	98	17:17	71	18:18	226		
14:14	223, 232	17:19-20	249	18:19	218–21		
14:24	243, 247	17:19	99, 102	18:20	218–20		
15:9	243, 247	17:21-23	103, 248	18:21	104, 218, 219, 226, 227, 229		
15:13-15	243	17:21-22	95, 248				
15:18	243, 247	17:21	221, 248				
15:19-20	223	17:24	228	18:22	218, 219, 227		
15:19	223	17:30	228				
15:24	243, 247	18–20	17, 214, 215, 217, 232–4	18:23	220		
15:28	243, 247			18:24	218, 219, 226, 227, 229		
15:29	223						

18:26	255	20:16	230	22–23	17, 95, 239,
18:28	220	20:17-19	229		246
18:30	218–20	20:17	228	22:1–23:30	250
18:31	220	20:18	228	22:1–23:20	215
18:33	220	20:19	228, 230,	22:1-15	262
18:37	255		260	22:1-11	251
19	214, 254	20:20	217	22:2	250
19:2-4	219	20:21	217	22:3-7	252
19:2	220	21	160, 234,	22:3	252
19:3	222		239, 240	22:4-7	222
19:4	220	21:1-18	76	22:4	253, 254
19:6	220	21:1-2	234	22:5	253
19:8	220	21:1	239	22:8	252, 254
19:9-13	253	21:2-7	240, 241	22:10	254
19:10-13	253	21:2	19, 239,	22:12-20	256
19:10	119, 218–		245	22:12-13	222
	20	21:3-7	235, 239	22:12	252, 254,
19:11	220	21:3	239, 240		256
19:14-19	219, 229	21:4	105, 239	22:13	218, 257
19:14	119	21:5	240	22:14	254, 256,
19:15-19	218, 232	21:6	19, 239,		259
19:15	220		240	22:15-20	256
19:16	119	21:7-18	249	22:15-17	256
19:17	220	21:7-16	239	22:15	256, 257
19:20	220	21:7-9	239, 240	22:16-17	244
19:24	226	21:7	245	22:16	257
19:32	220	21:8-15	235, 239,	22:18-20	256, 261
19:35	220		244	22:18	256, 257
19:36	220	21:8-9	239	22:19	218, 260
20	215	21:9-18	243	23	94
20:1-11	13	21:9	240, 243	23:1-15	260
20:1-7	260, 261	21:10-15	239	23:1	252, 262
20:1-6	229	21:10-14	239	23:2	262
20:1	159	21:11-15	236	23:3	262
20:2-3	160, 218,	21:11-12	244	23:4-15	262
	219, 229	21:11	218, 222,	23:4-10	263
20:3	232		240, 242	23:4-5	105
20:6	220, 229	21:13	119	23:4	240, 252,
20:12-19	15, 215,	21:14	55		254, 262,
	221, 228,	21:16	222, 240,		263
	229		241	23:5	240, 263
20:12	228	21:17-18	235, 239	23:11-15	263
20:13	228, 229	21:17	222	23:11-12	263
20:14-15	228	21:20	55	23:13-15	263
20:14	228, 230	21:21-22	119	23:13	263
20:16-18	228, 230	21:23	118	23:15-20	87, 95, 100

2 Kings (cont.)

23:15	86, 264	11:21	79	*Job*	
23:16-20	90, 263, 264	12:12	71, 118	1:9	266
		12:14	71	32:7-9	74
23:16	95, 263, 264	14–16	63		
		21:6	131	*Psalms*	
23:17-18	157	22:2	131	15	2
23:17	263	22:10–23:45	131	24	2
23:19	263	23:13	262	35:13	117
23:20	263	24	63	48:5	163
23:21-30	264	28	19-21	51	32, 48
23:21-27	264	28:5-15	20	69:11	117
23:21-25	265	28:16	20	99:8	15
23:21	252, 263, 264	28:17	20	139	139
		28:18	20	139:7-12	139
23:24	264	28:19	20		
23:25	218, 247, 250, 264, 265, 267	28:20	20	*Ecclesiastes*	
		28:21	20	4:13-14	74
		28:22	20	5:7	163
		28:23	20		
23:26-27	264, 265	28:24	20, 21	*Isaiah*	
23:26	264, 265	28:25	20	3:5	209
23:27	264	28:26-27	19	5:5-10	14
23:28-30	264	28:27	20	11:10	54
23:29	266	29–32	215	14:3	57
23:30	266	29–31	216	30:1-5	228
23:33	223, 232	32	214	31:1-3	228, 232
23:35	223, 232	32:1-23	216	36–39	215
24:1–25:21	215	32:26	118	36–37	214
24:4	242	33:12-19	20	36:1	216
24:13	223	33:12-13	118	36:2	216
25:4	232	33:18-19	241	36:3	226
25:13-16	223	34–35	215	37	214
		34:14	255	37:36-38	216
1 Chronicles		36:12	242	38:1-8	13
2:7	110	36:14-19	242	38:9-20	216
22:7-16	45			39:1	228
22:9	55	*Ezra*		42:3	228
28	45	16:7	34	59:7	242
				59:16	163
2 Chronicles		*Nehemiah*			
1	30	13:26	64	*Jeremiah*	
1:3	30			2:8	88
10–12	63, 70	*Esther*		2:23	88
11	70	4:1	117	2:36-37	232
11:1-4	24	4:16	266	4:9	163
11:4	70			7:6	242

7:9	88	*Jonah*		*James*	
8:2	240	1–2	143	5:17-18	140
9:4-9	209	1:1-3	142	5:17	135
11:10	88	4	142		
14:9	163	19:5	143	TALMUDS	
19:4	242	*Micah*		*b. Baba Meṣi'a*	
19:13	240	1:13	99	87a	158
22:3	242	7:5-6	209		
22:17	242			*b. Berakot*	
26:15	242	*Habakkuk*		55a	54
		1:5	163		
Ezekiel				*b. Megillah*	
16:26	68	*Zephaniah*		14b	259
20:16	88	1:5	240		
23:20	68			*b. Šabbat*	
29:6-7	228	*Malachi*		56a	40
37:22-23	101	3:23-24	166		
				b. Sanhedrin	
Daniel		*Ecclesiasticus*		22a	44
1:4	67	48:12	160	47a	157
1:10	67	48:13	155	107b	158
1:13	67	48:14	160		
1:15	67			MIDRASH	
1:17	67	NEW TESTAMENT		*Midrash Tehillim*	
3:18	266	*Matthew*		I 26 7	157
3:24	163	1:6	48		
		8:27	164	*Pirqe Rabbi Eliazer*	
Hosea		9:33	164	33	156
2:13	104	15:31	164		
4:2	207			*Qoheleth Rabbah*	
5:10	207	*Mark*		8.10	157
5:11	88	5:42	164		
7:11	232			JOSEPHUS	
12:7-8	207	*Luke*		*Antiquities*	
12:8-9 MT	207	5:9	164	7.131	41
		7:16	164	8.212-224	66
Amos		8:56	164	8.246-265	66
2:6-8	207			9.8.6	155
5:8-12	207	*Acts*		10.1.2	226
7:10-17	28	3:10	164	10.2.2	231
8:10	117				

Index of Authors

Aberbach, M. 86
Ackerman, S. 123
Adelman, R. 38
Alter, R. 94, 221
Amit, Y. 72, 106, 115, 127, 128, 237
Anderson, J. E. 216
Angel, H. 108
Appler, D. A. 109, 116
Arendt, H. 200
Ashkenasy, N. 46
Attardo, S. 168
Auld, A. G. 18, 23, 29, 208
Avioz, M. 258, 266

Bal, M. 42, 121, 122
Bar-Efrat, S. 7, 36, 67
Barnes, W. H. 217, 220, 231
Barré, L. M. 183, 185
Barth, K. 84, 87, 91, 92, 97, 98, 101
Barton, J. 1, 2, 251, 266, 267
Beach, E. F. 123, 127
Becker, E. 165
Begg, C. T. 230–2
Ben Barak, Z. 126
Ben Zvi, E. 239
Benson, J. 41
Bergen, W. J. 154, 156, 181
Berlin, A. 202, 203, 235, 236
Berman, J. 93
Betlyon, J. W. 223
Beverley, J. 199–201
Bhabha, H. 201
Biddle, M. E. 170
Birch, B. C. 2
Bodner, K. 25, 44, 46, 67–9, 73, 74, 78, 80, 86, 94, 154, 156, 207, 217
Boer, R. 68, 69, 73, 77, 94
Booth, W. C. 10
Boring, E. G. 155

Bostock, D. 222, 225–7, 229, 230
Bosworth, D. A. 94, 98, 99, 101
Bowen, N. 47, 48
Branch, R. G. 183, 185–9, 191–3
Brandes, Y. 43
Braude, W. G. 157
Brenner(-Idan), A. 122–4, 127, 170
Brettler, M. 62
Brichto, H. C. 112
Brinton, D. G. 156
Brodie, T. L. 143, 144
Brooks, G. 40
Brooks, S. S. 7
Brosh, B.-Sh. 59
Brueggemann, W. 45, 46, 73, 139, 147, 149, 156, 229, 231

Calvin, J. 35, 42
Camp, C. V. 183, 187, 188, 195
Carroll R., M. D. 2
Chan, L. 212
Chaney, M. L. 207
Chastellain, G. 165
Chesnokova, A. 161
Childs, B. 216
Chirichigno, G. C. 206, 207
Chun, S. M. 250–6, 258, 261, 266
Clarke, S. 200, 203
Cogan, M. 62, 67, 69, 72–4, 86, 95, 99, 164, 183, 187, 194, 215, 220, 229, 238, 239, 248, 249, 253, 259
Cohen, A. 157, 192, 193, 195
Cohen, S. 182
Cohn, R. L. 50, 94, 156, 162, 179, 185, 188, 195, 208, 210, 252, 254, 262
Cranz, I. 238
Critchley, S. 167
Cronauer, P. T. 124
Cross, F. M. 97, 239

Darr, K. P. 227
da Silva, F. C. 123
Daube, D. 37
Delamarter, S. 266
Delitzsch, F. 38
DeVries, S. J. 66, 68, 70, 73, 75, 86, 89
Di Lella, A. A. 155
Dorp, J. van 90
Dozeman, T. B. 99
Dray, C. A. 157
Driver, S. R. 35
Duffy, E. 166
Dutcher-Walls, P. 105, 123, 183–8, 191, 192

Ebeling, J. 128
Edelman, D. 259
Elliot, J. H. 68
Emery, B. 38
Eslinger, L. 255
Evans, P. S. 221
Exum, J. C. 34, 39
Eynikel, E. 90, 239, 240

Feldman, L. H. 66, 226
Fleishman, Y. 127
Floriani, A. 201
Forster, E. M. 3, 4, 10
Franklin, N. 128
Freedman, D. N. 39
Fretheim, T. E. 185, 187, 190, 208, 261
Freud, S. 163, 164
Friedlander, G. 156
Friedman, R. 239
Frisch, A. 51, 52, 54, 55, 57, 58, 61
Fritz, V. 72, 188, 189, 195, 240
Frymer-Kensky, T. 35

Gaines, J. H. 123
García-Treto, F. O. 118, 170–2
Garsiel, M. 46, 56, 93
Gehman, H. S. 53, 124, 126, 159
Gericke, J. 72, 73
Gesenius, W. 87
Gilmour, R. 154
Ginzberg, L. 158
Glover, N. 137, 146
Goldingay, J. 92
Gordon, R. P. 94, 101

Gray, J. 74, 86, 89, 104, 124, 130, 204, 239, 248, 259
Gray, M. 39
Greenberg, J. 161
Greenberg, M. 56
Gross, W. 86, 92, 99
Guillaume, P. 127, 128
Gunn, D. M. 8, 35

Hackett, J. A. 259
Hadjiev, T. S. 113, 114, 117, 136
Hakola, R. 165, 166
Halpern, B. 235, 244, 245, 257
Hamilton, V. P. 156
Handy, L. K. 183, 254
Hayes, J. H. 182
Hays, C. B. 214
Hazleton, L. 123
Heller, J. 41
Henry, M. 42
Hens-Piazza, G. 145, 147, 188, 193, 195, 209
Herrmann, W. 104
Hill, S. D. 156
Hobbs, T. R. 158, 159, 177, 227
Hokenson, J. W. 167
Holstein, J. A. 85
hooks, b. 211
Hoover, T. R. 208
Hutcheon, L. 203
Hyers, C. 170

Iser, W. 49

Jackson, M. 170
Jang, S. 229
Janzen, D. 227, 229, 231, 252
Japheth, S. 70, 71
Jeon, Y. H. 59, 61
Jobling, D. 94
Johnson, B. J. M. 38
Jones, G. H. 159, 208
Jones, P. H. 85, 92, 98
Joseph, A. L. 95, 235, 242, 243, 247, 251

Kaufmann, Y. 59
Keen, S. 161
Keil, C. F. 38, 89, 91
Kermode, F. 33

Keulen, P. S. F. van 260
Kim, U. 37
King, G. 170
Kirk-Duggan, C. 43
Kissling, P. J. 141, 142, 150, 151
Kitz, A. M. 128
Klopfenstein, M. 89, 92
Knight, D. A. 2
Knoppers, G. N. 50, 53, 95, 218, 221, 261, 264
Koenig, S. 11, 32, 35
Konkel, A. H. 252
Koosed, J. L. 123
Kren, T. 34
Kuhl, C. 95
Kuloba, W. R. 183, 186, 187, 190–2, 194, 196

Lamb, D. T. 40, 215, 222, 224, 225
Lange, J. P. 37
Lapsley, J. E. 2
Lasine, S. 84, 104, 116, 119, 152–5, 157, 159–62, 165, 166, 235, 242, 244, 250, 258, 261, 265
Lee, K. S. 183, 188
Leithart, P. J. 104, 141
Lemaire, A. 52
Lemke, W. E. 95, 97, 99
LeMon, J. M. 214
Leneman, H. 36, 41
Létourneau, A. 40
Leuchter, M. 257
Liddon, H. P. 117, 118
Lipka, H. 68, 69
Liver, J. 52
Lohfink, N. 251, 252
Long, B. O. 67, 86, 106, 119, 159, 208
Long, V. P. 135
Longacre, R. E. 263
Longman III, T. 135
Lowery, R. H. 252
Lumby, J. R. 47
Luther, M. 37

Machinist, P. 214
Maier III, W. A. 136
Maier, W. A. 108, 117
Marcus, D. 45, 48, 181
Mazar, A. 259

McCarter, P. K. 44
McCarthy, D. 97
McGraw, A. P. 168
McKenzie, S. L. 35, 95, 97
McKinlay, J. E. 123
Meyer, W.-U. 162
Miller, J. M. 182
Miscall, P. 93
Moberly, R. W. L. 101, 102, 163, 164
Montgomery, J. A. 53, 124, 126, 159, 177
Morreall, J. 167, 168
Mowrey, M. E. 165
Mullen, E. T. 183, 187–9, 222, 225

Na'aman, N. 225
Nahkola, A. 93
Nelson, R. D. 56, 66, 70, 74, 175, 183, 194, 195, 208, 235, 239, 240, 257, 258, 262, 265
Newsom, C. A. 2
Nicol, G. 33, 39, 47
Noth, M. 53, 243, 245
Nünning, A. 33

O'Connor, M. P. 86–8
Oatley, K. 162
Ojwang, G. O. 127
Okyere, K. 73
Olley, J. W. 145
Organ, B. E. 73, 75, 77
Otto, E. 1
Overholt, T. 156

Parker, S. 175
Paynter, H. 114, 115, 118, 170, 174, 179, 181
Pearson, P. D. 201
Person, R. F. 94, 95
Pinker, A. 152, 164
Pippin, T. 123
Piven, J. S. 164
Plein, I. 72
Plöger, O. 96
Porten, B. 56
Postell, S. D. 94
Provan, I. 46, 135–7, 159, 208, 256, 260–2
Pruin, D. 124
Pyszczynski, T. 161

Rad, G. von 100, 237
Radday, Y. T. 170
Revell, E. J. 254, 257
Rice, G. 89
Rimmon-Kenan, S. 32
Rivers, F. 48
Robinson, J. 124
Rofé, A. 67, 73, 74, 94, 128
Römer, T. 50, 95
Rosenberg, A. J. 157
Russell, S. C. 128

Schenker, A. 23
Schiff, R. 51
Schipper, J. 231, 232
Schmidt, B. 166
Scholz, S. 39, 40
Seibert, E. 63
Seitz, C. R. 227, 228
Seow, C.-L. 45, 46
Shaw, C. S. 71
Shemesh, Y. 127, 154, 156, 165, 204
Shulman, A. 253
Simon, U. 88, 140
Skehan, P. W. 155
Slotki, I. W. 253
Smagorinsky, P. 201
Small, B. C. 4
Smelik, K. A. D. 235, 242
Smolar, L. 86
Solomon, S. 161
Solvang, E. 35
Spivak, G. C. 200
Springer, M. 161
Stanton, C. 43
Stavrakopoulou, F. 236, 241, 242, 244
Sternberg, M. 32, 49, 51, 61, 84
Steussy, M. 36, 39
Stipp, H.-J. 153
Stone, K. 187, 189
Sugirtharajah, R. S. 203
Sun, C. 42
Sweeney, M. A. 22, 23, 50, 67, 71, 75, 84, 112, 182, 187, 190, 220, 226, 231, 248, 253, 256, 257

Tadmor, H. 164, 183, 187, 194, 215, 220, 229, 238, 239, 248, 249, 253, 259
Talshir, Z. 22, 71
Tatar, M. 163
Tierney, R. J. 201
Todorov, T. 163
Trible, P. 123
Tsumara, D. 75

Van Peer, W. 161
Van Seters, J. 92, 95
Van Winkle, D. W. 89, 95, 99
Vanderhooft, D. S. 214, 235, 257
Vargon, S. 228, 231
Viviano, P. A. 106

Walsh, J. T. 50, 58, 66–70, 75, 88, 95, 100, 101, 104, 110–12, 114
Waltke, B. K. 86-8
Warner, J. 168
Warren, C. 168
Weems, R. J. 259
Weinfeld, M. 62, 75, 237
Weisman, Z. 67, 72, 73, 79, 80
Weiss, M. 63
Wellhausen, J. 96
Wenham, G. 2
Wertsch, J. 201
Whedbee, W. J. 170
Whybray, N. 33
Williams, J. G. 93
Williamson, H. G. M. 216
Witte, M. 66
Wray Beal, L. M. 104, 113, 114, 118, 119, 137, 139, 143, 150, 172, 177, 180, 225, 229, 231
Würthwein, E. 164
Wyatt, S. 138, 144

Yamada, F. 39
Yee, G. 48, 106, 123

Zakovitch, Y. 52
Zalewski, S. 53, 54
Zevit, Z. 50

www.ingramcontent.com/pod-product-compliance
Lightning Source LLC
Chambersburg PA
CBHW050323020526
44117CB00031B/1593